THE
ORIENTATION
OF ANIMALS

KINESES, TAXES
AND
COMPASS REACTIONS

BY

GOTTFRIED S. FRAENKEL

PROFESSOR OF ENTOMOLOGY,
UNIVERSITY OF ILLINOIS, URBANA, ILLINOIS
(FORMERLY LECTURER IN PHYSIOLOGY IN THE DEPARTMENT OF
ZOOLOGY AND APPLIED ENTOMOLOGY, IMPERIAL
COLLEGE OF SCIENCE AND TECHNOLOGY, LONDON)

AND

DONALD L. GUNN

DIRECTOR, TEA RESEARCH INSTITUTE,
ST. COOMBS, TALAWAKALE, CEYLON
(FORMERLY LECTURER IN ZOOLOGY
UNIVERSITY OF BIRMINGHAM)

DOVER PUBLICATIONS, INC.
NEW YORK

This new Dover edition, first published in 1961, is an expanded version of the first edition published by Oxford University Press in 1940. The following new material has been added to the Dover edition:
Appendix: Additional Notes Added December, 1960
Supplementary Bibliography, 1940–1960

Standard Book Number: 486-60786-0
Library of Congress Catalog Card Number: 61-65082

Manufactured in the United States of America

Dover Publications, Inc.
180 Varick Street
New York 14, N.Y.

PREFACE TO DOVER EDITION

THIS book, after a long and exhausting gestation, appeared early in World War II. On its day of publication—August 22, 1940—the Battle of Britain was raging, London was ringed by pillars of smoke from burning aircraft, and the first bombs fell on London itself. It is hardly surprising that the original publishers, the Oxford University Press, printed only a small number. Only about 250 copies left for the United States and we do not know how many of them successfully crossed the Atlantic; and half that number went to the rest of the world. In March, 1949, the book was sold out and soon fetching more than the original price when it could be got secondhand (Swan, C. K. 1955. *J. Soc. Bibliogr. nat. Hist.*, Vol. 3, pp. 117–126). It could not be immediately reprinted because the type metal had been wanted during the war and the type had been broken up; and we were both too fully occupied to produce a revised edition, although there had not been much new work published in the decade since the original manuscript went to press. There the matter lay until Dover Publications, Inc., decided to make it possible for everyone to have and to read the book itself, instead of depending on quotations, which only too often betray incomplete reading or comprehension.

When this book appeared, it was well received by all the reviewers except only the late Professor S. O. Mast (1941, *Science*, Vol. 93, pp. 619–20). Some of his criticisms were sound (for example, *Arenicola* larva has indeed two eyes and not one, though that does not affect the argument); some were hardly fair (for example, regarding our not quoting him on one statement regarding *Euglena*, when we quoted him five times in three pages around the statement), and some suggested that he had not read the whole book and, for example, appreciated that a kind of memory could depend simply on sensory adaptation. We were the more sensitive to his remarks because he, more than any other research worker, had weaned us from the simple mechanical ideas against which he fought so long. But these were the last rumblings of the old controversies, and today hardly a single zoologist will use the word *tropism* for behaviour of motile animals; indeed the tendency in the last two decades has been to go even farther than we have done away from Loeb's ideas. Today, research workers often abandon the safety (and, they say, the sterility) of an objective attitude towards animal behaviour and adventure into the subjective. The revival of this book may provide a corrective to the bolder flights of fancy.

To some extent, we may be blamed for the turn towards subjectivity. In our original preface we said that 'the success of the book may be measured by the new ideas and experimental work which it stimulates.' In the event, it seems to have tidied up the basic concepts to such an extent that almost every subsequent contribution in the narrow field that it deals with, namely the mechanisms of simpler orientation reactions, has been discussed in the words and spirit of the definitions and terms that we selected; but, on the whole, attention has now turned towards wider fields of more complex kinds of behaviour such as instincts (e.g., Tinbergen, 1951, *The Study of Instinct*), learning (e.g., Thorpe, 1956, *Learning and Instinct in Animals*), navigation and homing (e.g., Carthy, 1957, *Animal Navigation*), on the one hand, or electrical phenomena underlying sensory reactions (e.g., 'Physiological Mechanisms in Animal Behaviour,' *Symp. Soc. exp. Biol.* No. 4. 1950) on the other. So what the book actually did was to round off an epoch in the study of the elementary orientation behaviour of animals.

Detailed expositions, sometimes critical, of the concepts of the book have subsequently appeared in several places, as in the article 'Animal Behaviour,' in the *Encyclopædia Britannica* (by the late W. C. Allee), in one by Soulairac (1949), and in the books of Tinbergen (1951) and Savory (1959), with careless inaccuracies. The scheme has been made the basis of the description of many phases of insect behaviour by T. C. Schneirla (1953) and forms almost the backbone of Carthy's (1958) *Introduction to the Behaviour of Invertebrates*. It was belatedly submitted by O. Koehler (1950) to a critical analysis as exhaustive as it was trenchant and caustic.

The main text of this edition is an exact photocopy of the original (but for corrections of misprints). Some actual mistakes have been referred to in footnotes. The literature which has grown up since the appearance of the book has been dealt with in a separate appendix at the end of the book, with references to such additions in footnotes at the appropriate places in the text. In this attempt at bringing the book up to date, it was not possible within the permitted framework to achieve complete coverage. The nature of these notes is further to explain, extend, or amplify the original text and to lead the reader to new developments. It has not been found possible to introduce entirely new concepts and ideas which have greatly developed since the book first appeared, as for instance the orientating effect of polarized light (amply discussed in Carthy's book 1958), or the effect of biological rhythms on the expression of orientation reactions (*Cold Spring Harbor Symposium on Biological Clocks*, 1960). All these matters do not seem to change the fundamentals or the framework of the subject. Moreover, there is little chance that the subject will be brought fully up to date within the foreseeable future by us, for one of us (G. S. F.) long ago went over to the study of insect nutrition, and the other (D. L. G.) first to research on locusts, then to their control in tropical Africa, and now to the administration of research on the production of tea.

We are particularly happy to record our appreciation to the President of Dover Publications, Inc., Mr. Hayward Cirker, for rescuing the book from a physical oblivion from which it could speak only through secondhand quotations, and restoring it to the shelves of the libraries and bookstores in a form in which it is accessible and financially available to all.

G. S. F.

D. L. G.

December 1960

PREFACE TO FIRST EDITION

THE object of this book is to give an account of those reactions of animals which used to be called 'tropisms'. The first part describes the main categories of these reactions in a manner suitable for undergraduates and teachers; the second part reviews recent work for advanced students and research workers. In places the book may be too advanced for most undergraduates and in places too elementary for research workers; this is due to its double purpose. Undergraduates might be well advised to confine themselves to Part I, with the addition of Chapters XIX and XX; advanced workers should need no advice on what to leave out.

The classification of reactions given in Part I is based upon that of Kühn (1919), with certain additional categories associated with the name of von Buddenbrock. We have attempted improvements by adding new categories and altering or abolishing old ones. The process of classifying should not need defending. It remains for future work to show whether the changes made are as economical as they seem to us to be. Whether they are or not, the success of this book may be measured by the new ideas and experimental work which it stimulates.

In the first part of the book there are two chapters (III and IV) which do not deal with animal behaviour directly, but with its physiological background. They have been included for two reasons. First, the subject-matter is needed for the understanding of the rest of the book; and secondly, the material in them is not commonly given in courses in zoology and there appears to be no book in which it is presented concisely, as it is here. For example, modern views on muscle tonus can be obtained only from original papers and reviews; these views could not be explained to students who have no previous training in physiology, except in a suitable context. We hope that context is not too sketchy.

Each of the two authors wrote about half of the book. One of us (G. S. F.) did Chapters I, VIII–X, XII, XIII, XV–XVIII, and the other (D. L. G.) did Chapters II–VII, XI, XIV, XIX, XX. We have, however, criticized each other's work and often compromised when we disagreed. We believe that the book now makes a reasonably consistent whole.

We wish to thank those who have been so kind as to help one or other of us in various ways. Dr. M. L. Johnson (Mrs. Abercrombie) read the whole of the manuscript and made many helpful suggestions. Prof. H. Munro Fox, F.R.S., and Prof. F. R. Winton helped in the same way with parts of the manuscript, while Mr. E. W. Bentley read the proofs very effectively. Miss Mary D. Unwin drew Fig. 17, and Dr. B. De Meillon, Dr. J. S. Kennedy, Dr. D. P. Pielou, and M. M. Volkonsky gave information about unpublished experiments and corrected our accounts of them. Permission to reproduce published illustrations was given by the Akademische Verlagsgesellschaft m.b.H for *Z. wiss. Zoologie* and for *Zool. Anzeiger*; by Messrs. Gustav Fischer for *Zool. Jahrbücher*; by the Cambridge University Press for *J. exp. Biol.* and *Biol. Rev.*; by Messrs. Christophers for Adrian, *Basis of Sensation*; by Messrs. J. & A. Churchill Ltd. for Winton & Bayliss, *Human Physiology*, 2nd edition, and Starling's *Principles of Physiology*, 6th edition (edited by C. Lovatt Evans); by Clark University for Crozier, *The Foundations of Experimental Psychology*; by the Columbia University Press for Jennings, *Behavior of the Lower Organisms*; by Messrs. Methuen & Co. Ltd. for Wigglesworth's *Insect Physiology*; by the Rockefeller Institute for Medical Research for *J. gen. Physiol.*; by the University of Chicago Press for *Physiol. Zoöl.*; by Messrs. John Wiley & Sons Inc. for Mast, *Light and the Behavior of Organisms*; by the Wistar Institute of Anatomy and Biology for *J. exp. Zoöl.*; by Verlagsbuchhandlung Paul Parey for *Z. angew. Ent.*; and by many individual authors. In many cases authors lent original photographs or original drawings, and they have thereby greatly simplified the work on the illustrations. Without their help this book would either have been more expensive or less well illustrated, and our thanks and those of the reader are due to them.

It is too much to hope that this book is wholly free from errors, but research workers will naturally refer to the original publications which we have quoted, and we hope that any authors whom we may have misrepresented will not be slow in telling us so.   G. S. F.

                                                      D. L. G.

March 1940

CONTENTS

PART I

I. INTRODUCTION I

II. ORTHO-KINESIS 11

III. PHYSIOLOGICAL MACHINERY 24

IV. REFLEXES 35

V. KLINO-KINESIS 43

VI. KLINO-TAXIS 58

VII. TROPO-TAXIS 76

VIII. TELO-TAXIS 90

IX. LIGHT COMPASS REACTION 100

X. DORSAL LIGHT REACTION 120

TABLE IV. TABULATION OF REACTIONS . . 133

PART II

XI. THE TWO-LIGHT EXPERIMENT . . . 136

XII. UNILATERAL BLINDING AND CIRCUS MOVEMENTS . 161

XIII. SKOTO-TAXIS. INTENSITY v. DIRECTION . . 174

XIV. TEMPERATURE REACTIONS 189

XV. GRAVITY REACTIONS IN GENERAL . . . 216

XVI. GEO-TAXIS 228

XVII. MECHANICAL STIMULATION 244

XVIII. CHEMICAL STIMULATION 270

XIX. VARIATION IN BEHAVIOUR 292

XX. GENERAL DISCUSSION AND CONCLUSION . . 305

TABLE VI. KÜHN'S CLASSIFICATION . . . 317

APPENDIX: ADDITIONAL NOTES ADDED DECEMBER, 1960 . 319

BIBLIOGRAPHY 336

SUPPLEMENTARY BIBLIOGRAPHY, 1940–1960 . . . 355

AUTHOR INDEX 362

SYSTEMATIC INDEX 365

GENERAL INDEX 369

LIST OF PLATES

Fig. 8	*facing page*		30
Figs. 85 and 86	,,	,,	182
Fig. 88	,,	,,	192
Figs. 90 and 91	,,	,,	194
Fig. 93	,,	,,	202
Figs. 100 and 101	,,	,,	218
Fig. 104	,,	,,	226
Fig. 107	,,	,,	232
Fig. 122	,,	,,	266
Fig. 130	,,	,,	284

THE
ORIENTATION
OF ANIMALS

PART I

I

INTRODUCTION

THE study of animal behaviour extends over a wide field; only a small part of it is covered in this book. We shall deal with the orientation of animals, the directions in which they walk or swim, and the reasons why particular directions are selected.

Generally speaking, the position normally adopted by an animal in relation to its surroundings is not completely haphazard. There is a posture and an orientation which can properly be regarded as normal. In its characteristic position, a dog stands on its feet with its belly downwards. Similarly, animals are not distributed at random over the area in which they live; each species tends to be found predominantly in a particular kind of habitat, in which the climate may be quite different from the climate measured by the local meteorologist. Even if you consider only the animals which can travel far, the seashore, the green valley, and the mountain-top have very different faunas. We include under the term *orientation* not only those reactions which guide the animal into its normal stance but also reactions which guide it into its normal habitat or into other situations which are of importance to it.

These two kinds of orientation can be illustrated by means of familiar examples. Most fishes have a normal position in which the dorsal surface is uppermost and the longitudinal axis is horizontal. This position can be abandoned at a moment's notice and succeeded by dives, twists, and all kinds of aquatic acrobatics; but eventually there is a return to the standard orientation, the position adopted by the fish when it is inactive, and the position from which active movement generally starts. This is what we call the *primary orientation* of the animal. Dead fish usually float at the surface with the belly or the side uppermost; this indicates that the maintenance of the primary orientation is an active process of balancing. It is a *reaction* which is normally controlled chiefly through the activity of the sense organs of equilibrium in the internal ear.

It is obvious that fishes living in streams do not usually get swept down into the sea but, on the whole, each fish keeps its place in the stream. Indeed, most of us have seen trout facing up stream and swimming just fast enough to keep a constant position relative to the banks. The fish orientates itself into the stream, and in some way the direction in which it faces must be due to the direction of flow of the water. This is a *secondary orientation* which is superposed on the primary orientation. As we shall see, the maintenance of position in a stream is not necessarily a simple or single reaction, but it is probably most often guided through the eyes.

The distinction between primary and secondary orientations is thus clear enough and is the first step in our classification. Primary orientations provide the basic position from which other reactions start, and they are most commonly concerned with the inclination of the vertical axis of the animal. Secondary orientations are usually not simply concerned with the direction in which the horizontal axis of the body points—as if it were a compass needle, for example—but they involve locomotion. The distinction is thus based upon the functions of the reactions. When, however, we classify orientation reactions according to their mechanism, we find that the two classifications cut across one another, so that two primary orientations may have mechanisms with little in common, while a primary one may have a mechanism which is practically identical with that of a particular secondary orientation.

Let us now turn to an animal having a manner of life very different from that of a fish, namely, the common bluebottle or blow-fly, *Calliphora erythrocephala*. When it is stationary or when it walks on a solid surface, the feet cling to the surface whatever its inclination to the horizontal. The direction of gravity is of practically no importance in determining the orientation of the body axes, and the primary orientation is not to gravity at all but to the contact of the surface. During flight, however, blow-flies adopt the usual position, with the dorsal surface upwards.

On summer days it is common enough to find a number of flies flying about at random in each room; if you flap a cloth violently amongst them, most of them make straight for the light of the window. This is, then, a secondary orientation.

If a piece of meat is left uncovered in such weather, especially if it is not quite fresh, within a short time blow-flies appear as if by magic and lay their eggs on it. No housewife would doubt that the smell of the meat attracts and guides the flies. On cool days in spring and autumn flies often collect on a sunny wall, and in these cases too we have examples of secondary orientation.

There is a large body of information, gained mainly during the last half century, about both primary and secondary orientations of animals, particularly in relation to the external factors which direct these reactions. This book is principally concerned with the way in which the various external factors—light, smells, currents, heat, and so on—operate the living mechanisms and lead to orientation.

The reactions of fishes and flies that we have chosen as examples are, as far as is known, spontaneous and inborn. They are performed by all the members of the species in question, without previous training or experience. In most of the large groups of animals a certain degree of learning by experience is known to take place, but in birds and mammals it becomes of great importance. Warm-blooded animals are not nearly so completely controlled by contemporaneous external factors as poikilotherms are, but are influenced greatly by internal factors and by past experience. Even in those animals which behave predominantly in more complex ways, however, there are still signs of more elementary behaviour, particularly in the more automatic functions like balancing and in the methods used to localize smells, sounds, warm places, and the like. We shall not deal with learning, but shall confine our attention to the more primitive orientation reactions; consequently, most of our examples will be taken from the invertebrates and from the so-called lower vertebrates.

Before the time of Darwin's theory of evolution, Descartes's view—that animals are automatic, thoughtless machines—dominated men's ideas about animal behaviour. There seems to have been little useful work done in the subject during that period, and zoologists were fully occupied with the anatomy and classification of animals. The publication of Darwin's *Origin of Species* in 1859 caused a great outburst of work in many fields; in behaviour it started a search for evidence of psychical and psychological relationships between man and other animals. Romanes, who did the best work of this kind, collected anecdotes about the behaviour of animals and interpreted them in such a way as to indicate the similarity between man and other animals. Not only were emotions attributed to animals but they were regarded as the factors operating them; this is what we call the anthropomorphic view of behaviour (ἄνθρωπος, man; μορφή, form). Moreover, behaviour was often described and explained in terms of subsequent events, results, purposes, and objectives, in teleological terms (τέλος, end, objective), almost as if animals had considerable fruitful experience or foreknowledge. The question of the validity of such points of view is not the subject of the present discussion, but it is clear that they are little concerned with details of the mechanism of behaviour. When the functional value of a reaction had been discovered and the emotion controlling it had been guessed according to the taste of the observer, the inquiry was at an end.

The remarks of Romanes (1883) about the flight of insects into a flame at night provide a typical example of the anthropomorphic treatment of a kind of behaviour with which we deal in this book. After comparing this behaviour with that of birds, when they dash themselves against the windows of lighthouses, he goes on:

'Here there can be no question about a possible mistaking of a flame for white flowers, etc., and therefore the habit must be set down to mere curiosity or desire to examine a new and striking object; and that the same explanation may be given in the case of insects seems not improbable, seeing that it must certainly be resorted to in the case of fish, which are likewise attracted by the light of a lantern.'

About the same time, there were signs of interest in the details of behaviour and of the beginnings of a new objective attitude in the writings of Bert (1869), Lubbock (1881, 1882, 1889), Graber (1883, 1884), and Plateau (1886). Although these authors still used the anthropomorphic terminology, it is difficult to decide to-day whether their outlook was entirely anthropomorphic. Lubbock appears to have used expressions like 'preference of *Daphnia* for yellow or green' in an entirely objective sense, though he regarded animals which reacted differently from the majority as possessing a 'difference of taste'. Graber commonly used expressions like 'liking' and 'fear', as in the suffixes -*liebend*, -*hold*, and -*scheu*; but it must be remembered that he took over this terminology from Strasburger, who, in his description of the photo-taxis of swarm spores, used the terms *photophil* and *photophob* as well as their German translations *lichthold* and *lichtscheu*. In describing and interpreting the reactions of animals to various colours, he wrote of *Lust- und Unlustfarben* and of *Helligkeitsgeschmack*, he discussed the question of the extent to which certain reactions are caused by *Lust-* or *Unlustgefühle*, and came to the conclusion, for example, that the *Unlust* of *phengophil* (φέγγος, light) animals for the dark is about as strong as the *Unlust* of *phengophob* animals for the light.

Meanwhile, almost unnoticed by zoologists, enormous progress had been made in the investigation of directed movements of plants and of freely moving unicellular organisms. Here there was no danger of obscuring the real problems with anthropomorphic phrases. The scientific conception of geo-tropism goes back to Knight (1806) and of photo-tropism to De Candolle (1832). The conception of these two phenomena which is current to-day is due to Sachs (1832–97). In the ten years before 1888 a remarkable series of important publications on the movements of unicellular organisms laid the foundations of the scientific treatment of sense physiology and the principal new terms were invented about that time. Strasburger (1878), in a fundamental study of the movements of swarm spores and flagellates in response to light, used the term *photo-taxis* to distinguish the locomotory reactions of freely moving organisms from the *photo-tropic* reactions of sedentary plants. Then Pfeffer (1883, 1884, 1888), in an equally fundamental series of investigations on the attraction of the sperm of ferns and mosses by chemicals, established the term *chemo-taxis*. Schwarz (1888) described certain behaviour of the green flagellates *Chlamydomonas* and *Euglena* as *geo-taxis*, though we now know that the term is inappropriate for these particular reactions. Jönsson (1883) first detected *rheotropism* in growing plants and in Myxomycetes, while Stahl (1884) described positive *hydrotropism* in Myxomycetes. Engelmann made two important discoveries, the *photo-kinesis* of *Amoeba* (1879), diatoms and *Paramecium* (1882), and particularly of *Bacterium photometricum* (1883), and the chemical attraction of bacteria to oxygen (1881). His work led to that of Jennings on the ciliates. *Thermotropism* was discovered by Wortmann (1883) for plants, and Verworn (1889) used the same term for reactions of *Amoeba*. Verworn (1889) was also responsible for the first use of the terms *thigmotropism* and *galvanotropism*.

The ground was thus well prepared for the prophet of the new movement, Jacques Loeb. Starting in 1888, he set his face against anthropomorphism and teleology in the study of invertebrate behaviour and began the attempt to describe all behaviour in physical and chemical terms. As a young colleague and intimate friend of the plant physiologist Sachs, at the University of Würzburg in Bavaria, Loeb was well acquainted with the progress already made in the study of the responses of plants and of unicellular organisms. This work had just been described in the second edition of Sachs's famous book *Lectures on Plant Physiology* (1887). The theory of the tropisms (τροπή, turn) of plants was the starting-point for Loeb's tropism theory of animal reactions. In 1890, he published a book entitled *Der Heliotropismus der Thiere und seine Uebereinstimmung mit dem Heliotropismus der Pflanzen*, and from that time until his death in 1924 his record is one of the most extraordinary activity.

Loeb's ideas are perhaps best put forward in his own words. In his last book on the subject, published in 1918, he wrote:

'The analysis of the mechanism of voluntary and instinctive actions of animals which we propose to undertake in this volume is based on the assumption that all these motions are determined by internal or external forces. Our task is facilitated by the fact that the overwhelming majority of organisms have a bilaterally symmetrical structure, i.e., their body is like our own, divided into a right and left half.

'The significance of this symmetrical structure lies in the fact that the morphological plane of symmetry of an animal is also its plane of symmetry in physiological or dynamical respect, inasmuch as under normal conditions the tension in symmetrical muscles is the same, and inasmuch as the chemical constitution and the velocity of chemical reactions are the same for symmetrical elements of the surface of the body, e.g., the sense organs.

'Normally the processes inducing locomotion are equal in both halves of the central nervous system, and the tension of the symmetrical muscles being equal, the animal moves in as straight a line as the imperfections of its locomotor apparatus permit. If, however, the velocity of chemical reactions in one side of the body, e.g., in one eye of an insect, is increased, the physiological symmetry of both sides of the brain and as a consequence the equality of tension of the symmetrical muscles no longer exist. The muscles connected with the more strongly illuminated eye are thrown into a stronger tension, and if now impulses for locomotion originate in the central nervous system, they will no longer produce an equal response in the symmetrical muscles, but a stronger one in the muscles turning the head and body of the animal to the source of light. The animal will thus be compelled to change the direction of its motion and to turn to the source of light. As soon as the plane of symmetry goes through the source of light, both eyes receive equal illumination, the tension (or tonus) of symmetrical muscles becomes equal again, and the impulses for locomotion will now produce equal activity in the symmetrical muscles. As a consequence, the animal will move in a straight line to the source of light until some other asymmetrical disturbance once more changes the direction of motion.

'What has been stated for light holds true also if light is replaced by any other form of energy. Motions caused by light or other agencies appear to the layman as expressions of will and purpose on the part of the animal, whereas in reality the animal is forced to go where carried by its legs. For the conduct of animals consists of forced movements' (pp. 13–14).

'Physiologists have long been in the habit of studying not the reactions of the whole organism but the reactions of isolated segments (the so-called reflexes). While it may seem justifiable to construct the reactions of the organism as a whole from the individual reflexes, such an attempt is in reality doomed to failure, since reactions produced in an isolated element cannot be counted upon to occur when the same element is part of the whole, on account of the mutual inhibitions which the different parts of the organism produce upon each other when in organic connection; and it is, therefore, impossible to express the conduct of the whole animal as the algebraic sum of the reflexes of its isolated segments' (pp. 21–2).

This statement will be discussed at the end of this book, when the material for the discussion has been marshalled; it should be pointed out here that it is by no means free from demonstrable error and unjustified dogma. Strangely enough, the reactions which were earliest found to be impossible to fit into this scheme were reactions of Protozoa.

However much in error Loeb may have been in his ideas, he

certainly stimulated an enormous amount of work and of discussion. It was perhaps unfortunate that he formulated his theory so early in his career, for he showed both stubbornness and vigour in defending it and refused to consider sound arguments against it. In the end, he gave what was superficially an extraordinarily clear picture of his 'Mechanistic Conception of Life' (1912), illustrated by his description of J. H. Hammond's 'artificial heliotropic machine'. This machine was fitted with photo-electric cells and it reacted to light in much the same way as a positively photo-tactic organism.

'It seems to the writer', he wrote (1918), 'that the actual construction of a heliotropic machine not only supports the mechanistic conception of the volitional and instinctive actions of animals but also the writer's theory of heliotropism, since this theory served as the basis in the construction of the machine. We may feel safe in stating that there is no more reason to ascribe the heliotropic reactions of lower animals to any form of sensation, e.g. of brightness or color or pleasure or curiosity, than it is to ascribe the heliotropic reactions of Mr. Hammond's machine to such sensations' (p. 69).

'The best proof of the correctness of our view would consist in the fact that machines could be built showing the same type of volition or instinct as an animal going to the light' (p. 68).

The writer 'is inclined to believe that with this enlargement [memory] the tropism theory might include human conduct also . . .' (p. 171.)

The principal objections to Loeb's all-embracing theory developed along three main lines. First, Jennings early showed that many reactions of Protozoa would not fit into the tonus theory and eventually Loeb admitted this (1918, p. 155), though he objected to their being called 'trial and error' reactions. Later, other reactions, now known as telo-taxis and the light compass reaction, were found which did not fit in, either because they could occur when the animal had been made asymmetrical experimentally or because they were essentially asymmetrical reactions. In the second place, many authors disapproved of the automaticity and the rigidity of the mechanistic scheme of reaction proposed by Loeb. These authors include v. Buddenbrock (1915 b), Bierens de Haan (1921), and, more recently, Russell (1938) and Alverdes (1932) and his school. In the third place, a number of weaknesses were found in the application of the tonus theory even in the most favourable cases (Mast, 1911, 1913, 1914, 1915, 1923, 1938). Bitter controversy continued right up to the time of Loeb's death, although many of the differences between the antagonists could have been composed in 1919, when Kühn published a new classification of elementary orientation reactions. This classification incorporated some of Loeb's ideas and some of those of his opponents. It was soon accepted in Germany and there led to a fresh outburst of original research in the subject, but it has been almost ignored in other countries. In the United States, in particular, it has failed to damp the old tropism fires completely. Crozier and his school still use the old terminology and defend the old ideas, while Mast, Loeb's most successful opponent, has little use for the new classification (Table VI, p. 317).

Kühn's classification of elementary reactions is described in his own papers (1919, 1929) and also in a review by Fraenkel (1931). During the past twenty years it has been shown to be weak in certain directions, though extremely useful as a summary of an enormous body of knowledge. It provides the basis for the classification which we are putting forward in this book, and a number of the alterations which we are making in it are presented here for the first time.

When Loeb began to use the term *tropism* to mean a directed movement, he intended to stress the supposed fundamental identity of mechanism in the curvature movements of plants and the locomotory movements of animals. For a considerable time, however, botanists have restricted the term *tropism* to the curvatures of plants and have used *taxis* for the directed locomotory movements of lower plants, such as algae, flagellates, and swarm spores. In the interests of clarity and consistency, it is obviously better for zoologists to adopt the botanical nomenclature, to this extent at any rate. Moreover, the term *tropism* has, in the course of time, come to mean not only a directed reaction but also such a reaction with the particular kind of mechanism postulated by Loeb.

Loeb himself used the term in two senses—in the general sense of an orientation reaction, and in the special sense of a reaction having his particular kind of tonus mechanism. This led Loeb himself into difficulties, so that in his last book (1918) on the subject he headed a chapter 'Thermotropism' and quoted only experiments which, as he admitted, revealed no tonus mechanism. To-day the term is used for locomotory reactions by Crozier and his school in the United States and by a few workers elsewhere, but it is being steadily replaced by the term *taxis*. In Germany only the bending movements of plants and sessile animals are called tropisms. Mast avoids the use of either term and writes of 'photic orientation' where others would use the term 'photo-taxis'.

We shall not write of tropisms in this book. There are a few bending reactions of sessile animals to which this term seems to have a superficial application. These reactions include the 'heliotropic' bending of the tubicolous marine polychaete, *Spirographis spallanzani*, and the hydroid *Eudendrium*. They were originally described by Loeb, but they have never been properly reinvestigated, and it seems of little use to repeat here once more accounts which have been given again and again in many books since 1890.

The term *taxis* is to-day used for directed orientation reactions. Thus, positive and negative photo-taxis mean respectively movement straight towards or straight away from the light. We use the word only for reactions in which the movement is straight towards or away from the source of stimulation. It has thus much the same sense as Pfeffer's (1904) term *topotaxis*, which has never come into general use.

Undirected locomotory reactions, in which the speed of movement or the frequency of turning depend on the intensity of stimulation, we call *kineses*. This is established usage as far as variations in linear speed are concerned. There are some directed reactions in which the animal does not go straight towards or away from the source, but at an angle to the line joining it to the source; these we call *transverse orientations*, and we include under this heading the *light compass reaction* (Santschi, 1911; v. Buddenbrock, 1917), the *dorsal light reaction* (v. Buddenbrock, 1914), and the *transverse orientation to gravity*.

We devote one of the following chapters to each type of orientation and then, in the second part of the book, we survey the available knowledge about such reactions under the titles of the external factors which control them.

II

ORTHO-KINESIS

IN the first chapter a certain amount was written about the attitudes adopted by various workers in their studies of behaviour. Our own attitude can best be shown by detailed consideration of a particular case, a case which will at the same time serve as the example for the first type of reaction. For this purpose, we shall consider the behaviour of an animal in relation to its natural habitat, though later on we shall have to confine our attention to laboratory work rather strictly.

Meteorologists measure temperatures, wind speeds, humidities, and the like in assessing the climate and the weather of the moment; but these are regional measurements, intended to avoid showing local peculiarities, and they are of very limited value in describing the climates and the conditions in which small animals live. In an ordinary garden the temperature and wind speed vary from point to point, and the air humidity is often much higher beneath a stone or in a rubbish heap than it is in a standard meteorological screen. In a garden there is a great variety of habitats for small animals, varying greatly from one another in physical conditions. There are many *micro-climates* or *eco-climates* (οἶκος, dwelling) (Chapman, 1931; Kirkpatrick, 1935). The animals are not uniformly distributed over the whole region—as if scattered by an enormous pepper-pot—but, as every student of natural history knows, each species tends to be found in a particular eco-climate. For example, woodlice are generally found in moist places under stones and pieces of decaying wood. Our experiments will try to find an answer to the question, Why are woodlice usually found in moist places?

The experiments have in fact been carried out on the common species, *Porcellio scaber* (Gunn, 1937), but there are indications that similar results are to be obtained from several other species. In the first experiment a batch of the animals is divided into two halves; one half is put into a chamber containing enough water to saturate the space with water vapour quickly, and the other into another chamber in which the air is dried by means of calcium chloride, phosphorus pentoxide, or any other desiccating agent. The chambers are kept at room temperature (15–20° C.). Most of the animals in the moist chamber soon come to rest and later walk about very little. They live for days, and their weights hardly change at all. In the dry air, on

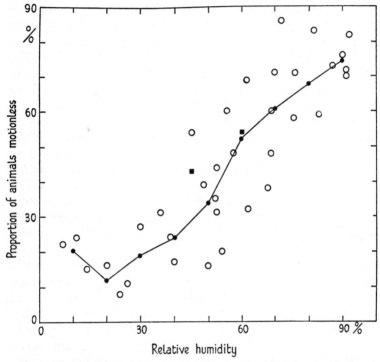

FIG. 1. Locomotory activity of the woodlouse, *Porcellio scaber*, in relation to humidity. Each point represents the number of animals motionless (expressed as a percentage of all the animals) in one experiment at constant humidity. The black squares represent experiments in which caustic potash and phosphorus pentoxide solutions were used instead of sulphuric acid. The line joins average points. (Gunn, *J. exp. Biol.* 1937.)

the other hand, the woodlice are almost incessantly active (Fig. 1), they die after an average of six hours, and by that time they have lost about a quarter of their original weight. Losses of carbon dioxide and faeces are relatively small, and the remainder is due to the evaporation of water from the body surface. It is this desiccation which kills the animals.

Thus *Porcellio* is quickly killed by dry air, while it remains alive a long time in moist; it walks about very much in dry air and hardly at all in moist.

In the second experiment some woodlice are put into a chamber in which there is, instead of a constant uniform humidity, a gradient of humidity (Fig. 2, p. 14). The chamber must be shallow; on one side of it are put dishes of water, and on the other, dishes of some desiccating agent. A perforated zinc platform is provided for the animals to walk on, so arranged that they cannot reach the water or the chemical below. Hygrometers can be put in to measure the humidities at the edges of the chamber, and an air-tight lid is put on. After 15–30 minutes a steady state is reached, with considerably moister air over the water than on the other side of the chamber. The animals are then dropped into the chamber through a small hole in the lid, and this hole is covered.

After a further quarter of an hour or so, most of the animals are seen to have collected in the moist side of the chamber, where they mostly stay still. From time to time one starts walking and goes into the dry side, but seldom or never does it stop there. The woodlice walk in both moist air and dry; they often stop and remain stationary for long periods in moist air, but they usually keep on walking in the dry. That is to say, their average linear velocity over the whole period, counting intervals of rest as well, is higher in dry air than in moist. Even under these artificial conditions, then, woodlice aggregate in a moist micro-climate rather than a dry one. Control experiments show that the animals really react to humidity and not to any smell of the acid.

We might say that woodlice like moist air and dislike dry, or that they seek the one and fear the other. But it is quite unnecessary to make any such assumptions about what goes on in the animals' minds. We can describe the behaviour in mechanical terms—actually by an analogy with motor-cars—because that involves only things that we can observe and demonstrate, while description in terms of the thoughts or emotions of the animals involves guesses and unjustifiable assumptions.

The mechanical analogy is a simple one, and it has some bearing on the traffic problem in towns. It is usual for through traffic to travel more slowly in towns than on main roads in the country. Suppose, for simplicity, that cars keep up a steady

speed of 40 miles per hour (m.p.h.) for 10 miles just outside a
town, then at the boundary the speed falls sharply to a steady

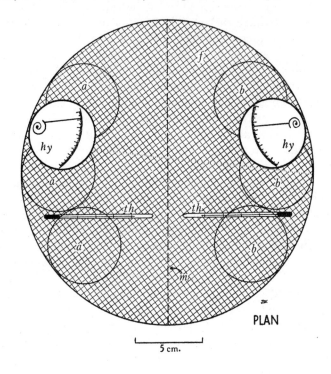

PLAN

5 cm.

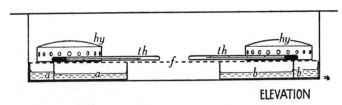

ELEVATION

FIG. 2. Alternative chamber, for testing locomotory reactions of small
animals to differences of humidity. Above, plan; below, elevation.
a, dishes of distilled water; *b*, dishes of sulphuric acid; *f*, perforated zinc
platform on dishes; *hy*, hygrometer; *m*, middle line; *th*, thermometer.
(Partly Gunn and Kennedy, *J. exp. Biol.* 1936.)

10 m.p.h. for the urban 10 miles, and then rises to 40 m.p.h.
again immediately on reaching the further boundary. Sup-

pose, further, that 100 cars are entering the area each hour, evenly spaced out.

It will take a particular car 15 minutes to cover the first 10 miles and, since the 100 cars per hour are evenly spaced out, during this quarter of an hour 25 cars will enter the 10-mile region behind it. At any one moment, then, there will be 25 cars in the first 10 miles. Similarly, it will take each car an

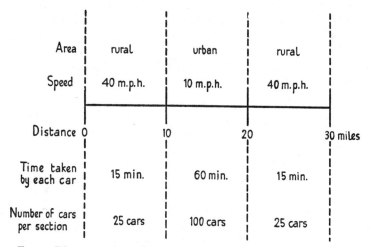

FIG. 3. Diagram to show the relation between the speeds of motor-cars and their concentrations. See pp. 13–15.

hour to get through the town, so that there will be 100 cars in that 10 miles, and again 25 cars in the further rural area. That is to say, a simple change in velocity causes a certain degree of aggregation in the region of low speed. As far as through traffic is concerned, it would hardly be correct to say that this is because the cars or their drivers like to linger in the town.

So it is with the woodlice. They move more quickly in dry air; their average speed is low in moist air, and they often stop altogether. The result of this dependence of velocity on humidity, which was observed in both of our experiments, is that they aggregate in moist air. Such a variation in linear velocity is called an ortho-kinesis (ὀρθός, straight, direct; κίνησις, movement) (Gunn, Kennedy & Pielou, 1937). The idea of *variation* in velocity is not implied in the Greek roots, but it is legitimate to put the idea into the compound technical term.[1]

[1] See also the exhaustive mathematical treatment of Gunn's *Porcellio* experiment, and of ortho-kinesis in general by Patlak (1953 a,b).

Although woodlice behave in another way which also contributes to the aggregation effect, the example will serve for the present purpose, for the ortho-kinesis alone would clearly lead to a certain degree of aggregation.

We have now some facts to help in deciding why woodlice are usually found in moist places. If they were scattered uniformly all over the country, and if they were to stay where they fell, some would fall on dry ground and desiccate to death, some would fall into water and would drown, and only those which fell in the moist places would live and reproduce. But we have learnt that they do not stay in dry places. They behave in such a way that they aggregate in moist ones, so that they are saved from premature death.

There are three popular kinds of answer to the question put forward on p. 11, if we disregard answers in terms of liking and fear. Two of these answers are almost valueless and even misleading, and the third is evasive.

1. They aggregate thus with the object of avoiding (or in order to avoid) death from desiccation. (The teleological answer.)

2. They aggregate thus because any ancestral woodlice which did not do so died young, and therefore left fewer offspring, while those which did behave in this way left more offspring, which inherited the beneficial behaviour. (The evolutionary answer.)

3. They aggregate thus because they are more active in dry air than in moist. (The mechanical answer.)

Consider these answers in turn. The teleological answer implies that either the animals themselves or some one or something can have a purpose or objective or end in view. There is no reason to believe that the animals learn this behaviour from experience, or that they hand on information from one to another or that they have insight into the situation. This answer depends on unjustifiable assumptions about the animals' minds or upon scientifically unjustifiable assumptions about outside control of or interference with the behaviour. It is an explanation in terms of what may go on in our own minds, based on the assumptions that woodlice have minds, and minds similar to those of men. Such an anthropomorphic explanation makes more difficulties than it solves, and is to be avoided, particularly for animals not closely related to man.

The evolutionary answer is a logical one. Though we can never *know* the historical details of the evolution of behaviour, it is just as evident that behaviour has evolved as it is that animal structure has done so. It is plausible to suppose that behaviour continually adapts to environment. But this answer is probably equally correct for almost every item of behaviour, and is the obvious answer in any investigation in which a correlation is found between the behaviour and the biological requirements of the animal. It does not lead to any systematic arrangement of our knowledge of the subject. It only attempts to tell us what went on in the past and gives no clue to what is going on during the present observations. It tells us, in effect, that they do so because they are what their inheritance makes them. It is interesting and instructive to find out correlations between behaviour in the laboratory on the one hand and natural habits and habitat on the other, and such correlations can follow the results of work on behaviour; they are not the essential material of the study of behaviour itself.

Perhaps, after all, there is no profitable answer to the question at all. Perhaps it is better to do what candidates sometimes do in examinations, and to answer a slightly different question which has not been asked—namely, *how* do woodlice aggregate in moist air? The answer to this question—though an incomplete one—is: by means of an ortho-kinesis. This is what we have called the mechanical answer, and it is the kind of answer given in this book.

It is trite to say that a thing is not explained by merely giving it a name; but names are convenient and economical for distinguishing things which are different and for showing the similarity of things which are similar, in behaviour and morphology and every other kind of science. No further justification is needed for erecting a classification. As for the name itself, the class of reaction must be given one of some sort and it is better to invent a new word, which can be given whatever meaning we choose, than to use a word already in the language and to distort its meaning to fit our purpose.

Photo-kinesis was the term used first by Engelmann (1882, 1883) for the mechanism of aggregation of *Bacterium photometricum* and certain other organisms in certain regions of the visual spectrum, but, as Mast (1911) has pointed out, that aggregation is not simply due to variation in linear velocity. The original experiment cannot therefore be used as the type of ortho-kinesis. Later, Loeb (1893) ascribed this type of reaction to *Unterschiedsempfindlichkeit*, or sensitivity to differences, the important factor being the intensity and not the direction of the stimulus. Mast (1911) seems to imply by *Unterschiedsempfindlichkeit* some kind of shock reaction which is dependent on rate of change of intensity and not dependent on direction, while Loeb used this word as a synonym of *kinesis*. In recent years, however, *kinesis* seems to have acquired the sense in which we use it, variation in intensity of locomotory activity which is dependent on the intensity of stimulation and not on the direction of stimulation (Patten, 1914). Shock reactions may be observable when the change of intensity is rapid enough, and there may be no reaction at all if sensory adaptation keeps pace with the change. We distinguish between *ortho-kinesis*, in which the rate of forward movement depends on the intensity of stimulation, and *klino-kinesis* (κλίνω, bend, incline), in which the frequency of turning depends on the intensity of stimulation (Gunn, Kennedy & Pielou, 1937). It is in the latter that shock reactions are often conspicuous.

These classifications of animal orientation reactions, Loeb's, Mast's, Kühn's, and the one put forward here, are all largely based on the externally observable features of the reactions. Classifications could be arranged on several planes or levels of refinement. The crudest method and in some ways the most satisfactory is simply to watch the animal under controlled conditions, as in the woodlouse experiment. It was in this sphere that Jennings and Holmes made their great contributions. The next refinement is to follow this up by interfering with the animal in such a way as to discover something about its internal machinery, to find out what part is played by the sense organs and their component parts, by the brain and nerves, the muscles, and so on. The most notable contributions to theory in this sphere have been made by Loeb, Mast, Kühn, and von Buddenbrock, and the emphasis has been on the mode of action of sense organs. Then one might go further, as Bethe, and Sherrington and his school have done, and investigate the reflexes and reflex co-ordination, or one might become still more fundamental and work on the mode of action of nerves and muscles as tissues.

The most fundamental investigations are concerned with the chemical and physical constitution and the organization of these organ systems. It is generally assumed that the properties of animal organs depend on the chemical and physical properties of their parts and on the organization of the parts into the whole, and that there is no divergence from the laws of non-living nature. Although this is pure assumption, the progress that has been made in physiology justifies it as a fruitful working hypothesis.

We are still far from being able to describe animal behaviour, even of the more elementary kind, in the fundamental terms of physics and chemistry or even in physiological terms. The greatest difficulty arises in the action of the brain. Fortunately it is not necessary to wait until a complete physical and physiological knowledge of animal activities is available before proceeding on the other levels of investigation. Just as the public analyst need know little of atomic physics, so the external characteristics of animal behaviour can profitably be observed and classified without much aid from the more fundamental sciences. At the same time, advances in physiology should contribute and are constantly contributing to advances in knowledge of behaviour.

Kineses are probably an important feature in the behaviour of many animals, particularly when the stimulus is of such a nature that it cannot guide the animal directly to its source. Thus light and radiant heat can give an immediate indication of the direction of the source, while smells can do so only in certain special circumstances. We might find out if kineses really are common by studying the literature on behaviour; but of course much of the work has been done with objectives other than the classification of reactions, or without present-day conceptions and criteria in mind. Consequently it is difficult to find many good examples; Wolsky (1933) gives some in discussing stimulatory organs.

Planarians have often been put forward as exemplifying photo-kinesis. Thus Loeb (1893) noted that *Planaria torva* is activated by light; he also pointed out, however, that these animals become active at night and are inactive in shadows in the day-time (Loeb, 1894). Pearl (1903) used *Planaria gono-cephala, P. dorotocephala*, and *P. maculata* and said in addition that very intense light causes a rise in the rate of locomotion, but he gave no figures. Walter (1907), in a very thorough piece of work, found that the rate of crawling of *P. gonocephala* in dark-ness was 0·50 mm./sec. and in light of intensity 38 metre-candles was 0·82 mm./sec. In another set of experiments he got 0·57 mm./sec. for darkness and average speeds varying irregu-larly from 0·63 to 0·75 mm./sec. for light intensities between 0·94 m.c. and 431 m.c. Welsh (1933) used a marine tur-bellarian, *Plagiostomum* sp., and found that very intense light of 1,500 foot-candles (1 ft.-candle = about 10 metre-candles) in-creased the rate of linear movement by 10–20 per cent. over the rate for 7·5 ft.-candles. Ullyott (1936) pointed out that *Dendrocoelum lacteum* is not inactivated by darkness and its normal period of activity is the evening. In some experiments on the training of the polyclad, *Leptoplana*, Hovey (1929) regularly found that the untrained animals started to move when the light was switched on.

All these flat-worms aggregate in the shadier parts of the available area and come to rest there. How, then, are all these observations to be reconciled? First of all, darkness does not stop movement, so the activity at night provides no problem. Second, an increase in light intensity tends to arouse stationary animals, and in addition they are periodically active in any case, whether kept in darkness or in light. During an active period the photic effect on the speed of locomotion can hardly have much aggregating influence, for the concentrations of animals in the various regions due to that are simply inversely proportional to their speeds, which differ by only about 30 per cent. at the most (cf. pp. 13–15). It is, therefore, clear that the aggregations observed have other causes. In fact it has been shown that the frequency of turning varies with the light intensity and that these animals are able to move straight away from a light source even when it is very dim and diffuse (Ullyott, 1936). These other reactions lead to aggregation, and the animals simply come to rest when the usual period of activity is over. The cessation of movement maintains an aggregation which has been reached mainly by other means. The general result of this is, therefore, that the animals will be found in the shadier places in the day-time. The other kinds of reaction mentioned here are dealt with in Chapters V and VII.

There has been some disagreement about photo-ortho-kinesis in the maggot larvae of various flies—*Calliphora*, *Sarcophaga*, and *Musca*. These maggots are strongly photo-negative (see Chap. VI). Mast (1911) reported a speed of 0·321 cm./sec. in 7 m.c. and 0·345 cm./sec. in 3,888 m.c., and concluded that the photo-kinetic effect was negligible. Herms (1911) recorded speeds of 0·416 cm./sec. in 325 m.c. and 0·469 in 1,057 m.c.; he thus found a greater increase in speed for a smaller increase in light intensity than Mast. These results have been discussed by Miller (1929); he stressed the importance of the local rise of temperature caused by intense illumination, and showed that the speed of locomotion in maggots is closely correlated with temperature. Detailed consideration of the various papers leads to the opinion that if the speed of maggots depends on light intensity at all, the effect is quite small.

Most, if not all, of the quantitative work on the speed of locomotion of land animals in relation to light intensity is subject to this criticism; intense artificial light raises the temperature, and it may be the rise of temperature which causes the animal to go more quickly and not the light at all. Experiments carried out with aquatic animals are not so weak in this respect, for their body temperatures must be kept fairly constant by the water, and the temperature of the water can be taken accurately with a thermometer. The work of Cole (1923) on *Limulus* in sea-water falls into this class. He recorded velocities of 178 cm./min. in 8,000 m.c. and 157 cm./min. in 900 m.c. Still, such slight variations in velocity seem unimportant in producing aggregations of animals, and attention should rather be directed to those cases in which movement ceases altogether in a certain intensity. Herms (1911) found that the movement of maggots (*Sarcophaga*) ceased altogether when the light intensity was below 0·000,07 m.c.; Patten (1917) found that the whip-tail scorpion, *Mastigoproctus giganteus*, began to move only if the light intensity rose above 0·16 m.c., while the velocity was constant between 1·18 m.c. and 120 m.c. Similarly, Young (1935) showed that lampreys aggregate in the darker part of a tank simply by remaining active in the light and coming to rest in the dark. This reaction is interesting in another way, for it is not initiated in ordinary eyes but in pigment spots on the tail which are supplied by the lateral line nerve.[1]

In all the foregoing cases there is more activity in light than in darkness. In its ordinary daily cycle of activity the cockroach, *Blatta orientalis*, is active in darkness and inactive in light (Szymanski, 1914; Wille, 1920). In setting up a standard terminology for this kind of difference, the obvious thing is to refer to high activity as positive and to say that lampreys show positive photo-kinesis; but lampreys, by this means, aggregate in darkness and so are photo-negative, so that confusion in the sign attributed to the kinesis might easily occur. It would be particularly confusing in describing reactions in a temperature gradient (see Chap. XIV), for some animals are active in both high and low temperatures and become stationary and aggregate in a middle region. We are therefore proposing to retain the terms *photo-negative* and *photo-positive* to describe behaviour which leads to aggregation in darkness or light respectively and not to use positive and negative to qualify kinesis at all. Instead, we propose that when activity results from high intensity or concentration of the stimulus, it should be called *high kinesis*, and when it results from low intensity or concentration, it should be called *low kinesis*.[2] Thus lampreys show high photo-kinesis and cockroaches low photo-kinesis. The latter case is complicated by a tendency to rhythmical activity, but that is beside the present point.

This terminology needs further explanation as applied to certain reactions to contact. A number of animals, including the cockroach, which remain in crevices during a great part of their lives, are always active when they are in open spaces and tend to become stationary only when a large part of the body surface is in contact with solid objects. Now we might say, on the one hand, that contact inhibits movement or, on the other hand, that lack of contact stimulates the animal to move. The former statement implies that the animal is always spontaneously active unless the inhibitory contact stimulus is applied, while the latter implies that the absence of contact is an adequate stimulus to some receptor (see pp. 29–30) and leads to locomotion. We cannot yet decide which of these is the proper formulation. A change of stimulation, either an increase or a

---

[1] See note 1, Appendix.
[2] See note 2, Appendix.

decrease, can be an adequate stimulus (Adrian, 1928; Fraenkel, 1932 a), but there is no well-established case of the continued absence of positive stimulation, without temporal or spatial contrast, acting as an effective stimulus. It seems probable, therefore, that the contact is the positive stimulus involved and that its action is inhibitory. In that case, *thigmo-kinesis* (θίγμα, touch) is the appropriate name for the reaction. Loeb used the prefix *stereo-* (στερεός solid). A high degree of contact causes low activity, so animals which remain stationary only when in crannies show low thigmo-kinesis—they are active when they have little contact.

If there is complete inactivity below a certain intensity of the stimulus and always locomotory activity above that threshold, then if there is no other reaction all the animals must eventually collect in regions of low intensity of stimulus and be trapped there. In fact, of course, other reactions always interfere and some animals eventually become active in the aggregation zone. The intensity of aggregation then depends on the proportion of animals which are thus activated, from whatever cause. A survey of the literature suggests that ortho-kinesis is seldom the sole mode of reaction to any stimulus, and that it usually reinforces some other kind of reaction to the same stimulus. The data available are, however, very scanty and have usually been obtained merely incidentally in work on other kinds of reaction. Direct studies of ortho-kineses themselves may well show that these reactions have much greater importance than has been realized.[1]

---

[1] See note 3, Appendix.

III
PHYSIOLOGICAL MACHINERY

ALTHOUGH the behaviour of a whole animal can seldom be described in detail in physiological terms, there are grounds for hope that such descriptions will become more common as knowledge increases. At the present time, it is usually possible to refer externally visible behaviour to internal machinery in very broad outline only, and not in detail. Information about this internal machinery is increasing rapidly and it is desirable to have some knowledge of it, if only to avoid the kind of mistake made by some of the earlier workers. The information provided here should be supplemented from the books mentioned in the reference list.

Muscle is the tissue which is responsible, at the last stage, for most of the movements of the larger animals, and it is also the part of the behaviour mechanism which is most easily studied in the laboratory. Muscle is thus the principal *effector* in animals; cilia, flagella, and pseudopodia are less common effectors.

Some simple experiments can be done to show the principal properties of muscle. The calf muscle (gastrocnemius) of the frog is dissected out with its attached sciatic nerve, and the resulting nerve-muscle preparation is kept moist with physiological salt solution. The knee joint is firmly fixed, and the tendo Achilles at the heel end of the muscle is attached to a lever with thread (Fig. 4). The apparatus is so arranged that when the muscle shortens, the lever records the change by scratching soot off smooth paper. The paper is fixed on to a drum which is turned at the required speed by a motor.

In the intact animal the shortening or contraction of this muscle is always initiated by impulses passing down the sciatic nerve from the spinal cord. In a nerve-muscle preparation a similar impulse can be started by applying an electric shock to the nerve. A shock of suitable size produces a *single twitch* (Fig. 5).

Starting with a shock which is too small to produce any nerve-impulse, and increasing it step by step, eventually a point is reached at which a slight contraction occurs. This is the *threshold* of stimulation of the preparation. Further increases in the

shock produce a quick rise in the contraction, and then no
further increase at all. That is to say, over a narrow range of

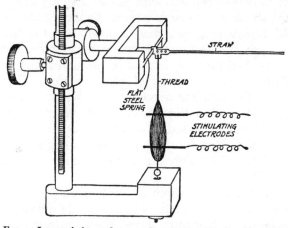

Fig. 4. Isometric lever, for recording the tension developed when
an isolated muscle is stimulated. The straw scrapes a white line on
smoked paper fixed to a rotating drum (see Fig. 5). The electrical
stimulus can be applied directly to the muscle, as shown here, or
to the nerve supplying the muscle. (Winton & Bayliss, 1935.)

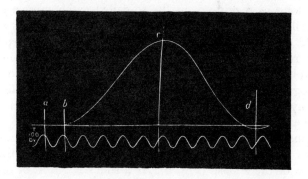

Fig. 5. Smoked drum record of a simple muscle twitch.
Time wave 1/100th sec. between crests. *a*, point of stimulation; *ab*, latent period; *bc*, period of contraction; *cd*, period of
relaxation. (Lovatt Evans, 1933.)

intensity of shock the intensity of the response is graded; on one
side of that range there is no contraction at all, and on the other
the maximum contraction always occurs. If, now, the nerve is
cut through progressively at some point between the electrodes

and the muscle, until only a single nerve-fibre is left intact, this grading disappears. The single nerve-fibre controls a small group of muscle-fibres, and they act as a single unit. As the size of the shock is increased, nothing happens at all until the threshold is reached, and then immediately the maximum response appears. The same is true for a single muscle-fibre which is shocked directly, instead of through its nerve. Both kinds of fibres, then, show the *all-or-nothing* effect. The graded response in the complete nerve-muscle preparation is due to the fact that the various fibres have slightly different thresholds, so that a shock can be found which will activate some fibres and not others; when the shock is a little stronger it passes the threshold for all the fibres, and the maximum contraction occurs.

The size of a single twitch is constant only as long as the conditions are kept constant. Changes in the initial length of the muscle, the weight of the lever, the temperature, the state of the muscle itself, and so on, can all affect the size of the contraction. The duration of the twitch is less variable, but it changes with the temperature and the state of the muscle. It varies in different muscles and different animals, so that it may be as long as 9 minutes in the so-called catch muscle of the lammellibranch, *Venus*, and as short as 1/300th second in a wing muscle of a fly or bee (Ritchie, 1928; Snodgrass, 1935). A fairly representative time for vertebrate skeletal muscle is probably about 1/10th second, the value for the calf muscle of the frog (Evans, 1933). The single twitch cannot, therefore, be the only motive force in the slow and controlled movements of whole animals.

If, instead of a single shock, a series of shocks is put in at regular intervals, the effect on the muscle depends on the frequency of the shocks (Fig. 6). If a shock is put in before the previous relaxation is complete, relaxation is replaced by a new contraction. A higher frequency of shock allows very little relaxation in between contractions and the result is *clonus*. When no relaxation occurs at all, and there is just one smoothly maintained contraction, the muscle exhibits *tetanus*. Tetanic contraction is the basis of normal movements in the whole animal and also of the maintained tensions of *tonus* (see Chap. IV) in skeletal muscle.

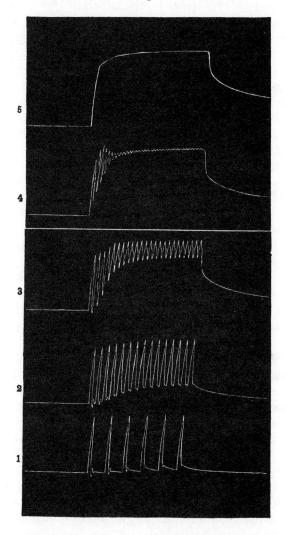

Fig. 6. The effects of repeated stimulation of a muscle. The records show progressive fusion of individual mechanical responses as the frequency of stimulation is increased from curve 1 to curve 5. 1. Complete relaxation between contractions. 2. Relaxation almost complete. 3 and 4. Clonus. 5. Tetanus. (Winton & Bayliss, 1935.)

In a slow limb movement in an intact animal, at first only a few nerve-fibres carry tetanizing impulses, each nerve-fibre to its own group of muscle-fibres. Since only a part of the whole muscle is involved, the force developed is slight and little movement results. Then, stage by stage, more and more nerve-fibres are activated from the central nervous system, and more and more groups of muscle-fibres are thrown into tetanus, so that the force developed and the extent of the movement increase progressively until a large part of the muscle may be involved. Although each new recruit to the active condition starts work suddenly and immediately exerts its full force, the whole change is gradual and smooth because there are very many fibres in the muscle and they are brought into action in progressively larger numbers. Control over the speed of the whole movement resides in the central nervous system, where the impulses originate.

When the movement is over, the limb may finish up in a position which can be maintained only by the continued application of muscular force. Muscles cannot hold a weight without expending energy—as a table carries dinner—and a muscle may be very active when its length and shape are not changing at all. Muscular fatigue from carrying a heavy object is a common enough experience. The active condition of a muscle without change of length, maintained isometric contraction, is called *tonus*. In tonus, a certain number of fibres are thrown into tetanic contraction. As they fatigue and begin to relax, other fibres take up the strain, so that the fibres become tetanized in relays. Co-ordination is carried out reflexly through muscle-spindles which send impulses to the central nervous system (see p. 33 and Chap. IV). This reflex tonus of skeletal muscle appears to be always present in the normal animal; it may be different from tonus in gut muscle and it can be distinguished as *tetano-tonus*.

It has been thought for a long time that the so-called catch muscle of certain lamellibranch molluscs had a mechanism other than the tetano-tonic one. This muscle keeps the valves of the shell closed, exerting a great force for a long time without apparent fatigue and with only a low consumption of oxygen at most. It has been shown by Ritchie (1928, pp. 77–86), however, that it is not necessary to postulate any peculiar mechanism and that the peculiar properties of this muscle are what might be expected as a result of the very long relaxation time and the low frequency of tetanizing impulses.

Most of these observations apply in principle to mammals and to the frog; it should not be thought that the machinery works in identical fashion in all the phyla of invertebrates. Indeed, some considerable differences are already known. It is unfortunate that our knowledge of nervous and muscular action is derived mostly from the study of vertebrates, while the elementary reactions dealt with in this book are seldom found in simple form except in the invertebrates. The study of the properties of vertebrate organs may, however, make it easier to grasp the principles on which invertebrate organs *may* work, and may shed some light on the subject by a kind of analogy; care must be taken to ensure that it is not a blinding light. It is clear that reactions which are superficially similar in Protozoa, Coelenterata, and Arthropoda cannot all be produced in the same way, because the effectors and the nervous systems differ so much. For example, inhibition takes place mainly in the *central* nervous system in the vertebrates, but in the Crustacea *peripheral* inhibition seems to be more important. In giving, in a few pages, a sample of physiological machinery it is clearly best to choose the type of machine which has been most extensively studied.

In the vertebrates practically all skeletal muscle is activated only by impulses travelling down efferent nerve-fibres from the central nervous system; these impulses are essentially electrical, though they are not electric currents. The nerve is rapidly restored after the passage of an impulse and becomes ready to transmit the next impulse. The process of restoration involves the consumption of oxygen and the appearance of heat and of carbon dioxide. The impulses themselves, even in a single nerve-fibre, can be recorded and measured by means of the cathode-ray oscillograph.

Anything which can make animal machinery start working is called a *stimulus*. The electric shocks applied to the nerve-muscle preparation are stimuli, though highly artificial ones. In intact animals the stimuli may be internal ones, such as hormones, or the strains applied to the muscle-spindles, or they may be external, such as changes in intensity of light, or pressure, or in the concentration of some chemical substance. Broadly speaking, any naked living tissue is sensitive to any kind of stimulation, provided it is intense enough. Some specialized tissues are particularly sensitive to one kind of stimulus; such a tissue is called a *receptor* for that stimulus.

Receptors take many forms. They may be aggregated together to form *receptor organs*, the familiar sense organs such as eyes, and provided with accessory structures like the lens and the iris, or they may be simply scattered free nerve-endings in the skin. Except in the Protozoa and the Porifera, which have no quick-conducting nervous system, receptors are linked with the nervous system. If an *adequate stimulus* is applied to the receptor—that is, a stimulus which is of the appropriate sort and of sufficient intensity—the receptor translates the stimulus into a different kind of energy and activates its afferent nerve.

Each receptor, then, has its own *specific function* and, while relatively unaffected by other stimuli, it may be extremely sensitive to its own kind of stimulus. Thus the dark-adapted human eye responds to about a dozen quanta of light energy of suitable wave-length, and some chemical receptors are activated by a few molecules of suitable substances. The idea of generalized receptors sensitive to all or several kinds of stimulus has been put forward, but no receptor of this kind is known. Protozoa, however, seem to be sensitive all over the surface to all stimuli, without much specialization.

The best way of obtaining direct information about receptor action is by recording the impulses in the afferent nerve. Using a suitable time-scale, the potential changes occurring are of the type shown in Fig. 7. When the time-scale is smaller, each impulse appears on the record as a spike arising from the base line (Fig. 8).

It is very difficult to interpret the impulses in a whole nerve composed of many fibres, and it is best to deal with a preparation of a single nerve-fibre, obtained by scraping away the other fibres in the nerve. If the receptor is appropriately stimulated, a series of impulses passes along the fibre; they are all the same size. An increase in the intensity of stimulation does not alter the size of the impulses; it alters their frequency. The impulses are very similar in character to those which occur in any other part of the nervous system.

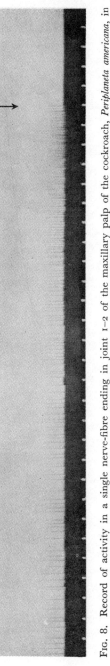

FIG. 8. Record of activity in a single nerve-fibre ending in joint 1–2 of the maxillary palp of the cockroach, *Periplaneta americana*, in response to forced flexion of the joint. Time marks $\frac{1}{10}$th sec. Record reads from *right* to *left*, and arrow marks start of movement. (*J. exp. Biol.*) (Pringle, 1938.)

We are now in a position to see the situation more clearly. First of all, when an impulse passes, nothing material passes along the nerve, just as waves in air, water, or the ether do not carry material with them. The impulse is like a fire passing along a train of gunpowder. The energy is obtained locally and the size of the fire at any point does not depend on the size of the fire which lit the gunpowder at the start. The gunpowder does not reconstitute itself ready for firing again, but the nerve does,

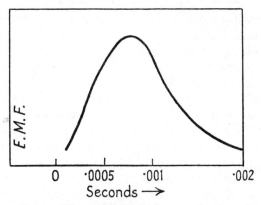

FIG. 7. Rise and fall of electromotive force in monophasic electric response (action current) of frog's sciatic nerve at 13° C. (Adrian, 1928.)

and after a very short *refractory period* it is ready to transmit again. A common frequency of impulse is about 100 per second. The impulses travel at about 100 metres per second (220 m.p.h.) in mammalian nerve.

An isolated preparation of the eye and optic nerve of the eel is almost inactive when unstimulated, i.e. in complete darkness. This is not true for some receptor organs, for the horizontal semicircular canal of the dogfish gives rise spontaneously to a steady train of impulses in its nerve; stimulation by rotation (angular acceleration) in one direction reduces the frequency of the impulses and in the other direction increases the frequency (Löwenstein & Sand, 1936, cf. pp. 223–7). Most receptors, however, appear not to initiate impulses spontaneously. When a light is shone into the eel's eye, after a short but appreciable time during which photo-chemical products are piling up in the retina, there is a great outburst of impulses in the nerve, many of the retinal cells being activated together. Within a few seconds the frequency of the impulses drops considerably, and then more and more slowly. This change is called *sensory adaptation*. It is distinguishable from fatigue and from accessory adaptation due to pigment movements, contraction of the pupil, and the like. Touch receptors adapt very rapidly, so that the impulses cease altogether a fraction of a second after the instant of application of a slight steady stimulus; the impulses start again if the stimulus is removed and applied again. For the eye, the impulses reach a very low almost steady frequency after 10 or 20 seconds. Muscle-spindles adapt so slowly as to be almost non-adapting. Other works (Adrian, 1928, 1930; Rawdon-Smith, 1938) should be consulted for a fuller account of receptor action.

It is apparent from what has been said that the intensity of stimulation can alter the impulses going to the brain in three ways—by altering the number of receptors and nerve-fibres involved, for the threshold of stimulation varies; by altering the impulse frequency in the fibres; and perhaps by altering the rate of adaptation. Actually the impulse frequency appears to be the most important variable, but the threshold effect is certainly significant in some cases. It is necessary to notice that in neither case is the total number of impulses reaching the brain proportional to the amount of physical energy which acts as the stimulus. In a single unit the impulse frequency diminishes owing to sensory adaptation while the external energy supply remains constant. Receptors are special tissues which translate the external energy into nerve-impulses, and the relation between the original and the translation is not necessarily either simple or constant. This fact spoils the simplicity of some of the statements made by Loeb.

Since the impulses in nerves are much the same wherever they occur, it is not immediately obvious how we receive the familiar varieties of sensory experience. A telegraphist might recognize the origin of a call by noticing which wire it arrives by. Similarly, the brain of a human being interprets the nerve-impulses according to the afferent nerve along which they arrive. All impulses passing along the optic nerve are interpreted as light, so that a violent blow on the eye, which stimulates the retina or the optic nerve mechanically, makes one see stars where none exist.

Receptors can be divided into three main groups—the

exteroceptors, which receive stimuli from outside the body; the *interoceptors* in the alimentary canal, which are responsible for belly-aches; and the *proprioceptors*. The last, the muscle-spindles of vertebrates and the campaniform sensillae of insects for example, occupy an anomalous position; they can be stimulated either from outside or from inside the body. They supply information about the distortions of the muscle-fibres and of the cuticle respectively, and therefore about the positions of the limbs. Muscle-spindles adapt slowly, so that one knows the position of one's legs even after a long period of quiescence in darkness. On the other hand, comfortable clothes cannot be felt without moving a few seconds after they have been put on, for the touch receptors show very rapid sensory adaptation. The proprioceptors are responsible for constantly grading and adjusting the muscle activities during movement and at rest. They are thus normally stimulated by the contractions of the muscles themselves, but they also come into action when a sudden external strain is applied, as when landing at the end of a jump, or when the knee is tapped to elicit the knee-jerk.

The exteroceptors are responsible for receiving external stimuli. *Photo-receptors* may take the form of eyes, which are often large and complex, or they may be free nerve-endings in the skin and they may not be externally recognizable. *Phono-receptors* take several forms, from the familiar ears of vertebrates to sensitive hairs in insects (Pumphrey & Rawdon-Smith, 1936). Indeed, it is difficult to make a hard-and-fast distinction between receptors for high-frequency vibrations, which we call sounds, and receptors for low-frequency ones which we feel with contact receptors in the skin. Thus the lateral line of fishes can be called a low-frequency sound receptor organ or a pressure receptor organ (p. 260). Other kinds of *mechano-receptors* (mechanical) are stimulated by contact, pressure of solids or fluids, angular accelerations (semicircular canals of vertebrates), or the force of gravity (statocysts).

Under the name *chemo-receptors* are included structures which we associate with the senses of smell and taste. We do not know whether the process of stimulation is really a chemical one or whether it is a physical one involving surface tensions or the like; the name is temporarily convenient. In vertebrates it is possible, by analogy with our own sensations, to distinguish between smell and taste because they involve different parts of the brain; even so, the layman is normally unaware that the 'taste' of his food is generally a compound of the taste in his mouth and the smell in his nose. Chemo-receptors are usually found round about the mouth, but they are also common in other regions, as on the antennae of insects. Receptors which are particularly sensitive to sugar solutions are even found on the feet of some Lepidoptera (Minnich, 1921; Marshall, 1935).

The stimulus provided by the humidity of the air can hardly be a chemical one, for water forms a very large proportion of all sensitive tissues and a little water more or less could hardly have much chemical effect; but since the term *chemo-receptors* is generally understood to be a cover for our ignorance, the class may for the time being be allowed to include *hygro-receptors* too. It is not economical to invent new terms until the position is clearer.

Lastly, *thermo-receptors* provide the animal with information about the temperature of its parts. They are probably present universally in animals, but their mode of action is almost completely unknown (Sand, 1938).[1] Indeed, our knowledge of the method of translation of stimuli into nerve-impulses is practically confined to the eye. The mode of action of accessory structures like lenses and vibrating ear-drums is fairly well understood in some cases, but the final stage of the translation is a practically untouched field.

The four great classes of external stimuli—photic, mechanical, chemical, and thermal—are not subdivisible to equal extents. Light may be of various wave-lengths—some of them invisible to us but visible to some other animals—and the flow of heat may be towards or away from the animal; but mechanical and 'chemical' stimuli may take one of many readily distinguishable forms. In the classification of taxes and kineses some of these are represented by prefixes, such as *geo-taxis* (gravity). It avoids confusion to use only two kinds of prefix—those indicating the class of externally observable mechanism of the reaction—such as *tropo-taxis, klino-kinesis*—and those indicating the physical nature of the stimulus—such as *photo-kinesis, thermo-kinesis*. It is undesirable to use prefixes like *horo-* (ὅρος, boundary) when the stimulus is not a simple physical one, for in such a case it is questionable whether the reaction is properly described as a taxis or not (p. 182).

[1] See note 4, Appendix.

IV

REFLEXES

WE know practically nothing about the transmission systems in Protozoa and Porifera. On the whole, the sensitive parts in these animals are very close to the effectors, so that even very slow messages must complete the journey in a short time. It has been shown that in a sponge, *Stylotella*, transmission takes place at about 0·2 to 0·8 cm. per second (Parker, 1919). Such transmission is called *neuroid* and is thus distinguished from *neural* transmission in nerve-fibres. The ciliary waves in *Paramecium* seem to move very quickly when observed with a microscope, but in fact they travel at the neuroid order of speed.

In all other animals quick-conducting nerves are found. In coelenterates the nervous system consists largely of a *nerve-net* under the ectoderm. This is rather like a layer of wire netting. When an activated receptor sends impulses into the nerve-net, they tend to spread fairly equally in all directions. In the anemone, *Calliactis*, for example, a single impulse started electrically does not, however, go very far, but is stopped in all directions by *synapses*. These are interruptions in the network where the transmission is sometimes stopped and in any case slowed down. Transmission across the synapse is probably chemical in nature, instead of being mainly electrical, as it is in nerve. An impulse which is stopped at a synapse does not leave that synapse unaltered, but prepares it in such a way that a second impulse arriving soon after can pass through. This phenomenon of preparing or clearing the way is known as *facilitation*. A series of impulses thus spreads in jerks from the initial centre, the leading impulse being lost at each ring of synapses. This arrangement differentiates between stimuli, so that a strong stimulus which starts a long train of impulses may affect a large part of the animal, while a weak one has only a local effect on the nerve-net. A certain variation in response is thus made possible (Pantin, 1935).

A nerve-net occurs in a number of other phyla, notably the Platyhelminthes and the Echinodermata, but in all phyla other than the Protozoa, Porifera, and Coelenterata there is also a central nervous system. The central nervous system consists

of a large or enormous number of nerve cell-bodies or neurones
and their fibres aggregated together. Now an animal which
received only one kind of stimulation and made only one kind
of response could have a direct nervous connexion between
receptor and effector and would not need a central nervous
system. If different kinds of response to one kind of stimulus are
possible, then there must be some means of turning the impulses
from the receptor into either of the several channels to different
effectors as occasion arises. This implies a set of connexions
between the various motor nerve fibres and the receptor fibre.
These connexions are the synapses. A synapse consists of the
ends of two nerve-fibres which come close together, in line, but
which are not actually continuous with one another. The gap
between the two fibres acts as a kind of valve, in the vertebrates
at any rate, so that impulses can cross it in one direction only.
Even when an impulse is transmitted across the synapse, the
speed of transmission is reduced while it is passing. There is
another kind of synapse in which the end of a nerve-fibre lies
close to a cell-body instead of to another fibre, but there seems to
be little difference between the two kinds in their activity.

The complexity of possible response in a series of animals
corresponds roughly with the number and degree of concentration of the nerve cell-bodies and the synapses. Concentration
of the cells reduces the length of fibre required for making connexions and is therefore economical of material. The importance of this can be seen by analogy with a telephone system.
A large town in which every house was connected with every
other by a separate wire would be a maze of wires and the
telephone system would be either lacking in privacy or would
require a complicated apparatus in every house. When each
wire goes to a central exchange, the system is more private and
more economical of material, at the cost of a little (synaptic)
delay in making connexions.

Recent work suggests that this analogy is far too simple to
suit the case at all completely. It throws a great deal of responsibility on the exchange operator, whatever that may represent
in the brain. There is evidence that some selection is carried
out by the muscles as well as the central nervous system, and a
resonance analogy is then invoked (Weiss, 1936; Lashley, 1929;
Coghill, 1929). The time is not ripe, however, to incorporate

this new work into a simple scheme, and we must confine our-selves here to the classical ideas, in spite of their deficiencies.

One of the simplest activities of the nervous system is exempli-fied by the mammalian response known as the *knee-jerk*. If one leg is crossed over the other in a sitting position, and the shin and foot are allowed to hang loosely, a sharp blow on or just below the knee-cap causes the shin and foot to jerk up sharply. In a normal person, no effort of will can completely prevent this response. The same reaction occurs in the decerebrate cat. If either the efferent or the afferent nerve is cut, the response disappears, so that the spinal cord must be involved in the reaction. Progressive removal of the spinal cord shows that only a small part of it is implicated. There is a very short time-interval between the application of the stimulus and the beginning of the response (0·0055 sec.), and there is evidence that only two synapses in the cord are involved (Jolly, 1910).

Most normal human beings give the knee-jerk, but it is ab-sent as a result of certain diseases. A few people who are quite healthy fail to give it unless they are at the same time engaged in pushing or pulling hard with their arms. The necessity for this reinforcement in some cases draws attention to the existence of individual variation, even in this most automatic and uncon-trollable reaction. It is therefore not surprising that great variation occurs with more complex reactions.

In the knee-jerk the stimulus is translated by the proprio-ceptors in the leg, goes to the central nervous system and is there, so to say, *reflected* back to the leg, where it is translated into effector action. The knee-jerk is thus a typical simple *reflex*. For simpler animals having no central nervous system the propriety of using the term *reflex* is very doubtful. At the other extreme, when a reaction involves many synapses and the so-called higher centres of the brain, it becomes too complex to call a reflex. The delay in the central nervous system is then too long for the impulse to be thought of as simply reflected. There is, however, no precise limit between reflexes and more complex activities, for one group shades into the other.

The phenomenon of *reflex tone* is also controlled by proprio-ceptors. These receptors are found, in the form of muscle-spindles, amongst the fibres of a muscle. They respond to a sudden stretching, such as is caused by striking the tendon of the vasto-crureus muscle in the knee-jerk test. The response to sudden stretching is a reflex contraction of those muscle-fibres which are associated with the stretched spindle. In tonus or tone some fibres are in a state of tetanic contraction. When they begin to fatigue and so to relax, there is a tendency for neighbouring fibres to be stretched; this stretching stimulates the muscle-spindles and initiates a reflex, so that the strain is taken up by the contraction of fresh fibres near the fatigued ones. This arrangement not only makes it possible for limbs to carry a weight, but it also acts as a resistance to any change.

Broadly speaking, any movable part of the skeleton has two sets of muscles—those which bend the limb and those which straighten it—and each flexor muscle has an *antagonistic* extensor muscle. If it were not possible to interfere with reflex tone, any bending movement would be rendered very difficult by the activity of the antagonistic muscles. In fact, however, the activity of those muscles which might hinder a co-ordinated movement is reduced or abolished. In reflex movements of the vertebrates, when additional impulses are sent from the motor neurones in the central nervous system controlling the active muscle, the activity of the motor neurones controlling the antagonist is reduced. The latter are said to be *inhibited*. Even the normal impulses of reflex tone are blocked to some extent, and this central inhibition is just as important in co-ordination as the central activation of the other neurones. In some Crustacea inhibition of the antagonist is not carried out centrally but peripherally, and there is an inhibitory nerve supplying each muscle, as well as sensory and motor ones.

We may thus imagine a stimulus being translated into nerve-impulses by the receptor; the streams of impulses may be re-translated at synapses several times in the central nervous system, but eventually there are at least two streams formed— the activating or exciting stream and the inhibiting one. There may also be other co-lateral streams which go through higher centres in the brain. These may eventually arrive at the motor neurones concerned by this roundabout route, and they may then interfere with these neurones in such a way as to alter the reflex. Interference of this kind becomes increasingly common and important in higher animals, it makes behaviour more variable and incalculable, and it is one reason for the rarity of simple repeatable orientation reactions in these higher animals. Such interfering impulses take longer to arrive, because they have to go through a larger number of synapses, where transmission is slowed down. Consequently, it may safely be said that sometimes the response starts before the brain has been informed at all. The knee-jerk starts before we are aware of it.

Reflexes are mostly activities which are carried out frequently during the life of an individual; they are often important in saving an animal from damage. The economy and the value of speed in such reactions, which need not involve the brain, is obvious. The relatively automatic reactions which the layman describes as 'instinctive' are generally either of this nature or somewhat more complex *acquired automatisms*. A true reflex is implicit in the structure of the nervous system and not learnt or acquired by exercise during the lifetime of the individual.

In the isolated nerve-muscle preparation there is a short interval—a few thousandths of a second—between the application of the shock and the beginning of the response, due to the conduction time in the nerve, synaptic delay in the neuromuscular junction, and the latent period of the muscle. In even the simplest reflex, like the knee-jerk, this delay is increased not only by similar factors on the afferent side but also by synaptic delay in the central nervous system itself. In a typical reflex like the extensor thrust in the cat, a response to pressure on the pad of the foot, or the flexor reflex in response to nocuous stimulation of the pad, the impulses do not simply go to the central nervous system and out again along a single line. A number of parallel paths are activated, and messages are relayed forwards to the brain and by other routes of various lengths to the motoneurones (Fig. 9, p. 40). The speed of transmission varies in the various parallel paths, so that the motoneurones do not all begin to be active at the same instant. Consequently, reflex contractions start smoothly, instead of abruptly like the contractions of isolated muscle. Moreover, a motoneurone may continue firing when stimulation of the receptor has ceased. This *after-discharge* tends to smooth off the decline or reversal of the original movement. Proprioceptive impulses from the muscle itself may contribute to a further smoothing and after-action. Even in the decerebrate preparation, then, reflexes are controlled movements.

Over a large saddle-shaped area of the back of the dog, a prick or an electric shock—simulating the activities of a parasite—initiates the *scratch reflex*. This can often be evoked in the normal dog by suitable tickling, and is probably familiar to most people. In the decerebrate dog, a steady unaltering stimulus leads to this repetitive response. There is thus an alternation of excitation and inhibition of the motoneurones controlling a whole series of flexor and extensor leg muscles. This alternation is not to be observed in the activity of the

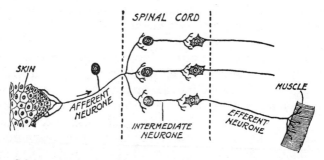

FIG. 9. Scheme of a simple reflex arc in a mammal. (Winton & Bayliss, 1935.)

receptors, but it arises in the central nervous system, in the series of neurones lying between the dorsal root ganglion and the motoneurones (Fig. 9). Again, the relatively complex activity of walking can be analysed into constituent reflexes, one of which leads to the next and so on in a chain. We conclude, therefore, that stimulus and reflex response need not be closely related in time and space, as they are in the knee-jerk, but the response may continue automatically for a considerable time after the cessation of the stimulus.

A particular muscle may be used by a large number of different reflexes. Each muscle is connected through intermediate neurones to many different receptors. A single muscle may contain tens of thousands of fibres, and to some extent different reflexes affect different groups of fibres in the one muscle, but each group of fibres is in fact used by more than one reflex. Impulses may thus converge on a motoneurone and its nerve-fibre, the *final common path*, from a number of different directions. A single final common path can, however, be used for only one set of messages at a time. In some cases the onset of one set completely obliterates a pre-existing one; in others an algebraic summation of excitation and inhibition may take place in the motoneurone, but in any case the resulting action is usually a co-ordinated one.

This co-ordination is made possible by the fact that each neurone in the grey matter is connected to a considerable number of others both on the sensory and on the motor side, so that there is practically a network connecting any receptor with any motoneurone. It is here that the most difficult problems arise. Why does a certain reflex take a particular path without activating all paths? That question is not yet answerable, but it seems probable that the answer will eventually be given in terms of properties of synapses, both for the cord and for the higher centres of the brain. When it is remembered that a single spinal nerve in man contains over 600,000 afferent fibres and 200,000 efferent ones, and that the corresponding dorsal root ganglion and motoneurone region form a relatively small part of the whole central nervous system, it will be seen that the enormous numbers of other neurones and their connexions which are present make possible an almost infinite variety of combinations of activities. Comparisons between the brains of different species are commonly made on the basis of mere bulk; the gross size of the brain must be interpreted rather in terms of the internal complexity which the size permits. The brain of man is said to contain about ten thousand million neurones.

Most of the reflexes so far mentioned, except the proprioceptive ones, have led to rather quick actions which are soon completed or succeeded by other actions. Such activities of the muscles are described as *phasic* as opposed to the *tonic* reflexes normally evoked by the proprioceptors and certain other receptors. Typical tonic reflexes are involved in the maintenance of the stationary upright posture in man and of the normal orientation to gravity in other animals. It seems possible that to some extent the red fibres in mammalian muscle are concerned mainly with posture and the white ones with phasic reflexes, but this distinction can hardly be a complete one. Thus slight deviations from normal posture are continually corrected phasically, and whole muscles are involved in some phasic reflexes. During normal walking two distinct sets of

reflexes are in action at the same time and in the same muscles—
the stepping reflex, with pressure on the soles of the feet as one
of the controlling stimuli, and balancing reflexes controlled
partly by the semicircular canals in the internal ear. It is not
known how far the combining of these reflexes occurs by the
summation of activities of two groups of fibres in the same
muscle and how far by the algebraic summation at the surfaces
of the motoneurones. In either case it is apparent that the
balancing during walking can hardly be due to a constantly
maintained tonus, but must be the result of continually adjusting
phasic activities. It is important to bear this in mind in considering Loeb's tonus theory of animal orientation.

The word *reflex* has been used above in its strict sense. Some
authors make a distinction between *partial reflexes*—that is,
reflexes in the strict sense—and *total reflexes*. The latter are
responses of the whole animal in its normal intact condition.
They probably represent a number of partial reflexes com-
pounded and co-ordinated; they may be regarded as automatic,
hereditary, and relatively invariable activities not involving
higher centres. In this book the word *reflex* is often used to
mean this kind of total reflex.

V

KLINO-KINESIS

THE earliest opposition to Loeb's tropism theory was put up by Jennings (1904, 1906) as a result of his work on Protozoa. The reactions of these animals could not be fitted into the tropism scheme, on the one hand because of asymmetries of structure and of response, and on the other hand because the reactions did not have the determinate and fixed appearance which was so important to Loeb. The semblance of forced action is greatest when an animal moves in a straight line which coincides with a ray of light; such reactions, which we now call taxes, provided the main support for Loeb's theory. On the other hand, Jennings demonstrated the occurrence of a number of aggregation reactions in Protozoa in which the direction of motion could not be related to the direction of the stimulus, reactions which we now call *undirected*.

In this kind of behaviour the direction of movement at any instant is completely random. Human locomotion is usually so purposeful that it is difficult at first to take in the idea of normally moving in undirected fashion. Almost all our steps are guided by what we can see in the near or far distance, by experience of what we expect to reach, or by information about the route to be taken. It is difficult to imagine what it would be like to have eyes which do little more than indicate the general intensity of light, to live so short a time that little experience can be gained, and to have no language or means of sharing experience and passing on tradition. In woodlice and many other animals, movements are very frequently random; for distance-receptors are often absent or temporarily ineffective, and the stimuli that the animal must then use arise in its immediate neighbourhood.

Although directed movements do occur in some Protozoa, in most cases locomotion is undirected. The classical example of this kind of behaviour is provided by *Paramecium*. If this animal swims into a hot region, it backs and turns and starts off again in a different direction; if it again reaches the hot region, the backing and turning are repeated and so on until it can swim forward freely (Fig. 16, p. 56). Identical reactions are shown when *Paramecium* swims into solutions of certain chemicals. This is what Jennings called 'trial and error' and Holmes 'the selection of random movements'. To most people both of these phrases have a somewhat anthropomorphic flavour—perhaps unnecessarily. Kühn substituted the term *phobo-taxis* (φόβος, fear) which was first suggested by Pfeffer (1904). Now it is important to notice that the new direction taken by *Paramecium* after a collision is practically unaffected by the angle at which it strikes the surface. There is no constant relation between the direction of the stimulus and the new direction of movement; the locomotion is thus undirected. When a number of individuals are doing it together, there is no semblance of drill or military manœuvres, so the word 'taxis' is not very appropriate. We are therefore using the name *taxis* for directed movements only. We can show, moreover, that it is possible to describe this kind of behaviour, objectively and quantitatively, as a type related to ortho-kinesis.

It is perfectly true that 'trial and error' can be understood as an objective description of certain movements, but it is also true that it is regarded as a subjective description by many people. In describing the same action in terms of reflexes, as we shall do, we do not pretend that all difficulties are thereby removed, but we consider that we are approaching the question in a manner which is likely to be more profitable.

The stepping reflex, which is the principal component in the act of walking, can be produced in a decapitated dog (pp. 40–2). It is well known that a fowl which has been decapitated for domestic purposes may run about for a short time. Walking is, in fact, a reflex act which may go on for a short time in the absence of the higher centres of the brain. There is nothing improper in speaking of such a complex co-ordinated action as a reflex, for we have already seen that there is a graded series of reflexes ranging from a single twitch-like response to a rhythmical response which continues even after the stimulus has ceased. It is clearly economical for an animal that an activity which is so constantly in use should be under automatic control, that it should involve few synapses, and those few in the lower parts of the nervous system.

In the woodlouse the reflex activity of walking occurs more often in dry air than in moist (Chap. II). In this case, walking may be described as a reflex response to the stimulus of dryness. The drier the air, the more the animal walks about, so that there is a rough proportionality between stimulus and response (Fig. 1, p. 12). This is the ortho-kinetic response. In some animals there is a *klino-kinetic* response, in which the rate of random turning, or angular velocity, depends on the intensity of stimulation.

In a uniform environment, where there is no reason why an

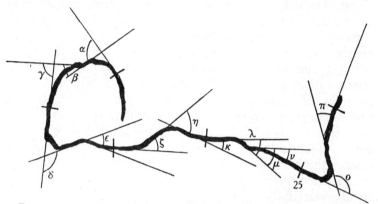

Fig. 10. The thick line represents the track of *Dendrocoelum*. The cross-lines mark half-minute intervals. The method of finding the values of the angles a, β, γ, &c., is shown. The amounts of turning in the five half-minutes shown were 215, 185, 90, 150, and 160° respectively. (Ullyott, *J. exp. Biol.* 1936.)

animal should turn at one point rather than at any other, turning nevertheless does occur. The direction of linear movement changes for no apparent reason. In some cases these random changes of direction occur often, so that the animal never goes far in a straight line. The planarian, *Dendrocoelum lacteum*, has been shown by Ullyott (1936) to behave in this way. When there is no suitable stimulus, like a current of water, directing the animal constantly, it does not go far in a straight line, but turns from time to time. Under uniform conditions there is a certain basal frequency of turning. Since the animal may change direction much or little at each turn, it is desirable to take account of the size of each turn instead of simply counting them, and to estimate the total of all the changes of direction in unit time. This gives a figure for the rate of change of direction (r.c.d.) (Fig. 10). The turns are added up irrespective of whether they are right or left turns, so it is perhaps inaccurate to call the r.c.d. an angular velocity. It must be understood that it is the *average* basal r.c.d. which is constant, for the r.c.d. varies from minute to minute. Similarly, the linear velocity varies from moment to moment, but the average is constant if a large enough number of minutes is taken into account.

If the intensity of the light shining on the planarian is increased, while everything else is kept constant, there is no change in the linear velocity, but there is a sudden increase in the r.c.d. There is no ortho-kinetic response, but there is an increased r.c.d. resulting from the increased light, a klino-kinetic response (Gunn, Kennedy & Pielou, 1937). The r.c.d., however, immediately begins to fall again, and after about 30 minutes or so has returned to the basal level (Fig. 11). This decay in the response in spite of the constancy of the physical stimulus strongly suggests sensory adaptation in the eyes (p. 32). Each time the light intensity is raised the same thing happens; the r.c.d. suddenly increases and thereafter falls slowly until it reaches the basal level again. On the other hand, a decrease in light intensity has no effect on either the linear velocity or the angular velocity.

Under suitable conditions this klino-kinesis can cause aggregation of *Dendrocoelum*, just as ortho-kinesis can cause aggregation in some other animals. In a suitable gradient of light these planarians collect in the darkest region and, even though they move about constantly, they do not leave this region. In order to discover whether this is a reaction simply to the *intensity* of light falling on the animal, or to its *direction* as well, the apparatus is arranged so that the animal moves about on a horizontal plane, and all the light comes from vertically above it. The room is dark, all the surfaces are dead black, and the graded series of lights shines down through a grid like an egg box. Thus the only object visible to the animal is the single patch of light above it (Fig. 12, p. 48). Any photo-reaction which the animal shows must then be a reaction either to the intensity of this single light or to the series of intensities of the single lights seen in turn. It cannot be a reaction to the direction of the light. If the gradient is of suitable steepness, the planarians, at first scattered evenly over the surface, after an hour or two collect in the dark end.

This aggregation of *Dendrocoelum* can be described in terms of the two components, namely, the alteration in the amount of

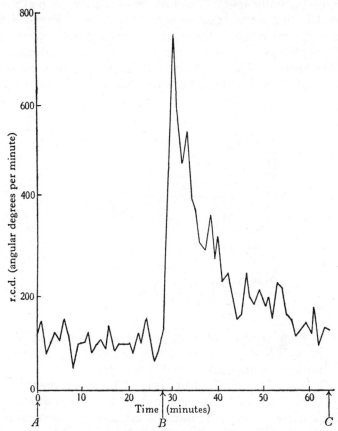

FIG. 11. Graph showing the relation between light intensity and the rate of change of direction (r.c.d.) of *Dendrocoelum*. *A* to *B*, in darkness, r.c.d. is basal. At *B*, light was switched on and left on. At *C*, with the light still on, the r.c.d. has returned to the basal value, owing to sensory adaptation in the eyes. (Ullyott, *J. exp. Biol.* 1936.)

reflex turning called klino-kinesis and the process of sensory adaptation in the eye. The strict mathematical treatment is too long to present here, because each animal may turn in any direction at any point and the analysis must be a statistical one. It is therefore necessary to present a simplified and idealized version![1]

[1] See also the exhaustive treatment of klino-kinesis by Patlak (1953 *a*,*b*).

The average basal rate of change of direction under the conditions used by Ullyott was just over one right angle per minute (actually 103°). The first simplification we make is to postulate that we are dealing with a mythical average animal, which always turns to the right, always through exactly one right angle (90°), and which spaces out these geometrical turns evenly in time. That is to say, if it has for the time being an r.c.d. of 90° per minute, it turns through one right angle at the

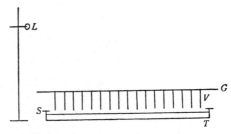

Fig. 12. Diagram of apparatus for obtaining non-directional gradients of light. *L*, source of light; *G*, opal glass; *V*, opaque black vanes; *T*, experimental trough, 35 × 110 cm.; *S*, cardboard, to stop reflection from sides of trough. (Ullyott, *J. exp. Biol.* 1936.)

end of each minute, rather than turning through 45° at the end of each half-minute or 180° at the end of 2 minutes or something more irregular.

With such an animal, when the r.c.d. increases, the time and the distance between these right-angled turns diminish. If the r.c.d. is quite constant, the animal keeps crawling round the sides of a square continually. When the light gets brighter, the r.c.d. rises, and the extent of the rise depends on the difference between the new light intensity and the intensity to which the eyes are fully adapted.

Consider our 'average' animal in a suitable gradient of light. Suppose that it starts somewhere near the middle, at *O* (Fig. 13, p. 49), fully adapted to the light on that cross-section of the gradient, and crawls across the gradient. The light intensity on the eyes remains constant, and the eyes were adapted at *O*, so the path *OA* before the first turn is the longest one possible, the length of path appropriate to the basal r.c.d. At *A* the first of the postulated right-angled turns occurs, taking the animal into brighter light, so that the r.c.d. is raised. The path *AB* must therefore be shorter than *OA*.

All along *AB* adaptation must be lagging behind the change in light intensity or the aggregation will not occur. At *B*, then, adaptation still lags behind. Let us make the simplifying

LIGHT   GRADIENT

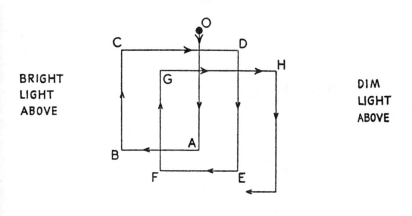

BRIGHT
LIGHT
ABOVE

DIM
LIGHT
ABOVE

FIG. 13. Path followed by the 'average animal' postulated in the text. *O* is the starting-point. *CD* is longer than *AB*, and *GH* longer than *EF*, &c., so that after each set of four turns the animal is a little nearer the dimly lit end of the gradient. For further explanation, see text, pp. 48-51.

assumption that in the constant light along *BC* adaptation becomes complete. The r.c.d. was high at *B*, and becomes basal at *C*, so the distance *BC* is shorter than *OA*. Along *CD* the animal is moving into dimmer light, so the r.c.d. remains basal, and *CD* is as long as *OA*. In similar fashion the animal proceeds along the line *DEFGH*, &c.

The lengths of *OA* and *BC* are not interesting except in constructing a consistent figure. The important fact is that *CD* is longer than *AB*, and *GH* is longer than *EF*, so that after each set of four turns the animal is a little nearer the dimly lit end of the gradient.

This theoretical treatment is, of course, far too simple and regular to apply directly to a real animal. The principal result of the treatment does apply, however, even when the simplicity is discarded; this result is that klino-kinesis with a suitable rate of

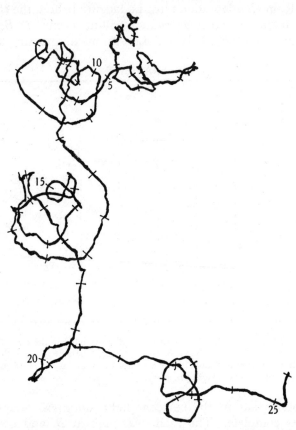

FIG. 14. Track of *Dendrocoelum* corresponding to the part *BC* of Fig. 11. The cross-lines mark half-minutes and the numbers give the time since the light was first increased. (Ullyott, *J. exp. Biol.* 1936.)

adaptation will tend to make pieces of track going towards dim light (*CD* and *GH*) longer than those going towards bright light (*AB* and *EF*). This account is in agreement with the kind of track made by *Dendrocoelum* in arriving at the darker end of a gradient. The animal faces in all directions in turn and wanders at random; but bit by bit it gets nearer and nearer to the darkness. It cannot see where it is going, for the experiment is arranged so that there is no horizontal light at all, and the reaction cannot be a directed one (see following chapters). Its only guide is this: if travelling in a certain direction leads to an increase in the light falling on the eyes, then that direction is the wrong one. This involves the act of comparing a certain light intensity in the present with another light intensity in the past. It is not necessary to postulate a mind making this comparison—the properties of the eye itself provide the mechanism of this rudimentary kind of memory. If the light falling on the eye is constant, no shift in the chemical equilibrium takes place there and the eye is fully adapted; if the light increases, there is a shift in the chemical equilibrium in the retina, and this acts as a stimulus to the afferent nerve. As soon as the new equilibrium position has been reached, and the shifting has stopped, the nerve is no longer stimulated and the reaction ceases.

It is therefore the photo-chemical equilibrium in the eye which is acting as 'memory'. A displacement of the equilibrium results from a change of light intensity, but the change inside the animal's eye lags behind the external change, and is fairly slow, so that the activity in the optic nerve goes on for quite a long time after the external change is over. The curve shown in Fig. 11, p. 47, shows how very slow adaptation is.

It is interesting to see what happens if there is klino-kinesis, but without adaptation or other complications. Suppose that for some animal, not *Dendrocoelum*, increase in light results in an increased r.c.d. which is then maintained at the new level. Suppose, simply, that for each light intensity in the scale there is an appropriate level of r.c.d., which is instantly reached and then maintained as long as the light is constant. Then, in the gradient, the animal would twist and turn in the light and make long straight excursions in the dark, but there would be no aggregation in the dark. Indeed, at first glance it seems as if there should rather be aggregation in the light, because once an individual gets there its path must become so tortuous that it would take a long time to get away (see below). If *Dendrocoelum* gets into intense light, it adapts, so that after a certain time it has its basic r.c.d. and can make the long excursions which give it a fair chance of getting away. In fact, our hypothetical non-adapting animal would remain uniformly distributed, for there is no factor postulated which would favour motion in one direction rather than another. At any point in the gradient there is no reason why such an animal should turn sooner when going up the gradient than when going down. On the average each animal which laboriously and deviously leaves the bright end will be replaced by another one approaching equally deviously. Adaptation, however, *is* a factor which favours motion in one direction. At a given point in the gradient, planarians going up the gradient will tend to have a higher r.c.d. than those going down. The reason for this is that the r.c.d. now depends on the past as well as the present light-intensity, because of the effect of the past light-intensity on the slow process of adaptation.

The point can be made clearer by a rather far-fetched analogy. Imagine that an animal must accumulate a certain quantity of light before it can turn, as if it were filling a jug. When it turns it empties the jug and then has to fill it again before it can turn once more. In the gradient the light is raining down, a downpour at the bright end and a drizzle at the dim end. All this is appropriate if the r.c.d. is dependent only on the light intensity at the moment, with no adaptation. In such a case, on going up the gradient the jug fills slowly at first and then more quickly, and on going down it fills quickly and then more slowly. If the animal crawls up a distance sufficient to fill it, on the return journey it will crawl exactly the same distance before turning, for the jug takes the same time to fill whichever way the animal traverses a particular stretch. Now if there were instantaneous adaptation, the jug would be expanded or contracted to suit the light, and it would always be filled in exactly the same time. The r.c.d. would be constant at all intensities, at the basal rate, and there would be no aggregation. *Dendrocoelum* compromises between the two and, unlike either of them, it does aggregate. It adapts slowly. As it goes up the gradient, the jug expands but not quickly enough to keep pace with the increasing rain, so the animal turns rather soon. When it is going down the gradient from C (Fig. 13, p. 49) its r.c.d. goes down to basal. The jug analogy becomes rather complicated here, for along CD adaptation is still lagging behind, but we must imagine the jug contracting as the rain diminishes. *Dendrocoelum* when going up the gradient turns sooner than an instantaneously adapting animal and later than a non-adapting one; going down the gradient it behaves as if it adapted instantaneously, though in fact it does not.

At this point it is interesting to compare ortho-kinesis with klino-kinesis. Pure ortho-kinesis, uncomplicated by any other reaction, is rather inefficient as an aggregating reaction. There is nothing in ortho-kinesis to stop the animal going to all the available places, and the aggregation zone is reached by sheer chance. The reaction consists of a relative delay in leaving this zone once it has been reached. In aggregation due to klino-kinesis with adaptation, on the other hand, there is always an extra tendency for the animal to turn aside when it is going away from the aggregation zone in a gradient, and to this extent it is guided back to that zone. Adaptation or some such complication is essential to klino-kinetic aggregation; adaptation would merely make ortho-kinesis even less efficient in producing aggregation.[1]

As we shall see in the following chapters, a still more efficient mechanism of aggregation is provided by *taxes*, or directed reactions, in which the animal goes directly towards the aggregation zone. For taxes, however, a more complex receptor system is required, so that discrimination of direction is made possible. For kineses, receptors which discriminate only intensity are sufficient. Nevertheless, kineses may be exhibited by animals which have direction receptors and which can show taxes under suitable conditions. *Dendrocoelum* itself is such an animal. It is for this reason that it is necessary to ensure that experiments on kineses are so arranged that there is no horizontal light component and taxes are impossible.

Although the highly artificial conditions of these experiments can seldom exist in nature, such conditions are required for the analysis of the mechanism of the reaction. In nature the light often takes the form of a patchwork with sharp shadow edges, instead of the ideal smooth gradients so far considered. Some of the earliest behaviour experiments by Graber were done in 'choice chambers' or 'alternative chambers', in which half of the field was light and half dark, with a sharp shadow edge between. Until recently, however, insufficient attention was

[1] See note 5, Appendix.

paid to the small amount of horizontal light reflected from the walls of the chamber and from surrounding objects in general. When all the effective light comes from above, the aggregation of *Dendrocoelum* in the dark side can be described in terms of the reaction just dealt with.

In this connexion the conception of net distance travelled

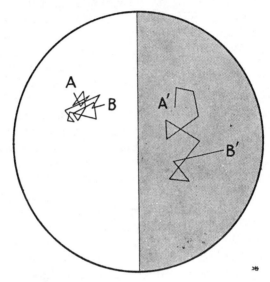

Fig. 15. An 'alternative chamber', with one half lit from above and the other in shadow. Showing the kinds of track to be expected from non-adapting animals on each side, in klino-kinesis.

is of value. Suppose an animal starts from a point *A* (Fig. 15) and travels by a devious path to another point *B*, the straight line joining *A* to *B* is the net distance travelled, while the actual distance is much greater. When the r.c.d. is high, the animal twists and turns and crosses and re-crosses its own path, and the net distance covered is small. When the r.c.d. is low, however, the average net distance (*A'* to *B'*) is considerably higher than in the former case.

If some specimens of *Dendrocoelum* are placed in such a chamber, they eventually collect in the dark. The original low net rate of travel in the light rises as adaptation proceeds, and the animals tend to reach the boundary sooner than they would if there were no adaptation. In the dark side the low r.c.d. results in the animals having a high net rate, so that they frequently reach and cross the boundary into the light. Immediately one does so there is a great rise in the r.c.d. (Fig. 11, p. 47), much twisting and turning goes on, so that mostly the animal by chance gets back into the dark. When it does so, it goes off in a straight line (low r.c.d.) and so remains in the dark. When, in spite of the high r.c.d., the animal goes farther into the light instead of regaining the darkness, re-entry is facilitated by adaptation, when that eventually goes far enough, giving a higher net rate of travel and a higher chance of reaching the boundary again. When the boundary is reached, crawling across from light to dark is uninterrupted. If there were no adaptation, the effect would be to trap each animal in the region where it had started, in the light because of the low net distance travelled in a given time and in the dark because of the tendency to turn back at the boundary, and the final result would be a uniform distribution of animals; but when adaptation occurs, the turning back into the dark is just the same, while the trapping in the light is reduced.

The striking part of the reaction as one observes it is the sudden rise in r.c.d. near the boundary, and it is upon this that attention has previously been focused. On reaching the light the animal turns. If this turn takes it back into the dark, it ceases to turn. If it does not, there is another turn, and so on. It looks as if the animal is avoiding the light, as if it tries one direction and, if that fails, then another (Fig. 16, p. 56). It is, therefore, not surprising that until recently the terms 'shock reaction', 'avoiding reaction', 'trial and error', and 'phobo-taxis' have been applied in such cases. As we have seen, it is unnecessary to postulate anything anthropomorphic in the behaviour of *Dendrocoelum*, and the reflex theory of klino-kinesis with adaptation provides the simplest available mechanism. Although the conception of 'trial and error' may be necessary in studying the behaviour of mammals, it appears to be unnecessary for the reactions discussed here. [1,2]

Rather a large amount of space has been devoted to examining Ullyott's results from various points of view because it is not at first easy to see how the reaction in a gradient works. The different points of view will probably suit different people.

[1] See note 6, Appendix.
[2] See note 7, Appendix.

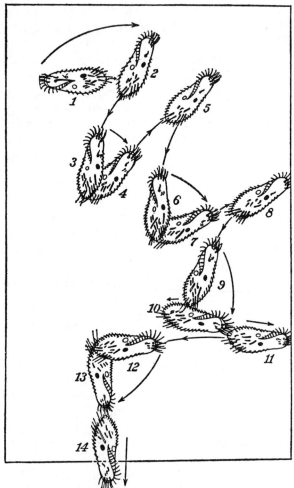

FIG. 16. Reaction of *Oxytricha* to heat applied at *x*. The organism moves backwards from position 2 to position 3, then swivels on its posterior end to position 4, and then goes forward to position 5. The set of movements 2 to 5 constitutes one turn. This turn did not take the animal out of the warmed area and turning was repeated in (5–8), (8–11), and (11–14). Evidently it was cooler at position 14 and the animal then went straight on. Notice that turning was always towards the aboral side. In this type of reaction the new direction taken after a turn is not dependent on the direction of the steepest gradient nor on any other property of the stimulus. (Jennings, 1906.)

Ullyott's results are too new to have been applied to other animals yet, and much reinvestigation is required in the light of his conclusions.   In a sense he put into measurable terms what was already known, so that there is reason to think that klino-kinesis, with some complication like adaptation, is the machinery of many 'phobo-taxes'.

The classical cases of this type of reaction are to be found in Jennings's (1906) book on the behaviour of Protozoa. The aggregation of *Paramecium* in a drop of slightly acid water is too well known to need describing in detail again here. The ciliates swim at random, getting into the drop purely by chance and not by a directed movement.   When they reach the boundary on the way out, however, they turn and so tend to return into the drop.   Within the drop, away from the edges, they turn little or not at all.[1]

Boundary reactions have since been reviewed by Mast (1911) and Rose (1929).   It seems of little use to go over them once again until more is known about their relation to the more generalized kind of reaction observed in a gradient that has no sharp boundaries.[2]

---

[1] See note 8, Appendix.
[2] See note 9, Appendix.

VI

KLINO-TAXIS

IT has already been shown that although kineses can result in aggregation, they do so by means of an inefficient and devious method. *Taxes* (τάξις, formal arrangement) can produce aggregation too, but much more efficiently. They result in the animal moving directly towards or away from the source of stimulation. When a single light acts as the stimulus, the animal either moves straight forward, with its body axis in line with the light rays, or locomotion is along this line in general, slightly complicated by regular symmetrical deviations. The kind of reaction in which these regular deviations are a necessary part of the orientation mechanism is here named *klino-taxis*, (κλίνω, bend, incline).

Generally speaking, the anatomical structure of an animal sets an upper limit to the efficiency with which it can respond to environmental factors. For example, there can be no response to a picture as such, if the eyes are incapable of form vision. We are so accustomed to our own very efficient eyes that it may be difficult to realize the disability under which other species are placed by having very simple eyes. A simple experiment described by Koehler (1932, p. 713) is revealing, particularly in relation to klino-taxis. A piece of wide tubing, blackened inside, was fitted with two pieces of ground glass 5 cm. apart, as if they were lenses in a telescope. This instrument was fitted to one eye of the observer and the other eye was covered, so that the only light visible came through the two pieces of ground glass. The observer was then like an animal with a single eye of a simple kind. As long as he did not move, he could see only a uniform field of light, an average of the light falling on the outer piece of glass. No form was distinguishable, and there was no information about the direction from which the light came. The observer could not tell which way he should turn in order to go towards the main light; but if he moved his head from side to side, he could distinguish changes in the intensity of light as he moved, he could stop when the light was most intense, turn his body in that direction, and so move towards the light. For continued accurate orientation, particularly in getting round or over obstacles, the pendulations of the head must be repeated at intervals or continuously. This is the kind of orientation reaction which we call klinotaxis.

The photo-negative behaviour of the maggot larvae of certain common flies was one of the earliest taxes investigated scientifically (Pouchet, 1872). It was the subject of controversy

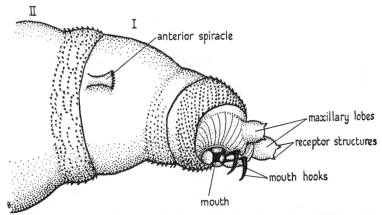

FIG. 17. Anterior end of maggot larva of *Lucilia sericata*. I and II, thoracic segments. For details of receptor structure see Snodgrass (1935) or Imms (1937). (After Ellsworth, 1933.)

among Loeb (1905, 1918), Holmes (1905 a), Mast (1911), Herms (1911), Patten (1914), and others during the early years of this century, and it is perhaps the most easily demonstrated behaviour of this kind. We therefore use it as our first example. The reaction is shown equally well by the larvae of a number of species, including *Musca domestica*, the house fly, *Calliphora erythrocephala*, the blow-fly or bluebottle, and *Lucilia sericata*, the green-bottle. In these maggots the greater part of the head proper is invaginated into the thorax but, when the animal is fully extended, part of the head carrying the maxillary lobes, the mouth hooks, and the mouth opening can be seen externally. In what follows this part will be referred to as 'the head', for the sake of brevity (Fig. 17). No photo-sensitive structures are known.

When the larva has finished feeding, it leaves the food and goes into a dark place, where it pupates. During the interval of 3–4 days (20° C.) between the cessation of feeding and the formation of the puparium, the animal is known as the full-fed larva. It is during the first of these days that the animal is most suitable for the experiments on the reaction to light; at other times the reaction is more variable and not so precise, and it disappears altogether before pupation (Herms, 1911; Patten, 1916). The larvae adapt to light and cease to react to it, so they must be kept in the dark for a time before testing (Mast, 1911).

In the early experiments the larvae were placed in direct sunlight near a window. Under these conditions they give a clear reaction, crawling straight away from the window. If a dozen or so larvae are tested together, they move together like a troop or team and show that the term *taxis* is an appropriate one. For precise analysis of the reaction, however, sunlight has two disadvantages: first, another stimulus—heat—is applied at the same time; and second, the stimulus is not presented in simple form, for there is some light coming from all directions, although most of it comes directly from the sun. The heat can be greatly reduced by interposing a glass tank of water as a screen between the window and the animal, or the experiment can be done in a dark-room, using screened artificial light and a matt black background. The animal still crawls directly along the light beam and away from the source (Fig. 18). This is called *negative photo-taxis*.

In order to analyse the reaction it is necessary to consider the method of locomotion. During steady crawling a series of waves pass forwards along the muscular body-wall of the maggot. The posterior end is fixed down to the substratum and the ventral surface just in front is raised. This elevation passes forwards, the body just behind becoming longer and thinner, while in front it is humped up. The wave reaches the head, which is thus picked up, thrust forward, and then put down again.

During steady forward crawling the head is sometimes put down symmetrically in line with the axis of the body, but from time to time it comes down alternately to the right and to the left. When the maggot first begins to crawl, these lateral deviations of the head are usually considerable, and may even result in the body assuming a U-shape.

In order to find out how the animal gains its orientated direction, a second light is arranged to throw a beam at right angles to the first (Fig. 19, p. 63). When the animal is steadily orientated to the first light (*m*), that is switched off, the second

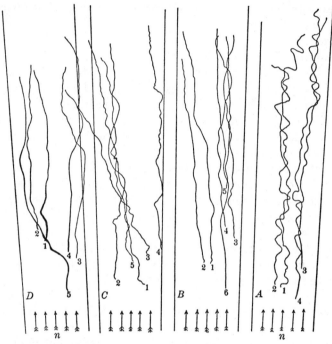

FIG. 18. Tracks of four maggots (*A* to *D*) in a beam of horizontal light. Direction of light indicated by arrows. Each maggot tested 4 to 6 times. The head movements are shown in detail in *A*. The maggots do not move quite 'as though . . . impaled on the ray of light'. (Mast, 1911.)

one (*n*) is switched on, and the method of re-orientation to the new light is watched. Under these circumstances, one of two things may happen, depending on the position of the head at the moment of switching over the lights. If by chance the next movement of the head is towards the new light (*c*), the head is swung across to the other side before the body moves up; if the next movement chances to be away from the light (*e*), the crawling goes on as usual, and at the following movement (*g*), which will normally be towards the light, the shifting over of

the head towards the dark side takes place. Two or more considerable head deviations to the same side (*e* and *h*) cause a
curving of the general path of the animal, so that the swinging
across of the head tends to turn the animal away from the light.
The shifting over of the head before the body moves up is repeated until the head is illuminated equally at two successive
head deviations, and then the animal is once more orientated
in line with the light (Mast, 1911). The movements of the
animal are illustrated in Fig. 19.

In this experiment, if the new light is very bright, so that it
shines right through the tissues of the animal, the head is swung
across immediately, even if it then becomes directed towards
the light. Several head movements and a swaying of the head
in the air may then take place before one of the head positions
is followed up by crawling.

If, when the new light is switched on, the head is by chance
being put down directly in front rather than to one side, the
response of the animal is to start to make head deviations. This
same response occurs in *any* increase in light, whether from
behind, above, or from the side. If the animal is not already
making lateral deviations, it commences to do so. It may crawl
on or it may stop, but the result is the same. The procedure
described above can then come into action.

The photo-receptive region of the fly larva is at the extreme
anterior end (Pouchet, 1872; Loeb, 1890; Mast, 1911; Herms,
1911; Ellsworth, 1933). Soon after orientation to the first light
has been completed, this sensitive region is thrust out to either
side alternately, so that, when the new light comes from one
side, the sensitive region receives either head-on illumination
or none at all. In the former case the head is swung across to
the other side; that is to say, the regular alternation is interrupted by a movement which results in reduction of stimulation
of the receptors concerned. The stimulus is the increase of light
intensity, compared with the intensity acting during the previous movement towards the other side; the response is a
swinging across of the head before the normal forward movement of the body is continued.

During orientated locomotion the fly larva from time to time
points its head to this side and to that, and this alternation can
be described as trial movements. Holmes (1905 *a*) described the

process as the selection of random movements, but the alternation of lateral positions of the head is too regular to be properly

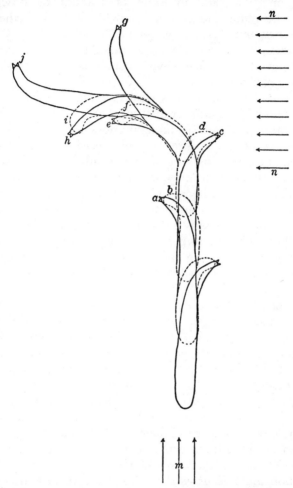

Fig. 19. Re-orientation in the maggot. The maggot expands to *a*, contracts to *b*, expands to *c*, &c., with the light *m* on. At *d*, *m* is put out and *n* put on. The lateral movement to *e* is somewhat larger than *a*; the next one (*g*) increases the light falling on the receptors and is corrected by a swing over to *h*. See pp. 61–2. (Mast, 1911.)

called random. Using the vivid terminology of Jennings, a *trial* movement which leads to an *error* is corrected; an *avoiding reaction* takes place. The vividness is lost, but there is a real gain in clarity if the description is more non-committal, less anthropomorphic, and in terms of a reflex response to a specified stimulus. Mast (1911, 1938) calls the response a *shock reaction*, but this term is not sufficiently specific. We call it *klino-taxis*, a directed orientation made possible by means of regular deviations and involving comparison of intensities at successive points in time.

In this case the response is clear enough; the real nature of the stimulus requires further discussion. First of all, the absence of elaborate eyes suggests—though it does not certainly show—that the receptors are incapable of precise discrimination of direction, and that as long as the head is stationary, they provide no clue to light direction but act as intensity receptors only. The body shades the sensitive region from behind, so that the receptive apparatus can be used as a direction receptor if the body or the head is pointed in a series of different directions. The light intensities from various directions can be compared, but the comparison is successive in time, not simultaneous such as our own eyes can carry out. (Compare, however, pp. 67–9.)

The exact location and form of the photo-receptors is unknown. Ellsworth (1933) reported that they are on the maxillary lobes (Fig. 17, p. 59), but Pouchet (1872), Patten (1914), and Gunn (unpublished) were unable to discover any change in reaction to light when these organs were removed. Snodgrass (1935) describes them as having the structure of chemo-receptors, and this has been confirmed experimentally by Welsh (1937). Our ignorance of the exact organization of the photo-receptors hinders analysis of their mode of action.[1]

Whatever the structure of the receptors, there is enough evidence of their anterior position to show that variation in stimulation must occur as the head is drawn in and covered by the succeeding segments, and then thrust out again. The head is very small, so that with horizontal light it may be completely shaded by the body at one instant, and then brightly lit as it is thrust out to one side. Thus the photo-receptive region does not pass straight from one side position to the next, but goes through a series of light intensities which include the comparative darkness of the contracted position.

[1] See note 10, Appendix.

In orientating, then, the animal seems to compare the intensities received at two different times, while actually the receptors may pass through a whole series of varying intensities between these two occasions. It seems probable, on the face of it, that this successive comparison by a kind of memory is of the same sort as that of *Dendrocoelum* (p. 51); that the state of adaptation depends on a whole series of previous intensities in a complex way; and that the reaction of swinging over the head only occurs when the new light-intensity is considerably above the recently passed intensities. These conjectures remain to be tested by further work.

Although fly larvae have no direction receptors, they can thus perform a directed reaction. Normally, in crawling away from a light, they reach a darker place; the light can, however, be arranged so that this negative photo-taxis leads them into a lighter place. Loeb (1890) did this by putting the larvae into a test-tube which was then placed at right angles to a window (Fig. 20, p. 66). A screen threw some shadow on to the half of the tube nearer to the window, while the other half was fully lit. The main direction of the light was away from the window, even in the shaded half. Starting at the window end the larvae all crawled away from the source of light, and thus towards the lighter region of the tube. Most of them continued across the shadow edge, with some hesitation there, and went to the brightest end of the tube. That is to say, in the main the animals reacted to the *direction* of the light, even when this reaction took them into *brighter* light. The hesitation occurred when about one-third of the body had been thrust out of the shadow, when the head was swung across in the usual way. In a few cases the swinging was so violent that the head actually got back into the shadow, and then this movement was followed up by the animal crawling back into the shadow *against* the direction of the light. Thus, although the resultant path of the larva is directed, the constituent steps are not, and during each step the animal is reacting to intensity changes only.

This conclusion can be neatly confirmed by tricking the animal, so to speak. Two lights are arranged in a dark room, both of them hanging centrally over a sheet of wet ground glass on which the experiment is to be carried out. One of them, a dim one, is left on all the time so that the operator can see the animal; the other is controlled by a bell push, so that it can be easily switched on for a moment. For this experiment maggots bought from a shop which supplies them to anglers as 'gentles' will do, but individuals must be selected for accuracy and speed of orientation in a horizontal beam. A picked specimen is

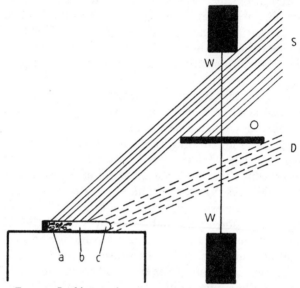

FIG. 20. Loeb's experiment antagonizing direction and intensity of light. The maggots go from *c* to *a*, away from the light, and in so doing they collect in brighter light. *abc*, tube containing the maggots; *D*, diffuse light from the sky; *S*, direct sunlight; *O*, opaque strip of wood; *WW*, window. (After Loeb.)

dropped on to the centre of the experimental field. The first movements of the head are lateral ones, and the animal commonly sways its head from side to side several times before forward movement starts. Each time the head comes over to (say) the left side, the bright light is switched on for an instant. When the animal begins to crawl it turns to the right, usually at an angle of 90° or more. When it has straightened out again, it can again be caused to turn fairly sharply in either direction by switching on the light when the head goes over to the other side. This control is easily carried out for a short period; but after a time the lateral head movements become very small and often imperceptible. During this later stage it is difficult to time the flashes so as to make them coincide accurately with the rapid movements of the animal (Gunn, unpublished).

The experiment shows that the animal gives the same responses to changes of intensity when the light is all from above, or uniform, and when it is presented as a horizontal beam. In the former case the changes of light are due to the observer and his switch, and in the latter to the alternate shading of the head and its emergence into the light, involved in the ordinary process of locomotion.

Circling movements can thus be caused by flashing a light every time the head goes over to a particular side. Circling— or circus—movements of various kinds are useful in discriminating between the several taxes. In certain reactions they occur after unilateral extirpation of the receptors, either in uniform light or in an imperfect beam of light as well; no one has so far succeeded in unilaterally blinding an animal which behaves exclusively klino-tactically. Herms (1911) reported that he succeeded in blinding maggots unilaterally and got circus movements, but it has been impossible to repeat his results (Gunn, unpublished), and no other author has confirmed them. The circus movements can be produced, however, by flashing up the light at each head deviation to one side in the fly larva. Such deviations do not occur in other kinds of taxes. Possibly a similar technique of simultaneous flashing will have this effect in other cases of klino-taxis; that remains to be seen.

Another test which is used to discriminate between the various taxes is to see what the animal does under the *simultaneous* action of two directed lights. The arrangement shown in Fig. 29, p. 82, can be used, with two beams at right angles. The fly larva crawls away from both of such lights, but not directly away from either. If the two lights are equal and at equal distances from the animal, it goes approximately halfway between the two beams. If one light shines more brightly on the animal—because it is either brighter or nearer—the track is more nearly in line with the brighter beam. In this two-light experiment the fly larva reacts to both lights simultaneously and goes between the two.

Although the description we have given is satisfactory for the orientation of maggots in one light or in two lights crossing at right angles, it is not clear if it applies to a special case investigated by Patten (1914). He arranged two beams in line, shining in opposite directions, so that each beam could usually illuminate one side of the animal only (Fig. 21). Each maggot was started off in a direction at right angles to the main beams by means of a dim light ('orienting light', Fig. 21), and when it reached *O* the dim light was turned off and the others were uncovered. The relative intensities of the two main lights

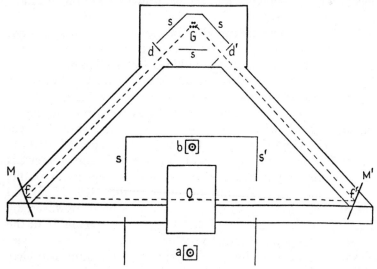

Fig. 21. Diagram of apparatus for producing two antagonistic beams of light in line. *a*, *b*, 'orienting lights' (2 c.p.); *G*, light source (1 to 5 lamps); *M*, *M'*, mirrors; *O*, centre of experimental field; *s*, *d*, opaque screens. (Patten, *J. exp. Zool.* 1914.)

could be altered by shifting the experimental field to one side or the other. The animal could not go away from either light without going towards the other to an equal extent; in fact, it diverged from the original line across the beams by an amount which depended on the relative intensities. Thus when the two intensities were in the ratio of 3:4 and the difference was thus 25 per cent. of the higher intensity, the average deflexion towards the weaker light was 8·86° (Table I).

Patten estimated the angle which a pair of flat eyes would have to make with the animal's axis to fit these figures, on the assumption that there are two such eyes which receive equal quantities of light in the orientated position (Patten, 1914;

Loeb, 1918). He found that it was nearly 41° for several ratios of intensity. He was careful to make it clear that the matter is too complicated to permit the bald statement that this is actually the angle of a real receptor-surface. Indeed, later authors have repeated the work using beams which cross each other as well as beams in line, and found that the estimated angle of the hypothetical surfaces depends on the angle between the beams and also on their relative intensities (Crozier and Kropp, 1935).

TABLE I. *The average angular deflexion of maggots (larvae of* Calliphora erythrocephala) *under the influence of two lights in line, at five different absolute intensities and nine relative differences of intensity. Based on 3,000 trails. (From Patten, 1914.)*

Number of lamps	Difference between the intensities of the two lights, as a percentage of the stronger one								
	0	8⅓	16⅔	25	33⅓	50	66⅔	83⅓	100
	deg.	deg.	deg.	deg.	deg.	deg.	deg.	deg.	deg.
1	−0·55	−2·32	−5·27	−9·04	−11·86	−19·46	..	..	..
2	−0·10	−3·05	−6·12	−8·55	−11·92	−22·28	..	..	..
3	+0·45	−2·60	−5·65	−8·73	−13·15	−20·52	−30·9	−46·8	−77·6
4	−0·03	−2·98	−6·60	−9·66	−11·76	−19·88	..	..	..
5	−0·23	−2·93	−5·13	−8·30	−10·92	−19·25	..	..	..
Averages	−0·09	−2·77	−5·75	−8·86	−11·92	−20·28	−30·9	−46·8	−77·6

When the beams are in line, Patten (1914) reported that the maggots may turn into the orientated position without any 'wig-wagging' of the head and without interruption of the regular alternation of lateral head positions; the deviation of the head to one side is simply larger than that to the other side, so that the track is a smooth curve (Fig. 22, p. 70). Thus Patten's observations are consistent with the idea that maggots *can* orientate by *simultaneous* comparison of intensities of stimulation on the two sides (tropo-taxis, Chap. VII) under suitable circumstances. They have no bearing on the *successive* comparison of intensities in a single light, and they are not necessarily inconsistent with the klino-tactic scheme. The smooth turning without corrections of head positions may be due to a delay in response, so that instead of swinging the head across to the other side at once, the maggot makes a larger deviation to that side when it occurs in the normal sequence.[1]

Klino-taxis can be performed by means of very different

[1] See note 11, Appendix.

apparatus from that used by maggots. The receptor-effector apparatus of unicellular or non-cellular organisms cannot have much in common with that of maggots, and yet in some Protista the same kind of tactics or manœuvres are used in orientating to light. *Euglena*, which serves as an example, is a green protistan which swims by means of an anterior flagellum or crawls

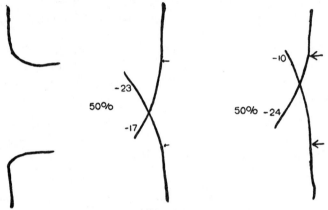

FIG. 22. Tracks made by maggots in the apparatus shown in Fig. 21, with lights in line. The lights came on when the maggots reached the points marked by arrows. The maggots were started alternately from *a* and *b* (Fig. 21); they diverged somewhat towards the weaker light (see Table I). The two trails on the left were made with only one light on, to test the accuracy of re-orientation. For the other four trails one light was twice as strong as the other. (Patten, *J. exp. Zool.* 1914.)

on the substratum. The flagellum has an enlargement at its base which is believed to be photo-sensitive (Tschakhotine, 1936). This flagellar enlargement is shielded on one side by a cup-shaped mass of brown pigment called the eye-spot or pigment shield (Fig. 23). The surface near which the pigment shield lies is for convenience of description called the dorsal surface; it is convex, and it is the blind side. The ventral surface is concave (Fig. 23), and the presumedly photo-sensitive surface is exposed towards this side.

Euglena is photo-positive in dim light, when either swimming or crawling, and photo-negative in bright light (Mast, 1911, 1938). If it is exposed to a single source, it goes directly towards it or away from it, and it thus behaves photo-tactically. In two lights it orientates between the two, travelling more nearly in line with the stronger beam (see pp. 145, 148). If it is going towards a single light and the intensity is increased without changing the direction of the light, there is no response; but if the intensity is sharply diminished, there is a change in the direction of motion—which is later corrected. This response to a *diminution* of light in positively photo-tactic *Euglena* is important in analysing the reaction.

The mechanism of crawling is imperfectly understood. The

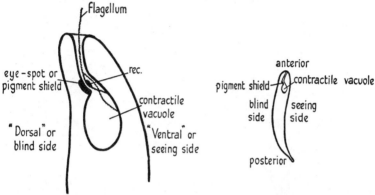

FIG. 23. Side views of·*Euglena viridis. rec.*, enlargement in flagellum believed to be photo-receptive. The terms dorsal and ventral are not fully justifiable, but are convenient. (After Mast, 1938.)

pointed posterior end is in contact with the substratum apparently all the time, and it describes a fairly straight path. The organism rotates on its own axis as it goes forward, like a banana rolling over and over, and the blind side is always turned towards the axis of the spiral which the anterior end therefore describes (Fig. 24, p. 72). There is no amoeboid movement, and Mast (1911) was unable to decide how or why these movements lead to continuous locomotion at all; during locomotion, both ends move back and forth, and this may be the clue to the problem.

The successive positions adopted by a photo-positive crawling *Euglena* when the direction of the light is changed are shown in Fig. 24. In positions *a* to *c* the organism is spiralling towards the light *o*, and at *c* that light is switched off and light *n* is switched on at right angles. No response occurs as long as the ventral surface faces the new light; when position *d* is reached, the pigment shields the flagellar enlargement from the new light and there is a response to this local decrease in intensity of illumination. The body is bent more towards the ventral surface (*d* to *e*) and so away from the light. According to Mast

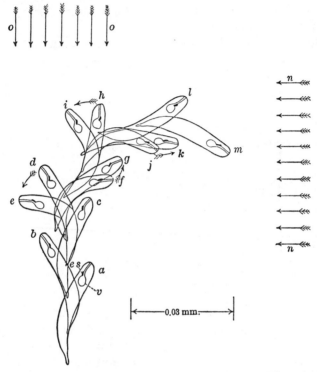

FIG. 24. Re-orientation of *Euglena* when crawling, When the organism is at *c*, the light *o* is switched off and *n* is switched on. See text, pp. 70–73. (Mast, 1911.)

(1911) this results in a curvature of the general path towards the light; it is unlikely that we shall understand exactly how a turn *away* from the light is responsible for causing the path to curve *towards* the light, until we know more about the mechanism of locomotion.

The similarity of this reaction to the klino-taxis of maggots is evident. *First,* a change of direction of movement can be induced by a simple change in *intensity* of light quite irrespective of *direction* of light, by an increase of light in the photo-negative maggots and a decrease in the photo-positive *Euglena*. It seems quite likely that *Euglena* could be induced to turn repeatedly in the same direction, if the light were diminished each time it lay on, say, its left side, as in the simultaneous flashing experiment with maggots (pp. 65–7). *Second*, the eyes of both forms are not known to be more than simple intensity receptors, and they are pointed out towards the two sides in regular alternation. *Third*, the direction of turning is determined by the position of the animal at the moment when the intensity of stimulation changes and not by the direction of the light; this is shown by the simultaneous flashing experiment. In normal circumstances (horizontal beam), however, the result of turning is orientation in the direction of the light. *Fourth*, both organisms orientate in line with a single light and between a pair of lights. In short, in both cases there is a comparison of two intensities of illumination of the receptors, and these two intensities stimulate at successive instants in time; the comparison can be used in performing a taxis because the stimuli act in two successive positions of the receptors which recur in regular alternation.

Although the orientation of *Euglena* while swimming is essentially the same, there are certain differences of detail (Jennings, 1904, 1906). The *dorsal* surface is on the outside of the spiral, and a diminution in light causes a swerve to the *dorsal* side. In this case, then, if the light is changed as in Fig. 24, the reaction occurs when the organism is on the side of the spiral nearer to the new light, and it swerves towards that light. A fresh swerve occurs at each turn, until orientation is complete (Fig. 25, p. 74).

A number of other cases of protistan behaviour which fit into the scheme of klino-taxis are described by Jennings (1906) and Mast (1911, 1938). Amongst the Metazoa, the post-trochophore larva of *Arenicola* (Mast, 1911) and the tadpole larva of the ascidian, *Amaroucium* (Mast, 1921), have each a single eye and swim along a spiral; they react just like *Euglena*, the similarity being extraordinary, while the kinds of structures involved are quite different.[1] Earthworms have scattered light receptors in the skin (Hess, 1925) and when moving rapidly they make pendular movements of the anterior end, like maggots. Under certain conditions they react very much as maggots do (Mast, 1938).

[1] See note 12, Appendix.

Hydra behaves in a way which is probably accurately described as klino-tactic. The positive photo-taxis of *Chloro-*

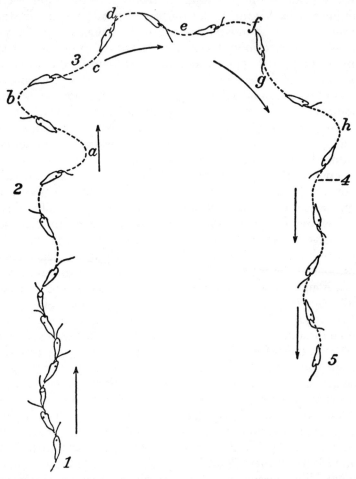

Fig. 25. Re-orientation of *Euglena* when swimming. From 1 to 2, light from direction of top of page; at 2, direction of light reversed. Each time the receptor is shielded by the eye-spot (Fig. 23), the organism swerves to the dorsal side (p. 73). Consequently it becomes re-orientated after a few turns round the spiral. (Jennings, 1906.)

hydra viridissima has been known for a very long time (Trembley, 1744) and has recently been investigated by Haug (1933). The animal has no discernible eyes. It moves along either by somersaulting or by looping. In reacting photo-tactically, before detaching the basal disk the animal swings the oral end round in complete circles, with the base as centre. This movement is not uniform in speed; it is 10–15 times faster when the oral cone is facing away from the light than it is in the semicircle towards the light; it is slowest of all[1] when the oral cone is directed straight at the light. The moment at which a looping or somersaulting movement starts is presumably purely random, but since the oral cone spends most of its time facing the light, locomotion is usually in this direction. The general path is a zigzag one.[2]

Klino-taxis is an uncommon type of reaction to light, for a reason which is not difficult to find. Light, as a stimulus, commonly has direction as well as intensity and many animals have developed photo-receptors which are capable of discriminating its direction instantly and without any kind of trial movement. With such receptors types of reaction which are more efficient than klino-taxis become possible; these are dealt with in the following chapters.

Klino-taxis is unknown as a reaction to gravity, for gravity varies little in intensity and has direction (Chap. XV). On the other hand, chemical stimuli have intensity but are essentially without direction. By means of a special apparatus, more complex chemo-reactions are sometimes possible, but klino-taxis is probably the most common one (Chap. XVIII). Even when other reactions are theoretically possible, klino-taxis may occur in early stages of orientation or in special circumstances, as when planarians make 'wig-wag' movements of the head (Taliaferro, 1920).[3,4]

The diagnostic features of klino-taxis are thus sufficient to mark it off clearly from other taxes. Moreover, there are enough examples, especially among the Protista, to justify the erection of this new class of reaction. It remains to be seen whether fresh work will show that it has an even wider importance than has been outlined above.

---

[1] And often stops for periods.
[2] See note 13, Appendix.
[3] See note 14, Appendix.
[4] See note 15, Appendix.

VII

TROPO-TAXIS

IN previous chapters we have dealt with the reactions in which the animal reaches a source of stimulation—or a region of least stimulation—by means of random movements (kineses), or by means of fairly regularly alternating deviations (klinotaxis). In the former the path is very devious, while in klinotaxis it is wavy. We now come to cases in which the path is straight, and directly towards or away from a source of stimulation (*tropo-taxis* and *telo-taxis*). These are the types of reaction usually associated with the term *photo-taxis*, formerly called heliotropism. The animal has been vividly described as moving 'as if spitted on the light ray'.

Kineses can be performed with even the most simple kind of receptor—a single purely intensity-receptive ending. Klinotaxis requires a somewhat more complex arrangement, in that the receptor must not be equally accessible to stimulation from all directions. The required inaccessibility is achieved by the shielding effect of the body, by a special pigment layer, for example, or by a deviation of the receptor from the ideal spherical shape. In tropo-taxis there must be at least two receptors, which are so arranged that they are not always equally stimulated. It is convenient to describe how this inequality of stimulation in the unorientated position can lead to direct orientation in the simplest theoretical case, and then to go on to real cases.

Consider a photo-positive animal which is provided with a pair of eye-spots, one on each side of the body. Suppose each eye can be reached by light from its own side or from straight ahead, but not by light from the opposite side. Suppose the animal is tested in a perfect dark-room, with no stray light at all, so that all the light comes from a single small source. If, now, the animal is set down athwart the beam, the eye which is turned towards the light will be more stimulated than the other. This asymmetry of stimulation starts turning reflexes (τροπή, turn) which continue until the two eyes are equally stimulated. The animal thus turns towards the light, that is towards the side on which the eye is stimulated. When stimulation becomes symmetrical, turning ceases and the animal moves straight forward to the light.

If this reaction is to be carried out successfully, it is necessary that the eyes should be so arranged that a slight accidental deviation from the straight path to the light leads to inequality of stimulation. The two eyes acting together then enable the animal to make a simultaneous comparison of intensities on the two sides, and so to correct the deviation, without trial movements. If the eyes are not well arranged from this point of view, then accidental deviations may be corrected only slowly, and then perhaps over-corrected, so that a wavy path may result; in that case, further tests are necessary to decide whether the reaction is tropo-tactic or klino-tactic.

In this theoretical animal stimulation of one of the eyes causes reflex turning towards the stimulated side. In the intact animal this turning eventually brings the other eye into action, and so might be expected to initiate an additional turning reflex in the opposite direction. What happens, in fact, is that in the central nervous system a balance is struck between the impulses from the two eyes. If there is an excess on one side, turning towards that side occurs; if there is equality, the two sets of impulses are cancelled out and the animal does not turn at all, but goes straight forward. These, then, are the essential features of tropo-taxis—*simultaneous* comparison of intensities on the two sides, and orientation according to the balance thus struck.

It is possible to interfere with the animal in such a way that this balance of stimulation becomes impossible. Thus, if one eye is put out of action—e.g. by means of black paint—using the other eye, the animal can turn until it faces the light. As long as that eye is stimulated in the least, turning continues, so that the animal turns too much, and then cannot see the light at all. After that it walks on as if in darkness. If, instead of a horizontal beam of light, an overhead light is used and the animal placed in a large white box, so that the intensity of light is roughly the same on all sides, then the animal turns to-wards the seeing side, as before; but however much it turns, the seeing eye is always stimulated to the same extent, so turning goes on. These continuous turning movements are the *circus movements* (*Manege-Bewegung*) characteristic of tropo-taxis. On unilateral blinding, when tested in uniform light, the animal turns continually towards the seeing side if it is photo-positive and towards the blind side if photo-negative. The paired receptors of an animal which behaves tropo-tactically have been compared with the paired reins of a horse; if one is pulled, the horse turns; if both are pulled equally, the horse goes straight. Each rein has a one-way turning action.

In tropo-taxis the animal can often no longer orientate properly in a beam when the photo-receptors of one side are eliminated. As we shall see, there are, however, some cases in which a two-way action of a single eye is possible to a certain extent, and then orientation may occur in a beam even after unilateral blinding (pp. 85, 155).

One more experiment is useful for discriminating between the types of reaction—namely the two-light experiment. Instead of a single light source in a dark-room, two sources are used and their beams cross in the experimental field. If the animal at first goes to one of the lights, with a balance of stimulation as far as that light is concerned, the other light must stimulate only one eye, so that the whole balance is upset. In tropo-taxis turning therefore occurs towards the second light, and a balanced orientation is reached when the animal goes *between* the two lights and not to either one directly. This also occurs in klino-taxis, though by a different mechanism. In telo-taxis the animal goes to one of the lights (see Chap. VIII).

When we come to compare this abstract ideal of tropo-taxis with real cases, we find difficulty in discovering a perfect example. In some cases the reaction is imperfect because of deficiencies in the receptors or in the central nervous system, and in other cases more complex kinds of reaction are combined with tropo-taxis itself. Indeed, the more complex the receptor-nervous-effector system, the more difficult it is to describe an animal's behaviour in terms of one of these simple types. In a particular case a kinesis may be the only possible kind of reaction because of the form of presentation of the stimulus or because of the simplicity of the receptor mechanism; but when the animal is capable of carrying out a more efficient reaction in the shape of a taxis, then it also has the anatomical arrangements necessary for kineses and may perform them too under appropriate circumstances. Indeed, there is an ortho-kinetic component in taxes, in that the stimulus leads to linear motion as well as to turning. Some animals turn towards a light without necessarily moving towards it (e.g. *Erax*—Mast, 1923; *Ranatra*—Holmes, 1916). The ortho-kinetic element is then absent, and the reaction is not a taxis but a posture reaction. Care must therefore be taken to avoid speaking of a 'tropo-tactic animal'. Tropo-taxis is a type of reaction, not a type of animal.

These points are well illustrated by reference to the behaviour of a tick, *Ixodes ricinus*. This arachnid is photo-positive, but it has no recognizable eyes. The sensitivity to light is diffuse and is probably located just under the surface cuticle and mainly at the anterior end of the globular body. In a beam of light, while the animal is still far away from the source, the track made is similar to that of *Dendrocoelum* (Chap. V, klino-kinesis) (Fig. 26). As the tick approaches the light

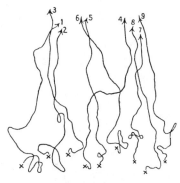

FIG. 26. Tracks of ticks towards light. The crosses indicate the starting-points. Notice that the initially convoluted path becomes wavy as the light is approached. (After Totze, 1933.)

source, the reaction changes from an undirected one to a directed one, and the track becomes wavy, as in klino-taxis. Finally, when the distance remaining is short, the track becomes straight. In this final stage there is none of the appearance of klino-taxis. In a two-light experiment the animal goes between the two, so that tropo-taxis appears to be the only possible identification of reaction for the last part of the journey. Unfortunately, the unilateral elimination of the unknown photo-receptors appears not to have been attempted (Totze, 1933).[1]

Again, the larva of the meal moth, *Ephestia kühniella*, is photo-negative (Brandt, 1934). On each side of the head there is an

[1] Totze's observations were not confirmed by Lees (1948), who never found *Ixodes* photo-positive.

eye composed of six closely grouped ocelli. Each eye covers a visual field which is cut off behind by the presence of the body, so that the animal cannot see directly behind or within an estimated angle of 20° on either side of the axis. Consequently, when reacting to a beam, the caterpillar may be as much as 20° off the direct line from the light and yet not receive the

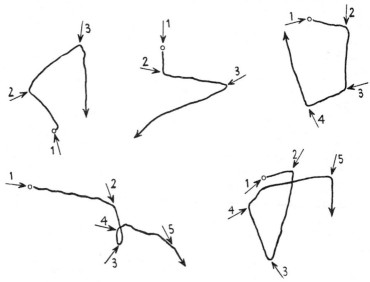

FIG. 27. Tracks of *Ephestia* larvae away from light. Each track starts from a small circle, with a light as shown by the arrow numbered 1. When the animal reached the point on the track indicated by arrow No. 2, the first light was switched off and a new light—the direction of which is indicated by arrow No. 2 —was switched on. Similarly for the other arrows. (After Brandt, 1934.)

information necessary to make the correction (Fig. 27). The extent of the errors shown in experiments on 125 caterpillars of this species is shown in Fig. 28. Thus about 40 per cent. of the tracks were within ±5° of the direction of the beam, while only about 13 per cent. involved errors of over 25°. In a two-light experiment these caterpillars do not go directly away from either light, but follow a path between the two beams. If one beam is more intense than the other, the path is more nearly in line with the stronger beam (Figs. 29, 30, pp. 82, 83). When the lights are equal the animals go half-way between them, for about 55 per cent. of them follow a path within 5° of the bisector, while only a few diverge by 30° or over (cf. pp. 157–9). Divergences from the ideal result are to be expected in behaviour, and statistical analysis can show whether or not they are important in identifying the type of behaviour. In this case the figures show that the divergences are statistically normal.

In the dark *Ephestia* larvae are dis-orientated; they wander

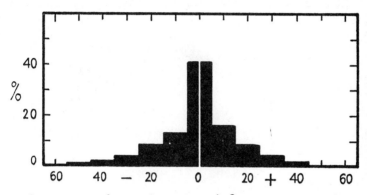

Divergence of path (in degrees) from direction of light.

FIG. 28. Graph showing the variation in the directions taken by 125 *Ephestia* larvae. The angle was measured to left (−) or to right (+) of the horizontal beam of light, and the number of larvae orientating at each angle to the beam is expressed as a percentage of 125. For example, 16 per cent. or 20 of the animals diverged to the right by between 5 and 15°. (Data from Brandt, 1934.)

at random. In light they orientate. The two-light experiment indicates that the orientation is either klino-tactic or tropo-tactic. The straightness of the path and the result of unilateral blinding indicate tropo-taxis (Fig. 31, p. 84). In a beam a caterpillar with one eye painted over starts by going away from the light and then curves round gently towards the blind side; this blind side is thus presented to the light source, so that no photic stimulation can occur. The apparatus—the painted eye—which could lead to correction is out of action. In overhead light the animal turns in circles towards the blind side.

These *Ephestia* larvae, when orientated to a single small source, cannot see the light at all; an accidental deviation must be of about 20° before it can be corrected, even when both eyes are acting normally. How, then, do simultaneous comparison and balance occur, as they have been described in the theoretical

part of this chapter? In the animal's normal life it is not subjected to such simple conditions as these, for the light then
comes from many directions and in varying quantities. The
two-light experiment shows that the caterpillar, so to speak,
sums up the light from the various directions and takes a
general direction away, being influenced more by the stronger

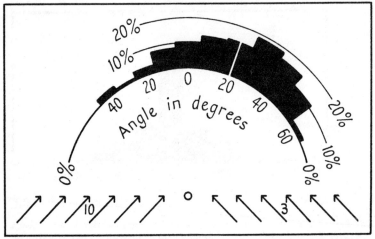

Fig. 29. Graph showing the directions taken by 127 photo-negative *Ephestia*
larvae under the influence of two beams of light crossing each other at right angles.
The directions were measured from the bisector of the right angle. The intensity
of the right-hand light was 3/10ths that of the left-hand one. (Data from Brandt,
1934.)

of the lights. Only light from almost directly behind is invisible,
and the balancing up involves all the other light. In nature,
then, the meal-moth larva can thus sum up the light and take
a general direction away from it.

Turning now to positive photo-tropo-taxis, the pill-bug
(*Armadillidium*) provides an interesting example. This land
crustacean lives under stones or decaying wood, often in
association with other woodlice. *Armadillidium* is not always
positively photo-tactic, but individuals can be selected which
are so for the time being. The positive reaction appears particularly after a sudden rise of temperature or a period of starvation or desiccation. Otherwise, the animal may be photo-
negative and often it is indifferent to light. There is a pair
of compound eyes, each consisting of only a few ommatidia

(about 25), and the two visual fields overlap a little in front. Fig. 32, p. 85, shows the tracks made by photo-positive specimens which have been blinded on one side (Henke, 1930). They fail

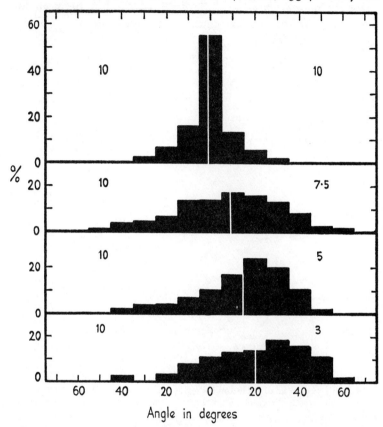

FIG. 30. Directions taken by *Ephestia* larvae in two lights (compare Fig. 29). The left-hand light was kept constant (10) and the right-hand one had relative intensities of 10 (top), 7.5, 5, and 3 (bottom). Each white line shows the average angle of orientation for the particular combination of lights. The lowest part of the figure (10:3) is a repetition of Fig. 29 on rectangular coordinates. For further explanation see Fig. 28. (Data from Brandt, 1934.)

to maintain a straight path to the light, and deviate towards the seeing side. In overhead light they perform circus movements for an indefinitely long time, again towards the seeing side.

In a two-light experiment intact photo-positive specimens

of *Armadillidium* on the whole react to both lights together (Fig. 33, p. 86), going between the two. Sometimes, however, an individual may go nearly directly to one of the lights; these cases are merely extreme variants about the line between the lights (Fig. 34, p. 87). We must postpone consideration of this to Chapter XI (pp. 157-9).

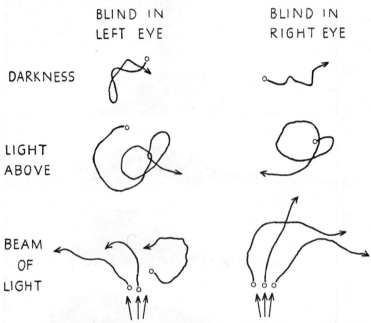

Fig. 31. Tracks of photo-negative *Ephestia* larvae blinded on one side, each track starting at the small circle and ending at the arrow head. The straight arrows below indicate the direction of the light for the adjacent tracks only. (After Brandt, 1934.)

In *Armadillidium* all the ommatidia of one eye are *qualitatively* similar, in the sense that when stimulated they all initiate turning in the same direction; the eye has a one-way action. As will be shown in Chapter XI, the angle of orientation between two lights (Fig. 34, p. 87) suggests that the ommatidia are not *quantitatively* the same. In many cases in which tropo-taxis is the predominant type of reaction initiated in the eyes, the ommatidia of one eye are neither qualitatively nor quantitatively the same. The best-known example of this is found in *Eristalis tenax* (see pp. 155-7) (Mast, 1923).

Eristalis, the hover-fly or drone-fly, and other members of the Syrphidae are commonly mistaken for bees or wasps. *Eristalis* itself is large and slightly bee-like, and can be seen hovering about flowers on sunny days; its aquatic rat-tailed maggot larva is well known. When the adult has been kept

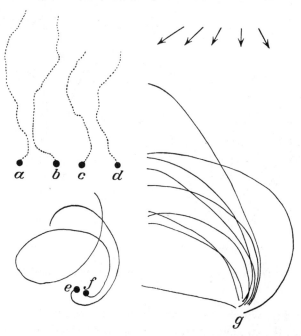

FIG. 32. Tracks of photo-positive *Armadillidium* blinded on the right side. *a–d*, in darkness; *e, f*, with the light overhead; *g*, in a beam, the direction of which is indicated by the arrows. (Henke, 1930.)

in the dark for an hour or so, it is strongly photo-positive and orientates with great accuracy. It flies or—if its wings have been clipped—walks straight to the light. It goes between two lights; after unilateral blinding, it makes circus movements in uniform light. In these respects it behaves typically tropo-tactically; but when tested in a beam after unilateral blinding, under appropriate conditions it can still go straight to the light, instead of deviating towards the seeing side. Under similar conditions in a two-light experiment it still goes between the two, provided they are sufficiently close together. This divergence from the type is due to the existence of two functionally different regions in a single eye, one of which initiates turning to the same side and the other in the opposite direction (Fig. 35, p. 88). To the left of the forwardly directed ommatidia of the right eye—that is, nearer the middle line—there are a few

FIG. 33. Tracks of photo-positive *Armadillidium* in two equal lights. (After Müller, 1925.)

ommatidia which look across to the left side, so that the visual fields of the two eyes overlap. These antero-median ommatidia, when stimulated, initiate turning to the left or contra-lateral side, so that they work in unison with those ommatidia of the left eye which are stimulated by the same light. All the other parts of the eye are connected with ipsi-lateral turning. It is these antero-median ommatidia which enable *Eristalis* to orientate in a beam of light when blinded in one eye; they are insufficient in number and in sensitivity to allow beam orientation when the hind ommatidia are dark-adapted, or to prevent circus movements in uniform light (Mast, 1923). The result is that a state of balance is possible even with only a single eye in action.

Eristalis thus presents a step in advance of the simpler tropo-taxis mechanisms in the direction of telo-taxis. The optical apparatus required for telo-taxis, an eye with a two-way action,

is present, but the central nervous phenomenon characteristic
of telo-taxis—namely, inhibition of one of the two lights—is

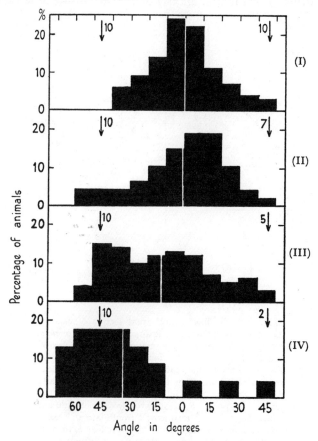

FIG. 34. Graph showing the behaviour of photo-positive
Armadillidium in two beams crossing at an angle of 92·5° and
of intensity ratios (I) 1:1, (II) 1:0·7, (III) 1:0·5, (IV) 1:0·2.
The angles are measured from the bisector of the angle between
the beams, and the arrows show the angular positions of the
beams. The ordinates give the percentages of animals tested
which orientated at each angle. Each white line shows the
average angle of orientation. (Data from Henke, 1930.)

absent. Similar conclusions have been reached for the behaviour
of *Notonecta*, the water boatman or back-swimmer, and *Dineutes*,
the whirligig beetle (see Chaps. XI and XII).

There is another observation on *Eristalis* which is important in discussing the tonus theory of orientation. The eye appears to be differentiated into regions not only according to sensitivity

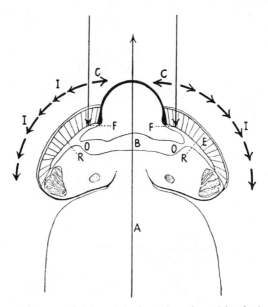

Fig. 35. Outline of horizontal section of head of *Eristalis*; with arrows showing direction in which turning tends to occur when the ommatidia under the arrows are stimulated. *A*, longitudinal axis of animal; *B*, brain; *C*, antero-median ommatidia which, when stimulated, tend to lead to turning to the other side (*contra*- lateral); *E*, eye, showing accurately the directions in which the ommatidia point; *F*, fixation or frontal ommatidia, which point directly forwards; *I*, fronto-lateral, lateral, and posterior ommatidia, which tend to lead to turning to the same side (*ipsi*-lateral); *O*, optic nerve; *R*, retina. (After Mast, 1923.)

or *intensity* of reaction and *direction* of reaction but also according to *kind* of reaction or the means by which turning is accomplished. Thus if a lateral ommatidium of *Eristalis* is stimulated by a single light, the fly walks round a curve towards the source; but if the hindmost region of the eye is stimulated, the fly turns without walking, the ipsi-lateral legs moving *backwards* and the contra-lateral forwards. It is hardly likely that a simple increase in tension or tonus would cause a leg to change from the movements required for forward walking to those required for backward walking, and we must therefore refer this mode of behaviour to specific reflexes rather than to a widespread tonic effect (Mast, 1923).

In this chapter attention has been directed mainly to experiments with arthropods; that is because they are, above all, the animals which have eyes suitable for tropo-tactic behaviour and also suitable for experimental elimination. The cup-eyes of planarians are also suitable in both of these ways, though less so, and indeed modern views on tropo-taxis owe much to the work of Taliaferro (1920) on *Planaria maculata*. Tropo-taxis is probably a very widespread type of reaction.

Loeb was greatly impressed with the importance of balance of stimulation in symmetrical sense-organs and balanced action in symmetrical effectors in the orientated position, and it was essentially for this type of behaviour that he carried over the term *tropism* from plant physiology into animal behaviour. In the main, the same criteria are satisfactory for our category of tropo-taxis, and it was therefore appropriate for Kühn (1919) to retain the prefix *tropo-* for it. We do not subscribe, however, to the idea that tonus is necessarily the mechanism of the reaction (see pp. 6–7; pp. 26–8), and tropo-tactic balance is now known to be possible even when there is asymmetry of receptors or effectors.[1]

---

[1] See note 16, Appendix.

VIII

TELO-TAXIS

KLINO-TAXIS and tropo-taxis are two orientation reactions in which bilateral balance is the essence of the reaction. The animals thus set themselves in the direction of the stimulus and move straight towards or away from it. It is the two-light experiment which demonstrates the existence of balance, for then the animals do not orientate to either light, but between the two along a kind of resultant. In the next category of reaction, *telo-taxis*, orientation in the direction of the source of stimulation occurs *without balance*.

A striking example of this is provided by the behaviour of the little mysid crustacean, *Hemimysis lamornei* (Franz, 1911; Fraenkel, 1931). Large numbers of this species are to be found in the aquarium tanks of the Marine Biological Stations at Plymouth and at Naples. When a single light is placed at the side of a glass tank containing *Hemimysis*, the animals swim to and fro continually, always keeping in line with the beam of light. They swim about 10 cm. towards the lamp, then turn sharply through 180° and cover about 10 cm. again before turning back towards the lamp, and so on. If an additional light is arranged so that the two beams cross at right angles, some of the mysids are quite unaffected in their behaviour while others switch over to this second light and behave as if the first one were non-existent. The result is that the mysids form two streams which, so to speak, flow through one another, crossing at right angles and not interfering with each other. Each individual is first positively and then negatively phototactic in rapid alternation. At any one moment, each orientates to *one* of the two lights only; consequently there is clearly no orientation to *balance* of stimulation. Since an animal from time to time switches over and orientates to the other light, and since the eyes are so large that both lights must be in the field of vision at one time, we can say that the animal disregards one light when it is orientating to the other. In contrast to the types of orientation in which balance occurs, in this case we postulate *central inhibition* of one of the two lights.

The value of the two-light experiment is that it indicates the mechanism of orientation to a single light, and it shows the importance of balance in klino-taxis and tropo-taxis. Since the mysid does not balance in two lights, we must therefore look for a different mechanism of orientation to a single light in this case.[1]

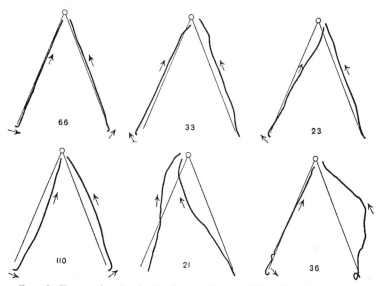

FIG. 36. Two tracks of each of six bees in directive light. The circles represent light sources and the arrow at one end of each track indicates the position from which the bee started. (Minnich, *J. exp. Zool.*, 1919.)

Let us now consider a case of photo-taxis in which balance is not the essential feature of orientation. The honey-bee is strongly photo-positive under certain conditions. A captured bee released in a room immediately flies straight to the window. In a dark room it flies or crawls in a straight line towards a light (Fig. 36). The mechanism of this reaction has been worked out by Minnich (1919) and Urban (1932), who generally used bees which had been deprived of their wings. In a dark-room with two lights the bees mostly crawl straight towards one of the lights. If the lights shine on the bee with equal intensity, it goes equally often towards either of them. If one of the lights is stronger, the bee crawls more often towards this one and less often to the weaker one. Frequently it starts

---

[1] See note 17, Appendix.

off in the direction of one light and then suddenly changes
over towards the other. Sometimes it changes direction several
times, so that it follows a zigzag course. All these phenomena—
and in particular the zigzag track—were first reported by
v. Buddenbrock (1922), who worked on a number of marine
animals. The tracks shown in Fig. 37 are characteristic of the
behaviour described here and hold equally well for the bee.
The behaviour of *Hemimysis* and of the bee are essentially

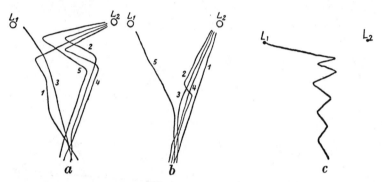

FIG. 37. Tracks of hermit crabs (*a* and *b*) and an isopod *Aega* (*c*) in a two-light
experiment. Each part of the track is directed towards one light only. (*a* and *b*,
after v. Buddenbrock, 1922; *c*, Fraenkel, *Biol. Rev.* 1931.)

similar. At any moment orientation is exclusively towards
one of the two sources of stimulation, the other source being
continuously or—in the case of the zigzag course—temporarily
disregarded.

It is true that in the first part of its track, before orientating
to one of the two lights, the bee occasionally takes a direction
between them (tracks 3 and 5, Fig. 37, *b*). In these cases balancing occurs temporarily and the bee thus also exhibits a tropo-
tactic reaction. This shows that a single animal may perform
either of two types of reaction, so that one cannot properly speak
of a *telo-tactic* or a *tropo-tactic animal*, for the bee is both. The
main conclusion remains, namely, that there exists in the bee
a mechanism of orientation in which the balance of stimulation
in the two eyes is not essential.

When a bee is orientating towards one light and disregarding
the other, the orientating light stimulates the two eyes symmetrically, while the disregarded light usually affects only one

eye. The orientating light stimulates the frontal ommatidia of both eyes, which look directly forwards and which lie parallel to the axis of the body; the disregarded light stimulates ommatidia farther back on the eye, which look out at an angle to the axis of the body, and it is this stimulus at least which is inhibited in the central nervous system. It is possible that only this posterior stimulus is inhibited or alternatively that the whole of the stimulation of that eye is ignored. In the former case, apart from the partial inhibition, the mechanism of orientation could be similar to tropo-tactic balance; in the latter case, no bilateral balance would be involved at all, and the animal would orientate just as well if one eye were put completely out of action.

The test of these alternatives is easily carried out with bees which have had one eye covered with opaque paint. In 'uniform' light—that is, an overhead light shining into a box with white walls and floor—the bee then deviates in loops, curves, and circles towards the seeing side, exactly as in typical tropo-taxis. This experiment is therefore not crucial, for it can be interpreted as simply calling forth the tropo-tactic response which has already been mentioned for the bee.

In a beam of light the unilaterally blinded bees start by looping towards the seeing side. As the experiment is repeated again and again with the same individuals, these loops become less and less curved and less and less frequent, so that eventually a bee with only one eye in action crawls straight towards the light with the same accuracy as a normal bee. Fig. 38, p. 94, shows this gradual straightening out of the tracks, which was first described by Minnich (1919) under the term 'modifiability through experience'. It was subsequently shown that this term is inappropriate, and that the phenomenon is due to sensory adaptation in the eye (Clark, 1928) (pp. 166–8).

Since a unilaterally blinded bee can orientate perfectly in a beam, it is evident that there must be some ommatidia which do not initiate any turning reflexes; these are the frontal ommatidia, which look straight ahead, and when they alone are stimulated the bee walks straight forward. There are other ommatidia on *each* side of these. This arrangement has already been described for *Eristalis* (pp. 85–8, Fig. 35). Considering the

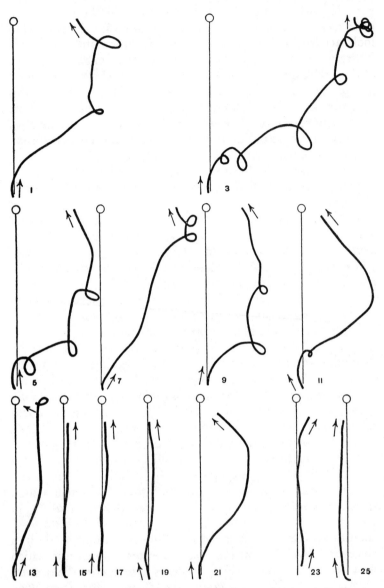

FIG. 38. Consecutive tracks of a bee with the left eye blackened, in directive light. The circus movements to the right in the first few tracks later gradually straighten and the animal eventually walks directly towards the light. (Minnich, *J. exp. Zool.*, 1919.)

left eye, there are other ommatidia which lie nearer to the middle line of the head than the frontal ones, and they look across the axis of the animal towards the right side. These antero-median ommatidia thus cover the same field as certain ommatidia of the right eye, so that there is a certain degree of binocular vision. All the ommatidia to the left of the anterior ones look out to the left in radiating fashion. It is easy to see that for distant objects the anterior ommatidia look at the centre of the binocular field; since this region of the eye is not concerned in initiating turning, and since it is the region stimulated when the bee is orientated, it is often called the *fixation region* and compared with the fovea of the vertebrate eye.

If, when a unilaterally blinded bee is walking straight to a light, that light is moved so that it shines on the lateral ommatidia, then the bee turns directly towards the seeing side. If it is the left eye which is still functional, the animal turns to the left just as in tropo-taxis, and the stimulus is thus transferred forwards to the fixation region. The animal re-orientates to the new position of the light. If now the light is shifted a little to the animal's right so that it stimulates the antero-median ommatidia, the animal again turns towards the light, but this involves a turn towards the blind side—i.e. towards the right. That is to say, the antero-median ommatidia initiate reflex turns to the contra-lateral side, the fixation ommatidia initiate no turns at all, and the majority of the ommatidia—the lateral ones—initiate ipsi-lateral turning. Thus orientation is attained by the action of reflexes which depend on the region of the eye which is stimulated. This kind of eye can be called a two-way eye, because it can initiate turning in either direction.

Bilateral balance is therefore not necessary to orientation, but an analogous condition of balance can arise in a single eye because of the differentiation of the eye into regions (strictly, the differentiation is in the central nervous system and not in the eye at all). On the other hand, the initial circus movements in a beam might be taken to indicate that bilateral balance is normally used by the bee in its telo-tactic orientation, and that the inhibition applies only to the posterior light and not to the whole illumination of one eye. It is not yet possible to decide this question.

We have seen that, in spite of the fact that in one eye there are ommatidia which cause ipsi-lateral turning and others which cause contra-lateral turning, circus movements nevertheless occur in uniform light. This means that the turning effects due to the two sets of ommatidia are not equal. This inequality might be due to the greater numbers of the lateral ommatidia; judging from detailed information about a rather similar case (*Eristalis*, Fig. 74, p. 157; Dolley & Wierda, 1929) the hindmost ommatidia initiate reflexes which are much stronger than those started in lateral ommatidia nearer the front, so that both qualitative and quantitative differences occur.

The behaviour of unilaterally blinded bees in a beam is explicable in terms of the information now available. It should first be understood that it is very difficult to arrange a darkroom so that all the light comes directly from the light source; usually a considerable amount of light is reflected from the background, and in order to get the best conditions it is necessary for the observer to wear black gloves and a mask, and for black velvet or something similar to be used to absorb light. In the experiments which have been described, the arrangements appear not to have reached this very high standard. Consequently, a certain amount of light could reach the hindermost sensitive ommatidia even when the bee was facing the light. When the bee turns towards a dim posterior light of this kind, the image of the main source passes from the fixation area on to the antero-median ommatidia. Here, then, is a situation suitable for setting up balance with a single eye, the strong light acting on the antero-median ommatidia producing an opposite effect to the weak reflected light acting on the very sensitive posterior ommatidia. When the bee is fresh from the complete darkness and so fully dark-adapted, the turning effect due to the posterior part of the eye is too great to be balanced at all, so that circus movements occur; later, as the eye becomes light-adapted, the threshold of stimulation of all the ommatidia rises and eventually the reflected light has no turning effect at all. The main source of light then has its full effect, and is brought on to the fixation region. Thus the disappearance of the circus movements is due simply to sensory adaptation and not to any kind of learning. It may reasonably be assumed that in a perfect dark-room with no reflected light the unilaterally blinded bee would go straight to a light at once, without any preliminary circus movements.

The photo-reaction of the bee can thus be ascribed to two important factors—the form of the reflex 'map' of the eye, including ipsi- and contra-lateral turning areas and a fixation region, and the occurrence of inhibition of a second light, in the central nervous system. The reflex map is to be found in animals which behave only tropo-tactically, like *Eristalis*. It is the central inhibition which is the additional factor. Such inhibition is clearly necessary before complex behaviour can appear. What is most interesting in the case of the bee is that while it is reacting to light as such—and not as coloured light, or as the signal of a flower—it calls this inhibition into action, as a component of a taxis. When a bee is visiting flowers it would soon be in a poor way if it behaved in a sort of tropo-tactic manner and went between two of them! Actually, of course, it goes to one flower at a time, and it is apparent that that one is a goal, an objective, just as there is a goal in football to which the players direct their steps from time to time. It was this feature of this type of orientation which led Kühn to call it telo-taxis (τέλος, end, objective). Kühn (1919) had a much wider conception of telo-taxis than we are advocating here. He included the orientation of a dragon-fly towards its prey and similar reactions; in this sense, a cricketer might be said to behave telo-tactically in running between the wickets, or in his long walk back to the pavilion, although these activities involve a complex set of motives, learning, and so on which are generally thought to be absent in the elementary reactions which we are considering. It is wiser, in fact, to restrict the term *taxis* to a reaction in which the stimulus is undifferentiated and does not involve form vision. Otherwise we should soon reach the absurd position of having to speak of floro-taxis, gyno-taxis, and perhaps even pub-taxis!

An animal cannot behave telo-tactically unless it possesses receptors which indicate the direction of each of several sources of stimulation simultaneously; it cannot ignore a source if it receives no information about its existence. For this reason such reactions can only be performed in response to radiant energy, through receptors like eyes. Cup-eyes, compound eyes, and camera-eyes can be sufficiently elaborate to satisfy the requirements, but eyes of the two former types are frequently not provided with a large enough number of elements—e.g. ommatidia. Further, the eyes must be sufficiently extensive for the animal to be able to look directly forward for positive telo-taxis or directly back for the negative reaction. In fact, most animals which behave photo-telo-tactically have binocular vision over the relevant field. Thus *Hemimysis* has nearly spherical compound eyes on movable stalks, so that it has binocular vision both in front and behind. Apart from the stalk-eyed crustaceans and a few insects like dragon-flies, few animals can see directly behind them, so that negative photo-telo-taxis is probably rare.

We have seen that *Eristalis* has all the machinery for performing telo-taxis. Presumably it can fly to a flower as to a goal and ignore neighbouring flowers; but *Eristalis* does not show inhibition when it is orientating to two lights in a dark-room, and it goes between them. It is able to orientate to a light when unilaterally blinded, so that each eye must have a two-way action. The bee is distinguished from *Eristalis* mainly by the fact that sometimes, though not always, it inhibits the second of two lights. Our criterion for telo-taxis is thus this central inhibition in orientating to one of two lights, and not the successful orientation to a light in the unilaterally blinded condition. After all, there is an obvious difference between (*a*) going between two sources and (*b*) going to one and ignoring the other, so that the normal behaviour of *Eristalis* and of the bee can be clearly distinguished. *Eristalis* behaves tropo-tactically, while *Apis* sometimes behaves tropo-tactically and sometimes telo-tactically. Kühn (1929) himself and v. Buddenbrock (1937) regard the straight course towards one light in the one-eyed animal as the criterion of telo-taxis, and consequently claim that this type of reaction is very widely distributed among animals. But if their criterion is accepted, a single antero-median ommatidium would suffice to transfer a reaction from tropo-taxis to telo-taxis, without any considerable change in the behaviour of the animal; on their criterion, too, animals which go to one light and ignore the other are lumped together with those which orientate between two lights.

Let us consider finally a rather aberrant case of telo-taxis.

Crabs and hermit crabs are able to walk forwards, sideways, obliquely forwards, and, for short distances, backwards and obliquely backwards. All these varied modes of progression, except those leading directly backwards, are used in the photo-tactic responses of these crustaceans (v. Buddenbrock, 1922; Alverdes, 1930). *Eupagurus bernhardus* goes towards a single light equally well when walking forwards, sideways, or in between the two. While moving, it sometimes changes over from one of these orientations of the body to another, without altering its general direction of locomotion at all. Although the angle between the axis of the body and the beam of light changes considerably, the general direction of locomotion is unaltered! The eyes have each a visual field of 360° in a horizontal plane, for the eye-stalk is attached below the equator of the nearly spherical eye. Removal of one eye makes not a scrap of difference to the orientation of the crab, nor to its varied modes of walking. Often the eye is pointed at the source of light, but sometimes it is pointed in other directions without interfering with the orientation. In a two-light experiment, whether with one eye or with two, *Eupagurus* follows the zigzag course which we associate with telo-taxis alone (Fig. 37, p. 92); occasionally for a time it may go between the two lights, but the fact that it *can* behave tropo-tactically is beside the point. The behaviour is generally typical of telo-taxis, but it does not fit well into the scheme which we have described for the bee because apparently any part of the crab's eye can act as the fixation area. It is therefore not possible to work out a reflex map of the eye in terms of rigid reflexes, and it seems that here we are forced to postulate a higher degree of co-ordination and perhaps plasticity (Bethe & Fischer, 1931). But that is another story.

LIGHT COMPASS REACTION

IN the directed reactions (taxes) which have been discussed so far the animal moves directly towards or directly away from the source of stimulation. In the undirected reactions (kineses) the animal follows a convoluted path which eventually takes it towards or away from the source. These are kinds of reactions which guide animals into dark places (planarians, maggots) or light places (*Eristalis*, *Apis*), or moist places (woodlice), for example; the places into which the animal is thus led are, on the whole, of ecological importance to that particular species under the particular conditions of the moment. The direction in which the animal goes is severely limited by the environmental conditions; if a ship had to be steered on similar principles on the high seas it would either follow a semicircular track by going towards the sun or the moon, or it would go either directly north or south if guided by the compass needle or the pole star.

Consider an animal which has a permanent home to which it returns after its excursions, and suppose it to be guided in its comings and goings by one of the taxes, using the sun. At any moment of the day it could make an excursion in one direction only. We know, in fact, that animals are not restricted in this way, and it was in connexion with the problem of homing that the new type of orientation, which is to be discussed in this chapter, was first discovered.

The homing of ants has been an interesting mystery for centuries. Judging from its behaviour, an ant appears to know, at each moment and at each position on the track, whether it is moving towards the nest or away from it; when food is found, it is immediately seized with the mandibles and taken towards the nest. We know to-day that this orientation is made possible by a number of sensory clues, of which optical, olfactory, and kinaesthetic ones are of the greatest importance. In this chapter we are concerned only with the part played by light in these reactions.

Many of the indefatigable observers of ant life—Forel, Lubbock, Piéron, Fielde, Cornetz—have marvelled at the 'infallible sense of direction' of ants, particularly when they are returning to the nest with food. Cornetz (1911) observed that ants which were lifted up when on their way home and put down again in another place then started off again in the original direction—that is to say, on a path parallel to the old one, whether this led them to the nest or not. Santschi (1911) repeated these experiments and recognized that it was the sun which directed the animal along its track. Since the tracks were not often directly towards or away from the sun, it was logical to look for some mechanism by which the sun could serve as a fixed point, whatever the direction taken in a particular excursion. The key to this problem turned out to be the peculiar structure of the compound eye of arthropods, in which a small source of light can stimulate only one ommatidium at a time, or at most a few ommatidia. Having once taken up a certain angular position relative to the sun, an arthropod has then merely to retain the image of the sun on the same ommatidium in order to remain orientated. Santschi compared this kind of eye with a compass, with the sun acting as the north magnetic pole. Just as a ship's navigator can maintain any desired direction simply by keeping a constant angle between the compass needle and the axis of the ship, so the ant can maintain a constant direction with respect to the sun simply by keeping the image of the sun on a particular ommatidium. There is one additional requirement if this method is to be effective in guiding the ant back to the nest; if the sun is shining on the front of the left eye on the outward journey, it must be kept on the rear of the right eye on the return journey. There must be some linkage in the central nervous system between ommatidia which are 180° apart on the horizontal plane.

In demonstrating the importance of the sun in the homing of ants Santschi carried out some novel and striking experiments. He stopped the sunlight from reaching the ants directly and then threw it on them from the opposite side by means of a mirror. The ants immediately changed direction so that the reflection of the sun came to occupy the direction previously occupied by the sun itself. In one case, when the ants were travelling northwards towards the nest, and the sun was in the west and so shining on their left sides at right angles to the track, when the sun was shaded and the reflection thrown from the opposite direction the ants turned right about and went southwards. The *reflected* sun was then in the east and on the left and shining at right angles to the track (Fig. 39). In another case, in which the sun was beyond the nest, by the same technique the ants could be induced to go in any direction by placing the mirror suitably, since they always travelled in the direction of the image of the sun in the mirror.

Brun (1914) repeated these experiments successfully and

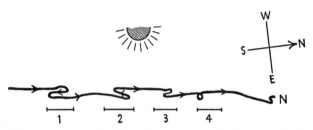

Fig. 39. An ant was returning to the nest with the sun on its left side. In four consecutive places 1, 2, 3, 4 the direct light from the sun was shaded and the image of the sun was projected from the animal's right-hand side by means of a mirror. The animal preserved its position relative to the sun or its image respectively by turning round. (After Santschi, 1911.)

added some very illuminating ones, of which the following is perhaps the most interesting. At 2.39 p.m. an ant was on its way back to the nest, approaching it in a more or less straight line (Fig. 40). The sun was shining on the ant's right side, making about a right angle with the axis of the body and with the general direction of the track. A box was then put over the ant, and it was kept imprisoned in this way for about $2\frac{1}{2}$ hours. When it was released, it started off in a new direction which deviated from the original one by an angle of about 37°. This was approximately the angle through which the sun had moved during the ant's period of imprisonment, so that the sun was still kept at right angles to the track. Of course the new path did not lead to the nest but deviated to the right by about 37°.

In another homing insect, the honey-bee *Apis mellifica*, a similar mechanism is sometimes involved in the return to the hive. Normally bees orientate themselves optically by means of conspicuous landmarks such as houses, trees, roads, and so on,

and can return from two or three miles away by this method
(v. Frisch, 1931). In an environment in which conspicuous
marks are absent, however, they use the sun as the ants do.
Wolf (1927) experimented with bees in a barren sandy waste (a
disused aerodrome). The bees were first trained to feed at a

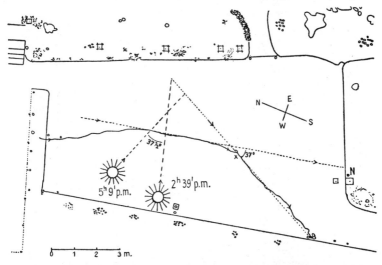

Fig. 40. An ant, *Lasius niger*, was returning to the nest (*N*) with the sun shining
from the right at an angle of about 90° to the animal's path. At the place *x* the
ant was imprisoned for 2½ hours. When released it deviated from its former path
by an angle which was exactly the angle through which the sun had travelled
during this period. The rays of the sun again made a right angle with the animal's
path. (After Brun, 1914.)

place 150 metres distant from the hive and they learned to go
to the food and to fly back to the hive. Some of them were then
captured at the feeding-place, transferred elsewhere, and then
released. They flew off in a direction parallel to the line joining
the feeding-place and the hive, covered the distance they had
been accustomed to travel between food and hive, and then
started to make random movements. This shows that the bees
had some means of telling not only the direction of the hive, but
also its distance away. Fig. 41, p. 104, shows diagrammatically
the behaviour of the bees when transferred from the feeding-place
to various other places. If the bees were imprisoned at the
feeding-place for some time, they behaved like the ants and

deviated from the proper direction by an amount which corresponded with the amount of movement of the sun during the period of imprisonment.[1]

The return of a spider from a meal at the centre of its web to

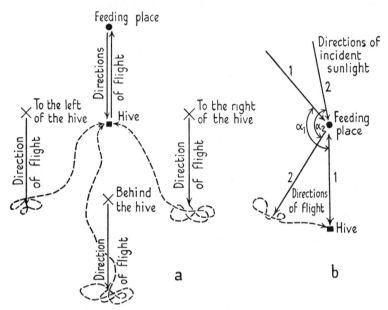

FIG. 41. (*a*) Routes taken by bees which have been caught at a feeding-place and released in different directions from the hive. In each case the bee flies off in the direction and for the distance which would have brought it straight from the feeding-place to the hive. (*b*) Bees imprisoned at a feeding-place for a certain period and then released deviate from the straight course to the hive by the angle through which the sun has travelled during this period ($\alpha_1 = \alpha_2$). (After Wolf, 1927.)

the lurking-place near the edge might be regarded as homing. The direction of the incident light plays a part in guiding the spider on this short journey (Bartels, 1929).

The general importance and wide distribution of this type of orientation reaction was first recognized by v. Buddenbrock (1917), who worked with animals which do not make nests or return to a home. His first experiments were done with the larva of *Vanessa urticae*, the small tortoiseshell butterfly. If this caterpillar is allowed to crawl on sooty paper in a dark-room, it leaves tracks which show that it wanders at random, crossing

[1] See note 18, Appendix.

and recrossing its own path and getting nowhere. When a small source of light is in sight, however, the animal maintains

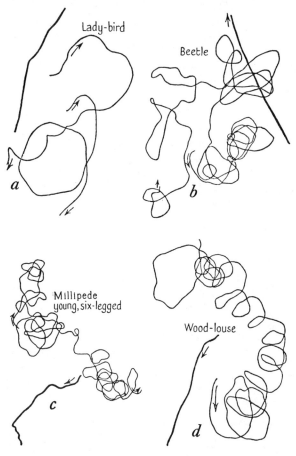

FIG. 42. Tracks of several arthropods in directive light (heavy lines) and in the dark (fine lines). *a*, Coccinellid (beetle); *b*, Chrysomelid (beetle); *c*, Julus (Myriapod); *d*, Oniscus (wood-louse). (v. Buddenbrock, 1917.)

a straight or only slightly curved path. Fig. 42 shows this type of behaviour for four different arthropods. In the experiment illustrated in Fig. 43, p. 106, the caterpillar crawls with its left side towards the light (L_1). This light (L_1) is extinguished and another light (L_2) is switched on. The caterpillar immediately turns, making a hairpin bend, so that its left side is once more illuminated—but by light (L_2) this time.

In the simple experiment with a single light the caterpillar may maintain one direction for nearly an hour, or it may give it up after a few minutes. It then stops, raises and waves its head, and crawls off in a new direction. Thus the particular angle of orientation can be changed spontaneously and is not fixed for any definite period.

This type of orientation, in which the animal need not travel in line with the light but in which the light is certainly used in the performance of a directed orientation, was called by v. Buddenbrock (1917) *Lichtkompassbewegung* (light-compass-movement). As we shall see later (Chaps. X, XV; Table IV, pp. 133–5) there are other *transverse orientations* (e.g. dorsal light reaction) in which the angle of orientation is 90° and fixed. The term *meno-taxis* (μένω, remain), introduced by Kühn (1919), means exactly the same thing as *compass reaction*. It is convenient, however, to reserve the term *taxis* for reactions in which the animal goes towards or away from the source of stimulation. The term *compass reaction* has the advantages of being vivid, self-explanatory, and, although in the common tongue, objective, and we propose to use it rather than its synonym *meno-taxis*. In compass reactions the source of stimulation serves as a fixed point by means of which an orientated path is maintained. The animal maintains a definite angle between the direction of motion and the line joining the source to the receptor. Generally speaking, this is done by keeping the stimulus on a particular point in the receptor apparatus. This point may be altered sharply from time to time. At any one moment different individuals orientate at different angles, so that the behaviour of a crowd does not look like a formal arrangement and the word *taxis* is therefore not very appropriate.

FIG. 43. A caterpillar crawling in a dark-room, with the light on its left, turns through 180° when this light (L_1) is replaced by a light on its right side. That is, it keeps the incident light on the left. (After v. Buddenbrock, 1917.)

Let us now consider a particular case of light compass reaction in greater detail. *Elysia viridis* is a small green opisthobranch mollusc which lives among algae in the Mediterranean. When tested in a dark-room under the influence of a horizontal beam of light, it crawls in more or less straight lines; when illuminated from above, its course becomes irregular (Fraenkel, 1927 *d*). This shows that straight crawling depends on the light. When the light is shifted to a new position, the mollusc immediately responds by crawling in a new direction; the new direction bears the same relation to the new position of the light as the previous direction did to the old position of the light. The angle between the axis of the body and the line joining the eye to the source of light is called the *orientation angle* (Fig. 44). We can therefore say that the mollusc keeps its orientation angle constant. Fig. 45 *a*, p. 108, shows a case in which an *Elysia* maintained an orientation angle of about 90° and kept its left side turned towards the light. Fig. 45 *b* illustrates another case, with an orientation angle of about 45° and with the animal's right side turned to the light. The orientation angle altered from experiment to experiment, but it was not without limitations; if crawling directly towards the light is reckoned as an orientation angle of 0°, then all the angles observed lay between 45° and 135°. This is easily explained by the structure of the eyes; they are cup-eyes with a lens and other arrangements such that only light falling within the angle 35° to 130° approximately can reach the retina. The animal cannot possibly see directly ahead or behind (Fig. 46, p. 109).

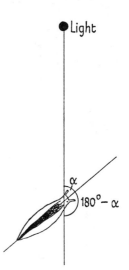

Fig. 44. Method of measuring the orientation angle which the longitudinal axis of *Elysia* makes with the incident light. (Fraenkel, 1927 *d*.)

In the experiments illustrated in Fig. 45, p. 108, the light was sufficiently far away for the rays striking the animal to be practically parallel; it is obvious that when the light is near by the rays are far from parallel, and the maintenance of any particular orientation angle must result in a curved path. In

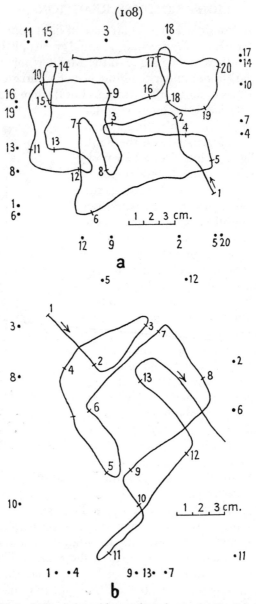

FIG. 45. *Elysia viridis* moving with an orientation angle of 90° (left) (*a*) and of 45° (right) (*b*) to the incident light. The figures on the curves indicate the moments at which the light was placed at the places indicated by the same figures in the margin. The distance of the animal from the light was much larger than is indicated in this figure. (Fraenkel, 1927 *d*.)

the case illustrated in Fig. 47, p. 110, the light was close up; the animal orientated with an angle of nearly 90° and with the light on its left side, and then switched over to 90° on the right side, making altogether more than four complete journeys round the light with the second of these orientation angles.

We have seen that anatomical reasons make it impossible for *Elysia* to use orientation angles greater than 130° and less than

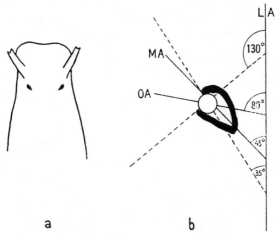

a   b

FIG. 46. Position of the eyes in the head of *Elysia*, showing that the only light that enters the eye comes in from an angle between 35° and 130° to the long axis. (Fraenkel, 1927 *d*.)

35°, and angles of 0° and 180° cannot occur. In other animals, however, such angles can and do occur. Table II and Fig. 48, pp. 111–12, show the theoretically possible types of light compass reaction. It is obvious that in parallel rays the tracks would be straight, and in radiating light they would usually be curved.

When an animal goes straight towards or away from a light, it is not possible to say immediately whether it is carrying out a taxis, on the one hand, or a light compass reaction with an orientation angle of 0° or 180° on the other. Indeed, it seems likely that the mechanism which maintains a compass reaction is often similar to that of telo-taxis, so similar that in the case postulated it might be equally correct to call the reaction either telo-taxis or light compass reaction. In both cases orientation depends on the maintenance of a particular distribution of

stimuli over the sensory apparatus. We might, therefore, expect
that in light compass reaction the same phenomenon of central
inhibition of one of two lights might appear. This is in fact the
case for *Elysia* (Fig. 49, p. 113). If the mollusc is orientated to
one light and an additional light is switched on, it sometimes
changes over to the second light; in most cases it continues to

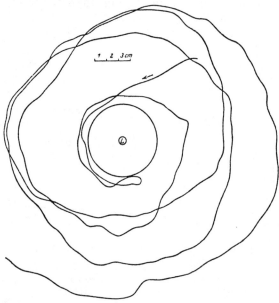

FIG. 47. *Elysia viridis* circling round a candle with an
orientation angle of about 90°, first on its left and then on its
right. (Fraenkel, 1927 *d*.)

orientate to the first light, even though that one is considerably
the weaker. In one case *Elysia* kept to the first light although the
second one acted upon the animal with an intensity 16 times
as great.

Elysia usually changes direction by means of a smooth curve.
If the light is moved round by a quarter of a circle, almost
invariably the animal turns through 90°, and only seldom does
it go round the other way (270°). If the light is shifted round
through 180°, smooth crawling is occasionally interrupted by
random movements of the anterior end of the body, with the
posterior end sticking to the substratum, and then the new
direction is suddenly taken up with astonishing precision. It

seems to be the rule that the new orientation is reached with as little turning as possible. This conclusion has been confirmed by v. Buddenbrock (1935) for a number of insects (Fig. 50, p. 114).

Light compass reactions have been described as occurring in a large number of insects (v. Buddenbrock & Schulz, 1933; v. Buddenbrock, 1937); they also occur in *Elysia*, as described above, and in the common snail, *Helix* (v. Buddenbrock, 1919),

TABLE II. (*From Fraenkel, 1931.*)

Size of the orientation angle	Path adopted in parallel rays of light	Path in diverging rays of light
0°	Straight line directly towards source (cf. positive photo-taxis)	Straight line directly towards source (cf. positive photo-taxis)
<90°	Straight line, obliquely approaching source	Spiral, eventually finishing at source
90°	Straight line, perpendicular to the rays	Circle, with the source as centre
>90°	Straight line, obliquely away from the source	Spiral, going away from the source
180°	Straight line, directly away from source (cf. negative photo-taxis)	Straight line, directly away from source (cf. negative photo-taxis)

in spiders (Bartels & Baltzer, 1928; v. Buddenbrock, 1931 a), and in Polychaeta (v. Buddenbrock, 1937). The reaction is therefore widespread and of general importance. Its function can be realized more vividly when one remembers the stories of men walking round in large circles when lost in barren places and without proper means of orientation. It might be possible for a strictly symmetrical animal to keep on a straight line while walking on a perfect horizontal plane; but in fact animals are seldom provided with such ideal conditions. They have to turn round obstacles and to go over irregular surfaces, and if no means of orientating were available, the total range of action would be greatly reduced.

It is therefore not surprising to find that some animals show a very high degree of accuracy in maintaining the orientation angle. Thus v. Buddenbrock & Schulz (1933) showed that insects can correct the angle if the stimulus merely passes from one ommatidium to the neighbouring one. This was demonstrated by means of two lights placed 4 metres away from the insect; the animal was first allowed to orientate to one of them, and then that light was put out and the other put on (Fig. 51, p. 115).

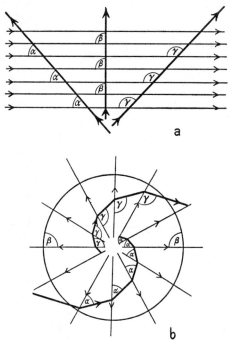

Fig. 48. Scheme of the theoretical cases of light compass reaction (*a*) in parallel light, (*b*) in light coming from a point-like source. Compare Table II, p. 111. (Fraenkel, *Biol. Rev.* 1931.)

When the lights were so close together that they illuminated the same ommatidium, no correction of the course occurred. When, on the other hand, the two beams illuminated two different ommatidia—and this could be determined by cutting sections of the eye—then a suitable correction of the course occurred when the lights were switched over (Fig. 52, p. 116).

In the type of compass reactions so far mentioned the mechanism is much like that of telo-taxis, for there is inhibition of a second light; these reactions are distinguished from telo-taxis by the fact that when orientated to a single light the animal does not move in line with the rays. Compass reactions involving a mechanism similar to *tropo-taxis* are also possible, as long as the balance is kept asymmetrical to a fixed extent. The caterpillars of *Lymantria (Porthetria) dispar* (the Gypsy Moth) crawl in the general direction of a single light in a dark-room, but seldom directly to the light. The path is kept at a constant divergence angle from the light rays, so that it takes the form of

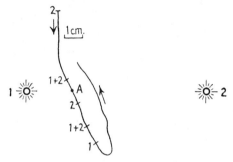

FIG. 49. *Elysia viridis* illuminated in turn by one light (1) and two lights (1+2). The centimetre scale applies only to the track. Distance *A* to light 1 = 9 cm.; *A* to light 2 = 36 cm. The mollusc orientated to the weaker light (2) and remained orientated to it when a much stronger one was present at the same time. (After Fraenkel, 1927 *d.*)

the logarithmic spiral characteristic of light compass reactions (Fig. 53, p. 117) (Ludwig, 1934). The angle of orientation is commonly 20–40°; it is seldom zero or as high as 90°; it usually remains constant for periods of days, though it may change either suddenly or gradually (Ludwig, 1933, 1934). This is all consistent with ordinary compass reactions. But in two lights the caterpillars do not inhibit one and orientate to the other; they maintain their divergence angle to some kind of resultant of the two lights. This means that both lights are taken into account, a state of balance is involved, but this balance is asymmetrical. It is therefore likely that when there is only one light there is a similar asymmetrical balance.

Ludwig (1934) discusses this in relation to what an animal behaving tropo-tactically would do if one eye were covered with a semi-transparent varnish. The covered eye would be less stimulated than usual by a given intensity of light. Consequently the animal would tend to turn to the side of the normal eye, even if its body were already in line with the light rays. This would lead to increased stimulation of the covered eye and diminished stimulation of the normal eye, and equality of stimulation could be reached by orientation at an angle to the

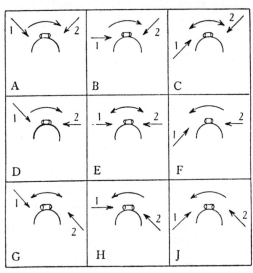

FIG. 50. Light compass reaction of the beetle, *Geotrupes*. Direction of turning (curved arrow) when the light from one direction (arrow 1) was changed to light from another direction (arrow 2). (v. Buddenbrock, 1935.)

rays. In the caterpillars of *Lymantria* it is unlikely that the asymmetry of the organism is an anatomical one of this sort, for although particular individuals kept the light always on the left side, for example, at a fairly fixed angle, most individuals changed not only the size of the divergence angle but also the sign of it, from one side of the body to the other. This lability suggests that the asymmetry is of a physiological nature and probably in the central nervous system. There may well be cases, however, in which some anatomical asymmetry leads to a genuine 'asymmetrical tropo-taxis' which could only be identified as such by the small and constant size of the divergence angle (cf. Chap. XI).

Ludwig calls this reaction *tropo-meno-taxis*. It is perfectly clear that it is somewhat different from the kind of compass reactions investigated earlier, for in those a second light can certainly be inhibited. Honjo (1937) investigated the conditions under which inhibition occurs in the dung beetle, *Geotrupes sylvaticus*, which had previously been shown to react well. When a second beam is thrown on the beetle at an angle of 90° or 180° to the first, it is usually inhibited even when it is much stronger; some-times it becomes the orientation light and the first light is then inhibited, as in the case of *Elysia*. If, however, the two beams cross at an angle of only 40°, the animal does not inhibit either but turns so that its divergence angle makes a line between them. If one eye is put out of action the reactions are the same, except that they are limited to one side of the animal.

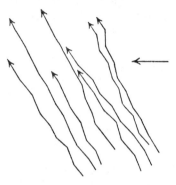

Fig. 51. Tracks of *Geotrupes* when the direction of the light was repeatedly changed by 3 degrees. (v. Buddenbrock and Schulz, 1933.)

The probable explanation of these results is as follows. When the lights are far enough apart, each eye can be stimulated by one light only; but when they are near together one eye can be stimulated by both lights, while the other need not be affected at all. With lights far apart inhibition occurs, while with lights near together it does not. It seems, therefore, that inhibition occurs only when one light stimulates only the eye which is not being used in fixing the divergence angle. When both lights stimulate the same eye, both influence the angle of orientation and neither is inhibited. In this case, then, as far as the one eye is concerned, we are dealing with a mechanism similar to that of tropo-taxis in *Eristalis*, in which balance can occur with a single eye in action, but of course the result is orientation at an angle to a line between the lights instead of along it. If we consider both eyes, then the parallel with *Eristalis* no longer holds. In *Geotrupes* it is the stimulation of the second *eye* which is inhibited, but inhibition of a *second light* on *one* eye does not occur.

Like telo-taxis, the usual type of compass reaction can be carried out only if the eyes are effective direction receptors. Such complicated eyes may be used for tropo-taxis, but they are not essential for this reaction. It is unlikely that the ocelli of a caterpillar are sufficiently effective to perform a compass reaction with a mechanism like that of telo-taxis; for such animals, inhibition of a second light is probably impossible simply because the optical apparatus does not give sufficiently accurate information about how many lights there are and where they are situated. It is thus interesting to find that a light compass

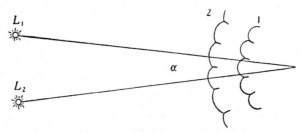

FIG. 52. Method of finding the minimum change of direction of the incident light required to show a light compass reaction. In case 1, the change from the light 1 to light 2 has no effect because the same ommatidium continues to be stimulated. In case 2, the light ray is shifted from one ommatidium to another and re-orientation may occur. (v. Buddenbrock, 1935.)

reaction can be performed by means of eyes which are not complex direction receptors but probably little more than intensity receptors, the mechanism of reaction being like that of tropo-taxis, instead of the more efficient telo-taxis. Further experimental work is required, however, to test this interpretation of the observations and to find out how common this 'tropo-meno-taxis' is.

Although the general character of the light compass reaction was recognized by Santschi (1911) for the first time, certain varieties of the reaction have been known for a longer time. If almost any vertebrate is tested on a rotating platform, it makes certain movements of the head and of the eyeballs which are known as compensatory movements (Löwenstein, 1936). These are in part due to the activity of the semicircular canals in the internal ear; but if that apparatus is put out of action, compensatory movements still occur as long as the animal can see.

In insects, too, compensatory movements occur in the turn-table experiment (Rádl, 1903). They are reminiscent of the behaviour of someone looking out of the window in a moving train; the eyes fix on some object in the middle distance and, as the train moves forward, the eyeballs slowly rotate back, and then suddenly flick forwards on to another object. Something like this sometimes happens in insects which have a very flexible neck, the movement of the whole head taking the place

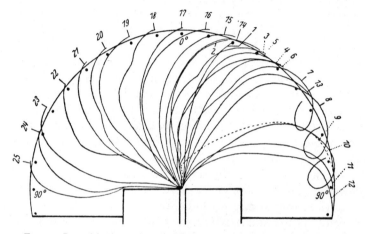

FIG. 53. Logarithmic curves towards one light placed in various positions, representing consecutive tracks of one caterpillar of *Lymantria dispar*, resulting from the orientation angle remaining constant for almost the whole track. Near the light, owing to the great light intensity, the track becomes a circle round the light. (Ludwig, *Z. wiss. Zool.*, 1934.)

of movements of the eyeballs. More commonly the insect rotates on one point so as just to counteract the rotation of the table, or walks or flies along a curve. In either case the general effect is to keep the optical field relatively constant. As we shall see, it is a fixation reaction, or compensatory movement or light compass reaction of this kind which is really in action in many cases of so-called 'rheo-taxis'.

An unusual type of light compass reaction is exhibited by *Daphnia pulex* (Eckert, 1938). *Daphnia* has a spherical compound eye which is movable by means of muscles. If the animal is fixed in a compressorium and a single movable light is shone on it, as the light is moved so the eye rotates in the same direction

(v. Frisch & Kupelwieser, 1913). There is a tendency to keep the image of the light on a certain median ommatidium. When *Daphnia* is swimming, if the light is not at first on this fixation ommatidium the eye is suitably rotated. The asymmetrical tensions in the eye muscles then provide the sensory impulses which initiate turning reflexes leading to orientation of the body in line with the light. In much the same way the labyrinth of mammals keeps the head in its primary orientation and unusual tensions of the neck muscles initiate righting movements of the legs and body. If there are two lights *Daphnia* looks at neither, but in between them. In swimming the animal goes between two lights. This rather unusual mechanism leads to a reaction which is essentially tropo-tactic. Occasionally, however, the correcting reflexes arising in the eye muscles fail to appear. The eye behaves normally and faces a single light or between two lights, but this time the eye muscles maintain a constant angle between the axes of the eye and the body. The animal then swims at a constant angle to the rays from a single light. In two lights, however, owing to the tropo-tactic orientation of the eye and the absence of inhibition of the second light, the path followed is more complex (Eckert, 1938). Eckert calls this reaction *klino-tropo-taxis*. *Klino-* here refers to the constant angle between the direction in which the fixation ommatidium points and the direction of motion of the animal, and has no connexion with the reactions which we call klino-kinesis and klino-taxis. Since this reaction of *Daphnia* is at present an isolated case, it seems a little premature to provide a new name for it. It is perhaps best regarded as an unusual compass reaction with a mechanism similar in certain respects to the mechanism of tropo-taxis.

When we come to consider the detailed mechanism of the usual kind of light compass reaction, difficulties arise immediately. Attention has already been drawn to a certain similarity between it and telo-taxis. In the case of the honey-bee a permanent fixation region in the front of the eye was postulated; stimulation of ommatidia to the left of this causes turning to the left, and stimulation of ommatidia to the right causes right turning. One thinks also of a fixation region in the case of light compass reaction, but a temporary rather than a permanent one. This implies that the whole reflex map of the eye can be suddenly adjusted when a change of the orientation angle occurs. The two conceptions—the reflex map and the fluidity postulated—have a certain inconsistency which is not universally acceptable. The fluidity which is required seems to be more in keeping with some sort of central organization of the optic field or, indeed, may be simply another way of expressing that very thing.

If, when an animal is showing the light compass reaction, the light is moved round, the animal always re-orientates by turning round the shortest way (Fig. 50, p. 114); this suggests that there is really a reflex map as in telo-taxis. The similarity between telo-taxis and light compass reaction is still closer when we take as the example of the former the behaviour of the crabs studied by v. Buddenbrock (1922), in which the crabs go towards the light but with no constant relation between the body axis or the axis of the eye and the direction of motion. Simple schemes all seem to break down in one way or another when we try to apply them to these reactions, so that for the time being their internal mechanisms remain mysterious.

In spite of the points of similarity of these two types of reaction, it seems worth while to keep them separate, for a simple and clear distinction can be made between them in practice. In telo-taxis the path followed is always in line with rays of light, while in the compass reaction it is usually not so. Another distinction can be made on completely different grounds; in photo-taxes the light is usually a token stimulus (see Chap. XIV) which commonly leads the animal directly into a more favourable place, while in compass reactions the light may be regarded as a token stimulus only in a more remote sense. It tends to keep the animal moving in a constant direction, and so to lead it to a *different* place, whether more favourable or not.[1]

---

[1] See note 19, Appendix.

DORSAL LIGHT REACTION

THERE are many aquatic animals which normally swim horizontally, with the dorsal surface upwards; many of these maintain this orientation *optically*, by keeping the dorsal surface perpendicular to the light which passes through the surface of the water. In some animals which normally swim on their backs (e.g. *Chirocephalus*) the position is reversed, so that the *ventral* surface is kept facing the light. This kind of orientation occurs very obviously in many animals which have no, static organs (see Chap. XV) and which are not in stable equilibrium—that is to say, which can only maintain the normal position with the back upwards by means of active movements; in other cases this kind of orientation is obscured because there are static organs in action or because there is stability of equilibrium at the same time, but the participation of the dorsal light reaction can still be demonstrated by experimental methods. This reaction was first detected in *Daphnia* (Rádl, 1901; Ewald, 1910). Later, its wide distribution and general importance were recognized by v. Buddenbrock (1914, 1915 *a*), who named it *Lichtrückenreflex*. We are calling it dorsal light *reaction* in order to avoid giving the impression that it is a simple *reflex*. This kind of behaviour has been observed in many groups of animals, as is shown in Table III.

The dorsal light reaction can be demonstrated in the following simple manner; the animal to be tested is put into a glass aquarium in a dark-room. It is first observed when the light shines from above; most animals then swim with the dorsal surface upwards. Then another light is substituted underneath the aquarium and, if the reaction is not interfered with by other reactions, the animal proceeds to swim upside-down. The same procedure applies in the case of a ventral light reaction, and the result is similar, *mutatis mutandis*.

This reaction is similar to tropo-taxis and telo-taxis in that the animal places itself symmetrically with respect to a single incident light, but it is unlike these taxes in that the animal does not move towards the light but—if it moves at all—at right angles to it. On the other hand, in the light compass reaction the animal does *not* place itself symmetrically but it *does*, as in the dorsal light reaction, move at an angle to the light rays. The dorsal light reaction is thus clearly not the same as any of these other reactions; its relation to them is worth further investigation. Although it has quite distinct characteristics, its mechanism might be similar to that of one or other of them.

TABLE III. *Sample distribution of the occurrence of dorsal light reactions in the animal kingdom*

Group	Genus	Author
Coelenterata (Medusae)	*Leuckartiara*	Fraenkel, 1931
	Charybdaea	Fraenkel, 1931
Annelida-Polychaeta	*Alciope*	v. Buddenbrock, 1937
	Tomopteris	Fraenkel, 1931
Crustacea-Branchiopoda	*Daphnia*	{ Rádl, 1903 { Schulz, 1928
	Chirocephalus, *Apus, Artemia* }	Seifert, 1930, 1932
Crustacea-Malacostraca	*Leander* and other shrimps } and prawns }	v. Buddenbrock, 1914 Alverdes, 1926, 1928
Insecta-Exopterygota	Nymphs of Ephemeridae and } of *Notonecta*	v. Buddenbrock, 1915 *a* Wojtusiak, 1929
Insecta-Endopterygota	Larvae of *Acilius*	Wojtusiak, 1929
Vertebrata-Pisces	*Crenilabrus*	v. Holst, 1935 *b*

In tropo-taxis we can distinguish two main types of mechanism, the one simply involving a balance of stimulation in the two eyes (*Armadillidium*, Chap. VII), and the other being somewhat complicated by the presence of a fixation area and the possibility of balance in a single eye (*Eristalis*, Chaps. VII and XI); in telo-taxis, too, there seem to be two main types, the one being distinguished from the condition in *Eristalis* only by the occurrence of central inhibition of a second light (*Apis*, Chap. VIII), and the other seeming to have no permanent fixation area but having both central inhibition and some kind of central organization of the optic field (*Eupagurus*, Chap. VIII). In the light compass reaction there is no permanent fixation area on the eye, but there is central inhibition and presumably central organization of the field; the fixation region is kept constant for a certain time. We can apply to the dorsal light reaction the same tests as were used in discriminating between these other types. We shall find, however, that the results are not always clear-cut, because the animals are frequently also photo-tactic and a mixed reaction has to be analysed. The experiments described below are selected with these points in mind and also to show how the reaction may be distinguished from mere stability of equilibrium and from behaviour controlled by static organs (Chap. XV).

Before proceeding to the experiments themselves, some theoretical considerations need to be elucidated. In taxes and in the light compass reaction the animal is usually treated as if it were moving on a horizontal plane; it has only one plane of movement, and all turning takes place about a vertical dorso-ventral axis. Aquatic animals, however, have three planes of movement, and can turn about any or all of three axes of the body. They can turn to the left or right about a vertical axis, they can roll over on one side and thus rotate on their own longitudinal axes, or they can pitch or turn front or back somersaults and thus rotate about a transverse axis. In taxes, only the first kind of rotation—turning—needs consideration, but in the dorsal light reaction we have to consider in addition the second and third kinds—rolling and pitching. In order to maintain the normal position in the water, the animal must neither pitch nor roll, and the reassumption of the proper orientation may necessitate the use of either of these rotations or of both of them. We may thus expect to find that the complete reaction involves two mechanisms; they may be distinguishable or they may be inseparable in practice. Although animals can often remain stationary in the water, corrections of body orientation are usually associated with forward swimming; consequently rolling becomes a movement similar to that of a screw being driven home, the axis of the animal coinciding with the axis of the screw, and pitching becomes back or front somersaulting, at least experimentally when it goes farther than the rhythmical pitching of a ship.

Now in animals which have two symmetrically placed eyes, rolling can conceivably be prevented by a mechanism very similar to that of tropo-taxis. Any tendency to roll over on one side must result in the two eyes being differently illuminated— always assuming that all the light comes from vertically above in parallel rays. This inequality of stimulation could lead to asymmetrical reflex movements tending to correct the balance of stimulation and so to restore the animal to its normal position (Fig. 54 *a*). That is not to say that this is necessarily the mechanism, for there is no *a priori* reason against the existence of a fixation area with the possibility of balance in a single eye, as in *Eristalis* and *Apis*. For pitching, on the other hand, no

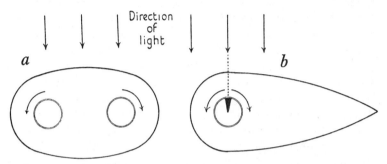

FIG. 54. *a*. An animal seen from the front. There is a symmetry plane for rolling, and the dorsal light reaction could be carried out by means of a mechanism involving symmetrical balance (cf. tropo-taxis of *Armadillidium*). *b*. An animal seen from the side. There is no symmetry plane for pitching, and a dorsal light reaction by pitching could only be carried out by a mechanism dependent on a two-way eye (cf. *Eristalis*).

plane of bilateral symmetry exists in most animals so that the fixation area mechanism seems absolutely essential (Fig. 54 *b*); no question arises in this case of reflexes from one eye balancing those initiated on the other, for in pitching both eyes are equally affected by any degree of rotation. At the very outset we must, therefore, postulate the existence of a reflex map in the eye as far as the antero-posterior vertical plane is concerned; we shall find, further, that in certain cases a similar map is required in the transverse vertical plane.

So far we have considered the dorsal light reaction in relation to tropo-taxis. We might equally well have compared it to the telo-taxis of the honey-bee, for unfortunately the discriminating test between tropo-taxis and telo-taxis (the two-light experiment) has never been applied to a dorsal light reaction. We have therefore no knowledge of whether animals which perform this reaction would inhibit one light or not. The only question which we can profitably discuss at present is whether there is in fact a fixation area for rolling, and if there is, how great is its importance.

If an animal is normally orientated, belly downwards, and the light is then placed immediately beneath it, the two eyes should be quite equally stimulated. Consequently, there would seem to be no reason why the new position should be attained by means of a rolling movement; if stimulation is perfectly symmetrical, there is no reason why the animal should roll to the left rather than to the right. On the other hand, it is easy to imagine the sort of reflex map in the eye which would lead to somersaulting; no question of balance need arise in this case. Consequently, it might be expected that when the light is transferred from above to below, or vice versa, the normal animal would ordinarily re-orientate by means of a somersault. In fact, of course, re-orientation under these conditions often occurs by rolling, and we must then assume that the light has not been placed absolutely symmetrically below the animal.

Let us now turn to actual cases. The cladoceran crustacean, *Daphnia*, has a movable median compound eye. If the animal is kept still in a compressorium and a light is moved about in the neighbourhood, the eye rotates in response (Rádl, 1901; von Frisch & Kupelwieser, 1913). The eye itself performs a fixation reaction (pp. 117–18) and this is probably involved in the loco-motory reactions, just as the neck reflexes are involved in the righting reaction of a falling cat. *Daphnia* is positively photo-tactic under appropriate conditions. It has no statocysts. When falling through the water, with its natatory second antennae held stiffly up, it is in stable equilibrium. In spite of these complications, a dorsal light reaction can be demonstrated, the actual orientation at any moment being due to a combination of this with the photo-taxis and the stability of equilibrium. When illuminated from above, *Daphnia* swims towards the light with the back directed obliquely upwards, the body axis being kept at 20° or 30° to the light rays; when the light is below, it swims down and the dorsal surface is underneath. When illuminated from the side it swims towards the light and, upon reaching the wall of the aquarium, keeps its back to the wall (Schulz, 1928).

The fish-louse, *Argulus foliaceus*, shows the dorsal light reaction very well. It always turns the dorsal surface towards the light, whether that comes from above or below or from the side. If the light is rapidly shifted from above to below, *Argulus* sometimes rolls over, but usually it turns a front somersault (Fig. 55). If one of the two eyes is destroyed, *Argulus* not only does circus movements towards the seeing side in a horizontal plane, which are to be expected because it reacts photo-tropo-tactically (positive), but it also makes continuous rolling or spiralling movements. The latter indicate that a balance of stimulation is involved in stopping rolling, and that as far as rolling is concerned, balance of stimulation enters into the dorsal light reaction in this species (Herter, 1927).[1]

Among the most striking examples of this reaction are those of some of the Anostraca and Notostraca (Crustacea, Branchiopoda) — *Chirocephalus*, *Apus*, and *Artemia* (Seifert, 1930, 1932). Unfortunately both *Chirocephalus* and *Apus* live in temporary fresh-water pools and are only rarely found, but

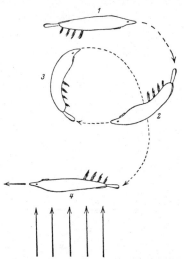

FIG. 55. A carp louse, *Argulus foliaceus*, performing a dorsal light reaction by pitching. (Herter, 1927.)

Artemia, which lives in very saline water, can easily be reared from resistant eggs and is excellent for demonstration purposes. *Apus* (*Triops*) *cancriformis* and *Lepidurus apus* always turn the dorsal side towards the light when swimming freely. *Apus* reorientates mainly by rolling; this can be repeatedly demonstrated by the arrangement shown in Fig. 56, p. 126, in which one-half of the aquarium is lit from one side and the other half from the other side. *Apus* has two compound eyes and a median eye on the dorsal surface. The median eye communicates by a kind of telescope with a window on the ventral surface, but the compound eyes cannot see ventrally. Thus if the light is placed below the animal, the righting reaction is started by the median eye, but the normal orientation is ordinarily maintained through the compound eyes. When one of these is painted

[1] See note 20, Appendix.

over, the animal does rolling and circling movements towards the seeing side.

Chirocephalus (Branchipus) grubei normally swims belly upwards and it performs a *ventral* light reaction, though not a very strong one. *Artemia salina* shows a strong ventral light reaction. When the light is moved from above to below the aquarium, *Artemia* either rolls or somersaults into its new orientation (**Fig. 57**). If one eye is removed, it rolls continually, moving

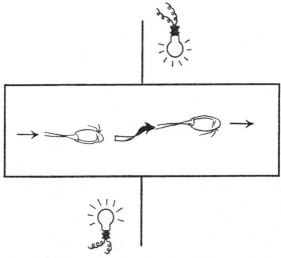

Fig. 56. *Lepidurus apus* performing a dorsal light reaction by rolling, seen from above. (After Seifert, 1930.)

along in spirals, while if both eyes are cut off, the light reaction disappears. Here, again, the importance of the two eyes in maintaining a balance about the longitudinal axis is evident. The nauplius larvae of *Artemia*, which have no compound eyes, do not show the ventral light reaction; the reaction appears at the same time as the compound eyes. In the adult there is a curious correlation between the photo-tactic reaction, which may be either positive or negative, and the manner of somersaulting, when re-orientation takes place by that method instead of rolling. When the light is changed over from above to below, individuals which are photo-positive turn a back somersault, while those which are photo-negative turn a front somersault. A little cogitation will make the reason for this clear (Fig. 57).[1]

[1] See note 21, Appendix.

Many of the free-swimming decapod crustacea, prawns and shrimps, show the dorsal light reaction under suitable conditions. Those species, like *Leander xiphias*, which have statocysts, only do so after the statocysts have been removed; of course, during normal life the reactions initiated in the statocysts and the eyes usually reinforce one another, and it is only under experimental conditions that the two reactions can be

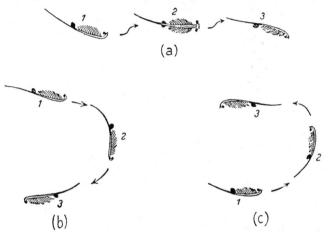

(a)

(b)   (c)

FIG. 57. Ventral light reaction of *Artemia salina*: re-orientation when the light is placed below, (a) by rolling, (b) by back somersaulting (pitching), and (c) by front somersaulting (pitching). (After Seifert, 1930.)

made grossly inconsistent with each other. *Processa caniculata*, which has no statocysts, always turns its back to the light (v. Buddenbrock, 1914). On the other hand, *Lysmata seticaudata* swims on its back and is then in stable equilibrium; it does not show a ventral light reaction. The mechanism of these reactions has been investigated by Alverdes (1926, 1928), his methods being similar to those used by Kühn for investigating the static reactions of the crayfish (see Chap. XV). In order to eliminate the interference of the backward darting due to the tail fan, Alverdes cut the ventral nerve cord just in front of the first abdominal ganglion. The animal was held firmly with forceps in such a position that it could not touch the walls or floor of the aquarium. The normal *Leander* uses its statocysts in maintaining the normal position with the belly down. When it is held obliquely, the legs on the lower side make repeated pushing, rowing, or scuffling movements, which would return it to its normal position if it were free to move (Fig. 58, I a & II a). Illumination from the side does not interfere with this statocyst reaction (Fig. 58, III a & IV a). If, however, the two statocysts in the bases of the antennules are removed, their function is taken over to some extent by the eyes. If the light comes from the side while the animal is held in its normal position, pushing movements are made by the legs on the side farther from the light (Fig. 58, III b). If the animal is turned over on its side, so that its back is towards the lateral light, the animal holds itself symmetrically and no pushing movements occur (Fig. 58, IV b). If the animal is allowed to rest on the bottom of the aquarium when the light comes from the side, it does not turn right over on its side, but compromises by turning through about 45° (Fig. 58, V b).

Processa caniculata, which has no statocysts, shows the same reactions as a *Leander* which has been deprived of statocysts. When resting on the bottom, in turning its back to the light it even lies on its side or on its back, so that the tips of the legs lose contact with the floor.[1]

Removal of one of *Leander's* two eyes spoils the dorsal light reaction, which shows that a balance of reflexes from the two eyes is involved in the normal reaction (Fig. 58, I c–V c). When held in the normal position, with the light above, such a specimen makes continual pushing movements with the legs on the seeing side, and the legs are held symmetrically and at rest only when the animal is tilted over at an angle of 45°, with the intact eye uppermost. The fact that symmetry can be attained at all is interesting and suggests that either a third receptor is concerned in the normal orientation or the reflex map in the eye is of a type not yet encountered. This problem remains to be solved. No experiments appear to have been done with the unilaterally blinded animal in uniform light or swimming freely, so we do not know if *Leander* will make righting movements in all positions in the former or roll perpetually to the blind side in the latter.

Processa caniculata reacts quite differently when unilaterally blinded; it behaves exactly like the normal animal. In this case complete balance can be maintained with one eye alone, so that the fixation region mechanism must be in action.

Very recently, dorsal light reactions have been detected and

[1] See note 22, Appendix.

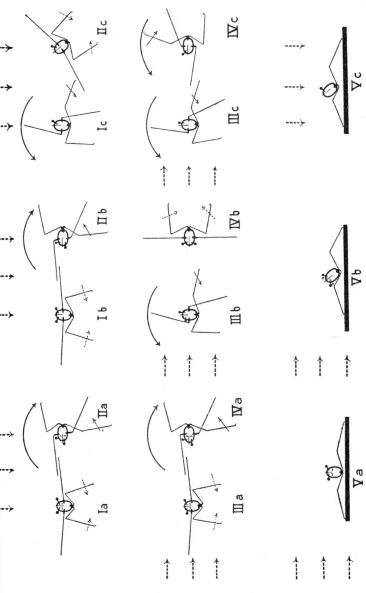

Fig. 58. Scheme of the orientation reactions of a prawn, *Leander xiphias*, in relation to light and gravity. *a*, animals intact; *b*, animals without statocysts; *c*, animals without statocysts and with only one eye. I–IV suspended freely. V resting on the bottom. Heavy broken arrows indicate incident light. Curved arrows indicate sense of turning. Small full arrows indicate direction of thrust of leg. Explanation in text, pp. 127–8 and 221–2. (After Alverdes, 1926.)

analysed in a fish, *Crenilabrus rostratus*, by von Holst (1935 *b*). If the light shines from the side in a dark-room, *Crenilabrus* inclines its back somewhat towards that side; if the light shines hori-

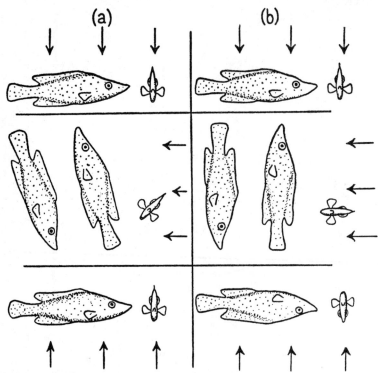

FIG. 59. Dorsal light reaction of a fish, *Crenilabrus rostratus*, when the light comes from above, from the side or from below. *a*, intact; *b*, without labyrinths. Seen from the side (large figures) and from the front (small figures). Without labyrinths, the position is entirely directed by the dorsal light reaction. With the labyrinths present, the fish becomes somewhat tilted when the light comes from the side, but does not swim on its back when illuminated from below. (v. Holst, *Pubbl. Staz. zool. Napoli*, 1935 *b*.)

zontally from in front, the fish tilts its body with the head down, and with the light behind it tilts its head up (Fig. 59 *a*). In none of these cases, however, is the body axis held at right angles to the rays of light; the orientation is a compromise controlled partly by the eyes and partly by the labyrinth of the internal ear. The static reactions of the labyrinth tend to keep the fish in its normal position, while the abnormally placed light tends to lead to an abnormal position. When the light is put beneath the fish, so that the two forces are directly opposed, the static reaction gains a complete victory and the illumination has no effect. When *Crenilabrus* is compromising between the two reactions, the effectiveness of the light depends on its intensity and the stronger the light the greater the inclination of the fish (Fig. 60). The matter is somewhat complicated—but in the expected direction—by the progress of sensory adaptation in the eye.

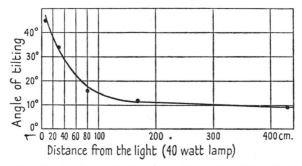

FIG. 60. Curve, showing the dependence of the tilting of the transverse axis of *Crenilabrus*, illuminated from the side, on the intensity of the light. Abscissa — distance from the light (40 watt); ordinate — lateral tilting from the vertical. (v. Holst, *Pubbl. Staz. zool. Napoli*, 1935 *b*.)

When the labyrinths of *Crenilabrus* are put out of action, the static reaction disappears and the dorsal light reaction is left in a pure state. In horizontal lateral light the fish turns through 90° and swims on its side or vertically up and down; with the light below, it swims upside-down (Fig. 59 *b*). When one eye is put out of action as well, it rolls towards the seeing side. This shows that a balance of stimulation is concerned. After a time, however, rolling ceases and the animal can maintain its normal optical orientation with a single eye only. This suggests that both ipsi-lateral and contra-lateral rolling can be started in a single eye in the normal animal, but that the ipsi-lateral rolling is then dominant; after removal of one eye, perhaps more notice is taken of the contra-lateral impulses, so to speak, in the central nervous system. Something rather like this appears to be the case in an allied recovery reaction (see pp. 225–6). This case of *Crenilabrus* is very remarkable, in that a whole set of movements and positions of the fins, eyes, and the whole trunk, which had previously been regarded as almost exclusively controlled by the labyrinth, can also be controlled by eyes when the labyrinth is out of action.

The question of whether or not dorsal light reactions are involved in the orientation of flying animals has aroused considerable speculation. A most important fact in this connexion is that stability of equilibrium differs greatly in the two media, air and water. In flying animals the suspension points—namely, the attachments of the wings—are rather high up and the centre of gravity is relatively low. The equilibrium is therefore stable, particularly because the air exerts only a very small upward thrust on the body (Principle of Archimedes). In aquatic animals, on the other hand, the upward thrust of the water is the main force counteracting the weight of the fish, and the centre of gravity being usually fairly near the centre of the body, the equilibrium is often meta-stable or even unstable. Consequently aquatic animals must make active movements in order to maintain their normal orientation, while in flying insects and birds the need is nothing like so great.

It is, therefore, not surprising to find that attempts to establish the occurrence of dorsal light reactions in insects during flight have failed (v. Buddenbrock, 1915 a).[1] A single case has recently been reported by v. Holst (1935 b). When the butterfly *Gonepterix rhamni* flies in the late afternoon, instead of keeping its body horizontal, it inclines it at an angle of 30 to 40°. A similar reaction has been described for locusts (pp. 192–5) and occurs in certain butterflies; when resting on the ground or on plants, they orientate the body to the sun's rays. There is good evidence, however, that in these cases we are dealing with an orientation to radiant heat, and it may well be that the reaction of *Gonepterix* is of the same sort and not a light reaction at all.

The dorsal light reaction resembles photo-taxis in that orientation is directed and symmetrical (pp. 120–1); but it differs clearly from photo-taxis in that orientation is transverse to the light rays instead of in line with them. On the other hand, the symmetrical dorsal light reaction is like the asymmetrical light compass reaction in that the body axis is placed across the light rays. These two reactions are therefore put together in the larger group of *transverse orientations* (Table IV, pp. 133–5).

[1] See note 23, Appendix.

TABLE IV

SUMMARY: TABULATION OF KINESES, TAXES, AND TRANSVERSE ORIENTATIONS

1 *General description*	2 *Form of stimulus* *required*	3 *Minimum form of re-* *ceptors required*

KINESES. Undirected reactions. No orientation of axis of body in relation to the stimulus.

ORTHO-KINESIS Speed or frequency of locomotion depen- dent on intensity of stimulation.	Gradient of intensity	A single intensity re- ceptor
KLINO-KINESIS Frequency or amount of turning per unit time dependent on intensity of stimulation. Adaptation, &c., required for aggregation.	Gradient of intensity	A single intensity re- ceptor

TAXES. Directed reactions. With a single source of stimulation, long axis of body orientated

KLINO-TAXIS Attainment of orientation indirect, by in- terruption of regularly alternating lateral deviations of part or whole of body, by comparison of intensities of stimulation which are successive in time.	Beam or steep gradi- ent	A single intensity re- ceptor
TROPO-TAXIS Attainment of orientation direct, by turn- ing to less or to more stimulated side, by simultaneous comparison of intensities of stimulation on the two sides. No devia- tions required.	Beam or steep gradi- ent	Paired intensity recep- tors
TELO-TAXIS Attainment of orientation is direct, without deviations. Orientation to a source of stimulus, as if it were a goal. Known only as response to light.	Beam from a small source of light	A number of elements pointing in different directions

TRANSVERSE ORIENTATIONS. Orientation at a temporarily fixed angle to the direction
is seldom directly towards or away from the source of stimulation.

LIGHT COMPASS REACTION Locomotion at a temporarily fixed angle to light rays, which usually come from the side.	Beam from a small source	A number of elements pointing in different directions
DORSAL (OR VENTRAL) LIGHT REACTION Orientation so that light is kept perpendi- cular to both long and transverse axes of the body; usually dorsal, but in some ani- mals ventral. Locomotion need not occur.	Directed light	Paired intensity recep- tors
VENTRAL EARTH (TRANSVERSE GRAVITY) REACTION Orientation so that gravitational force acts perpendicularly to long and transverse axes of body. Dorsal surface usually kept uppermost. Locomotion need not occur.	Gravity (or centri- fugal force simulat- ing gravity)	Statocysts with a num- ber of elements, as is usual with statocysts

4 Behaviour with two sources of stimulation	5 Result of unilateral removal of receptors	6 Formerly called	7 Examples
Locomotion random in direction.			
Reaction to whole of the gradient	No effect? Reduced intensity of reaction?	Simply kinesis	*Porcellio*; Chap. II
Reaction to whole of the gradient	No effect? Reduced intensity of reaction?	Phobo-taxis; avoiding reactions; *Unter-schiedsempfindlichkeit*	*Dendrocoelum, Para-mecium*? Chap. V
in line with the source and locomotion towards (positive) or away from (negative) it.			
Orientation between the two, curving into one when close to sources See Chap. XI	Usually impossible; no effect? Reduced intensity of reaction?	Part of tropo-taxis; avoiding reactions; phobic mechanism	Fly larvae, *Euglena*, larvae of *Arenicola, Amaroucium*; Chap. VI
Orientation between the two, curving into one when close to sources See Chap. XI	Circus movements in uniform field of stimulus and often also in beam or gradient	Tropo-taxis, but klino-taxis excluded, and cases with two-way eyes added from telotaxis	Woodlice, *Ephestia* larvae, *Eristalis, Notonecta*; Chap. VII
Orientation to one at a time; animal may switch over to the other at intervals, giving a zigzag course	Not known, because often the same animal can behave tropo-tactically, and the circus movements which occur may be the result of tropo-taxis	Telo-taxis, but excluding cases which always orientate between two lights before curving into one of them and excluding reactions to specific objects and form reactions	*Apis, Eupagurus*; Chap. VIII
of the external stimulus or at a fixed angle of 90°. Locomotion need not occur and in any case			
If each light affects one eye only, orientation is to one alone; if one eye is affected by both lights, orientation to both combined	No effect, except in limiting the possible angles of orientation	Meno-taxis	*Elysia*, ants, bees; caterpillars of *Vanessa urticae*; Chap. IX
Not known	No effect in some species; produces screw-path in others	Dorsal light reflex (*Lichtrückenreflex*)	*Argulus, Artemia, Apus*; Chap. X
A statocyst combines the forces mechanically and orientation should be determined by the resultant	No effect in some species; produces rotation or lateral tilting in others	?	*Leander*, Crayfish; Chap. XV

PART II

XI

THE TWO-LIGHT EXPERIMENT

THE notion of vibrations in the ether is familiar. The wavelength of such vibrations can be great or small. The longest of the known ones are of the sort used in radio transmission, up to thousands of metres long (say 10^6 cm. or about 6 miles), and the shortest are observed in cosmic rays, down to about 10^{-12} cm. long. In this vast range there occurs a narrow band of vibrations which we recognize as light (about 4 to 7×10^{-5} cm. long) and as radiant heat. Light can be recognized as such and so distinguished from radiation of other wave-lengths only by means of living eyes, and the band of wave-lengths used as light differs in different species of animals. Within the visible spectrum, the normal human being differentiates between lights of different wave-lengths by means of their colour. Bees' eyes are insensitive to red light, but they see farther into the ultra-violet than human beings do (3×10^{-5} cm.) and the ultra-violet is a distinct colour to them.

When radiation strikes suitable matter, if it is absorbed it tends to cause a rise of temperature and it is recognizable by that property. All light is also radiant heat, but, in relation to its stimulating effect on the human retina, blue light has much less heating effect than red. That is to say, the photochemical effect is not proportional to the total energy if different wavelengths are compared. In experiments on the responses of animals to stimulation by light, it is usual to eliminate as much as possible of the red and infra-red part of the spectrum, so that the results shall be complicated as little as possible by responses to local rises of temperature.

Leaving aside altogether the heating effects, light does not commonly have much direct effect on animals. It can be beneficial, as when it is responsible for the synthesis of vitamin D in the skin of man; in great intensity it can be damaging, as when it causes sunburn. Broadly speaking, however, the importance of light to animals is of quite a different kind. It acts as a signal providing information about factors in the environment other than light itself; it acts as a token stimulus (see pp. 189–91). Thus in nature a dark place is commonly also cool, moist, and safe; in ponds the lightest place is near the water surface, where the gas content of the water may be most favourable, and so on. Evolution must have occurred in behaviour just as much as in structure, so we should expect to find that on the whole an animal's behaviour helps it in the struggle for existence. In particular, it is in fact found that when there is *usually* a correlation between light intensity or direction and some important factor in the environment, animals react to the light and reap the benefit in relation to that other factor.

As we have seen (Chaps. V–IX), the uses to which eyes can be put depend on their structure; they may be merely intensity receptors, they may be direction and movement receptors as well, or they may be capable of form-vision. In this book we are concerned only with reactions to intensity and direction.

In this connexion light is a very convenient stimulus to use, for its direction and intensity can be fairly easily controlled and measured. Partly because of this, and partly because almost all animals respond to light at one time or another, the greater part of the experimental work on the principles of elementary animal behaviour has been done with light as the stimulus. A short account of some of the physical properties of light is therefore not out of place.

When a single source of light is used, the light is either allowed to radiate from the source or it is bent by means of lenses to form a parallel or a convergent beam. In the former case, if a surface is exposed at right angles to the light near the source and then moved progressively away, the intensity of illumination of the surface decreases rapidly, and is inversely proportional to the square of the distance from the light (Fig. 61, p. 138). With a strictly parallel beam, however, the intensity does not vary with the distance from the source, provided no significant amount of light is absorbed by the medium through which the light is passing.

Considering first a single radiating source, it is easy to see that when an animal carries out an efficient positive photo-taxis it goes straight to the light in the most direct way; it travels in line with the light rays striking its anterior end; and it goes up the steepest gradient of light intensity which is available. When two sources are presented to the animal simultaneously, however, there is no longer merely a single light-direction and the gradient of light intensity is complicated.

FIG. 61. Lines of equal intensity of light around a source of luminosity of 100 candle-power. If the scale line represents 10 cm., then the figures on the iso-lux represent ten-thousands of metre-candles; if the scale line represents 10 metres, then the figures represent metre-candles. The lines are drawn from calculations based on the inverse square law. Notice that the intensity falls very rapidly at first and then more slowly.

As we have seen (Chaps. VI–VIII), different species of animals react in different ways under such conditions. Fig. 62 shows how the lines of equal intensity are arranged around two sources of unequal intensity. This figure was constructed by calculating the amount of light falling on a hypothetical mote in the air, using the inverse square law.

Consider an animal which has a spherical eye which is photo-sensitive all over its surface and equally exposed to light in all directions. Suppose that the animal behaves photo-positively in such a way that it always moves straight up the steepest intensity gradient that is available in its immediate neighbourhood. That is to say, when the animal is about to take a step, there is one direction in which that step will subject the eye to a higher intensity than any other. This direction— the maximum gradient direction—is given by the lines normal

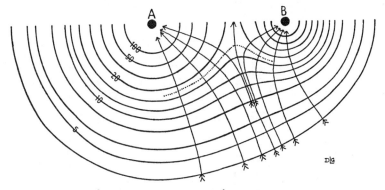

Scale 10 cm. Intensities in ten thousands of metre-candles
Scale 10 m.   Intensities in metre-candles

Fig. 62. Iso-lux round two sources of luminosity 256 (*A*) and 64 (*B*) candle-power, calculated and drawn graphically from the inverse square law (Trotter, 1911). If the scale line represents 10 m., the intensities are in metre-candles; if it is 10 cm., the intensities are in ten-thousands of metre-candles. The curved arrows represent paths up the steepest gradient, and are normal to the iso-lux.

to the lines of equal intensity. Some of these maximum gradient lines have been inserted in Fig. 62. On most of these lines the animal would start off towards some point between the two light-sources, but would later curve round and finally go almost directly to one source. If Fig. 62 is regarded as a contour map of two mountains, then the lowest point on the line joining their peaks represents the head of the pass, and the pass leads down to the valley. If our hypothetical animal starts in the bottom of the valley, it will climb up and nearly reach the head of the pass, but will then turn fairly sharply and make directly for either light. On all lines to the left of this it will eventually reach the stronger light, and on lines to the right, the weaker one.

Although no animal with such a simple eye exists, it is relevant to ask how, in any case, it could receive the necessary information for following the steepest gradient. It is difficult to provide an exclusive answer to this question, but it is probable that the direction of the light is always of some importance,

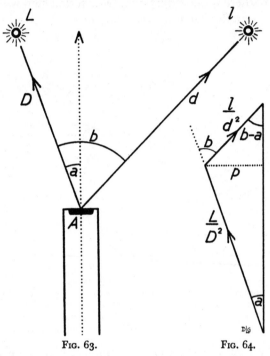

FIG. 63.   FIG. 64.

FIG. 63. Geometrical relations between a hypothetical flat cyclopean eye, not divided into separate elements, and the light from two sources. A, area of eye; L and l, luminosities of the two sources; D and d, their distances from the eye; a and b are the angles shown. The animal is assumed to orientate in such a way that the illumination of the eye is maximal.

FIG. 64. Triangle of forces for the case shown in Fig. 63, regarding the light intensities as forces drawing the animal forwards. Two of the sides are parallel to the two beams striking the animal's eye and proportional to their intensities in length. The third side represents the resultant force—in this case simply the direction of motion of the animal. p is the length of the perpendicular on the resultant. The sizes of the angles are filled in from Fig. 63 according to elementary geometrical principles.

and that no animal reacts purely to intensity when making a directed reaction. Before considering the possible performance of various real kinds of eyes it is interesting to deal with the properties of light in relation to another limiting shape of eye— a flat one.

Consider an animal with a flat frontal cyclopean eye, placed at right angles to the normal direction of motion. When this eye is looking straight at a source of light, the illumination is maximal; as the animal turns, less and less light will fall on the eye until, when the eye is edgeways on to the source, no light reaches it at all. In the same way the size of the shadow thrown —that is, the amount of light stopped—by a piece of paper varies with its angle to the rays of light. Suppose this animal arranges its body axis—say by means of numerous very minute trial movements—in such a way that the illumination of the eye is always maximal, and suppose that it moves towards the light, always maintaining this maximal illumination. With a single light-source it will move directly towards this light; with two, it will at first face between the lights and then curve in towards one of them. The precise path which it will follow can be calculated—as long as this hypothetical animal, unlike real animals, keeps precisely orientated.

Let A be the surface area of the eye (Fig. 63), and let D and d be the distances from the animal of two sources of luminosity L and l. Let a be the angle between the axis of the animal and the light falling on its eye from the source L. Let b be the angle between the rays from the two sources at the centre of the eye. Using the inverse square law, and remembering that the quantity of light falling on the eye depends on its area and its inclination to the rays, then the illumination of the eye due to the source L is

$$\frac{L}{D^2} A \cos a.$$

Similarly, the illumination due to the source l is

$$\frac{l}{d^2} A \cos(b-a).$$

Therefore $\dfrac{\text{total light}}{A} = \dfrac{L}{D^2} \cos a + \dfrac{l}{d^2} \cos(b-a)$. Expanding the second term in the usual way, we get intensity of illumination

$$= \frac{L}{D^2} \cos a + \frac{l}{d^2} \cos b \cos a + \frac{l}{d^2} \sin b \sin a.$$

Differentiating this equation, remembering that all the

quantities are constants except a, and putting the resulting intensity of illumination differentiated for maximum equal to zero, we get

$$0 = \frac{L}{D^2}\sin a - \frac{l}{d^2}\cos b \sin a + \frac{l}{d^2}\sin b \cos a.$$

Collecting the terms and rearranging, we get

$$\frac{L}{D^2}\sin a = \frac{l}{d^2}\sin(b-a).$$

Let us leave this equation for the moment and look at the matter from another point of view. Make the fantastic postulate that the lights are forces drawing the animal towards the two sources, like magnets attracting a piece of iron, and suppose that the resultant of those forces gives the line along which the animal moves. Then draw the usual triangle of forces, making the arrows which indicate directions follow each other round the triangle. In Fig. 64 this is done, and the lengths of two of the sides and the sizes of the known angles are filled in. Let the length of the perpendicular from the apex of the triangle on to the resultant be p. Then in the usual way,

$$p = \frac{l}{d^2}\sin(b-a) = \frac{L}{D^2}\sin a.$$

That is to say, we get the same angle of orientation a from the triangle of forces and from a calculation based on the assumption that the animal orientates to maximal frontal illumination. The animal's path can be predicted without calculation, simply by using the graphical construction of the triangle of forces. This is what is known as the *resultant law*, in the strict sense, the animal's path being predictable as the resultant of the two light-intensities regarded as forces.

The calculated paths, when one light is four times as strong as the other and the animal is started at various points, are shown in Fig. 65 For the same case, on Fig. 62 there have been constructed short lines showing the directions calculated from the triangle of forces rule, as illustrated in Fig. 66, p. 144. From this it can be seen that orientation up the steepest gradient and orientation according to the triangle of forces rule are practically indistinguishable, except in one small region.

The short lines in Fig. 66 are mostly nearly normal to the curves of equal intensity, the exceptional lines being those near the peak of the dotted line. In this region there are points from which animals going up the steepest gradient would go to the weaker light while those following the triangle of forces rule would go to the stronger one.

As far as is known at present, only one species of animal fits this triangle of forces calculation. That is *Phyllothalestris mysis* (Fraenkel, 1927 *a*), a copepod with a frontal eye. Its behaviour has not yet been investigated from the mechanism point of view to discover whether or not it makes lateral deviations or trial movements, and the eye is perhaps a little too complex to be regarded as simply a flat intensity receptor (Sars, 1911).

Fraenkel's experiments (1927 *a*) were carried out in a circular dish 30 cm. in diameter. Two electric lamps were so arranged that their beams crossed at right angles in the centre *M* of the dish (Fig. 67, p. 146). One was kept 50 cm. away from *M*, while the distance of

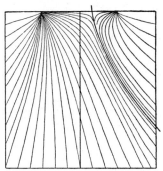

FIG. 65. Theoretical paths of an animal which orientates to two lights in conformity with the triangle of forces rule and which starts at various points. One light is four times as strong as the other. (Ludwig, *Z. wiss. Zool.* 1934.)

the other was varied between 20 cm. and 50 cm. so as to change the intensity of the light it cast in the dish. There was a scale marked in degrees of angle beneath the dish, centred at *M*, and a piece of thread was attached beneath the glass at this point. The copepods were collected in large numbers into a pipette and released at *M*; they streamed away at an angle between the two lights. This angle was measured by alining the thread with the stream and then reading off the angle made by the thread with the line joining the stationary light to *M*. Each reading thus represents a rough average value for several hundred animals. Table V, p. 145 shows the results and also the angles of orientation calculated from the triangle of forces relation. The average values obtained agree quite well with the calculated angles (Fig. 69, p. 148).

In the equation of the triangle of forces, if the angle b between the beams is 90°, then $\sin(b-a)$ is equal to $\cos a$.

Therefore
$$\tan a = \frac{l}{L}\frac{D^2}{d^2}.$$

In this form the triangle of forces rule is known as the *tangent law*. It has only a limited application and requires special

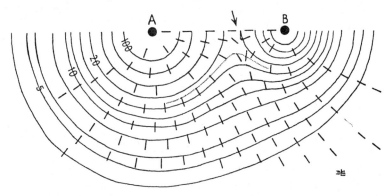

FIG. 66. Superposed on the intensity gradient shown in Fig. 62 are short lines showing the angles of orientation according to the triangle of forces relation. Notice that the paths far from the source are much the same as they would be if they led up the steepest gradient, but this similarity breaks down nearer the lights, especially near the right-hand end of the dotted line. The directions were obtained graphically. The receptors are assumed to be at the ends of the lines nearer the lights.

arrangements (see p. 155), for as the animal moves the angle between the beams changes (Fig. 70, p. 150).

Another hypothetical case is also interesting in the same way. Suppose the animal has a flat intensity receptor on each side and parallel to the direction of normal movement (Fig. 68, p. 147). Suppose that in two lights the animal orientates so that the two eyes receive equal amounts of light. (The tropo-taxis of an animal with flat eyes of this kind is called *pedio-tropo-taxis* (πεδίον, plain) by Eckert (1938) to distinguish it from the *profil-tropo-taxis* (*profil*-silhouette) of animals with more complex eyes of the *Eristalis* type.) Using the same symbols as before, we

find that
$$\frac{L}{D^2}A\sin a = \frac{l}{d^2}A\sin(b-a).$$

Here once more we have the equation of the triangle of forces,

so that such an animal which orientated to equality of illumination of the two eyes would also follow the resultant law. No
such animal is at present known, but there is, nevertheless, a
case which approximately fits the calculation. This is *Euglena*
(Buder, 1917; Mast and Johnson, 1932). *Euglena* has an enlargement of the base of the flagellum which is believed to be
photo-sensitive, and a shallow cup-shaped pigment shield which
shades it from behind and from the dorsal surface (Fig. 23, p. 71).

TABLE V. *Orientation of the copepod* Phyllothalestris mysis
between two lights

Distances in centimetres		Measured angles between stream of animals and L_1M	Averages	Angles calculated from triangle of forces
L_1M	L_2M			
50	50	46, 43, 45, 48, 47	45.8	45
50	45	48, 47, 48, 46, 49	47.6	51
50	40	54, 55, 58, 58, 54	55.8	57.5
50	35	68, 65, 66, 63, 66	65.6	64
50	30	72, 73, 72, 72, 73	72.4	70
50	25	78, 75, 76, 80, 76	77	76
50	20	81, 79, 81, 83, 81	81	81

The pigment shield makes an angle of about 45° with the body
axis (Mast, 1911, p. 90), and during crawling the axis is bent at
about the same angle. Consequently, the pigment shield is kept
roughly parallel to the direction of motion. The smallness of
Euglena makes a more precise description of the eye impossible,
but since the animal rotates on its own axis during forward
movement, the eye could possibly act like a pair of flat receptor
surfaces parallel to the direction of motion. The one eye looks
in the two directions at different times instead of simultaneously
and the comparison must be successive in time, but the calculation on the preceding pages is not invalidated by that.

Euglena conforms to the triangle of forces rule; it does not fit
the case of maximal frontal illumination because of the structure
of the eye and the mode of re-orientation; it may fit the case of
equality of illumination of parallel surfaces. It is interesting to
observe that if paired flat eyes are not parallel, and if each eye
is lit by one of the lights only, orientation to equality of stimula-

tion would not lead to conformity with the triangle of forces rule. According to Mitchell and Crozier (1928), however, if each eye is illuminated by *both* lights, then conformity with the rule would result.

This triangle (or parallelogram) of forces rule or resultant law has been the cause of much controversy. Some authors take the view that if an animal orientates between two sources of light, it thus conforms to the triangle of forces rule. In fact, there are several animals which behave tropo-tactically or klino-tactically and which do not conform to the rule in any strict sense. Fig. 69, p. 148, shows the angle of orientation of various species of animals plotted against the angle calculated from the rule. In general, the animals are more affected by the weaker light than they would be if they conformed to the rule. It has been held at one time or another that the rule

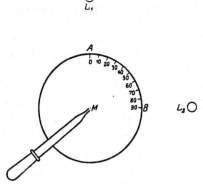

Fig. 67. Arrangement of the apparatus in the experiment with *Phyllothalestris*. L_1 and L_2 are the two lights and M is the middle of the dish. (Fraenkel, *Biol. Rev.*, 1931.)

applies to most of the species dealt with in the figure, though inspection of the angles shows that it does not, except in the case of *Euglena* and *Phyllothalestris*. Indeed, it has even been claimed (*not* by Patten) that it applies to blow-fly maggots, the data being obtained from experiments in which the angle of orientation was measured when the maggot was on the line between the two lights (pp. 67–70); the triangle of forces properly drawn for this experiment would therefore have two sides parallel! A study of the literature reveals no justification for the claim, even when the lights are suitably arranged.

The triangle of forces rule, then, applies only to very few cases. In most cases the eyes are not sufficiently simple in shape, and even with flat eyes the surfaces must point in one of two directions only. In many cases, of course, not only is the eye surface curved but the eye itself is composed of a number of separate elements which have different sensitivities and which may even initiate opposing reflexes with unilateral stimulation (two-way eyes).

The term *resultant law* may perhaps be interpreted in a wider sense than *triangle of forces rule*. When an animal goes between

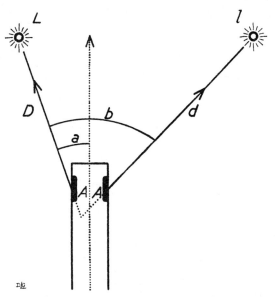

Fig. 68. Geometrical relations between light from two sources and a hypothetical animal with two lateral flat eyes parallel to its axis. Conventions as in Fig. 63. The animal is assumed to orientate in such a way that the two eyes are equally illuminated, each eye by only one light.

two lights, its precise path results from the action of both of the lights and in that sense is a resultant path. As long as this resultant is not thought to be calculable simply from the triangle of forces rule, the use of the term is harmless but not particularly useful.

When an animal is not supplied directly with information about the direction of the brightest light—either because it has not suitable receptors or because all the light comes from vertically above (Chap. V)—it can only react to the intensity gradient. It can then only reach the brightest (or dimmest) region by making trial movements of some kind—either the random movements of kineses or the alternating movements of klino-taxis. Even klino-taxis is only possible when the gradient is so steep in relation to the size of the trial movements that the

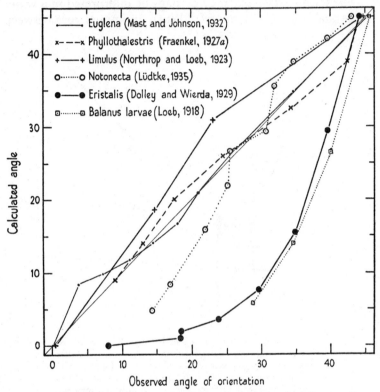

FIG. 69. Angles of orientation of various animals under the influence of two lights. Ordinates—angle calculated from triangle of forces rule. Abscissae—actual angles of orientation. The 45° diagonal shows what would be obtained from perfect conformity with the rule. Only *Limulus* was photo-negative.

receptor is capable of differentiating between immediately past and present intensities. Most animals, however, can respond to both intensity and direction (klino-taxis and tropo-taxis), while some are relatively indifferent to intensity and respond mainly to direction (telo-taxis and light compass reaction).

It has already been pointed out, without explanation (p. 139, Figs. 62, 65), that animals which orientate between two lights usually curve round to one of them when they get near the

lights. As an animal approaches a light, the intensity of the
light falling on its surface increases, and increases with an acceleration which is expressed in the inverse square law (Fig. 61,
p. 138). In an experiment with two lights of equal intensity,
a positively photo-tropo-tactic animal which starts equidistant
from the two sources commonly makes a straight track and
strikes the line joining the sources at its mid-point. As long as
the animal behaves perfectly, the whole picture is symmetrical.
But if the animal does not start on this line, or if it accidentally
deviates from it, or if the two lights are not equal in luminosity,
the track is not straight (Figs. 65, 66, 72). Consider the case
when the lights are equal but the animal starts nearer to one
than the other. In conformity with the inverse square law,
the nearer source will throw a higher intensity of light on the
animal than the further source, so that the animal will aim
more nearly at the nearer source. Consequently, as it walks, at
each step it will approach the nearer light a little, but will
approach the further light by a smaller amount. Therefore,
after each step the disparity between the stimulating effects of
the two lights must increase, so that the animal curves round
more and more until it goes straight into one of the two lights.

The expected path of a photo-positive animal under such
conditions is shown in Fig. 70. The animal is assumed to
start at A and, knowing the distance and luminosity of each of
the lights and using the parallelogram of forces construction, a
short piece of the path AB is drawn. The distances of the two
lights are different now that the point B has been reached, so
another construction is required for the next piece of path BC,
and so on. When the whole path has been constructed in this
way for a particular pair of lights, the smoothed curve derived
from it represents the theoretical path based on the triangle of
forces rule. In Fig. 71, p. 151, are shown curves obtained experimentally with *Phyllothalestris mysis* (Fraenkel, 1927 *a*, 1931),
one light being kept stationary while the other was moved for
each trial (cf. Table V, p. 145, and Fig. 69).

Although the calculation of the paths corresponding to
triangle or parallelogram of forces orientation is very complicated and inconvenient, it is not difficult to construct them
graphically. These paths are in fact identical with the lines of
force in an electric field set up by two charges of like sign, so that

for a simple case like equality of luminosity (charge) the figure can be taken from text-books of electricity. These lines are constructed as curves normal to the lines of equal potential. The simple case of two equal lights is not, however, the most valuable, for it does not give a very vivid picture of the difference

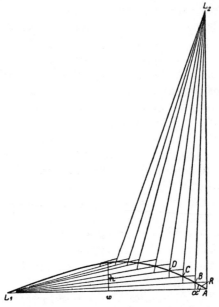

FIG. 70. Construction of the curve to the stronger (or nearer) light, using the parallelogram (or triangle) of forces construction. For explanation, see text, p. 149. (Fraenkel, *Biol. Rev.* 1931.)

between orientation up the steepest gradient and orientation in conformity with the triangle of forces rule. Since the potential is proportional to the inverse of the distance from the charge and the intensity is proportional to the inverse of the square of this distance, it is clear that the equal potential and equal intensity curves cannot be identical. The normals to them cannot, therefore, be identical, so the two kinds of orientation, namely up the steepest gradient and according to the triangle of forces, do not result in identical paths. The paths are, however, very similar indeed (cf. pp. 142–3), and it is only in the immediate neighbourhood of the two lights that the difference becomes apparent (Fig. 66, p. 144). Fig. 72, p. 152, shows the two cases.

It would be very difficult to decide in practice which kind of orientation is adopted in a particular case (Fig. 72, p. 152), particularly because of the variability of biological material. As has been pointed out above (p. 140), however, we know of no way in which an animal could obtain the information necessary for moving directly up the steepest gradient. On the other hand, there are at least two simple kinds of eyes which can lead to

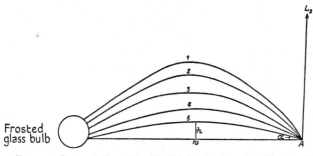

FIG. 71. Curves followed by *Phyllothalestris* when the distance of the light L_2 is varied. See Table V and pp. 143, 149. (Fraenkel, *Biol. Rev.*, 1931.)

orientation in conformity with the triangle of forces rule, as we have shown trigonometrically (pp. 140–6). Although the experimental measurements for *Euglena* and *Phyllothalestris* are probably not sufficiently refined to discriminate between the two kinds of orientation, we therefore prefer the view that these organisms orientate in conformity with the triangle of forces rule.

In the simple case when the two lights are equal and equidistant, any animal which orientated perfectly—klino-tactically or tropo-tactically—would go straight to the middle of the line joining the two lights (Fig. 72, p. 152). The whole picture is symmetrical, a point which Loeb stressed. In practice, animals orientate imperfectly and accidental deviations occur. Once an animal leaves the axis of symmetry of the picture it is unlikely that it will return to it exactly, so that curved paths to one light or the other are common (Fig. 73, p. 153). Nevertheless, cases do occur in which the animal actually passes the line between the lights. Ludwig (1934) pointed out that owing to the fact that the lights are not mathematical points, the middle line is really a middle strip, so that these cases are explicable. Once the lights are behind the animal, orientation is unstable, so that the slightest turn in one direction may lead to a further sharp turn

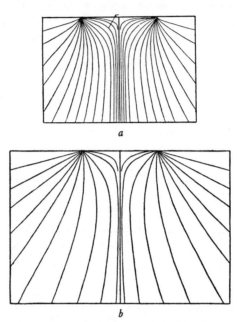

FIG. 72. Theoretical paths of animals which orientate (*a*) according to the triangle of forces rule, and (*b*) up the steepest gradient of light intensity. The two lights are equal in luminosity. (Ludwig, *Z. wiss. Zool.*, 1934.)

in the same direction and an almost straight path to one of the lights. In other cases, posterior illumination results in inhibition of locomotion and the animal ceases to swim and sinks to the bottom (*Corophium*, Fig. 73).

These middle paths in the immediate neighbourhood of two lights are not very common. Deviation from the middle path may be simply accidental, due to a somewhat erratic mode of locomotion. On the other hand, there may be asymmetries in the animal that give a bias to its locomotion. If one eye is in a different state of adaptation from the other, if the muscles of one side are fatigued, or if there are slight structural asymmetries, the maintenance of the middle path is not to be expected. Such asymmetries need not seriously interfere with orientation (Mast, 1923), but they can do so. The extreme curves in Fig. 73 do not, therefore, require any further explanation, nor do they indicate a mechanism different from tropo-taxis (Fraenkel, 1927 *a*, 1931). The importance of statistical treatment of results, when deviations are common, has already been touched upon in connexion with *Ephestia* (Chap. VII), and another possible cause of variability of orientation is dealt with below (pp. 157–9 and Fig. 75).

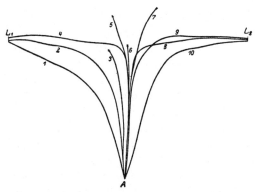

FIG. 73. Paths followed by a marine amphipod, *Corophium longicorne*, in two equal lights. Four paths end in a cross (3, 5, 6, 7). These represent cases in which the animal sank to the bottom and ceased to swim. (Fraenkel, *Biol. Rev.*, 1931.)

There has been, in the past, some confusion about this divergence from the middle line near the lights. It has even been held that behaviour changes over from tropo-taxis to telo-taxis, though it is now clear that no such assumption is required. At one time v. Buddenbrock considered that the deviation from the middle line took place at an angular distance from the lights which is characteristic of the species. He called the place where the deviation usually began the *Entscheidungspunkt* or 'decision point'. In the light of the above analysis it is unnecessary to discuss this further, particularly as v. Buddenbrock (1937) seems to have abandoned this view.

When it is required to measure the direction of orientation of an animal in a two-light experiment, it is necessary either to draw the tangents to the curve followed by the animal or to arrange that the curvature of the path should be so slight that it can be regarded as straight. The latter can be done either by having the light sources far away or by arranging, with the aid of lenses, to have two wide beams of parallel light.

Turning now to the relation between eye structure and possible modes of reaction, we have seen that a single flat eye can act as a direction receptor only if the animal faces in various directions in turn and compares the intensities at successive points in time. With two suitably placed flat receptors a simultaneous comparison of intensities could be made, so that the animal is provided with the information necessary to turn in the direction of the higher intensity. In many animals—notably arthropods, vertebrates, cephalopods, and some planarians, for example—the eye is composed of a number of separate elements, each of which is stimulated from a particular direction. Consequently, by comparing the intensity of stimulation of the various elements, such an animal can be informed—instantly and without any movement—of the direction of the strongest, or the weakest, or any other light. This will be subjectively familiar to the student, and can be objectively demonstrated in the case of the fire-fly, *Photinus pyralis*. During the night the female flashes her light and the male finds her by means of the flash. Mast (1912) has described how he observed these beetles starting to turn after the flash was over, but turning just the right amount to face straight towards the female. The male could not act in this way if the eyes were not such perfect direction receptors. The importance of direction reception is further shown by the behaviour of the toad, *Bufo americanus* (Mast, 1911). The normal animal orientates towards one of two lights, when tested in an otherwise dark room (telo-taxis). If the lenses of the eyes are removed, so that the eyes become mere intensity receptors, this toad orientates between two lights. Telo-taxis is obviously dependent on the presence of direction receptors, and intensity is of minor importance.

The absence of direction receptors prevents the occurrence of telo-taxis or of compass reactions with the same sort of mechanism; but the mere presence of such receptors is not in itself a guarantee that any of these reactions will occur. The reactions depend for their occurrence on the whole of the receptor-nervous-effector system. The same must be said for the precise form which a reaction takes; receptor structure is one and only one of the limiting factors.

The triangle of forces relation is known to hold in very few cases, though many animals orientate between two lights; the kind of factor affecting the precise direction in such an orientation is well illustrated by the case of *Eristalis tenax* (see also Chaps. VII and VIII). In the experiments by Dolley and Wierda (1929) the two lights were presented in the form of two wide beams of approximately parallel light crossing at right angles. The intensity of one beam was kept constant and the other was varied; the angles of orientation of the paths of flies walking under the action of the two lights were measured many times, and representative average values obtained for each value of the variable intensity. Horizontal sections through the head of *Eristalis* showed the arrangement of the ommatidia (Fig. 74, p. 157).

These experiments showed that for each pair of light intensities there was a characteristic angle of orientation (Fig. 69, p. 148). The reflex effect of the stronger light shining on the left eye was balanced by the reflex effect of the weak light shining on the right eye, so that the fly walked in a nearly straight line, not heading for either light but for a point between them. This point was nearer to the strong light than the weak one. In this balance, there are two main variables—the intensity of light striking the eye surface and the direction of the light. Now only those ommatidia which are parallel to the rays are stimulated (apposition eye, Imms, 1934; Snodgrass, 1935); and since the ommatidia are arranged radially, a particular direction of light corresponds to a particular ommatidium, or to a small number of ommatidia making up a certain region of the eye.

Thus, when the fly is orientated, a more forwardly directed ommatidium is stimulated by the stronger light and a hinder one by the weaker. Therefore the hinder ommatidia must produce a greater turning reflex *per unit of illumination* than the front ones. The intensity of the turning reflex per unit of illumination may be regarded as the 'sensitivity' of the ommatidium, though strictly speaking this sensitivity may reside either in the eye itself or in the central nervous system. Then the total turning effect of a given light is the product of its intensity at the eye surface and the sensitivity of the region of the eye which it stimulates. Actually, it is unlikely that the reflex effect would always increase linearly with the intensity, and we probably have to deal with a sensitivity which changes with the intensity. When the fly is orientated in a balanced position, knowing the angular arrangement of the ommatidia and the intensities and directions of the two lights, we can therefore make an estimate of the ratio of sensitivities of the two regions which are stimulated. This estimate is not a highly reliable one, because of the rapidity with which the eye becomes sensorily adapted, and because we do not know whether or not the relation between intensity of illumination and intensity of reflex turning is a linear one. The quantitative results are not highly reliable as such, but they provide a good and reliable picture qualitatively. The general conclusion is that the ommatidia which look straight forward have a sensitivity of zero, in the sense that stimulation causes no turning even though they are optically functional. Passing backwards over the eye, the sensitivity gets rapidly higher, so that it soon increases by scores of times. It should be clearly kept in mind that sensitivity here means *reflex sensitivity*; a small light acting on a posterior ommatidium initiates a reflex which quantitatively balances and cancels out the reflex produced by a much stronger light acting on a forwardly placed ommatidium.

It has just been stated that the sensitivity map of the eye of *Eristalis* is not quantitatively reliable. Apart from the difficulties already mentioned, the fly deviated by 8° where there was only one light and it is possible that the animal was allowed insufficient time to orientate completely (Fig. 69, p. 148). Nevertheless, the gradient found is of considerable interest and value for comparison with gradients for other insects. The map made up by Dolley and Wierda (1929) (Fig. 74) indicates a rise of 55 times in the sensitivity on passing back over only a part of the eye (23°). In *Notonecta* Lüdtke (1935) found a gradient of the same sort, but the corresponding increase of sensitivity was only 3·5 times. Yagi (1928) has done some qualitative work on the eye of the stick-insect, *Dixippus morosus*, and Clark (1933) on *Dineutes*. (Perhaps owing to a slip repeated in four lines near the bottom of Table I in Clark's paper, v. Buddenbrock (1935) appears to have misinterpreted his results.)

Consideration of sensitivity maps or reflex maps of this kind leads to some interesting conclusions. In the first place, if *Eristalis* becomes accidentally dis-orientated when exposed to a single light-source, the larger the dis-orientation the larger is the reflex correction applied; with increasing dis-orientation, increasingly sensitive ommatidia are stimulated, and the correct-

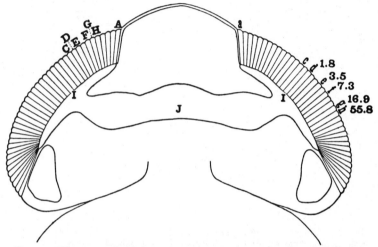

FIG. 74. Diagrammatic horizontal section through the head of *Eristalis*. Pairs of letters show which ommatidia are stimulated by two beams crossing at right angles; thus *C* is stimulated by one light and *c* by the other. The numbers show the relative 'sensitivities'; thus *h* is 55·8 times as 'sensitive' as *H*. *I*, retina; *J*, brain. (Dolley and Wierda, *J. exp. Zool.*, 1929.)

ing effect thus becomes rapidly stronger. As orientation approaches completion and the light passes forwards over the eye, it stimulates less and less sensitive regions in turn, so that the reflex turning dies out gently and does not go too far.

Consider now the effects on orientation in two lights of the three theoretically possible simple kinds of reflex maps or sensitivity gradients in compound eyes. For the *Eristalis* type, in two lights as in one, orientation is stable and at a relatively fixed angle between the two (Fig. 75 *a*, p. 158). After accidental dis-orientation, the reflex tending to increase dis-orientation is decreased ($W < X$) and that tending to decrease it is increased ($y > x$); a correcting reflex turn is thus effective. A second point about this type of gradient is that, when the two lights are unequal, the turning effect of stimulation by the weaker light is magnified by the high sensitivity of the hinder ommatidia. Consequently, the curve into one of the lights (Figs. 65, 66, 72) is delayed and the animal frequently reaches the line joining the sources (Mast, 1923). The weaker light has a greater effect

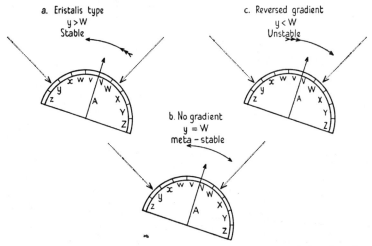

Fig. 75. Diagram to show the effect on orientation to two lights of various simple hypothetical sensitivity gradients. *A*, long axis of animal, arrow-head pointing anteriorly. Five ommatidia are represented in each eye, and their 'sensitivities' are represented by *v* to *z* in the left eye and *V* to *Z* in the right. The dotted lines represent two equal beams of light. The animal is disorientated and the curved arrow shows the direction in which further turning is expected to occur. The orientated paths expected are (*a*) half-way between the lights, (*b*) nearly to either light or anywhere between, (*c*) to one of the lights. See text, pp. 157-9.

than would be expected from the triangle of forces relation, and this has also been found to be the case with a number of other photo-positive animals (Fig. 69).

If the sensitivity were uniform over the whole eye (second simple type), the turning effects of two equal and equidistant lights could be in balance whatever two regions of the two eyes were stimulated (Fig. 75 *b*). An animal with eyes of this type would be expected to follow a path nearly directly to either light or anywhere in between them. Orientation would thus be meta-stable—that is, there could be balanced orientation whatever the direction, as long as each eye is affected by only one of the lights. This state of affairs has not been recognized experimentally, but the variability of orientation of *Ephestia* larvae and of woodlice (Chap. VII) might be partly due to the reflex maps approximating to this type, with very little difference in sensitivity in different parts of the eye.

The third possible type of gradient is the reversed one, with the highest sensitivity at the front of the eye. In two lights, if a photo-positive animal with this kind of eye at first orientated between them, orientation would be unstable; a slight accidental dis-orientation would bring one light on to a more forwardly directed ommatidium which, being *more* sensitive, would tend to produce an increasing turn in the same direction (Fig. 75 *c*). Thus the animal would turn towards one light and orientate almost as if the other light did not exist. No example of such a reversed gradient in a photo-positive animal has ever been recorded. Unfortunately this scheme does not provide a simple mechanism for telo-taxis, for in that reaction the animal often suddenly switches over from one light to the other, thus following a zigzag course (Chap. VIII). We therefore have to postulate switching inhibition as the mechanism of telo-taxis.

In animals behaving photo-negatively, uniform sensitivity would again lead to meta-stable orientation, but for stable orientation a *reversed* gradient is *required*, with the most sensitive ommatidia in front. [1]

An unusual kind of sensitivity gradient has recently been found by Eckert (1935, 1938) in *Daphnia pulex*. *Daphnia* has a roughly spherical median eye with a rather small number of ommatidia. In that plane of the eye which is concerned in tropo-tactic orientation the sensitivity rises to a maximum in the ommatidia which look out at an angle of about 45 or 50° to the median plane and then *declines* in the ommatidia behind. Some consequences of this arrangement are dealt with by Eckert (1938) in an elegant discussion of the theory of tropo-tactic paths.

In this chapter attention has been concentrated on the physical conditions resulting from the simultaneous action of two lights. The study of these conditions shows how animals can react and explains some of the apparently anomalous kinds of reaction. Examination of the physical conditions alone, however, is not enough; it becomes necessary to make some

[1] See note 24, Appendix.

assumptions about the internal machinery of animals. The formal explanation of the angle of orientation of *Eristalis* in terms of a gradient of so-called sensitivity in the eye is really little more than a special assumption for this particular experiment. It should not be mistaken for the assumption that visual acuity is greatest in the hinder parts of the eye, or anything of that kind. The whole subject of sensory capacity is in too rudimentary a condition to permit a general synthesis to be made as yet.

XII
UNILATERAL BLINDING AND CIRCUS MOVEMENTS

UNILATERAL blinding and the two-light experiment have always been the principal tests for discovering the mechanism of orientation of animals towards light. The circling movements which many animals make when blinded in one eye provided one of the principal pillars of Loeb's tropism theory, and even to-day they are regarded as one of the chief criteria for the kind of orientation known as tropo-taxis. Not only is the occurrence of circus movements regarded as a proof of tropo-tactic action, but their absence is commonly regarded as an indication of telo-taxis.

Actually, the issue is not quite so simple as that. We have seen that under suitable conditions of light an animal which behaves only tropo-tactically, like *Eristalis*, does not necessarily make circus movements when unilaterally blinded (pp. 85–6), while an animal which can behave telo-tactically, like the bee, may make them (pp. 93–5). One of the principal factors which determine whether circus movements shall appear or not is the manner in which the light is presented, and two other factors are the nature of the reflex map of the eye and the state of light or dark adaptation in the eye. All these factors must be considered in detail if circus movements are to be used to distinguish between tropo-taxis and telo-taxis.

It is necessary to bear in mind the three main ways in which the light can be presented. First, there is perfect beam-illumination; the light comes from a fairly small source in a dark-room, and is absorbed on dead-black surfaces; even the operator's hands must be gloved and his face masked in black, so that all the light which can reach the eye of the animal comes straight from the lamp. Second, there is uniform light; it is impossible in practice to make the light exactly equal from all directions, and the usual arrangement is to have the lamp above, and all the walls and the floor of the experimental chamber are covered with white paper. Third, there is the imperfect beam, which has some of the qualities of each of the other two kinds of illumination; with this, there is a considerable amount of reflection of the original light from the floor of the experimental field and perhaps from other directions as well.

Consider first the behaviour of unilaterally blinded animals in uniform light. Under these conditions practically every animal which behaves tropo-tactically or telo-tactically towards light makes circus movements; it has not so far been possible to blind unilaterally any of the animals which behave only klino-tactically. Positively photo-tactic animals turn towards the seeing side and those which react negatively turn to the blind side. This experiment provides part of the logical basis for the tropo-tactic mechanism postulated in Chapter VII. Each eye alone leads to turning towards one side, so that when both eyes are in action a state of perfect balance can occur, particularly when the stimulation of the two eyes is perfectly symmetrical. But when one eye of a photo-tactic animal is blinded, even when the reflex map is such that turns in either direction can be initiated in a single eye, no case is known in which light falling uniformly on all the parts of the single remaining eye has no resultant turning effect.

The term *reflex map* is used in those cases in which the turning effect produced by a light somehow depends on the position of the ommatidia which are stimulated by it; in these cases the magnitude of the turning effect also depends on the intensity of the light, as has been shown in Chapter XI. These relationships, which are usually complicated by the state of adaptation of the eye and are not in any case simple or direct proportionalities, were an important constituent of Loeb's theory. This was because any kind of repeatable mathematical relationship was regarded as evidence against 'free will' hypotheses of animal behaviour and in favour of mechanical hypotheses; it is now realized that this may be true without providing any support for the particular mechanical theory known as the tropism or tonus theory.

In this connexion a number of workers have subjected unilaterally blinded animals to overhead light of a series of known intensities and measured the radius of the resulting circus movements. Garrey (1918) did this for the robber-fly, *Proctacanthus*, and v. Buddenbrock (1919) for the edible snail, *Helix pomatia*; they showed qualitatively that the radius of circling becomes smaller with increasing light-intensity. Crozier and Cole (1929) obtained quantitative results for the slug, *Limax maximus.* In this animal turning is due to the parietal muscles, while locomotion is due to the muscles of the sole of the foot, so that it is one of the very few cases in which turning may be due to a steadily

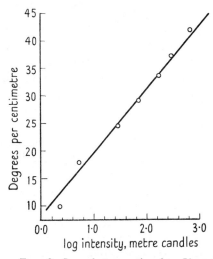

FIG. 76. In a photo-negative slug, *Limax,* one eye-bearing tentacle has been amputated; illumination is from directly above. The measure of circling used is the angular deflexion per unit length of path. Mean values of this quantity are plotted against corresponding values of log I, where I is the intensity of the light at the photo-receptive surface of the remaining tentacle. The curvature is proportional in magnitude, over the range of illumination used, to log I. (Crozier, 1929.)

maintained tonic contraction. *Limax* is thus one of the few animals which fit into Loeb's tonus mechanism of turning. The turning effect of the light, called the 'photo-tropic effect' by Crozier and Cole (1929), was measured as the angular degrees of turning per centimetre of linear distance travelled, and it was found to be proportional to the logarithm of the light intensity over a fairly wide range (Crozier, 1929) (Fig. 76). A similar relationship was established by Clark (1933) for the gyrinid beetle, *Dineutes,* up to an intensity of 1·3 m.c. Clark also found

that the rate of turning is dependent on the size of the source of
stimulation as well as on the intensity of light.

It has already been pointed out that animals which behave
telo-tactically make circus movements in uniform light when
unilaterally blinded. There is nothing inconsistent about this.
First of all, it is not possible for the light to be fixed and used as a
guide when it comes uniformly from all directions, so telo-taxis
cannot come into action. Secondly, animals which on occasion behave telo-tactically, sometimes also possess the tropo-
tactic mechanism, which comes into action on other occasions,
and they may therefore demonstrate their possession of this
mechanism when blinded and tested in uniform light. Thirdly,
even when we deal with an animal which never behaves tropo-
tactically, it is to be expected that the telo-tactic mechanism
will depend on a reflex map. The complication of inhibition
of lights other than that one which is fixed—i.e. kept on the
fixation ommatidium—may be completely ineffective when
there are no discrete lights, and unless the opposite turning
effects released in the single eye in uniform light happen to
balance exactly, it seems that circus movements are to be
expected. For those animals, like the bee, in which telo-
taxis seems to have essentially the same mechanism as the
tropo-taxis of *Eristalis*, circus movements are consistent with
telo-taxis even when tropo-tactic orientation is absent. The
superiority in numbers and in sensitivity of the ommatidia
behind the fixation region may thus lead to circus movements,
as long as there is no discrete light-source which can be brought
on to the fixation region and so lead to inhibition of other light.

Turning now to the behaviour of unilaterally blinded animals
in a horizontal beam of light, there are first of all a number of
animals which turn to the appropriate side and continue to do
so for an indefinitely long time; there appears to be no recovery
of any sort. This group includes the larvae of the meal moth and
the woodlice, which were dealt with in Chapter VII, and also
the snail, *Helix* (v. Buddenbrock, 1919), the silver-fish, *Lepisma*
(Meyer, 1932), and the millipede, *Julus* (Müller, 1924). If the
beam of light is perfect enough, negative photo-taxis in these
animals leads to turning towards the blind side which continues until the light is outside the field of vision; then the path
becomes relatively straight, and the reaction is described as a

curving away from the light rather than circus movements proper. This does not, however, involve any fundamental difference of mechanism, but it takes the animal out of the beam. If the animal is repeatedly replaced in the beam, it keeps making the same sort of curve instead of going more or less directly

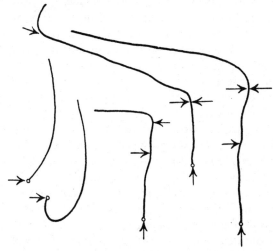

Fig. 77. Turning movements to the left side in *Julus fallax* (Diplopoda), blinded in the left eye, with horizontal light. There is no reaction if light is falling on to the blinded side or is coming from behind; if the remaining eye is illuminated, a turning movement towards the blind side occurs. Start of a path indicated by a small circle. Arrows indicate direction of light in subsequent positions (cf. Fig. 27, p. 80). (Müller, *Zool. Jahrb.*, 1924.)

away from the light source (Fig. 77). When the beam is less perfect, ordinary circus movements occur. In either case, the repeated turning towards the blind side in animals which are negatively photo-tactic and towards the seeing side in those which are photo-positive provides a valid criterion of tropo-taxis, for in this experiment there is present a discrete source of light suitable for the performance of telo-taxis.

The position is more complicated with certain other animals; at the start of the experiment normal circus movements occur, but, as time goes on, the turnings become less and less marked until eventually the animal goes fairly straight towards the light, almost as if it had two eyes in action. This has already been

described for both *Eristalis* and the bee, so that it is quite
compatible with purely tropo-tactic behaviour and with telo-
tactic behaviour as well. In both of these examples one eye alone
can lead to proper orientation towards a light; this is due to the
presence of a patch of forwardly directed ommatidia which are
not linked with any turning movement at all, on the two sides
of which lie ommatidia which initiate turning in opposite
directions. It is only with such an arrangement that telo-taxis
becomes possible, but telo-taxis is not inevitable, as *Eristalis*
shows. Consequently, if circus movements occur at first and
later cease, or if they occur occasionally and not at other times,
then this experiment is not a criterion of either tropo-taxis or
telo-taxis. Circus movements in a beam after unilateral blinding are diagnostic of tropo-taxis, therefore, only if they go on
continually and show no recovery. A distinction between the
tropo-taxis of *Eristalis* and the telo-taxis of the bee cannot be
made with this experiment, for the mechanism of reaction in
these two cases is essentially identical except for the inhibition
of stimulation of the second eye in the bee. In this experiment
such inhibition cannot come into action because the second eye
has been blinded, and the two types of reaction are therefore
indistinguishable as far as this particular test goes.

The phenomenon of circus movements which diminish and
disappear during the course of the experiment was originally
described by Holmes (1905 *b*) for *Ranatra* and *Notonecta*, and later
by Dolley (1916) for *Vanessa antiopa*. These authors ascribed
the change in reaction to learning by experience, a view which
was taken later by Minnich (1919) for the bee(Fig. 38, p. 94).
The clue to the real solution was implicit in the results of
Garrey (1918) for the robber-fly, in which the state of adaptation of the eye was shown to be of great importance in determining the rate of turning in circus movements. It was Clark
(1928), working on the backswimmer or water-boatman, *Notonecta*, who provided the solution. Although an aquatic insect,
Notonecta crawls along quite well in air; on a horizontal surface
it goes very directly towards a light. It has been used for
experiments on photo-taxis by a number of workers, including
Holmes (1905 *b*), Clark (1928), Schulz (1931), and Lüdtke
(1935, 1938).

Clark (1928) used as a light-source a ground-glass plate behind which a screened lamp was placed, and precautions were taken to prevent reflection from the walls of the dark-room. The backswimmers used had one eye covered with asphalt

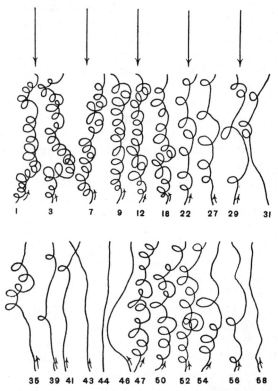

FIG. 78. Circus movements of a unilaterally blinded *Notonecta* in horizontal light. The tracks gradually straighten out in the course of successive trials numbered 1–46. Path 47 shows the reappearance of circus movements after a further period of 15 minutes in darkness. In the following trials in light the tracks straighten out again. (Clark, *J. exp. Zool.* 1928.)

black and were then left in darkness for between 6 and 24 hours. When tested after this period of dark adaptation, the animals always made circus movements when placed in the beam, but in doing so they approached the light-source progressively (Fig. 78). As the experiment with a particular individual went on, the number of circus movements per trial decreased and their radius increased, until eventually the animal went directly to the light. After this, continuation of the trials yielded no more circus movements. So far, the elimination of circus movements might possibly be ascribed to learning by experience; but Clark brought some of the dark-adapted animals into the beam and fixed them down so that they could not move at all, and showed that the elimination of circus movements depended on the time they had been exposed to the light whether they moved or not. Thus when an animal was not fixed down at all, it took 48 minutes to eliminate circus movements; when it was fixed down for 10 minutes, elimination took 34 minutes, making a total time in the light of 44 minutes. Similarly, when fixed in the light for 20, 30, 40, and 50 minutes, elimination took 18, 18, 7, and 1 minutes respectively, so that for all six tests the total time required was 48, 44, 38, 48, 47, and 51 minutes. These figures do not fit in with the hypothesis of learning by experience, for the duration of experience varied from 1 to 48 minutes, but they do fit in with the idea that elimination depends on light adaptation, for the total time in the light up to complete elimination varied only between 38 and 51 minutes and that irregularly. Moreover, if the intensity of the adapting light was varied in the proportions 100, 50, 25, 10, and 0, the times required for elimination were 2, 1, 2, 19, and 36 minutes respectively. The effects of the state of adaptation of the eye on circus movements were thus established.

The importance of adaptation in circus movements is neatly shown by means of two experiments in which the circling is induced in animals which actually have both eyes in action, though in different states of adaptation. The first of these is due to Boring (1912), who worked with planarians. The animal crawled about on the bottom of a dish, and around the dish six electric lights were arranged at equal intervals. By means of a suitable arrangement of switches, the one light which shone most directly on the left side of the animal was put on, however the animal moved. The animal was not fixed down or interfered with, but by this means the left eye became light-adapted while the right eye remained relatively dark-adapted. After a certain period a less intense light was substituted above the dish. The result was a series of circus movements towards the left side. These planarians are photo-negative, and when the two eyes were equally illuminated from above, the light-adapted and therefore less sensitive left eye initiated a smaller turning effect than the more dark-adapted right eye, so that turning to the left occurred. Thus circus movements may be due to a decreased sensitivity in one eye, without the reduction amounting to actual blindness.

The second experiment was described by Garrey (1918). The paint which he used to cover the eyes of his robber-flies eventually becomes brittle and can be scaled off. When this was done with flies which were light-adapted, the immediate result was a turning to the side of the previously blind eye. Clark (1928) obtained the same result with *Notonecta*. Both of these animals are normally photo-positive, so that when the previously covered and therefore fully dark-adapted eye was exposed, the ommatidia were in a very sensitive condition and immediately led to a turn which could not be balanced through the other light-adapted eye, a turn towards the more sensitive side. Although in both these animals each eye includes ommatidia for turning in each direction, the backwardly directed ommatidia were evidently sensitive enough to override the contra-lateral turning effect of the antero-median ommatidia. Of course, the formerly covered eye soon became light-adapted and the circus movements then ceased. In *Notonecta* Clark (1928) found that the time required for elimination of these circus movements was much the same as in the experiments previously described, in which unilaterally blinded animals were tested.

In uniform light it is to be expected that the radius of the circus movements of a unilaterally blinded animal will increase progressively as light-adaptation proceeds (Garrey, 1918); but, unless in the fully adapted state the same intensity of light is below the threshold, there seems to be no reason why circus movements should cease altogether. In a beam of light, however, the expectation is quite different. Consider an animal like *Eristalis* which has both ipsi-lateral and contra-lateral ommatidia in each eye, and imagine it placed in a perfect beam facing the light; even when unilaterally blinded, the reflex map would be satisfactory for keeping the animal facing and moving towards the light. In practice, however, it is almost impossible to get a perfect beam, and in all the experiments which have been described by a number of authors some circling does occur. The reason for this is that there is a certain amount of light reflected from the background on to the very sensitive back-wardly directed ommatidia. This causes ipsi-lateral turning until those ommatidia become more light adapted, when the re-flected light falls below their threshold of stimulation. If the beam is far from perfect, the backwardly directed ommatidia never become sufficiently light-adapted. Thus Dolley (1916) found that *Vanessa* with one eye covered could eventually go straight to a light in a dark-room, but they made continual circus movements in front of a window, where there was much scattered light.

The importance of the scattered light in circus movements in a beam was demonstrated by Clark (1931, 1933), using the gyrinid beetle *Dineutes assimilis* (Fig. 79). These whirligig beetles commonly swim in the surface of the water so that part of the head and body is actually in the air above the water surface. Each eye is divided into two parts, the upper one emerging into the air and the lower one being submerged. Like *Notonecta* they can crawl on land, and they behave in much the same way. Unilaterally blinded specimens tested in a beam at first made circus movements towards the seeing side (Fig. 79 A), and then gradually straightened out. Eventually they crawled *diagonally* across the beam in a straight line, the blind side being on the side of the light (Fig. 79 B). This diagonal path must have been due to some stimulation of the sensitive posterior ipsi-lateral ommatidia, so that, even after adaptation had oc-curred, the contra-lateral antero-median ommatidia had to be brought into action to produce balance.

Now, during the diagonal crawling, if the intensity of the light source was suddenly increased, the animals turned rather more away from the light, while if it was decreased they turned more nearly towards the light (Fig. 79 C). Presumably the increase in the intensity of the main light would be equally effective on all the ommatidia *which were already being stimulated*, but in the posterior region of the eye, where the light was very dim indeed, it would bring into action additional ommatidia. Low though the thresholds of these ommatidia might be, the scattered light could easily be too dim to stimulate some of them. An all-round increase in intensity of light does, in fact, cause a slight ipsi-lateral turn, and a fresh position of balance is then reached. Similarly, when the light was decreased in

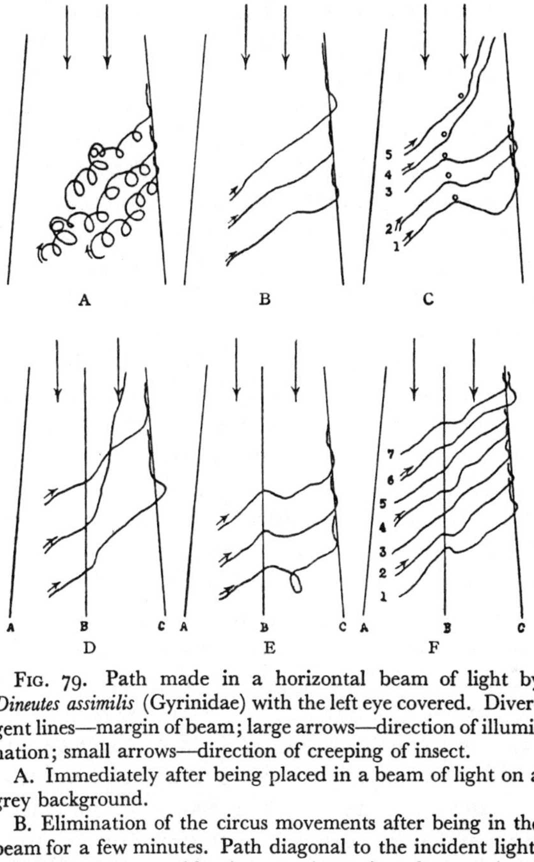

Fig. 79. Path made in a horizontal beam of light by *Dineutes assimilis* (Gyrinidae) with the left eye covered. Divergent lines—margin of beam; large arrows—direction of illumination; small arrows—direction of creeping of insect.

A. Immediately after being placed in a beam of light on a grey background.

B. Elimination of the circus movements after being in the beam for a few minutes. Path diagonal to the incident light.

C. Reactions to sudden increase (1, 2, 3) or decrease (4, 5) of illumination after circus movements had been eliminated. Circles indicate points at which intensity of light was changed.

D. Response to a sudden change of intensity of light reflected from the background without change in the intensity of the light from the source. Intensity diminishes. A–B background with a coefficient of reflection X. B–C background with a coefficient of reflection $X/10$.

E. As D, but intensity increases. A–B background with a coefficient of reflection X. B–C background with a coefficient of reflection $10X$.

F. Response to a sudden increase of intensity of light from the source. A–B background with coefficient of intensity X. B–C background with coefficient of intensity $X/10$. If the change of intensity takes place at precisely the same time as the crossing of the boundary from the lighter to the darker background, as in 3 and 5, no reaction occurs. (Clark, *J. exp. Zool.*, 1931.)

intensity, some of the posterior ommatidia would go out of action because their thresholds were too high, and a slight turn towards the light would be expected.

To clinch the matter, the surface on which the beetle crawled was covered with two pieces of paper of different shades of grey, so that the animal passed over the boundary on its diagonal journey. Although the main illumination was not changed this time, the animal swerved in the expected direction after passing over the boundary (Fig. 79 D, E). This shows clearly the importance of the light reflected from the background.

This diagonal path with *Dineutes* is only obtained when the floor or the background generally scatters the light on to the posterior ommatidia. On a good black surface the unilaterally blinded animal eventually goes directly to the light; on a white surface it never does so, and the conditions then approximate to uniform light. With a white surface the scattered light is so considerable that the threshold of the posterior ommatidia is always too low for them to become inactive.

Clark went on from this to estimate the amount of scattered light required to cause circling in a beam. He used a black surface for the animals to walk on, and the scattered light was reflected from small square pieces of white cardboard held behind the animal and at right angles to the beam. A piece of card 1 cm. square held 2 metres behind the animal did not interfere with the straight path to the main light. A piece 2 cm. square held 3 metres away caused occasional circus movements, while the same card at 2 metres caused circus movements which were only eliminated after thirty-six trips to the light. After that the usual diagonal path was followed. When the same piece of card was held 10 cm. away from the animal, it caused continuous circus movements.

The explanations we have given are thus adequate to the experimental results so far, although they may seem complicated to the beginner. It has been shown by Lüdtke (1935), however, that more complicated explanations will eventually have to be provided. Lüdtke used *Notonecta* and painted over the whole of one eye and sometimes parts of the other as well. When the whole of one eye and the antero-median part of the other are covered, one would expect balance and a straight path to be impossible, and the animal should circle continuously to the seeing side even in a beam. When one eye and the posterior part of the other are covered, one would similarly expect continuous circus movements to the blind side, initiated in the antero-median ommatidia. Lüdtke found that in the main these expectations were fulfilled, but there was much variation and some plastic adaptation to the new conditions. He found it necessary to postulate that the *direction* of the turning initiated in certain ommatidia depends on the *intensity* of light stimulating them, and in particular that light just above the threshold has an effect opposite to that due to stronger light. According to Lüdtke, it is the stronger light which acts in the directions mapped out by Clark (1928). Moreover, the situation is complicated not only by the process of adaptation in the eye but also by a fluidity in the reflex map of an adaptive sort. When the variables postulated are as many as this, the erection of artificial systems becomes rather unprofitable and insecure, and it is doubtful if much progress can be made along these lines. In this book we are dealing with certain fairly stereotyped forms of behaviour and, while we recognize the occurrence and importance of plasticity and adaptability of various kinds, we are not attempting to cover these subjects of study.

Considering all the experiments which we have discussed in this chapter, we conclude that tests for circus movements after unilateral blinding may yield valuable data for classifying a reaction as tropo-taxis or telo-taxis, but they do not always do so. In uniform light circus movements occur as a result of a tropo-tactic mechanism, but they may also appear in cases of telo-taxis. In a beam a straight course to the light is possible not only with a telo-tactic mechanism but also with a tropo-tactic one, provided the animal has a two-way eye. If continuous circus movements do occur in a perfect beam, then we can safely decide that a tropo-tactic mechanism is in action; as long as there is a discrete source telo-taxis is possible, involving the straight path to the source and the inhibition of other light, so that continuous circling alone provides a clear-cut criterion of the type of reaction.

XIII

SKOTO-TAXIS. INTENSITY *v.* DIRECTION

A. Skoto-taxis

IN dealing with photo-taxis we have usually taken as examples experiments in which the animals go towards the light. This is convenient because all three main types of photo-taxis can then be considered. Owing to the fact that few animals can see directly behind themselves, negative photo-telo-taxis must be rare. Inability to see behind while the body is kept straight does not matter in klino-taxis, because there are often regular deviations, in this kind of orientation, that expose the photo-sensitive parts to posterior light. On the other hand, if a single light-source is present, orientation by negative photo-tropo-taxis usually cannot be maintained perfectly. If the animal is perfectly in line with the rays it cannot see the light at all. Consequently accidental deviations are not corrected until they become large enough to bring the light into the field of vision. Such deviations have been recorded, for example, by Taliaferro (1920) for *Planaria maculata* and by Müller (1924) for *Julus*. When there are two lights or a constellation of lights suitably placed, negative photo-tropo-taxis can occur without these deviations.

When an animal behaves photo-tropo-tactically, it takes into account, so to speak, all the lights in its field of view and orientates accordingly. If it is photo-negative, it then goes towards a darker part of the field. We have regarded such behaviour as a movement away from light, but a number of workers have regarded it as an orientation towards darkness and called it *skoto-taxis* (σκότος, darkness) (Alverdes, 1930; Dietrich, 1931). This may seem like hair-splitting, but it raises some important questions. Can the absence (darkness) of the positive stimulus (light) act as a stimulus? Is there a clear distinction between stimulation by light causing contra-lateral turning and absence of stimulation by light causing ipsi-lateral turning? Is it not possible to make this distinction by analysis of reflex maps in the eye? As we shall see, it is not easy, if it is possible at all.

As early as 1905 Bohn reported that the marine gastropod

Littorina littorea goes straight to a black screen. When two black screens were suitably arranged, Bohn said that the winkles headed between them, just as many animals orientate between two lights. If the reaction towards darkness is important in the life of *Littorina*, then its inefficiency when the situation is complicated by a second black screen requires an explanation. The explanation put forward by Bohn (1909) and taken up by Loeb (1911) was that the animal was forced to orientate symmetrically in the field of stimulation, and this view fitted nicely into the tropism theory. When the subject was reinvestigated, however, Bierens de Haan (1921) working with *Littorina* and v. Buddenbrock (1919) with *Helix* confirmed the orientation towards a single screen but could not get orientation between two screens. No difficulty arises in any of this work if the reaction is described as negative photo-taxis, since no sufficiently crucial experiments were done.

The subject was taken up again about 1930 by Alverdes and his pupils, using such animals as shore crabs, terrestrial isopods, snails, myriapods, and earwigs. Most of the experiments were carried out in an arena with white walls, lit from above. When a piece of black paper was fixed to the wall, the animals walked towards it. In most cases, however, orientation was much less accurate than is usual with animals going towards a light. Dietrich (1931), who worked with the woodlice *Oniscus asellus* and *Porcellio scaber*, attributed this to the fact that the intensity difference between black and white is usually much less than the difference between darkness and the light from a lamp. Thus *Oniscus* walked from 32 cm. away to a rectangular figure 10 cm. wide and 7 cm. high, but failed to orientate to one 5 × 7 cm. in size. The performance was much improved if four black rectangles were equally spaced round a circle and the animal started in the centre (Fig. 80 *b*). But in this case, in whichever direction an animal started off, it would soon approach one or other of the rectangles and could then correct its direction. Thus, as indeed in all cases of so-called skoto-taxis, the black area forms a large part of the visual field. When there is no black screen at all, the paths are not at all straight (Fig. 80 *a*).

If the animal has its left side towards a black area, and the whole of the visual field of the left eye is occupied by that area, it will normally turn to the left. If the reaction is really skoto-taxis, the reaction is initiated in the left eye, whereas if it is negative photo-taxis, it is initiated in the illuminated right eye. When the animal is orientated, it may either be fixing the dark area anteriorly in a tropo-tactic or telo-tactic way, or it may be treating the light from the light walls as two sources of light and orientating between them. The experiments mentioned above

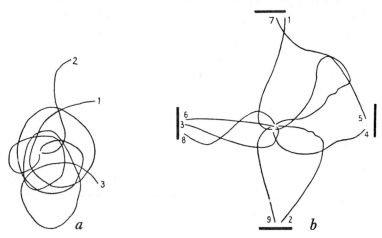

FIG. 80. *a.* Tracks of a photo-negative woodlouse, *Porcellio*, in an arena surrounded by white walls and illuminated from above. *b.* Tracks of *Porcellio* when there are four black screens in the experimental field. (Dietrich, *Z. wiss. Zool.*, 1931.)

do not discriminate between these possibilities. Once the animal is near one of the black areas, the others are too far away to have much effect.

In another experiment Dietrich (1931) started the woodlice midway between a black screen and a light (Fig. 81 *a*). Five of them went straight to the screen and seven passed it on one side or the other. It seems unnecessary to assume that the five reacted in a special way, differently from the other seven, and the whole lot can be regarded as performing negative photo-taxis.

In a further experiment the screen was so arranged that the woodlice could go directly away from the light and walk parallel to the screen, or go to the screen and walk at right angles to the rays of light (Fig. 81 *b*). In the event three went fairly straight away from the light, two went straight towards the screen, and three compromised, going in the general direction of the screen but missing it because they turned too much away from the light. Now when woodlice are in a photo-positive condition, their orientation is markedly inaccurate (Chap. VII), and if we assume a similar inaccuracy in negative photo-taxis,

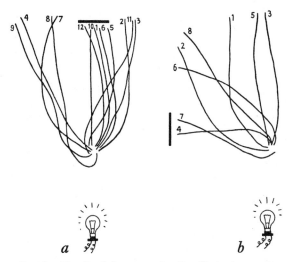

FIG. 81. Tracks of photo-negative *Porcellio* in the presence of one light and one black screen. *a*. The woodlice start on the line between light and screen. *b*. Direction of light and screen form a right angle at the starting-point. (Dietrich, *Z. wiss. Zool.*, 1931.)

it is unnecessary to postulate skoto-taxis at all. The fact that none of the animals deviated directly away from the screen is perfectly compatible with this view, when it is remembered how the whole field of vision can be taken into account in tropotaxis.

Geismer (1935) carried out similar experiments with *Helix* and concluded that skoto-taxis really occurred. In the two-screen experiment the rectangles were 24×20 cm. in size. The snails were started at a distance of 25 cm. away from them and were placed facing between the two. They kept this initial direction for a time and then curved off towards one screen or the other. When the snails were placed midway between a lamp and a screen, facing across the line joining them, the majority turned in a long curve to the screen. In these experiments the background was light in colour and so could be regarded as a constellation of lights contributing to negative photo-tropo-taxis; the screens were very large and the distances crawled were small. Moreover, the animals were started off facing a particular direction, they turned very slowly, and

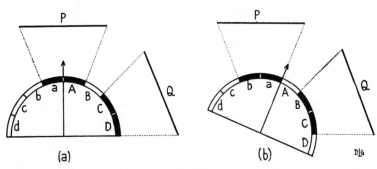

(a)   (b)   D|G

FIG. 82. Arthropod head, schematic, with paired compound eyes. The arrow indicates the animal's long axis. *P* and *Q* are black screens. The letters *a* to *d* represent the 'sensitivities' of the respective groups of ommatidia in the left eye, and *A* to *D* those in the right eye. Compare Figs. 35, p. 88; 74, p. 157; 75, p. 158. Explanation in text, pp. 179–80.

their reactions were very variable. Consequently the results were unsuitable for precise analysis and do not help to solve our problems.

Klein (1934) tested a number of arthropods by similar methods and *Julus* particularly gave some interesting results. At 41 cm. distance from two dark screens, each 10 × 7 cm. in size, the animals sometimes started by going between the two and sometimes by going straight towards one of them. In the former cases they sometimes later went straight towards one screen. After reaching one screen *Julus* sometimes changed over and went to the other, and even changed back again (Fig. 83). This is slightly reminiscent of the zigzag path in photo-telotaxis and seems to be inconsistent with the usual machinery of negative photo-taxis. It is not particularly consistent with skoto-taxis or any other elementary reaction when, after reaching the goal, the animal abandons it and makes for a distant but otherwise similar goal. The same kind of behaviour was shown occasionally by *Lithobius* and *Forficula* (Klein, 1934), even when unilaterally blinded.

Apart from this alternation between two screens, we have so far no evidence which is inconsistent with negative photo-taxis. Even the orientation to one of two black screens instead of between the two can be seen, on examination, to be consistent with the ordinary tropo-tactic mechanism. Assume that the eyes are of the type required for stable negative photo-tropo-taxis, with the anterior ommatidia most sensitive and with a gradient down to the least sensitive posterior ones (Fig. 82). Ommatidia which are not facing a black screen are facing a light background and consequently initiate contralateral turning. In Fig. 82 the letters *a*, *b*, *c*, *d* represent the amount of turning effect caused by the four groups of ommatidia when stimulated by the uniform light from the background, *a* being the largest and *d* the smallest. In

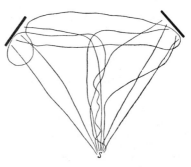

FIG. 83. Tracks of the photo-negative *Julus* in an arena surrounded by white walls and illuminated from above. There are two black screens inside the arena. (Klein, *Z. wiss. Zool.*, 1934.)

an experiment with two equal screens, suppose one is straight ahead of the animal and the other is on the right side (Fig. 82 *a*). The total turning effect towards the right is $(b+c+d)$ and the left-turning effect is simply B. Cancelling the symmetrically placed values B and b, we find a resultant right-turning effect of $(c+d)$. Thus the stimulation is both asymmetrical and unbalanced, and a turn to the right is expected. As the animal turns, as soon as the screen P just passes out of the field of vision of the right eye, the situation becomes quite different (Fig. 82 *b*). The right-turning effect is now $(c+d)$ and the left-turning effect is $(A+D)$. Cancelling D with d, the resultant left-turning effect is $(A-c)$. Since the anterior region (A) is assumed to be more effective than the posterior (c), the animal is expected to turn to the left. In Fig. 82 *a* the animal turns to the right and in Fig. 82 *b* it turns to the left. Somewhere between these two positions of orientation there will therefore be a stable position; there will be a balance of turning effects, though an asymmetrical one, and the animal will go straight towards a point near the right-hand edge of screen P.

It is easy to show by this technique that even if the animal at first orientates midway between the two screens, any slight accidental deviation will lead to a stable orientation towards the edge of one screen or near the edge. Thus a reaction having the appearance of skoto-telo-taxis can be described quite easily in terms of negative tropo-taxis, the light background acting like a constellation of lights.

In a similar way the reactions to the combination of a screen and a light can be described in terms of negative photo-tropo-taxis. Suppose the light is on the right and the animal orientates to the left-hand edge of the screen. The turning effect due to the light acting on the insensitive posterior ommatidia may then be balanced by the sum of the effects of (a) the background light on the corresponding ommatidia of the other eye, and (b) the background light on those sensitive anterior ommatidia of the left eye which correspond with the right anterior ommatidia facing the screen. If the anterior ommatidia are not sensitive enough to permit this balance, the animal will turn more to the left until the light goes off the field of view.

At first sight it looks as if the same sort of explanation could be applied to the behaviour of *Carcinus maenas* and *Eupagurus bernhardus* (Alverdes, 1930). The reactions towards two screens and to a light and a screen were similar to those illustrated in Figs. 81 and 83, but orientation was more accurate. There were, however, two important differences. These animals moved towards the goal backwards, forwards, or sideways, just as they do in photo-telo-taxis (p. 99); and during locomotion the antennules continually beat up and down, keeping to a plane which passed through the goal. When the crabs orientated between two screens, the antennules beat first towards one of them and then towards the other. This behaviour shows that the two goals were clearly seen by the crabs as separate objects. We have not reached a conclusion of this kind about any kind of taxis except telo-taxis. In accordance with the principle of parsimony, we do not postulate organization of the optic field unless it is necessary to fit the facts; it seems to be necessary in describing the behaviour of the crabs.

This conclusion raises two further questions. Are we justified in including amongst the reactions to uncomplicated physical stimuli these reactions involving rudimentary form-vision? If not, then the term *taxis* is not suitable and skoto-taxis is a misnomer. Nevertheless, reactions do not fall naturally into sharply defined classes capable of being named *elementary* and *complex*. The skoto-taxis and telo-taxis of crabs lie in a doubtful zone, and it remains a matter of personal taste whether one uses these terms or not. The second question arises from the results of Klein (1934) in experiments with two or more screens, when *Julus*, *Lithobius*, and *Forficula* occasionally abandoned one screen after reaching it and went to another. This behaviour is more understandable as a response to form-vision than as negative photo-taxis. If we are extending the use of the term skoto-taxis to cover these cases, should we not go further and apply it to the behaviour of woodlice? Our classification is simpler and more consistent if we do not do so. At present we have no reason to postulate form-vision for woodlice, but we do not deny the possibility that woodlice perform skoto-taxis; we merely await satisfactory evidence that their reactions are different from negative photo-taxis.[1]

There are some other reactions which are similar to skoto-taxis, but they can confidently be regarded as reactions to shapes. The caterpillars of the Black Arches Moth, *Lymantria monacha*, have been found to crawl straight towards vertically placed dark-coloured sticks (Hundertmark, 1936, 1937). If the sticks are imitated by vertical black stripes on a white background, the caterpillars react in the same way. If four equal stripes are equally spaced round a circle and the animals are started in the centre, approximately equal numbers go to the four stripes (Fig. 85). When the stripes are of different widths, more animals go to the wider stripes than to the narrower (Fig. 84). In all these experiments each caterpillar goes straight from the start to one stripe; there is no indication of orientation between two stripes or of switching over from one to another. Moreover, if the stripe is very broad—making an angle of 60° with the starting-point—the animal does not go towards the middle, as one would expect in photo-taxis, but makes for one edge. If one edge is taller than the other, fewer animals go to the shorter edge than to the taller (Fig. 86).

[1] See note 25, Appendix.

The importance of form is further shown by the fact that these caterpillars go to the edge of a single white stripe on a black background, although in this case orientation is not so rapid or precise. It is thus clearly the vertical black-white boundary which is aimed at.

There is an apparent inconsistency here in that in Chapter IX it was suggested that the eyes of *Lymantria* caterpillars are too

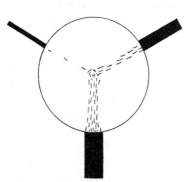

simple to carry out ordinary light compass reactions by a mechanism like that of telotaxis, while here we postulate their capacity for form-vision. The former would, however, require a fairly large number of discriminating optic elements covering at least a quarter of a circle on each side of the body, while the reaction described in this chapter requires such discrimination only straight ahead.

FIG. 84. Tracks of caterpillars of *Lymantria monacha* towards dark screens of different area. The screens stand upright on the experimental field, but for the purpose of this drawing they are shown leaning outwards. (Hundertmark, 1937.)

Here we assume that the caterpillar needs to recognize a fairly upright dark-light boundary straight ahead only; presumably orientation takes place by means of trial movements. An examination of the relation of the structure of the eyes of caterpillars to various reactions to light (Lammert, 1925; Ludwig, 1933, 1934; Hundertmark, 1936, 1937; Oehmig, 1939) is very desirable.[1]

Kalmus (1937) has recently described similar reactions of first-stage nymphs of the stick insect, *Dixippus* (*Carausius*) *morosus*. When placed on a surface that has black stripes painted on it, these insects aline themselves with the stripes. If the stripes are very broad, the alinement is along their black-white edges. Kalmus (1937) tentatively suggested the name photo-horo-taxis (ὅρος, boundary) for this behaviour, but he recognized that form-vision was involved and that the reaction is therefore rather too complex to be called a taxis.

A very clear case of a reaction to shapes has been recorded by Knoll (1922). The Humming-bird Moth, *Macroglossa stella-*

[1] See note 26, Appendix.

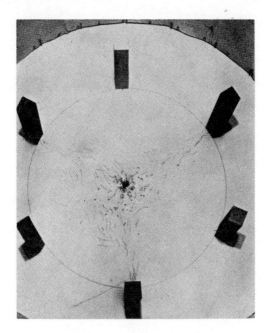

FIG. 85. Photograph of first-stage caterpillars of *Lymantria monacha*. They start from the middle of an experimental field surrounded by six dark blocks and are seen to crawl in almost straight paths towards these blocks. (Hundertmark, 1936.)

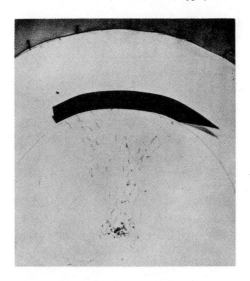

FIG. 86. Photograph of caterpillars of *Lymantria monacha* crawling towards a black figure of the shape of a trapezium. Most of them crawl towards the left vertical border, while the oblique border on the right is avoided. (Hundertmark, 1937.)

tarum, flies in the autumn towards dark objects and overwinters in crevices. In its reaction towards dark objects it prefers spots of 3–6 cm. diameter. It does not react towards darkness as a general stimulus but towards dark shapes within certain size limits. Again, according to Weyrauch (1936) the cicindellid beetle *Notiophilus* reacts positively to a light but is diverted from its course towards a small black screen 4 cm. square. This orientation towards a small black screen is unchanged by the simultaneous presence of a large black screen. Clearly this is not negative photo-taxis, for the animal is at the same time reacting photo-positively; nor is it a simple reaction to darkness, for a small dark screen is preferred to a large one. The size of the screen is important, so we must call it a simple kind of reaction to form.

We thus reach the conclusion that some reactions which have been called skoto-taxis can equally well be described as negative photo-taxis. Others can hardly be called taxes at all because they involve form-vision of a primitive sort.

B. INTENSITY *v.* DIRECTION

During the period when the tropism theory of animal conduct was dominant, the question of whether animals respond essentially to the direction of light or to its intensity was very much discussed. De Candolle (1832) is said to have been the first to attribute the photo-tropic curvatures of plants to differences of light intensity on opposite sides of the stem. Sachs (1887) rejected this hypothesis and considered that the curvatures depend on the direction taken by the light rays through the tissues. Loeb (1888) at first took over for animals the view of Sachs, then reverted to De Candolle's ideas (1906 *a*), and later he seems to have used both. Mast (1911) discussed the problem and laid down the main lines of modern views.

It is convenient to consider the matter under two heads. First, there are the relations between the direction of movement of the animal and (*a*) any gradients of intensity of light, and (*b*) the direction from which light comes; these relations can be studied by direct observation of the paths taken. Secondly, there are the relations between the mechanism or means by which the animal is able to make use of the stimulus presented to it and the direction and intensity of the light striking the various parts of the animal's surface; the study of these relations requires information about the structure and mode of action of the eyes and about the animal's manœuvres.

Consider the gross movements of the orientated animal first. It has already been pointed out that light radiating freely from a source like a candle or an electric lamp diminishes rapidly in intensity as it passes outwards (Fig. 61, p. 138). This is due to the fact that it is covering an increasing area. A photo-positive animal can, therefore, follow the direction of the rays and go up the steepest gradient of light intensity simultaneously, and it is not possible to know straight away whether it is reacting to the direction or to the gradient. It is possible to separate the two factors by using, first, a parallel beam, so that there is no gradient, and secondly, graded light shining at right angles to the plane to which the animal is confined, so that the light has no effective direction. Apparatus for producing this kind of gradient has been described, for example, by Mast (1911), Spooner (1933), and Ullyott (1936) (see Chap. V). The use of a gradient set up by passing the light through a triangular prism, filled with ink or the like, is not desirable because some light is then scattered and the animal may be able to make out the intensity of light some distance away. The light has then, in fact, an effective resultant direction and the factors of direction and intensity cannot thus be separated. There are plenty of examples of animals going straight towards the source in a parallel beam, so that a gradient of intensity is often not necessary. At the same time, it is also possible for some animals to collect at one end of a gradient even when the direction of the light does not help them, but they cannot then go straight to the place of aggregation (klino-kinesis, Chap. V). No information is supplied which could enable them to orientate their bodies in the correct direction. In a pure gradient, then, aggregation can take place by kineses, which are rather inefficient mechanisms. Planarians, which can perform taxes when the light is suitable, will aggregate in this way when the light is unsuitable for taxes. It would be interesting to know if other photo-tactic animals, like *Eristalis* and *Notonecta*, can aggregate by klino-kinesis too.

Instead of separating the two factors—direction and intensity —it is possible so to arrange them that they should produce movement in opposite directions. An experiment of this kind has already been described on p. 65. A test-tube held at right angles to a window is so shaded that the light is more intense at the inner end, although the light comes from the window (Fig. 20, p. 66). Loeb (1890) described how the photo-positive caterpillars of *Porthesia* (*Euproctis*) *chrysorrhoea* went towards the window in such a test-tube, although by so doing they went into weaker light. This experiment impressed Loeb with the importance of ray direction, though he later came to see the importance of intensity as well.

A more satisfactory way of antagonizing direction and intensity was described by Spooner (1933). The animals were first tested in ordinary or in parallel light and then in a convergent beam. Spooner used various planktonic animals from the Plymouth region—various copepods, decapod larvae, annelid larvae, and *Sagitta*. They all showed the same kind of behaviour and swam according to the direction of the light. Photo-positive specimens swam towards the light, first in the divergent part of the beam, right through the focus and then in the convergent beam, so that the light gradient was clearly unimportant (Fig. 87, p. 186). Photo-negative specimens went away from the light even though they then swam into the bright focus of the beam.

There are thus some reactions—kineses—which are controlled by intensity alone, and there are others—taxes—in which the animal moves along the light rays. In taxes photo-positive animals go towards the light source, even if the intensity is lower there, and photo-negative ones go away from the source, even if they then reach a higher intensity; it looks as if intensity is unimportant. This brings us to the second heading—the relations between mechanism of orientation on the one hand and intensity and direction on the other. Kineses are not in question here, and only taxes need be discussed.

In the chapters on klino-taxis (VI) and tropo-taxis (VII), it was stated that the animals orientate to equality of intensity of stimulation on the two sides—successive equality in the former and simultaneous equality in the latter. Now we say that the orientation is essentially to direction of light and not to the gradient of intensity. How are these two statements to be reconciled? The clue lies in the fact that the intensity of light

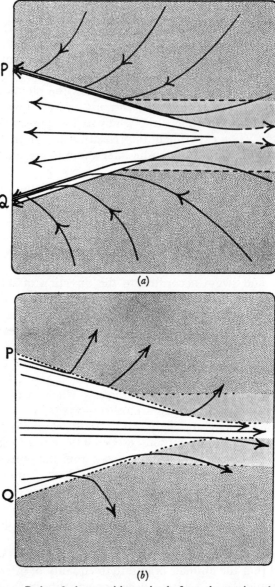

FIG. 87. *a.* Paths of photo-positive animals from the marine plankton in a convergent beam of light. *PQ* = entrance of the convergent beam. In going in the direction of the light, the animals move from high light intensity into low. *b.* Paths of photo-negative specimens of a planktonic copepod, *Nitocra typica*, in a convergent beam of light. By going in the direction of the light and away from the source, they move from lower into higher intensity. (Spooner, 1933.)

at a certain point in space is not necessarily the same as the intensity of light stimulating the receptors of an animal at that point.

It is obvious that the final stimulus is delivered as the quantity of light producing photo-chemical change, and that the intensity of stimulation of a particular receptor unit depends only on that quantity. Direction is important because it determines how much of the available light shall produce photo-chemical change. If a flat eye is held at right angles to the rays, the maximum amount of light reaches the sensitive surface and produces chemical change, while if such an eye is held parallel to the rays, there can be no stimulating change of this sort at all. Similarly, a tubular ommatidium cannot be stimulated at all except when it is nearly in line with the rays and facing the source. As the animal turns round, the shadows of its whole body and of specially pigmented parts of it continually alter the quantity of light falling on the photo-sensitive units. It is because the turning of the body alters the intensity of stimulation in this way that animals can react at all to ray direction.

This principle is illustrated in all the organisms we have studied, from *Euglena* and maggots to arthropods with compound eyes. Sometimes there is differential reaction to localized stimulation, as in *Eristalis*, so that stimulation of one photosensitive unit produces one kind, direction, and strength of response, while stimulation of another unit produces a response different in each of these respects. Sometimes, as in *Euglena*, the receptor is less complex and the kind and direction of the response are fixed, so that turning is always towards a certain side of the animal (e.g. the dorsal side); the response occurs when the normal rotation of the body results in a suitable change in the intensity of stimulation. When orientation is complete no such change occurs during the rotation. For the performance of taxes, then, the light must first have a direction which the animal can follow; then there must be co-ordination between the structure and action of the receptors and the activities of the effectors, so that variations in simple intensity of stimulation can lead to discrimination of direction of rays and orientation to that direction.

In *Eristalis* we have seen that the quantity of light reaching the eye is not the only factor determining the intensity of reaction;

the various units of the eye have different sensitivities. In telo-taxis and light compass reactions having a similar mechanism, there is a further complication that light which certainly reaches the photo-sensitive material may for a time produce no reaction at all. That leads on to kinds of reactions called skoto-taxis and to higher behaviour, where the intensity of physical stimulation may bear very little relation indeed to the intensity of reaction and where the form of the stimulating object is all-important. It is beyond the scope of this book to follow this out or to discuss the enormous differences in the reactions of a man to the minute differences in physical stimulation which occur when one person is present rather than another.

XIV

TEMPERATURE REACTIONS[1]

THE physical factor of temperature is very important to animals. They are killed by cold if the body temperature falls a little below the freezing-point of water, and by heat long before the boiling-point is reached. Compared with the range of temperature existing in the universe, the limiting temperatures for life are very close together, and those limits are often exceeded on the earth's surface. Within the extreme limits, animals vary greatly in their susceptibility, but temperature changes always have some effect. Poikilotherms—the so-called cold-blooded animals, in which the external and the body temperatures are usually close and fluctuate together—are like chemical reactions in that the speeds of many of their processes vary directly with body temperature. This holds over a range of temperature which depends on the species, and outside that range sub-lethal or lethal effects begin; within the vital range, all sorts of activities are affected, including reproduction and growth.[2] In the homoiotherms the effects of external temperature do not take the same form, but they are not unimportant.

The earth can be divided into geographical regions having certain temperature characteristics. Such a division deals with broad climatic conditions and does not attempt to describe local variations. Within any small region and at one instant, there is often an irregular patchwork of temperature conditions; it is hotter in the sun than in the shade, and there are warmer places and cooler places in an ordinary dwelling-house. For any one species there is a temperature which is most favourable. The optimum temperature for speed of growth is not the same as the optimum for length of life, but we can conceive of a general optimum which is best for the maintenance of the species, even if we do not know its exact value. Given the patchwork of temperature conditions and the existence of some kind of optimum, it would be surprising if animals did not react to temperature at all, if they took no steps to place themselves in favourable temperatures. In fact, many animals aggregate in regions of favourable temperature if given the opportunity.

When animals aggregate in a favourable temperature zone,

---

[1] The temperature reactions of insects have been exhaustively treated in a book by Herter (1953).

[2] Body temperatures in poikilotherms have been reviewed by Gunn (1942).

temperature is both the stimulus and a physical factor which greatly affects their lives. Reactions to light are generally not of this kind. Light is seldom intense enough to be damaging, although there are cases in which it can be beneficial or damaging according to its intensity. The effect of sunlight on the human skin is an example of such direct action. Generally speaking, light has an altogether different significance; it is a *token* stimulus (token—a sign, something which represents something else).

The caterpillar larvae of *Porthesia* (*Euproctis*) *chrysorrhoea* are positive to light when unfed (Loeb, 1890); starting from the ground, they therefore climb up plants and reach the leaves on which they feed. In the laboratory, if the light is put below, the larvae go the other way—down. Again, animals which use the light of the sun or the moon for making compass movements are enabled by this means to travel fairly directly over uneven surfaces, instead of twisting and turning as they do in the dark. In artificial light the effect of the reaction may be just the opposite, as when moths flutter round a lamp instead of going straight. In these cases, if reaction to light were to cease, the light itself would seldom do harm, for it is seldom sufficiently intense. The animals would, however, suffer in other ways that are fortuitously connected with light in natural conditions. That is why we then refer to the light as a token stimulus. There is an association between many light reactions and the lives of animals, though it need not be supposed that this is a mental association in any anthropomorphic sense. The association can be interpreted more safely in evolutionary terms (see Chap. II).

Although in temperature reactions the temperature is usually not just a token, there are some cases in which it has token value. All of our examples of this are taken from the behaviour of insect parasites of warm-blooded animals. In these cases temperature is one of the stimuli guiding the animal to its host.

The question naturally arises of why temperature is not more widely used as a token stimulus. Gravity is of great value as a token stimulus, because of its constancy of direction, and odours are too, because of their specificity, particularly in relation to food. Light is so valuable because its source is usually above, because it is reflected in varying degrees from different objects, and because it travels far and in straight lines. Light is the factor above all others which can give instant reliable information about what is happening at a distance. Many animals have developed very sensitive receptors which are able to take advantage of the directional properties of light.

When we come to consider temperature, we find an important difference; light is a form of energy, but temperature is a measure of the energy level. Heat is the corresponding form of energy. It is the temperature that affects the speed of metabolic processes; it is the transfer of heat that acts as a stimulus in behaviour. The rate of general metabolic processes certainly affects behaviour, but we will leave that for the moment and deal with the transfer of heat as a stimulus.

Heat may be transferred in four main ways—by radiation, conduction, convection, and evaporation. It may also be transformed from or into other forms of energy in chemical processes. Any kind of radiation may be transformed into heat on striking suitable matter, but only those radiations in a certain band of wave-lengths are familiarly and conveniently—but inaccurately—known as 'radiant heat'. This band includes the visible part of the spectrum and its neighbourhood, particularly in the infra-red region. This provides part of the answer to our question; *radiation* is used as a token stimulus. It produces photo-chemical change in the eye and only part of it appears as heat. Our eyes are so sensitive to it that we give it a separate name and call it light. Radiation does not, however, have a stimulus intensity dependent only on its amount of energy; the stimulus intensity also depends on the wave-length, and infra-red rays are invisible. These invisible rays are—as far as we know—rather little used as a token stimulus, presumably because the heating effect they produce can seldom be distinguished from local heating due to conduction and convection.

Conduction is the transfer of heat between two materials in contact. We test temperatures roughly with the hand; if heat flows into the hand, it stimulates thermo-receptors and we realize that the hand is touching something warmer than itself. In hot sunshine stone gets hotter than metal, because its heat is not rapidly conducted into the interior, but the metal feels hotter because heat is rapidly conducted to the place cooled by the hand. Our own sensations are not, therefore, very reliable guides to temperature, and perhaps animals in general are not very good thermometers.

Convection is the carriage of heat by the diffusion or flow of the molecules of a fluid. In this case the final transfer of heat to or from the animal is by conduction through contact. A stream of warm air or water can inform an animal of the direction of a source of heat provided that it has receptors suitable for discriminating the direction of flow of the fluid. It is possible to get a gradient of temperature in air or in water due to the diffusion from the hot source of heated molecules; although this gradient does not instantly inform an animal of the direction of the source, there are certain manœuvres which make it possible for the source to be reached economically.

Evaporation, removing heat from the animal, seems to be of more importance as a temperature-regulating mechanism than as a stimulus; the reverse process of condensation is probably not important.

We will first consider the reactions of animals to heat reaching them in the form of radiation. It is a familiar fact that many animals, both on land and in the sea, bask in the sun as if enjoying the heat. It was reported by Weese (1917) that the horned lizard, *Phrynosoma modestum*, not only does this but also turns and tilts its body, on cool mornings, in such a way as to set the dorsal surface as nearly as possible perpendicular to the rays of the sun. If the temperature gets too high or too low, this lizard buries itself in the sand of the desert in which it lives. Krüger (1931) has shown that the body temperature of a lizard may be 11° C. higher in the sun than in the shade, air temperature being unchanged, and orientation behaviour may be expected to make the difference still greater.

A similar case has been worked out more thoroughly by Fraenkel (1929 *b*, 1930). The desert locust, *Schistocerca gregaria*, is in a state of cold stupor below 17° C. and begins to move about between 17 and 20° C. When the air temperature has risen to this level in the early morning, the hoppers (nymphs) form dense aggregations on walls and slopes facing east and on the eastern sides of bushes. These aggregations are no doubt partly due to the well-known reaction of one locust to another, when they are of the migratory phase, but that would not explain their aggregation in places fully exposed to the sun. It is hardly

Fig. 88. Photograph showing the orientation of adult desert locusts perpendicular to the sun's rays. The lines on the board show the horizontal projection of the rays (arrow). Notice how the locusts lie on their sides. (Fraenkel, 1930.)

likely that there are suitable temperature gradients to guide the
hoppers to these basking-places, especially when there is a wind.
It is therefore probable that they wander at random until they
reach a warm sunny spot and then they react by becoming
immobile. Basking lasts until the air temperature rises to about
28° C., and then the locusts start to migrate. The same sort of

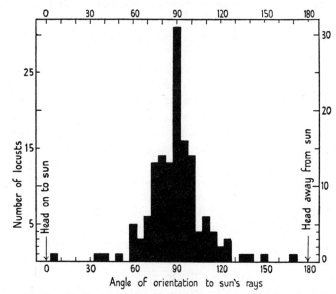

FIG. 89. Graph showing the distribution of the angles between the
body axes of 142 adult locusts and the projection of the sun's rays
on the horizontal (see Fig. 88). (Data from Fraenkel, 1930.)

thing happens when the temperature is falling in the evening,
but the aggregations then form on surfaces facing west.

During basking the locusts place themselves with their bodies
roughly parallel to one another and at right angles to the direction of the sun's rays (Fig. 88). Adults not only orientate the
body axis in this way (Fig. 89) but they tilt the median plane
over so that their sides catch the maximal amount of radiation.
If the sun mounts high in the sky before the air temperature
reaches migration-point, the locusts may practically lie on their
sides.

This response to sunshine is so striking that it was at first
thought to be purely a reaction to light, but locusts with their

eyes painted over still orientate, though not so accurately or quickly. If one eye is put out of action, usually but not always the seeing side is turned to the sun. If part of the body is shaded, the animal walks forwards or backwards out of the shadow; the delay is greater when the abdomen is shaded than it is when the head is shaded. All these experiments indicate that the eyes take some part in the normal reaction but that they are not essential. The temperature receptors are not known, but the shading experiments show that they must be spread widely over the body surface.

The mechanism of re-orientation when an artificial source of radiation is moved has been analysed by Volkonsky (1939). As the elevation of the lamp was slowly increased, the locust followed the movement by rotating its head in small jerks, twisting the neck in so doing; when the head had turned a certain amount, the inclination of the body was suddenly changed to conform to the head. Accurate and rapid re-orientation was dependent on the action of the compound eyes, for if they were put out of action, or if the source of radiation emitted mainly infra-red rays, re-orientation was not efficient, even when it occurred at all. Blinded animals, when they re-orientated at all, did so by means of a series of trials and not by a direct turn into the new position. With third-stage or younger nymphs, the importance of the eyes seemed to be less; it is perhaps possible that the precise visual orientation is secondary to the heat orientation, making it more precise, and that it has become so important in adults that it may occur even when there is little or no heating effect.[1]

If the air temperature rises above 40° C., as it may at noon in the locusts' habitat, there is a corresponding reaction which reduces the heating effect of the sun. The locusts not only face the sun but they often rear up on stones or sticks or climb to the tops of bushes, so that only the front of the head receives direct sunlight (Figs. 90, 91) (Fraenkel 1929 b).[2]

These are directed responses to radiant energy, but they are not locomotory. If a kinetic component could be added to the posture reaction, a taxis or a compass reaction would result, but in fact both Phrynosoma and Schistocerca keep still while basking, even normal movements being inhibited. If these animals are stimulated into walking the posture is abandoned. The animals

[1] Further work on this has been done by Volkonsky (1942) and Clark (1949).
[2] See note 27, Appendix.

FIG. 90. Postural orientation of hoppers of the desert locust sitting on the ground parallel to the sun's rays during noon-day heat. Photographed against the sun. (Fraenkel, 1929 *b*.)

FIG. 91. Postural orientation of hoppers of the desert locust sitting on a bush during the middle of the day. Notice how they hang parallel to the sun's rays. (Fraenkel, 1929 *b*.)

go into a state of akinesis; our terminology of low and high kinesis is not convenient here, for the assumption of immobility does not appear to depend much on the intensity of the radiation and the temperature at which it occurs is neither extremely high nor extremely low. According to Volkonsky (1939), the basking and the head-on reactions combine with heating effects of activity in such a way as to tend to produce a steady body-temperature. By analogy with meno-taxis and telo-taxis, this author calls the two reactions *men-akinesis* and *tel-akinesis*.

Examples of locomotory reactions to radiant heat are rather hard to find. This is not because invisible heating radiations are rare. Every object on the earth is radiating and receiving radiations all the time; but the radiations are noteworthy only if they come from objects warmer than their surroundings. The bodies of mammals are almost always warmer than the surroundings, especially in temperate and cold climates, and this fact is used by some parasitic insects. Martini (1918) reported that body-lice (*Pediculus humanus* var. *corporis*) will aggregate under a dull source of radiant heat, even if that involves their movement from the warmer to the cooler part of an iron bar. Homp (1938) reinvestigated the reactions of the same species, making very full and careful temperature measurements with a thermo-couple. She recorded plenty of reactions to the heat from an artificial finger, but was unable to get any reaction in an experiment so arranged as to give approximately parallel radiations and a minimal heating effect on the floor. She remarked on the unexpectedness of this, particularly because a blinded louse moving towards a warm 'finger' abandons its orientation at once if the 'finger' is quickly withdrawn. It is difficult to explain the differences in these results of the two workers.

Working on the bed-bug, *Cimex lectularius*, Rivnay (1932) and Sioli (1937) reported reactions to warmth, with receptors located on the antennae. Sioli (1937) obtained a reaction to sudden onset of invisible radiation (hesitation in walking), but he could detect no orientation reaction in which use was made of the directional and radiant property. He concluded that tropo-taxis was not involved (e.g. no circus movements after unilateral amputation) but that attainment of the source was by trial and error. The behaviour seems to fit well into our category of klino-taxis, the lateral deviations being made by the antennae and not by the whole body. As Sioli pointed out, the success of this technique requires proprioceptors or receptors giving similar information about which way the antennae are pointing when they are most stimulated.

Wigglesworth and Gillett (1934) worked on the large South American blood-sucking bug, *Rhodnius prolixus*. They found that blinded specimens could go straight to a test-tube of warm water from a distance of 3–4 cm.; the heat of the tube was the only possible stimulus. The reaction disappeared when the antennae were removed.[1]

This behaviour of *Rhodnius* is important in another connexion. The classification of taxes was designed for reactions to light, and it is sometimes difficult to fit reactions to other stimuli into the same scheme. In the case of *Rhodnius*, experiments are available for making the attempt. Considering first the receptors, it is rather unlikely that each sensory ending, if kept stationary, is capable of discriminating the direction of radiant heat, and in any case Wigglesworth and Gillett (1934) concluded that it is the temperature of the air and not radiant heat which is the effective stimulus. The stimulus cannot, therefore, be considered as having direction, but only a gradient of intensity.

The stimulus probably takes the form of concentric rings of diminishing temperature around the heat source (cf. Fig. 61, p. 138). With one antenna held stiffly in front, it is hardly likely that the temperature difference between the two sides of this thin appendage would be perceptible, but the gradient along the antennae could be. That is to say, by simultaneous comparison, the bug could receive information about the steepness of the temperature gradient. This information would be relatively useless for guiding the animal to the source, unless compared with other information—from the other antenna or from the same antenna pointed in a different direction. Since the reaction can be carried out with a single antenna, it is apparent that waving movements of the antenna are required before orientation can occur. These can make successive comparisons of temperature and lead to a klino-tactic response.

In fact *Rhodnius* does make lateral 'testing' movements with its antennae (or with the single antenna if the other is cut off), but only before it starts to move. It then takes up a direction

[1] See note 28, Appendix.

and walks straight forward to the source. Although a simultaneous comparison of intensities of stimulation is theoretically possible in the intact animal, it looks as if the reaction conforms more nearly to klino-taxis, with some increase in efficiency of a tropo-tactic sort. After unilateral removal of an antenna, there are no circus movements, but there is a slight tendency to turn towards the intact side when very near the source, and this supports the suggestion of a tropo-tactic element; but an experiment in which the uni-antennate animal turns either way towards the source shows that the reaction cannot be entirely tropo-tactic. In either case, it is probable that the animal tends to orientate towards maximal stimulation rather than simply to equality of stimulation on the two sides.

Here, again, the two-source experiment is interesting. Assume, for simplicity, that there are no draughts or convection currents, and that the heat is carried from the sources by diffusion outwards of warmed air molecules. A graph of lines of equal temperature around these two sources would be like a contour map of twin mountains—the pass leads to a valley. In a two-light experiment a generally similar graph results from plotting the intensity of light falling on a hypothetical mote in the air (Fig. 62, p. 139).

An animal which orientates between two equal sources—klino-tactically or tropo-tactically—goes along the bottom of this valley, if it is started equidistant from the two sources. In so doing, it goes up the steepest gradient, for the steepest gradient lines are normal to the equal intensity lines, but it does not take the shortest path to either source. If the animal's receptors or its movements are at all asymmetrical, it will not reach the pass but will turn towards one source or the other before it gets there. Moreover, if the animal is large in size compared with the distance between two sources, the moving antennae can investigate the gradient some distance away, and the animal can take a short cut to the source instead of following the usual curve. Therefore, just as the curve to the stronger light is neither indicative of photo-telo-taxis nor inconsistent with photo-tropo-taxis, so orientation to one of two heat-sources is not necessarily an indication of thermo-telo-taxis.

In the experiments of Wigglesworth and Gillett (1934) the centres of the two sources were 5·5 cm. apart and the bugs were started 3–4 cm. away from each source. Consequently, from the start they were well within that part of the gradient in which tropo-tactic or klino-tactic orientation is very unstable; a slight movement of even a small animal to one side or the other may be expected to make a big difference to its orientation (see Figs. 62, p. 139; 65, p. 143; 72, p. 152), and the movements of just the antennae of a large animal are equivalent to quite large lateral movements of the whole body of a small one. Consequently we have no difficulty in describing the orientation of *Rhodnius* as klino-tactic. Wigglesworth and Gillett (1934) describe it as 'a reflex pursuit of the antennae', to the source of stimulation, which, combined with the lateral movements of the antennae, is much the same thing.

It seems, therefore, that if a two-source experiment is to be used as a test for telo-taxis, care must be taken to ensure that the animals are started well outside the region of unstable orientation. This appears to be difficult with these parasitic insects, for the temperature stimulus is then often too weak to elicit a response at all. In any case, it seems to be physically impossible for an animal to inhibit one source in a gradient in which the stimulus is not truly radiant; the latest direction taken by a diffusing molecule is no indication of the direction of its origin.

The most recent work on token orientation to temperature has been done by Homp (1938). She set up a concentric temperature gradient by means of an 'artificial hot finger'. This consisted of a glass tube, set up vertically, through which warm water was circulated. Thermo-couple measurements were made of the temperatures of the floor, of the air, and of a freshly killed body-louse at various distances from the 'finger'. The value of the results was somewhat marred by the variability of the general environmental temperature, and of the 'finger' temperature, but they show the way for future work. At 0·5 cm. from the 'finger' the paper floor was warmed more than the air or the louse; beyond 1 cm. away the louse temperature rose most, while air and floor had roughly equal temperatures. A blackened thermo-couple showed much the same readings as the one inside the louse, and it was clear that direct radiation was heating the louse even when the 'finger' was no hotter than 49° C.

The lice were blinded with paint so that they could react

only to the temperature. The paths they followed when going towards the 'finger' were wavy and consistent with klino-taxis. With two 'fingers', the lice went at first between the sources and then usually curved round to one or other of them (Fig. 92). At some short distance from the 'finger', usually less than a

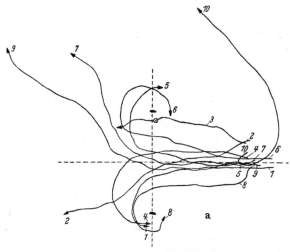

FIG. 92. Tracks of human body-lice towards two warm artificial fingers, whose position is shown by the black ovals on the dotted line. Environmental temperature—18·9° C., 'finger' temperature—66·5 to 71·3° C. The lice were started on the right. No. 10 did not react at all, but all the others first went between the two sources; Nos. 2, 3, 7, 9 went on too far, but the others curved round to one source or the other. (Homp, 1938.)

centimetre, they often went round and round it. Homp (1938) interpreted this as *thermo-meno-taxis*. It is difficult to accept this interpretation, particularly since she concluded that lice do not react to radiant heat. The circular paths occur near the source, where the temperature gradient must be steepening rapidly, and it is possible that the lice were simply creeping within their preferred temperature zone (see below) by means of klino-kinesis, reacting against both the higher temperature nearer the source and the lower temperature away from it (cf. Fig. 96, p. 204, and Fig. 132, p. 287). The data given are not altogether consistent with this view and we must await further investigation before accepting such an unexpected conclusion.

In these cases of parasitic insects, temperature is used as a token stimulus; that is shown clearly by the fact that at a certain point in the reaction the insects frequently bring the proboscis into the position for sucking blood and may even attempt to pierce the floor or the artificial finger (authors quoted above, and also Krijgsman, 1930). There is some disagreement about how far radiant heat is the orientating stimulus, but the transfer of heat in the air appears to be mainly responsible. Homp's (1938) measurements show that attention should also be paid to the gradient of temperature in the floor.

Most of the experiments on reactions to temperature have involved gradients of floor temperature and the resulting gradients in the air, without much probability of direct radiation from a distance being involved. Shelford and Deere (1913) devised an apparatus in which three currents of air, at different temperatures and humidities, were passed across a long rectangular box so that the floor took its temperature from the air. This apparatus was subsequently used by Hamilton (1917), Chenoweth (1917), and Heimburger (1924), but most of the later workers have avoided rapidly moving air. A similar technique has, however, been used for the reactions of fishes to temperature gradients in water (Shelford & Powers, 1915; Doudoroff, 1938). With very small animals in water, like *Paramecium*, physical difficulties of measurement are rather great and may account for some of the inconsistencies in the results (Mendelssohn, 1895, 1902; Zagorowsky, 1914; Alverdes, 1922; Koehler, 1934; Horton, 1935; Bramstedt, 1935). For land animals the most usual apparatus consists essentially of a metal bar, heated at one end and cooled at the other and so giving a gradient of temperatures in between. This method appears to have been used first by Martini (1918). Herter (1924) erected a glass box around the bar, and in this form the apparatus has been widely used under the name of Herter's *Temperaturorgel*. It has the grave disadvantage, for some purposes, that the temperatures of air and floor may be very different (Gunn, 1934). Variants of this type of apparatus have been described by Fulton (1928), Grossmann (1929), Nieschulz (1933), Totze (1933), Gunn (1934), Herter (1934), Adams (1937), and Campbell (1937).[1] Most recently, Thomson (1938) has returned to the earliest type of apparatus described by Graber (1887), in which the animal is given the choice of two temperatures rather than a whole series in a gradient. In any case, the objective is to find the temperature at which the animals aggregate when they are given a choice.

It has already been pointed out that animals die if they get too hot or too cold. For most animals there is a range of not much more than 40° C. within which life can go on and for some animals the range is much smaller (Bělehrádek, 1935). The range of body temperatures within which growth and reproduction can take place is still narrower than this. The question naturally arises of what is the best or optimum temperature for the life of a particular species. The answer depends on the criterion used. At 28° C. *Daphnia magna* lives 26 days and reproduces well; its rates of respiration and of heart-beat are lower both at higher and at lower temperatures. Thus at 8° C. all processes are slower but the animal lives proportionately longer (108 days) (MacArthur and Baillie, 1929), so that the total number of times the heart beats during a lifetime is about 15 million at either 8° C. or at 28° C. Which of these is the better temperature? The optimum body temperatures for low death-rate during development, high reproductive rate, high activity, and long life may be quite different from one another, so that it is always necessary to specify which kind of optimum is meant. Janisch (1931) considers that there is an absolute optimum, but this is too difficult to define at present for practical purposes.

In the two large groups of homoiothermal animals, the mammals and the birds, the body temperature is kept roughly constant at somewhere between 35° and 40° C. by means of complex anatomical and physiological arrangements. In hive-bees, co-operative control keeps the hive temperature fairly steady at 36° C. during the breeding season. In most animals, called poikilothermal or 'cold blooded', the body temperature fluctuates widely with the environmental temperature. Some degree of control occurs by behaviour mechanisms, as distinct from metabolic mechanisms, as in the locust (pp. 192–5).

Generally speaking, however, behaviour regulation of body temperature in poikilotherms takes the form of a locomotory

[1] See also Deal (1941).

reaction. If an insect is too cold, its easiest way of getting warmer is to move to a warmer place. This is the kind of behaviour which can be investigated by means of the various kinds of temperature gradient. The kind of result obtained is shown in Figs. 93, 94.

The temperature region in which aggregation takes place has been given various names, of which *preferred temperature* (*Vorzugstemperatur* or *Wahltemperatur*) and *thermal* or *temperature pre-*

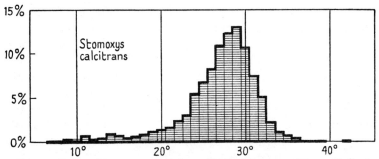

FIG. 94. Preferred temperature of the stable fly, *Stomoxys calcitrans*. Ordinate —percentage of individuals at each temperature (° C.). Nearly all the records fall between 24° and 32° C. (Nieschulz, *Z. angew. Ent.* 1934.)

ferendum (*Präferendum*) are in most common use (Herter, 1926, 1932; Bodenheimer & Schenkin, 1928). *Temperature optimum* is not specific enough and indeed such terms (e.g. *thermo-tactic optimum*) carry implications about the goodness or suitability of the temperature and about the mechanism of reaction (tactic) which are not implicit in the experiments. *Indifference zone* is also used. *Eccritic temperature* (ἐκκρίνω—pick out) can be employed if *preferred* is thought to be too anthropomorphic (Gunn & Cosway, 1938).

Some of these terms seem to imply that the temperature in question can be given to a fraction of a degree, unqualified, but a glance at Figs. 93–95, which are fairly representative, shows that the preferred temperature is a zone and not a point. For showing the peculiar features in each case, therefore, a block diagram is the best and is always necessary; but shorter summaries of the experimental results are often required. If the limits of the range are specified, as 18° to 30° C., then the figures given are unduly weighted by the few scattered observations at the end

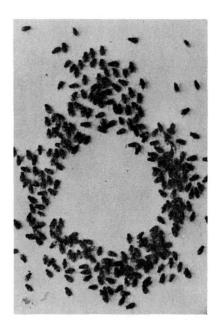

Fig. 93. Temperature preference of blow-flies (*Phormia terranovae*). There was an electric lamp alight behind the vertical sheet of opaque blotting-paper shown; the flies did not collect in the hottest region just opposite the lamp, nor in the cooler outer region, but in a zone of middle temperature at about 30°C. (Original photograph by Fraenkel & Hopf.)

of the block diagram, where it tails off. A more useful method is to give the range within which 50 or 80 per cent. of the observations occur (Bodenheimer & Schenkin, 1928; Bodenheimer & Klein, 1930). The arithmetic average preferred temperature is the shortest summary, but it gives no indication of the extent of the preferred range. If the block diagram is similar in shape

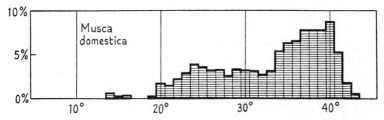

FIG. 95. Preferred temperature of the house fly, *Musca domestica*. Notice how wide is the temperature range (cf. Fig. 94) and how sharply it is cut off at about 40° C., which is near the upper thermal death point. (Nieschulz, *Zool. Anz.* 1935.)

to the statistical curve of normal variation, the standard deviation $\left(\pm \sqrt{\dfrac{\sum d^2}{n-1}} = S.D.\right)$ is a proper measure of this; from the standard deviation, the standard error $\left(S.E. = \dfrac{S.D.}{\sqrt{n}}\right)$ of the average can be worked out and then used to test the significance of a difference between two averages. Sometimes, however, the block diagram turns out to be markedly asymmetrical (Fig. 95) or to have two widely separated peaks, and then more complex methods may be required.[1]

Rather little attention has been paid to the mechanism of the reaction in preferred temperature. The stimulus is not presented as a radiating source, so telo-taxis is not in question; as a rule the apparatus is long and narrow, so that little room is allowed for manœuvres, and consequently tactic behaviour has not been reported. Even the two kinds of kineses, which are probably the most common mechanisms of the reaction, have received little attention. An avoiding reaction (*Schreckreaktion*) has been stated to be important in several cases. In short, the animal turns back and goes the opposite way when it reaches a very hot region. Thus Herter (1924) gives 36·5±0·90° C. as

[1] See note 29, Appendix.

the upper temperature at which the house cricket, *Acheta domestica*, turns back.

In the simplest cases the animal is large compared with the width of the apparatus, so that it can go only a very short distance across it; the animal can thus walk only towards or away from the hot end, and complex manœuvres are not possible. It is quite unknown how well this turning back fits the klino-

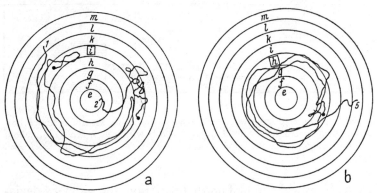

FIG. 96. Tracks of ticks in a concentric temperature gradient. At the end of the observation the animal came to rest (black dot). A square has been drawn round the letter (*h*, *i*) in the ring which is at the preferred temperature. Notice how the wavy track keeps a fairly constant distance from the warm centre. (Totze, 1933.)

kinesis scheme, as typified by *Dendrocoelum* (Chap. V). Totze (1933) used apparatus suitable for such an investigation; instead of being long and narrow, this was circular, heated at the centre, and cooled at the rim, so that it offered a large area for manœuvres. Fig. 96 shows the tracks of the ticks (*Ixodes ricinus*) tested by Totze. They show a series of avoiding reactions at both higher and lower temperatures so that they are consistent with klino-kinetic behaviour. The fact that the preferred temperature depended on the temperature at which the ticks had been kept during the previous two hours is reminiscent of the adaptation which is necessary to aggregation in the klino-kinesis of *Dendrocoelum*. Unfortunately Totze (1933) did not record the beginnings of the tracks, so we have no information about the mechanism of reaching the preferred zone.[1]

The dependence of the preferred temperature on the temperature to which the animals had previously been subjected or on

[1] See note 30, Appendix.

the general external temperature has been reported by Herter
(1924) for the ant, *Formica rufa*, by Bodenheimer & Schenkin
(1928) for the confused flour beetle, *Tribolium confusum*, and by
Henschel (1929) for the cheese mite, *Tyrolichus casei*, as well as
by Totze for ticks. In some of these cases the shift of preferred
temperature might be due to factors other than the previous
temperature. In any case, no one seems to have investigated
this relationship further, to see if individuals from various

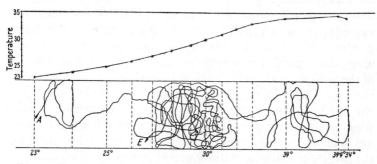

FIG. 97. Tracks of human body-louse in a temperature gradient. Temperatures shown in ° C. *A*, start; *E*, end. Homp gives the preferred zone as 26·4° to
29·7° C. Notice the much convoluted path just above 30° C. (Homp, 1938.)

temperatures would finally aggregate in a single temperature
region if given time, or to find out whether the effect is due to
sensory adaptation or to some metabolic change.

The difficulty of manœuvring in an apparatus only a few
centimetres wide is reduced if the animals are very small. For
cases of this kind, tracks have been published by Henschel (1929)
for the cheese mite, *Tyrolichus casei*, by Weber (1929) for the hog
louse, *Haematopinus suis*, and by Homp (1938) for the human
body louse, *Pediculus humanus corporis* (Fig. 97). Here again, the
aggregations appear to depend on repeated avoiding reactions
and were described by Homp (1938) and Henschel (1929) as
phobic (i.e. klino-kinetic). Similar conclusions can be drawn
from the illustrations published by Shelford (1913) and his
colleagues.

When the animal is very small, it seems likely that the
gradient is not steep enough to allow a directed reaction. For
thermo-taxis, the animal must be differently stimulated when
it lies athwart the gradient, either on its two sides for tropo-taxis

or when it swings from side to side for klino-taxis. With the gradients which have usually been used, only a large animal is large enough to have a sensible difference of temperature on the two sides, and the gradient is usually too narrow for a large animal to go across the gradient in any case. It will be interesting to see if thermo-taxis does occur when the appropriate methods are applied.

There remains one more kind of simple aggregation mechanism, namely, ortho-kinesis. This possibility requires detailed consideration. For simplicity, imagine a temperature aggregation which has no other mechanism. In order to produce collection of most of the animals in the preferred zone, the average linear velocity there must be a small fraction of the velocity in the other regions available. This is the case for the cockroach (Gunn, 1934), if the tests are carried out during the day-time, for in its preferred range the cockroach remains stationary for long periods; during the night, when these insects are normally active instead of hiding in their retreats (Szymanski, 1914), continuous activity makes this mechanism of aggregation practically ineffective, and observations of preferred temperature cannot be made by this method. That is to say, the method in which only the temperatures at which the experimental animals remain stationary are recorded is a method which is applicable only if the speed of movement does become zero in the preferred range. This method cannot be used at all when the animals remain active all the time, and it then becomes necessary to count the animals at each temperature at intervals, whether they are moving or not. Suitable observations may still demonstrate an ortho-kinesis of lesser importance, even if the animals never become quite stationary.

Most terrestrial poikilotherms become torpid at fairly low temperatures, between freezing-point and 15° C. In the absence of some mechanism other than ortho-kinesis, it would therefore seem that aggregation should occur in the cold stupor region; thus any animal which by chance penetrates into the cold region of the gradient may get cold enough for torpor to set in before it can regain the warmer regions. Although such a complication actually occurs (Fig. 94, p. 202), it is not the predominant factor, and the subject requires further analysis.

According to Krogh (1914): 'In studying the influence of temperature upon metabolism, we have to distinguish between the influence upon the central nervous system and the influence upon the reaction velocity of the metabolic processes in the tissues themselves.' Although Krogh was primarily concerned with attempts to get repeatable measurements of rate of oxygen consumption, undisturbed by struggling or other movements of animals, this conception has some value in the study of behaviour, too. We can thus distinguish between a *metabolic* effect of temperature and a *behaviour* effect, the latter caused directly by the interference of the nervous system. The two effects may work together or against one another; in the latter case, discrimination between them is easy, but it is not so in the former. Even in the absence of a behaviour effect, a metabolic effect may cause an aggregation like that of gas molecules into the coolest part of a temperature gradient. Temperature may produce the behaviour effect either through specific receptors or by direct action on the nervous system. In either case, the behaviour effect may be expected to be superposed on the metabolic effect, so that the resultant effect on *locomotory* activity could not be predicted.

When the metabolic effect of temperature is assessed by measuring the rate of oxygen consumption of the normal animal, rejecting all those readings for experiments in which the animal moved at all, it is found that respiration increases progressively with rising temperature, and then falls suddenly as damaging and irreversible effects of high temperature set in. Broadly speaking, the effect of activity on the part of the animal is to steepen this curve of rate of oxygen consumption. In considering preferred temperature, however, we are concerned with the locomotory activity rather than total activity. Several attempts have been made to measure this (Bělehrádek, 1935). Crozier (1924 a) measured the speed of walking of a millipede, *Parajulus pennsylvanicus*, and found that it increased with rising temperature in much the same way as oxygen consumption does. It should be noted, however, that the measurements which were included in Crozier's graph were selected ones. Cases in which the animal did not walk at all, or stopped, or even hesitated, were not included, so that Crozier's figures are not suitable for our purpose. They represent the average activity of those animals which were active, not the average for all the animals, and it is the latter figure which we require.

Nicholson (1934) approached the question from another direction, estimating the proportion of a batch of animals which move at each temperature and leaving aside the question of their velocity. Working with a blow-fly, *Lucilia cuprina*, he

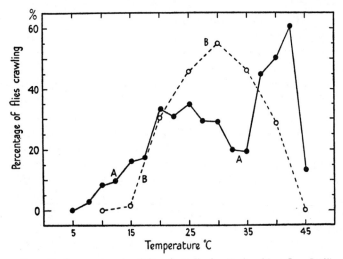

FIG. 98. Locomotory activity (crawling) of the blow-fly, *Lucilia cuprina*, in relation to temperature. For curve A the temperature was raised at about 7° C. per hour and the proportion of the animals crawling was assessed at intervals. For curve B the temperature was kept constant for 12 hours before the activity was assessed. (After Nicholson, 1934.)

erected three grades of activity—'rest', 'movement' (fidgeting, or activity other than locomotory activity), and 'crawling'— while the frequency of flying was estimated in a parallel series of experiments. In the first set of experiments Nicholson raised the temperature progressively at the rate of about 7° C. per hour. The change of temperature was thus not nearly as rapid as it could be when an animal walks along a temperature gradient in the laboratory, when a range of 20° or 30° C. may be covered in a minute or so. Consequently the results are not fully applicable to preferred temperature experiments, but they provide part of the essential background. When the average activity figures (proportion of animals 'crawling' at any instant) are plotted against temperature (Fig. 98 A) it is at once clear that the effect of temperature on locomotion is not a simple metabolic one. Activity increased from zero at 5° C. to a first maximum at 20° C., remained steady to 30° C., and then fell slightly to 35° C. before rising steeply to a second maximum at 42° C. Above that temperature there was a rapid fall in the frequency of crawling and lethal effects began to appear. In rather crude experiments Nicholson found that the preferred temperature range of the same species was about 20° or 25° to 35° C. That is to say, then, activity is fairly constant and high in the preferred temperature region, and falls just outside this range; in addition to this, activity is very high at temperatures near the thermal death-point. The high-temperature peak of activity can be regarded as an ortho-kinetic response to temperature, a response which would effectively keep the animal from staying long near the lethal temperatures in a temperature gradient; but there is no such peak of activity at low temperatures, so that if Nicholson's results were to be taken as giving a true indication of the behaviour in a temperature gradient, one would expect to find a minor aggregation at about 35° C. and most of the animals collected at about 5° C. and in a state of cold stupor. In fact, of course, the rate of change of temperature was too low to justify such an application of the results. They are valuable as an indication of the difference between metabolic and behaviour effects of temperature on locomotory activity, and, in combination with a second series of experiments by the same author, they show the importance of the time factor. The temperature-activity curve is quite unlike the usual temperature-oxygen consumption curve, or the temperature-velocity of walking curve of Crozier. If the temperature-velocity effect is presumed to be superposed, giving an increasing velocity of movement as the temperature rises, then the repelling effect at the high-temperature peak must be great. Nicholson's results for frequency of flight are similar to those for frequency of crawling, so that even in the absence of any other mechanism these blow-flies are amply protected by their behaviour from the danger of heat stroke in a temperature gradient. On the other hand, no evidence is available in these experiments of an ortho-kinetic protection against low temperatures.

In his second series of experiments Nicholson kept his flies for 12 hours at the constant temperature at which their activity was to be assessed. This ensured that the effects of the initial *change* of temperature would have worn off, and the effects of the *constant* temperature could thus be isolated and determined (Fig. 98 B, p. 208). At 45° C. all the flies were dead at the end of the preparatory period of adaptation. At the other temperatures no deaths occurred. The highest proportion of flies crawling occurred at 30° C., which is approximately the centre of the preferred temperature range, and the curve fell symmetrically about that point. A very similar curve was obtained for flight activity in similarly adapted animals. In these curves there is no sign of a peak of activity at about 40° C.; that is to say, the ortho-kinetic response is absent, so that we may presume that this response in the earlier experiments was a result of the recent *change* to a high temperature and not of the high temperature itself. [1]

The only work on the effects on activity of changes of temperature as rapid as those experienced in a temperature gradient has been done by Kennedy (1939 a). He used hoppers of the solitary phase of the desert locust (*Schistocerca gregaria*) in the Sudan and carried out experiments of a laboratory type in the field. The body temperature of one locust was taken by means of a thermo-couple and the activity of other similar locusts, undergoing similar changes in a cage, was recorded at the same time. The locusts were fully exposed to the sun for about half an hour, then shaded for a similar period, then exposed again, and so on. In the shade the body temperature varied from 26° to 31° C. on different days, and in the sun from 32° to 39° C. At the change-over, the first 1° C. change in body temperature occurred in 10 to 15 seconds and the whole change, amounting to 4° to 10° C., was completed within 5 minutes, faster than in any other experiments. The first effect of a rise of temperature was an almost instantaneous increase in locomotory activity, an increase which reached its peak at once but declined rapidly after about 5 minutes. On the other hand, a fall of temperature led to a slow increase of activity which reached its height in 5 to 10 minutes and was then maintained for 10 minutes or more. Kennedy's observations suggest that these particular experiments exaggerated the effects of a rise of temperature, so that the conclusions may boil down to this—that the locusts are stimulated to activity by a sudden drop in temperature. Such

[1] See note 31, Appendix.

a conclusion has a clear application to behaviour of locusts in the field. This work should be extended to other temperatures and to other animals.

We must thus distinguish between a metabolic effect of temperature on general metabolic activity and on speed of locomotion, a behaviour effect of temperature when the animal is fully adapted, and a second behaviour effect of *change* of temperature. It is the last of these which is likely to be the most important ortho-kinetic mechanism.

To summarize our knowledge of the mechanism of temperature aggregation, we may say that avoiding reactions (klinokinesis) have been observed in several cases and can lead to aggregation without immobilization. An ortho-kinetic reaction is theoretically possible, and this could be reinforced by a purely metabolic effect at the high temperature end. Little evidence is available to suggest that ortho-kinesis comes in as a protection against cold-stupor trapping, and usually only avoiding reactions appear to do that. Taxes have not been recorded in temperature gradients, except as responses to token stimuli.

Although the whole mechanism of reaction is not yet very clear, the fact that animals have preferred temperatures is clear enough. Most of the work done on preferred temperature has been concerned with the relation between the behaviour of the species investigated and their natural conditions of life. The differences between the methods used, however, make it difficult to compare the results of the various workers. Thus Thomsen & Thomsen (1937) tested maggots in the dung in which they feed, thus providing a fairly uniform relative humidity and natural conditions; but, as these authors point out, the animals were not only reacting to temperature itself but also to the chemical alterations in the dung caused by the temperature changes. Most of the other workers gave the animals neither food nor drink during an experiment. This does not provide quite such natural conditions in respect of other stimuli as might be thought, apart altogether from the possibility that the temperature reaction may change as starvation continues.

Thus it is a familiar fact that when a sample of air is warmed it becomes more effective as a drying agent. Similarly, if there is free communication throughout the air in a temperature gradient, that air will have a higher drying power and a lower relative humidity in the warm region than in the cold. Consequently, in the usual type of temperature gradient made of metal and glass and containing no humidity controlling material, there must be a humidity gradient too. Some animals do not alter their preferred temperature by reacting at the same time to this humidity gradient (Herter, 1925; Bodenheimer, 1931; Nieschulz, 1934), but some do (Lufti, 1936; Gunn, 1937; Gunn & Cosway, 1938).

Apart from graded factors other than temperature, the temperature itself may vary inside the apparatus as a result of changes in external temperatures. Thus in Herter's apparatus (1923 a, 1924), which has been widely used, there are gradients of temperature in a vertical direction and across the apparatus as well as along it. These are due to convection currents from the cool walls, and other complications, and the temperature situation is far too complicated to be properly shown by a few stationary thermometers. With such an arrangement, interpolation between thermometers is unsafe and comparison of results from different workers is unreliable. Thus Bodenheimer & Schenkin (1928) give 20·4° C. as the average preferred temperature of nymphs of the common house cricket, *Acheta domestica*, in Palestine, while Herter (1923 b, 1924) gives 26·5° C. for the same species in Germany. It is not possible to decide whether this discrepancy is due to the errors of the apparatus alone or to a real difference of behaviour in the two countries. Similar difficulties arise in comparing the results of Graber (1887), Bodenheimer & Schenkin (1928), H. Z. Klein (1933), Gunn (1934, 1935), and Gunn & Cosway (1938) for various species of domestic cockroaches. Further complications arise from individual differences between animals (Gunn & Cosway, 1938) and from the action of external factors which are difficult to investigate.

Nevertheless, valuable and proper comparisons can be made between different sets of experiments, using one piece of apparatus under standard conditions, provided the animals do not differ greatly in size. For example, using a modified form of his original apparatus, Herter (1934, 1935, 1936), and Herter & Sgonina (1938) have demonstrated differences between species of rodents in the floor temperatures preferred, and Lufti (1936) has done similar work on various species of reptiles. Similarly,

Krumbiegel (1932 *a*) has shown that geographical varieties of the beetle *Carabus nemoralis* have different preferred temperatures and that there is a correlation between these and the mean annual temperatures in the districts from which they come.

In order to overcome this complex temperature situation in the apparatus, two main precautions must be taken—to minimize convection currents from end to end by having the apparatus as shallow as possible, and to minimize transverse convection currents and other transverse temperature gradients by having the utmost thermal insulation, so that as far as possible the only flow of heat is from one end of the apparatus to the other (Nieschulz, 1933; Gunn, 1934). This arrangement has a further advantage in that it makes the fall of temperature per unit distance nearly uniform. When the temperature gradient is not uniform, it is to be expected that the results will be prejudiced in favour of any region where the gradient is least steep. The reason for this statement can be deduced by a theoretical comparison of the results of the usual type of control experiment, in which the temperature is uniform along the apparatus, and of an experiment with a hypothetical animal, having absolutely no preferred temperature, tested in a gradient of varying steepness (Deal, 1939).

Two examples may be taken of the relation between preferred temperature and natural conditions. Thomsen & Thomsen (1937) tested the larvae of various Diptera in their natural food (decaying faeces). The young maggots of the common house-fly (*Musca domestica*) had a preferred range of 30° to 37° C.; in separate experiments (Thomsen, 1938) it was shown that the larval development took place most quickly at 34° C., being slower at higher as well as lower temperatures. When pupation was about to begin, the preferred temperature fell to below 15° C. So low a temperature is not to be found in the dung-heap itself, and in fact the house-fly pupae are found in the earth near its outskirts. During the larval stage, when feeding is taking place, the animals are, in fact, found fairly near the surface, where the temperature is between 30° and 40° C.[1]

The larva of *Stomoxys calcitrans* (stable-fly), on the other hand, lives in the droppings of calves kept in stalls, where temperatures of 20° to 30° C. were recorded; the preferred temperature range of these maggots was 23° to 30° C. Presumably the

[1] See note 32, Appendix.

temperature reaction comes into action in this case if external causes raise the temperature of the faeces either locally or
generally.

Similar differences occur between the adults of these two
species (Nieschulz, 1934, 1935) (Figs. 94, p. 202, and 95, p. 203).
These differences are further related to the effects of temperature on activity, as determined by a technique of observation
when the temperature is raised fairly rapidly (5° to 10° C. per
hour). Thus heat paralysis begins to set in at 36° C. in *Fannia*

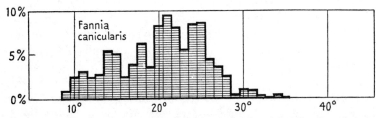

FIG. 99. Preferred temperature of the lesser house-fly, *Fannia canicularis*.
Compare Fig. 95 (*Musca*). *Fannia* appears earlier in the year than *Musca*.
(Nieschulz, *Zool. Anz.* 1935.)

canicularis, the lesser house-fly, and this temperature is found to
be outside the preferred range (Fig. 99). For *Musca domestica*, the
block diagram of preferred temperature (Fig. 95) has its peak at
40° C., while heat paralysis begins at 43·5° C. It is therefore not
surprising that this block diagram falls away very steeply from
40° to 43° C., and is markedly asymmetrical. On the other
hand, for *Stomoxys calcitrans* adults (Fig. 94) the figure has its
peak at 29° C. and extends to 36° C., while heat paralysis starts
at 43° C. The observed symmetry of this diagram is thus made
possible by the large difference between the preferred temperature and the heat-stroke temperature.

In connexion with the work on the preferred temperature of
the human body-louse, it is interesting to notice that Lloyd
(1919) has described experiments showing that more lice migrate
from a febrile man (trench fever) to his normal bedfellow than
from a normal man to a normal bedfellow; this response to the
body temperature of the host must have the effect of spreading
trench fever.

Most of the papers describing laboratory determinations of
preferred temperatures have been quoted above or by Herter

(1926, 1932). Field observations on temperature reactions of all sorts are sparsely but widely scattered through the literature. Two main research lines in this field may be expected to be fruitful in the near future: investigations of the mechanisms of locomotory reactions to temperature, and investigations of the relation between laboratory observations and eco-climates.

XV
GRAVITY REACTIONS IN GENERAL

THERE are two main kinds of orientation responses in which gravitational force is the stimulus, namely, *geo-taxis* proper and the maintenance of bodily equilibrium in the sense of the common phrase. In the former the animal moves along the lines of gravitational force, towards the centre of the earth in positive geo-taxis and away from it in negative geo-taxis. The latter, on the other hand, is usually a transverse orientation like the dorsal light reaction and need not involve locomotion at all. What one might call the 'ventral earth reaction' thus takes its place by the side of the dorsal light reaction in helping animals to maintain their *primary orientation*, in which locomotion is normally in a horizontal direction and the belly is downwards. In many animals this primary orientation forms a basis on which the other reactions are built up. In some animals, particularly aquatic ones, birds, and mammals, the normal position is an unstable or meta-stable one, so that active movements are required to maintain it (Chap. X); the maintenance of this normal equilibrium is partly controlled by gravity receptors.

These two types of orientation to gravity are closely analogous to two kinds of reaction to light. Geo-taxis corresponds to photo-taxis (Chaps. VI–VIII, XI, XII), and, like photo-taxis, it may be either positive or negative; the transverse gravity orientation corresponds to the dorsal light reaction (Chap. X), and in both cases there are a few species which normally keep the ventral side of the body uppermost instead of underneath. It has already been pointed out that the word *taxis* is to be restricted to those reactions in which the animal moves towards or away from the source of stimulation, so that it does not apply to the maintenance of normal equilibrium. This restriction is particularly valuable here, for it makes a distinction between the primary orientation, which is always in action except when it is temporarily interfered with by other reactions, and the locomotory reaction, which is itself characteristically temporary.

Gravity reactions are exhibited by animals moving about in three main kinds of situation—(*a*) on a surface, which need not be flat or horizontal; (*b*) in a simple fluid, namely air or water; and (*c*) in a fairly homogeneous soft medium, simulating a fluid, like sand or mud. The two kinds of gravity reaction are unevenly distributed in these three situations; the maintenance of equilibrium is very important for land animals which are raised on stilt-like legs, like the mammals and birds, and which are therefore unstable, and also for aquatic animals, which are frequently in meta-stable equilibrium.

Birds in flight use the semicircular canals as well as gravity receptors, both being located in the internal ear; in insects in flight, equilibrium seems to be mechanically stable (see p. 132) without any receptor action at all, except in the Diptera, in which the halteres act as equilibrium receptors (Fraenkel & Pringle, 1938).[1] Geo-taxis is to be found in all three situations. It is most strikingly shown by animals which live in sand or mud, but it is also to be observed amongst planktonic animals and terrestrial ones. In one set of cases of orientation on inclined planes, it is not yet agreed whether we are dealing with geo-taxis or with maintenance of equilibrium (see p. 235 *et seq.*). In the radially symmetrical planktonic coelenterates and ctenophores the axis of symmetry is normally kept vertical, so that movement is usually straight up or down. As soon as locomotion is superposed on to the primary orientation, therefore, these animals carry out negative or positive geo-taxis, so that their reactions can be classified under both headings (p. 228 *et seq.*).

There is one very important difference between light and gravity as stimuli. Light can vary, both in its intensity and its direction, and two lights differing in these respects can be used simultaneously. Gravity, on the other hand, is practically almost invariable, both in intensity and direction, and it cannot be presented in the form of two differently arranged stimuli. This statement is substantially accurate as far as animals in nature are concerned, but it requires a little modification for experimental conditions. These points can be made clearer in the light of a knowledge of the general structure of gravity receptors.

The typical gravity receptor is called a *statocyst*. In the past it has often been called an otocyst, simply because the statocysts of vertebrates are located in the ear. It consists essentially of a heavy solid object, the *statolith*, enclosed in a fluid in a chamber. The statolith either rests on or hangs from special sensitive cells, frequently supported by hair-like threads. When the statocyst is tipped over, the statolith comes to rest on different sense-cells, or it pulls on some of its suspending threads more and on others less than it did before. In static reactions (i.e. reactions initiated in the statocyst) this change in the distribution of the stimulation over the walls of the statocyst initiates suitable specific reflexes of limbs, &c., tending to correct the orientation and restore the statolith to the normal position.

Considering the case of a single statolith, for simplicity, we see that the actual stimulus is the pressure (or pull) of the statolith on the sensory cells. The size of this pressure can be varied only if the statocyst wall starts to move—or has an acceleration; the wall confers the acceleration on the statolith and exerts a force on the statolith in doing so. A very effective way of applying an acceleration to the statolith is to submit the animal to the so-called centrifugal force. In an animal which is able to resist being flung off by the rotation, the statolith is subjected to the combined force due to gravity and the rotation. This experi-ment has actually been carried out with the acoelous turbel-larian, *Convoluta roscoffensis* (Fraenkel, 1929 a), an animal which fits into our theoretical case in having only one statocyst. *Convoluta* is at times strongly positively geo-tactic, and then it crawls vertically downwards on a vertical wet glass plate (see pp. 231–2). Such a glass plate was mounted on the vertical axis of a centrifuge and rotated on this axis (Fig. 100). The tur-bellarians, under the simultaneous influence of the two forces, deviated from the vertical by an angle which corresponds with that calculated from the triangle-of-forces rule (Fig. 101). In this case, the centrifugal force combines with the force due to the weight of the statolith so that a *single resultant force* is actually applied by the statolith to the statocyst wall. That resultant can be calculated from the triangle-of-forces rule on purely mechanical principles, and it has nothing whatsoever to do with the activity of the nervous system or the shape of the receptor; it is a purely physical matter, and not a biological one like the triangle-of-forces orientation to light (see p. 142). That leads us to our first conclusion, namely, that in a single statocyst the stimulus can have only one direction at a time. With a com-

Fig. 100. Arrangement for testing the reactions of a positively geo-tactic animal, *Convoluta roscoffensis*, when acted upon by centrifugal force. The animals creep on a vertical glass plate mounted on a hand centrifuge. (Fraenkel, 1929*a*.)

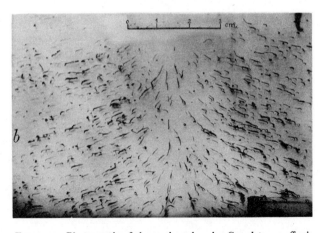

Fig. 101. Photograph of the paths taken by *Convoluta roscoffensis* under the action of centrifugal force. They orientate along the resultant of the gravitational and centrifugal forces. In the short period which elapsed between stopping the centrifuge and taking the photograph the head ends became directed vertically downwards. (Fraenkel, 1929*a*.)

pound eye stimulated by light there can be several stimuli, differing in intensity and direction, at one time, but however many and complex the forces applied to a statolith, the stimulation of the sense-cells is always single in direction and intensity. Consequently no question of telo-taxis can arise; the animal cannot inhibit one of two simultaneous stimuli on a single statocyst, for there never can be more than one.

It is theoretically possible to supply two different stimuli to the two members of a pair of statocysts. Kreidl (1892) substituted iron filings for the calcareous body in both of the statocysts of a crustacean. If a similar substitution could be carried out with one of the statocysts alone, leaving the normal statolith in the other, then a magnetic force could be applied to the one so that the stimuli applied to the two statocysts would differ in direction and intensity. By this means the test for telo-taxis could be applied. It has not been done so far, so that the usual classification of taxes cannot be made in the case of gravity reactions.

It has been pointed out above that the intensity of gravitational stimulation in nature can vary very little. The intensity of gravitational attraction changes according to the inverse square law, so that when one goes to the top of a mountain the statolith becomes slightly lighter; but such changes are so small that they can be left out of account in connexion with animal behaviour. Only accelerations, then, can change the intensity with which the statolith presses on the statocyst wall. Such accelerations undoubtedly occur in animals in nature, but it is difficult to study them under natural conditions. They have been studied experimentally, to some extent, especially in the vertebrates (Löwenstein, 1936).

One result of this relative invariability of the intensity and direction of the gravity stimulus is that geo-kinesis is unknown. For not only is the stimulus always directed so that the animal *can* always orientate without random movements as long as it is provided with direction receptors; but, in addition, the amount of vertical movement which an animal can make in a reasonably short time is too small to make any appreciable difference to the intensity of the stimulus, so that the gradient of stimulation, to which kineses are a response, is never available.

The gravity and acceleration receptors of vertebrates (statocysts and semicircular canals) can lead to two distinct kinds of reflex activity—tonic reflexes and dynamic (phasic) reflexes. Dynamic reflexes are active and often repetitive movements such as occur in all of the taxes so far considered; in tonic reflexes the part of the body concerned is kept in a certain constant position as long as the stimulus is unchanged. In the latter case, we have to deal with a steady unchanging state of contraction of the muscles concerned, a genuine condition of reflex tonus in the modern sense of the word. Much of the force of Loeb's tonus theory of animal orientation was derived from the few cases in which this tonic component is of considerable importance, as in the fishes. In some animals which move in a fluid medium— water or air—and in a few other cases (e.g. snails) the muscles which are responsible for steering the animal are partly or wholly different from those involved in causing forward movement. To use an analogy, these animals are propelled by oars and steered by a rudder, while perhaps the majority of animals are both propelled and steered by oars. The position of the rudder may be maintained by tonic contractions, while locomotion is effected by phasic ones. To take a well-known example, if a fish is rotated on its own axis and held in an abnormal position, shortly after the movement has ceased the dynamic reflexes are no longer observable; the fins are, however, held motionless in asymmetrical positions, such that if the animal were allowed to move forward these fins would rotate the animal into its normal position. In this case, then, a tonic component is concerned in the attainment of the transverse gravity orientation. Tonic reflexes also play a part in maintaining certain positions of the eyes during abnormal positions of the body, but these are not relevant to the present exposition. Tonic reflexes are also concerned in the posture reaction of *Spirographis* (Loeb, 1918) and in the geo-taxis of another polychaete, *Branchiomma* (v. Buddenbrock, 1913).

Let us now consider particular cases of transverse gravity orientation, leaving geo-taxis to the next chapter. There are a certain number of radially symmetrical planktonic animals (ctenophores and medusae) which normally keep the axis of symmetry vertical and which move up or down in a vertical direction. These cases could be considered under either heading; they are unusual in that the geo-taxis necessarily involves the maintenance of equilibrium instead of the two reactions being alternative. We shall consider them under geo-taxis.

The static reactions of the crayfish, *Potamobius astacus*, were first described by Kühn (1914) and have since become the standard example (Fig. 102). When a crayfish is swimming in the ordinary way, both the longitudinal and transverse axes are

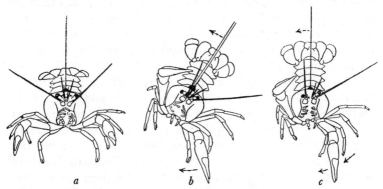

FIG. 102. The static reactions of the fresh-water crayfish, *Potamobius astacus*, *a*. Normal position. *b*. Inclined towards the left. The appendages on the lower side make rowing movements, those on the upper side are held up. *c*. After removal of the right statocyst a crayfish held in the normal position behaves as if it were inclined towards the left. (Kühn, 1914.)

kept horizontal, and the appendages are extended in a symmetrical way. If the animal is tilted over to the side, the appendages on the upper side are held up stiffly, while those on the lower side make repeated pushing or rowing movements which tend to return the animal to an even keel. Such movements have already been mentioned in connexion with the dorsal light reaction (pp.127–8). If one statocyst is removed by cutting off an antennule near the base, the crayfish makes these rowing movements even when it is on an even keel. The legs on the operated side are held up stiffly, while those on the side which still has a statocyst make the rowing movements, so that the animal behaves as if it were tilted over on to the intact side. This has been interpreted in the following way: each statocyst initiates reflex impulses to both sides of the body; those impulses which go to the same side of the body cause the rowing movements and those which go to the opposite side inhibit rowing movements.

Both of these sets of impulses are initiated in most positions of the statolith, including its position when the animal is on an even keel; but in that case the excitation and inhibition from the opposite sides are cancelled out. As the animal is tilted over, the statolith moves over a reflex map of a simple kind, so that both excitation and inhibition impulses from the lower statocyst increase in strength, while both sets of reflexes arising from the upper statocyst decrease in strength. The result is that only the reflexes due to the lower statocyst actually appear. When one statocyst is removed there are no impulses to balance those of the remaining organ, so that the animal behaves as if tilted on to the unoperated side.

The normal mechanism of the transverse orientation to gravity in this animal thus involves a balancing out of the excitation and inhibition from the two symmetrical receptors. It is, therefore, closely comparable to the mechanism of orientation to light in *Armadillidium* (p. 82). Since this gravity reaction is not a taxis, for it does not involve locomotion in the direction of the stimulus, we cannot say that the mechanism is tropotactic, but the similarity of mechanism is apparent. The striking fact is that in both cases each receptor organ initiates turning in one direction only, or has a one-way action. When the animal is symmetrically stimulated, the static reflexes do not come into action; they are initiated by asymmetry of stimulation, and they lead back to the symmetrical position.[1]

Another decapod crustacean, *Leander xiphias*—which has already been mentioned in connexion with the dorsal light reaction (p. 127)—gives a different result. According to v. Buddenbrock (1914) and Alverdes (1926) the static reactions are very similar to those of the crayfish (Fig. 58, IIa, p. 129); but when one antennule is removed, no change occurs in the reactions at all. One statocyst is sufficient to control the whole system of reflexes, and, unlike that of the crayfish, it must therefore have a two-way action. This is reminiscent of the photo-tropo-tactic mechanism in *Eristalis* and the photo-telo-taxis of the honey-bee, which can work when only one eye is in action. We therefore assume that there is a kind of neutral position for the statolith in the statocyst; when the statolith is in this position no reflexes are released from that organ. This neutral position can be compared with the fixation region in the eye of *Eristalis* or *Apis*. When the

[1] See note 34, Appendix.

statolith is shifted to one side, reflexes causing rotation in one
direction begin, and when the statolith is on the other side,
reflexes in the opposite direction are brought into action; we
therefore postulate a reflex map in the statocyst similar to that
in the two-way eye of *Eristalis*; but in this case only one stimulus
can possibly be presented at one time, so that lesser stimulation
of other parts of the receptor organ cannot upset the normal
orientation in the unilaterally amputated animal, as it does with
the light reactions of *Eristalis*. Bilaterally symmetrical stimulation of the receptors is thus not required for *Leander* to perform
its transverse gravity orientation perfectly.

It would appear from the older literature that most cases of
transverse gravity orientation are similar to that of the crayfish.
Rolling round the longitudinal axis has been reported to be the
result of operative removal of one of the two statocysts in the
planktonic heteropod mollusc, *Pterotrachea* (Tschachotin, 1908),
cephalopods (Delage, 1887; v. Uexküll, 1894), mysids (Bauer,
1908), and in many vertebrates. More recent investigations
have shown that while the immediate effect of the operation is
to cause rolling, in the course of time an operated individual
frequently regains the ability to orientate perfectly. According
to v. Buddenbrock (1914), after removal of the statocyst from
one of the two uropods, mysids still orientate perfectly. Friedrich
(1932) showed that, after the removal of one statocyst, *Pterotrachea* has a tonic bend of the whole body towards the operated
side, leading to rolling when the animal moves forwards; after
a mere 5 minutes, however, this symptom disappears and the
animal orientates perfectly, although it has only a single statocyst. A possible explanation of this recovery is put forward
towards the end of this chapter.

In the vertebrates equilibrium is controlled in a complex way,
but the main receptor concerned is almost always in the internal
ear (Fig. 103). The labyrinth is divided into two main parts, the
pars inferior, which is concerned with hearing alone (v. Frisch &
Stetter, 1932; v. Frisch, 1936), and the *pars superior*, which is
concerned with balance (Löwenstein, 1932, 1936). The *pars
superior* has, as far as we are concerned, two main parts: the
statocyst in the utriculus, which is broadly comparable with the
statocysts of invertebrates, and the semicircular canals, which
seem to have no parallel in other phyla. The semicircular

canals are bent tubes with an expanded chamber, the ampulla, at one end; the ampulla contains the receptor apparatus. The

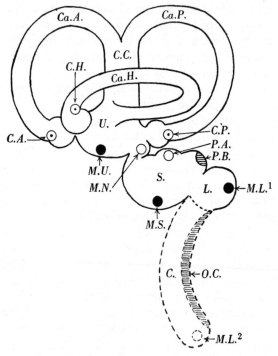

FIG. 103. Diagrammatic combination of the characters of the membraneous labyrinth in all vertebrate classes. *C.*, cochlea; *C.A.*, crista anterior; *C.H.*, crista horizontalis; *C.P.*, crista posterior; *C.C.*, crus commune; *Ca.A.*, canalis anterior; *Ca.H.*, canalis horizontalis; *Ca.P.*, canalis posterior; *L.* lagena; *M.L.*[1], macula lagenae in fishes and amphibia; *M.L.*[2], macula lagenae in reptiles and birds; *M.N.*, macula neglecta, papilla neglecta; *M.S.*, macula saculi; *M.U.*, macula utriculi; *O.C.*, organ of Corti; *P.A.*, papilla amphibiorum; *P.B.*, papilla basilaris; *S.*, sacculus; *U.*, utriculus; The ductus endolymphaticus is omitted for the sake of clarity. (Löwenstein, 1936.)

semicircular canals are not stimulated by being kept in abnormal positions, nor by linear movements or accelerations; only angular accelerations are effective. Broadly speaking, the statocysts respond to abnormal positions of the body by initiating and maintaining tonic reflexes, while the semicircular canals respond to angular accelerations by making the phasic responses of dynamic reflexes. This is not the whole story, however, and a recent review should be consulted for further information (Löwenstein, 1936). Strictly speaking, the semicircular canals are not gravity receptors at all. They are mentioned here for two reasons: their activities are closely connected with those of the statocysts, and a piece of work has been done on them which throws light on the process of recovery.

In early experiments on the equilibrium function of the labyrinth, the whole internal ear was removed on one side or it was put out of action by cutting the eighth cranial nerve. Such an operation results in asymmetries of both static and dynamic reflexes, in the assumption of asymmetrical postures and in abnormalities of locomotion. For example, fishes swim in a spiral course. This means that the normal maintenance of equilibrium involves a balancing of stimuli from the two sides of the body. An animal which is in unstable or meta-stable equilibrium must balance itself by thrusting out on both sides, but that is not what is meant here; the balance referred to is a balance of stimulation in the central nervous system which is converted into inactivity of the effectors as long as there is no excess on one side. This balance must occur, for if a fish with one labyrinth removed is held in its normal position, so that no correction is required, the fins are nevertheless held asymmetrically. There is no room here to go into detail about the functions of the various parts of the labyrinth and, since that is required if any further conclusions are to be drawn, we will leave the matter there except for one experiment. This has an important bearing on the question of recovery from unilateral extirpation of receptors.

If one labyrinth of a fish is removed, some of the symptoms just mentioned may be reduced or may even disappear within a few moments of the fish being put back into the water; others persist longer, but it frequently happens that, a couple of months after the operation, an operated fish cannot be distinguished from a normal one by ordinary inspection. If the fish has been blinded as well, recovery takes longer, but it still occurs. That is to say, when put to it, one labyrinth can do the work of two. The work of Löwenstein & Sand (1936) is very suggestive in this connexion.

These workers used an oscillograph to record the action currents in that branch of the eighth cranial nerve of the dogfish which supplies the horizontal semicircular canal. When the receptor was not stimulated there was nevertheless continuous activity in the nerve. Ipsi-lateral angular accelerations resulted in a considerable increase in these action currents, while contralateral ones led to a diminution *below the original level* (Fig. 104). If we may make so bold as to suppose that a similar both-ways effect is to be found generally in the fishes, then we can reach a valuable hypothesis. Generally speaking, in a recently operated fish the dynamic reflexes appear in response to rotations towards the intact side; rotations towards the operated side have no effect, or the responses are very weak. But we have seen that the animal is supplied with information about contra-lateral rotations, for the action currents *diminish* as a result of them. In the normal animal this diminution is probably of little importance, for the increase in activity on the other side is much greater; but for the operated animal the diminution in action currents is important. It seems that the animal ignores the diminution when it is intact, but when it has been operated on it takes more and more notice of it. As time goes on, assisted by the co-operation of the eyes and contact receptors, it slowly learns *how much* importance to attach to the reduction in action currents resulting from contra-lateral rotation (towards the operated side) and so is able to make the compensating movements efficiently. When this learning is complete, recovery is complete.

It is possible that we shall find a number of receptors which *can* have a two-way action but which have only a one-way action as long as both members of the pair are intact. There is a certain similarity between the case just described and the case of the eye of *Eristalis*. Each eye has a two-way action, but this is not discernible in the normal animal because appropriate parts of the two eyes work together and not antagonistically, just as in the dogfish. The reflex map is fully revealed only by unilateral extirpation. A clear distinction must be made between the two kinds of recovery in the two cases, however. The elimination of circus movements in *Notonecta* has been clearly shown to be due to sensory adaptation and to that alone (Clark, 1928); sensory adaptation does not occur in the semicircular

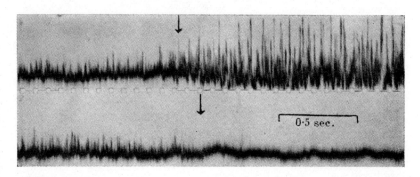

Fig. 104. Oscillograph records from the nerve-branch from the left horizontal ampulla of the dog-fish. Above: response to ipsi-lateral rotation (anti-clockwise). Below: response to contra-lateral rotation (clockwise). The arrows mark the beginning of rotation. Note the spontaneous discharge before rotation commences, and the decreased discharge on contra-lateral rotation. Records read from left to right. (Löwenstein & Sand, 1936.)

canals of the dogfish, and recovery is presumably due to the much more complex process of learning.

There are some reactions to gravity in which statocysts play no part (p. 235 et seq.). In other cases orientation is stable and the animal need make no effort to maintain it. In such cases there is, in fact, no reaction at all. Insects in flight have already been mentioned as an example of this phenomenon (pp. 132, 217). There are a few cases among the siphonophores (coelenterates) in which the animal is kept near the water surface and nearly erect by a gas-bladder at its upper end. The mechanically stable orientation of *Lysmata* has already been mentioned (p. 127). In some cases (e.g. *Chirocephalus*) reactions occur in spite of the fact that equilibrium is already stable.[1,2,3]

Most animals, if placed on their backs, will turn on to the ventral surface again as quickly as possible; these righting reactions are not always controlled by gravity, either through statocysts or through pressure on the animal's surface. They are often due to the absence of contact stimulation of the feet; they are dealt with in Chapter XVII under the heading of mechanical stimulation. The reactions which are properly called geo-taxis are dealt with in the following chapter.

[1] See note 35, Appendix.
[2] See note 36, Appendix.
[3] See note 37, Appendix.

XVI

GEO-TAXIS

THE general remarks about gravity receptors and about gravity reactions in general have mostly been made in the previous chapter. This chapter will be devoted to examples of geo-taxis involving statocysts and to certain similar reactions in which statocysts are not always involved and which are probably not geo-tactic at all.

Let us consider first a case which is most interesting not only because of its superficial simplicity but also because it does not have the normal reflex basis which we have usually postulated for these elementary reactions. The ctenophores cannot strictly be said to have reflexes at all, for they have no elaborate central nervous system. Among the ctenophores which have been shown to behave geo-tactically are *Beroë* and *Pleurobrachea*. *Beroë* has been studied mostly in the Mediterranean and it is not common in northern waters; *Pleurobrachea* is common in the northern Atlantic and in the North Sea. They are beautifully transparent globular or bell-shaped creatures with octa-radial symmetry. The single statocyst is situated at one pole of the animal and the locomotory organs—eight rows of comb plates—radiate from that pole like the lines of longitude on a terrestrial globe. The single statolith is suspended on four pillars formed of fused cilia. The nervous system consists mainly of a nerve-net, but there are also through-conduction nerves radiating from the vicinity of the statocyst.

In the normal position of these ctenophores, the axis of symmetry is vertical, the mouth is uppermost, and the eight rows of comb plates of cilia beat equally vigorously; consequently the animal moves vertically upwards. This negative geo-taxis can be reversed by suitable conditions, and then the animal swims vertically downwards. If one of these animals is gently tilted over, some of the rows of cilia either stop beating or beat less effectively; in a specimen which is geo-tactically negative, the cilia which remain active are those in the lower row and in a positive animal those in the upper rows (Fig. 105). It is easy to show that this asymmetry of activity is initiated by the statocyst. If a *Pleurobrachea* is fixed with the statocyst uppermost, and if the statolith is pushed to one side with a fine needle, all the rows of cilia stop beating except one or two. That one is either the row towards which the statolith has been pushed or the one diametrically opposite. If the statolith is removed altogether by sucking it out with a pipette, orientation to gravity ceases altogether (Verworn, 1891; Bauer, 1910). It is known that the only way in which these plates of cilia can be interfered with is in the direction of inhibition, causing them to cease to beat (Göthlin, 1920), and if the nervous system is put out of action they go on beating uniformly and continually. It therefore seems that when the statolith presses or pulls asymmetrically on its supporting pillars, the cilia are partly or completely inhibited except in one row (or two rows) on one side or the other. That row bears one of two relations to the asymmetrical action of the statolith, according to the sign of the reaction; it is either the row nearest to the statolith, in its displaced position, or it is the one farthest away.

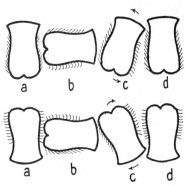

FIG. 105. Scheme of the geo-tactic responses of *Beroë*. *a*. Above: vertical position with the oral pole upwards. Below: vertical position with the oral pole downwards. After tilting (*b*) either the upper row of cilia stops beating and the lower row continues to beat (*b*, above) or the lower row stops beating and the upper one continues to beat (*b*, below). By this means *Beroë* is turned back into its vertical position (*c* and *d*). (Bauer, 1910.)

It is easy to see that the resulting asymmetrical action of the cilia would tend to restore the animal to its normal position. If the statolith could be kept in an asymmetrical position by artificial means, it seems likely that these ctenophores would loop the loop continually. In fact, when two neighbouring pillars, out of the four supporting the statocyst, were cut, four of the eight rows of cilia were disconnected and equilibrium could be maintained no longer. *Beroë* treated in this way tended to turn continuously towards the damaged side (Verworn, 1891).

In attempting to classify this geo-tactic reaction we immediately come up against the difficulty that a single statolith can never stimulate the statocyst in more than one direction or with more than one intensity at a time. It is therefore impossible to test for telo-taxis. It seems, however, that little difficulty arises if we call the reaction tropo-taxis. One supposes that the sensory epithelium inside the statocyst is divided into four regions, each corresponding to one ciliary pillar and two rows of ciliary comb-plates. The normal orientation results from the equal action of these four receptor-effector groups, each of which has only a one-way action. If one group is put out of action, permanent asymmetry and circus movements result; if the animal is tilted, the receptor asymmetry leads to asymmetry of effector action, and that to a return to the normal orientation. The whole thing is like tropo-taxis, but unfortunately it is clearly impossible to do the equivalent of the two-light experiment, for the statocyst combines all forces mechanically into one.

The classification of taxes was designed mainly for reactions to light, and there is frequently difficulty in adapting it to reactions to other stimuli. The classification is based largely upon the externally observable mechanisms or manœuvres of reactions, so the fact that these ctenophores have no central nervous system does not in itself cause difficulty; internal mechanisms must certainly be very different in the klino-tactic behaviour of maggots and of *Stentor* (Chap. VI), but we can classify these reactions together because of the common features of the manœuvres. The difficulty in this particular case is due to the peculiar structure and properties of statocysts which prevent the crucial tests from being carried out.

In the Scyphomedusae, instead of a single apical statocyst there are eight. They are arranged around the margin of the radially symmetrical animal. As in the ctenophores, in the normal position the axis of symmetry is kept vertical. Locomotion is due to muscular contractions of the umbrella of the medusa. If the medusa is tilted over, the lower side makes stronger contractions than the upper, tending to return the animal to its normal position (Fraenkel, 1925). The asymmetry of contraction is due to the fact that the uppermost statocyst releases into the nerve-net a greater excitation (probably impulses go on longer or occur more frequently) so that the neighbouring muscles do not relax fully after each stroke (Fig. 106). Consequently, at the following stroke these muscles cannot contract as much as the lower ones, so that less water is shifted by the upper part of the umbrella than by the lower. Extirpation of several neighbouring statocysts results in permanent disorientation. Here again, orientation is the result of the eight symmetrically (radially) placed parts of the receptor-effector system. Each sense organ has a one-way action, and if the state of equilibrium is upset, the upper and lower sides work against one another. The removal of several neighbouring statocysts destroys the balance, just as the blinding of one of a pair of one-way eyes does. We can therefore call the reaction geo-tropo-taxis.

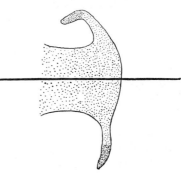

As far as bilaterally symmetrical animals are concerned, geo-tactic reactions are found almost entirely among animals living in water or in sand or mud. These reactions lead such animals towards or away from the surface of the water or other medium and, since the external conditions change sharply at boundaries of this kind, the reactions may be of great importance to the animals concerned.

FIG. 106. Geo-tactic response of a medusa, *Cotylorhiza tuberculata*. After being tilted so that the long axis is horizontal, at the end of a beat muscles on the lower side relax completely, while the muscles of the upper side only partly relax. During the following beat, the contraction of the lower side is consequently more effective than that of the upper side. This brings the medusa back into its normal position. (After Fraenkel, 1925.)

The small turbellarian, *Convoluta roscoffensis*, is only known to occur in small areas on the north coast of Brittany. At low water it is to be found on the surface of the sand and when the tide comes in it goes down into the sand. It has been shown by Gamble & Keeble (1903) and Fraenkel (1929 a) that these movements up and down are geo-tactic. If the animals are brought into the laboratory and put on sand in a dish they immediately disappear from the surface. If left alone for a few minutes, they crawl up out of the sand and up the walls of the dish until they reach the surface of the water. If the dish is tapped or shaken, they crawl or swim straight down again. Positive geo-taxis is thus released by mechanical stimulation, while if the animals are left alone they are negatively geo-tactic.

This can be shown more conveniently by allowing the animals
to crawl on a vertical glass plate which has been thinly covered
with a gelatine-sea-water mixture to give them a foothold.
They crawl downwards; if the plate is rotated in its own vertical
plane, the head end of each worm is turned sharply by just the
right amount and the rest of the body follows round this bend
as it reaches it, like a regiment of soldiers turning a street
corner (Fig. 107). If they are undisturbed for a few minutes,
the animals suddenly turn round and all start crawling up again.
When the plate is now very cautiously turned, avoiding all
mechanical shocks, again they compensate for the rotation and
keep going upwards.

Convoluta has a single statocyst, embedded in the brain and
inaccessible to operation. The whole worm can, however, be
cut into two parts and both parts will continue to crawl. Only
the part containing the statocyst continues to react geo-tactically.
It is reasonable to suppose that the statocyst is the receptor concerned in the reaction, but that cannot be demonstrated con-
clusively. Assuming that it is so, it is clear that the statocyst
must have a two-way action, like the single statocyst of the
ctenophores. The remarks made about the classification of the
reaction in that case apply equally well here.

The gravity reactions of the polychaetes *Arenicola grubei* and
Branchiomma vesiculosum, both of which live in sand, have been
studied by v. Buddenbrock (1912, 1913). The method of investigation is to put the animals into a glass-sided aquarium so
narrow that they can always be seen from one side or the other,
even though they are buried in sand. In such an aquarium both
Arenicola and *Branchiomma* always burrow vertically downwards.
Each time the aquarium is turned the worms respond by
making a compensating turn in their direction of burrowing.
In either animal, if one of the paired statocysts is removed, the
reaction is unaffected; if both are cut out the reaction is completely abolished. Each statocyst, therefore, has a two-way
action, but once more we cannot test for telo-taxis because we
cannot present a complex stimulus.

The details of the reactions are somewhat different in the
two cases. *Arenicola* burrows with its head and the statocysts lie
very near the head end. Consequently when the aquarium is
rotated all that *Arenicola* has to do is to move the head until the

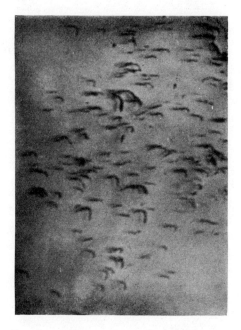

FIG. 107. The acoelous turbellarian, *Convoluta
roscoffensis*, creeping down a vertical glass plate.
The plate has just been turned by 90°, and
Convoluta turns by an angle of 90° to regain its
previous relation to gravity. (Fraenkel, 1929 *a*.)

statolith lies once more on the neutral position or fixation region and then to continue burrowing. *Branchiomma*, on the other hand, burrows with its posterior end (Fig. 108). When the aquarium is rotated, the head, which contains the statocysts, is not at first moved at all. The tail makes the compensating movements and, until the head reaches the part of the burrow

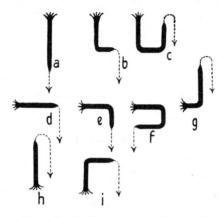

FIG. 108. Positive geo-taxis of the marine polychaete, *Branchiomma vesiculosum*. The worm is kept between two glass plates, the space between which is filled with sand. From each position the worm burrows vertically downwards with the tail end (broken lines). The worm is put into the various initial positions by turning the aquarium. (After V. Buddenbrock, 1913.)

where the tail was when the aquarium was rotated, the head remains disorientated (Fig. 108). This remote control of the tail implies a complex reflex map in the statocysts, comparable to that in the eye of *Eristalis*. The co-ordination involved appears to be of a high order, for the bend in the body moves forwards as the animal burrows, and a second re-orientation may occur before the animal has completed the first.

There are a number of animals which have statocysts in positions inaccessible to operations and which orientate geotactically in sand or mud; a clear demonstration of the function of these statocysts is not possible, but it is reasonable to argue by analogy and to suppose that the statocysts are involved in the geo-taxis. The razor-shell, *Solen*, inserts the foot vertically into the sand and burrows by characteristic movements (Fraenkel, 1927 c). The holothurian, *Synapta*, has five statocysts close to the nerve-ring; it burrows vertically, head first (v. Buddenbrock, 1912). The archaic brachiopod, *Lingula*, which lives in vertical holes in the floor of the Indian Ocean, has a pair of statocysts. In the isopod crustacean, *Cyathura carinata* (Langenbuch, 1928) and the larva of the dipteran, *Limnophila fuscipennis* (v. Studnitz, 1932), geo-tactic responses can be destroyed by extirpation of the statocyst, but statocysts are rare in the isopods and the insects.

In a number of cases, particularly in the non-burrowing gastropods, geo-tactic responses occur, but it is doubtful whether statocysts are involved or not. Thus *Littorina neritoides*, which lives on rocky coasts just above the water-line in the Mediterranean and near high-water mark in the British Isles, is strongly negatively geo-tactic (Fraenkel, 1927 b). The land pulmonates, *Helix* and *Limax*, show a strong negative geo-taxis when they are put under water. If placed on a seesaw they crawl up it and turn promptly when the beam tips under their weight (Baunacke, 1913). When on land they also react to gravity, but contact receptors and proprioceptors are supposed to be involved under these conditions (see pp. 235-43).

Attempts have been made to complicate the stimulus applied to the statocyst in various ways; the theoretical background of these has been dealt with on pp. 218-19. Kreidl (1892) replaced the statocysts of a prawn by iron filings and then subjected the animal to the action of a magnet. It reacted so as to orientate perpendicular to the resultant force acting on the artificial statoliths, a force which could be calculated from the magnitudes of the magnetic and gravitational effects by using the triangle-of-forces rule. Geo-tactic reactions have been tested by rotating the animal on a turn-table and so adding a centrifugal component to the force acting on the statolith. Using this method, Fraenkel (1927 b) showed that *Littorina* crawls towards the centre of a turn-table rotating in a horizontal plane. The same author (1929 a) tested *Convoluta* on a vertical plate which was rotated on a vertical axis (cf. p. 218).

There are a few cases known of animals which react geotactically to gravity without statocysts. As early as 1891 Loeb observed that the sea anemone, *Cerianthus*, does so in burrowing into the sand, and Fraenkel has observed a similar reaction in the sea-pen, *Pennatula* (unpublished observation). The most striking case of this sort is provided by *Paramecium*. A number of authors have worked on the negative geo-taxis of this animal. Some authors claim that the hind end is denser than the front, so that mechanically it is easier to swim up than down (e.g. Dembowsky, 1929), while others take the view that the inclusions of the food vacuoles act just like statoliths or like statolith-starch in the roots of plants. An experiment of Koehler's (1922) seems at first sight to support this view; he fed *Paramecium* with iron powder and then subjected the treated animals to the action of a magnet. It must be remembered, however, that the pull of the magnet on the iron filings in this experiment might easily be as great as the whole weight in water of the animal, so that the experiment is really very different from that of Kreidl (1892) with a prawn. The most recent work on this (Merton, 1935) should be consulted for further details of the controversy. It is worth while noticing, however, that *Paramecium* is sometimes geo-positive (Fox, 1925).

There is a large group of experiments on animals without statocysts which react to gravity when placed on an inclined plane. Mostly the animals react negatively and the reaction often lasts a long time. The echinoderms provide some of the best examples (Loeb, 1891); starfishes, sea-urchins, and holothurians crawl straight up the walls of an aquarium until they reach the water surface. Kalmus (1929) and Crozier (1935 *b*) have investigated this reaction particularly in *Asterina gibbosa*. *Asterina* creeps vertically upwards on a vertical surface; in dilute strychnine sulphate or when mechanically stimulated it creeps downwards. If a large cork float is attached to the animal, so that a strong upward pull is applied, it goes down in the negative condition and up in the positive. It is concluded from this that it is the pull of the weight of the animal on the attaching tube-feet which directs the movement. In the usual geo-negative condition, when placed on a horizontal rotating turn-table, *Asterina* creeps towards the axis of rotation. This again is consistent with the same explanation. We have no information about the mechanism connecting the tensions in the tube-feet and the precision of orientation. Examination of the details of the movements of the tube-feet might be helpful. Possibly they tend to maintain actively that angle with the under surface which is impressed on them in the first place by the applied force. That is probably too simple a mechanism, for starfishes often rotate slowly on the axis of symmetry during linear movement, but complex central control is unlikely to be in action in these 'reflex republics' (von Uexküll).

Since about 1925, Crozier and his collaborators have collected a large mass of data on what they call the 'geo-tropic' responses of various animals on an inclined plane. When the plane is sloped steeply (over 70° to the horizontal), on the whole these animals move straight up the steepest way; but when the plane is less steep they do not particularly favour the steepest path available. This is perhaps unexpected for a true geo-tactic reaction. If α is the inclination of the plane to the horizontal and θ is the angle between the animal's track and a horizontal line on the plane (Fig. 109), then the average angle θ at which white rats crawl is related to the angle α in the way shown in Fig. 110. The rats used by Crozier & Pincus (1926 b) were 13–14 days old, so that the eyes had not opened. Their results were not identical with those shown in Fig. 110, though similar; unfortunately in none of a long series of papers have they shown graphically the straightforward relation between α and θ, so Fig. 110 is taken from the work of another author. On the assumption that the component of the animal's weight (g) acting along the steepest line down the plane ($g \sin \alpha$) is the important component for orientation, they wrote: 'The extent of orientation θ is not directly proportional to the gravitational component in the creeping plane but to its logarithm. The graph in Fig. 2 shows that the equation

$$\theta = K.\log(\sin \alpha)$$

gives a satisfactory account of the observations. . . .'

Now it is conceivable that the component of gravity mentioned could be an important factor in orientation. The introduction of the logarithm, however, converts the equation into an empirical one with an appearance of having a sound theoretical basis. The Fig. 2 quoted (Crozier & Pincus, 1926 b) shows a straight line conforming reasonably well with the points, but it was later found that this line is always really sigmoid, as shown in Fig. 111. That is to say, K is not constant. It is therefore questionable if the continued use of this formula is justified, but Crozier & Pincus were still using it in 1936. In the meantime, a large number of papers had been published on this kind of orientation of rats, mice, slugs, snails, a caterpillar (*Malacosoma*), a beetle (*Tetraopes*), and a fiddler crab (*Uca*). A complicated theory of the proprioceptive basis of the reaction was elaborated

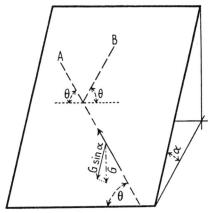

Fig. 109. Diagram showing terms used in description of orientation of rats creeping upon a wire grid inclined at α to the horizontal. The position of orientation is defined by the angle θ, the active component of gravity being *g* sin α. (Crozier & Pincus, 1926 *b*.)

and followed through various cross-breeding experiments with rats. No authors outside Crozier's own school seem to see eye to eye with him on the matter and the alternative accounts which have been put forward by Hunter (1927, 1931), Hovey (1928), Piéron (1928), v. Buddenbrock (1931 *b*), and Jäger (1932) have received rather cavalier treatment (Crozier & Stier, 1929; Crozier & Pincus, 1929, 1933, 1935; Crozier, 1935 *a*, *b*).

The aim of Crozier and his colleagues seems to be to express reactions in mathematical equations, but many zoologists find these equations difficult to interpret in zoological terms. The fact that some equation can be fitted to a particular kind of behaviour simply means that there is something orderly about the behaviour. That orderliness may be statistical rather than individual, so it need have no bearing on the old problem of free will. Free will is generally supposed to have considerable influence on birth-rates, but birth-rates can quite well be expressed in equations. No doubt a variety of different equations could be fitted to the data on the behaviour of animals on inclined planes; it does not follow that the separate terms in these equations would have any direct application to the component parts of the reactions concerned.

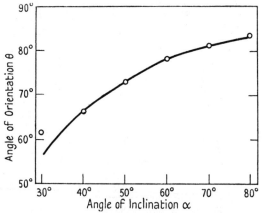

FIG. 110. The mean angle of upward orientation (θ) increases as the inclination of the creeping surface (α) becomes greater. Angle of orientation θ is plotted against angle of inclination α. (Hovey, 1928.)

The problem in this case is why certain animals creep at certain angles up inclined planes. The angle (θ) of crawling is not really constant for a particular inclination (α); indeed, the average values of θ given by the various authors are not central values of normal distributions. It seems that the animals studied are in some way hindered from crawling along a horizontal line across the inclined plane, and that the minimum deviation from this line increases as the tilt of the plane is increased. The explanation put forward by Crozier (1929) is that 'stable orientation on the inclined surface is achieved when the tension excitations due to the pull of the animal's weight are the same, within a threshold difference, on the legs of the two sides of the body'. In animals like snails, which have no legs, other suitable excitations are invoked. As long as the angle θ exceeds a certain threshold value for a particular value of α, creeping is unhindered (Fig. 112). Crozier & Pincus (1928) hold this view, although their Fig. 8, p. 799, indicates an avoidance of values of θ near 90°. The proper measure of the limitation of this orientation would therefore seem to be the *lowest* value of θ, averaged for different animals or sets of tests (Hunter, 1931).

The unpublished work of De Meillon is of some importance in

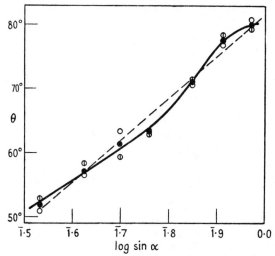

FIG. 111. Upward orientation on an inclined plane of two series of rats of a particular strain (open circles and circles with bar). The averages are represented by solid circles. Explanation of the terms in Fig. 109. (Crozier & Pincus, 1928.)

this connexion. He used a tick, *Rhipicephalus sanguineus*, which swells up enormously when it has had a meal of blood. Unfed ticks crawl over sloping or vertical surfaces freely in all directions. When fed, they always crawl upwards, and more steeply upwards the steeper the surface. Now the body of a gorged tick is greatly swollen *behind the region of the legs*, so that the centre of gravity of the whole animal is well behind the legs from which it is suspended. Consequently, when it walks on a steep incline the posterior weight swings the animal round passively and mechanically. It can be shown that the difference between fed and unfed ticks is simply due to this weight, for if a lump of plasticene is attached to the posterior end of an unfed specimen it behaves just like a gorged one. Imagine what would happen if a gorged tick tried to walk horizontally on a vertical surface. The twist due to weight of the blood would continually tend to push the lower legs forwards and pull the upper ones back. Each time a leg is lifted, the other legs on the same side would be subjected to a still greater strain and would tend to give way a little. The body would therefore swing round a little and the

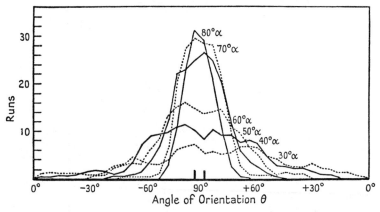

Fig. 112. The curves represent distribution of angles (θ) of creeping of rats, both to the left and to the right, at each of six angles of inclination of the creeping surface. Each curve was smoothed with a moving average of 3. Each approximates, roughly, to a normal frequency curve. (Hovey, 1928.)

leg would be put down in a position slightly different from that which it would have occupied if the body had not rotated. In the absence of an active correction of this slight swing of the body, it would actually be confirmed, so to speak, by the new position of the legs. This view, that the swinging round of the gorged tick on a vertical plane is mechanically imposed and is not a reaction of the animal at all, is in accordance with all the known facts. All the animal does is to walk. The orientation taken up by the body need be no more an organic reaction than is the orderly flight of a feathered arrow through the air. At the same time, it is still possible that the animal does respond to the asymmetrical tensions in the legs and does turn on to a vertical path more quickly than it is forced to do mechanically. The behaviour of the beetle, *Tetraopes tetraophthalmus* (Crozier & Stier, 1929), is similar to that of *Rhipicephalus*, but it cannot be described in purely mechanical terms. Forced slewing round, due to the posterior weight of the abdomen, is not the only factor involved, for θ still varies with α when the whole abdomen has been cut off.

There are a number of other cases in which the existence of a lower limit of θ cannot be explained on a purely mechanical basis. For example, when crawling on an inclined plane, rats are supported by four legs placed approximately at the corners of a rectangular body, so that the body would not be expected to swing round passively. Hunter (1931) pointed out that $g \sin \alpha$ is not the only important component of gravity in action. The other component perpendicular to the plane—$g \cos \alpha$—is the force holding the animal down on to the plane. When α is large so that $g \cos \alpha$ becomes small, if the animal is not to slip back it may have to supplement the frictional force (proportional to $g \cos \alpha$) by clinging on. Since the claws of rats are directed backwards, the action of clinging might easily lead to an active or passive orientation. Hovey (1928) observed that young rats going down often slip. This component of gravity may therefore be a factor in orientation.

Now the force $g \sin \alpha$ indicates the size of the force causing the animal to slide back. It can itself be resolved into two components parallel to the plane, one along the axis of the animal and one at right angles to it. The former—$g \sin \alpha \sin \theta$—measures the force against which the animal is working and which must be exceeded if it is to progress; the latter—$g \sin \alpha \cos \theta$—measures the force tending to roll the animal over on its side, for the feet are on the plane and the centre of gravity is above the plane. This rolling force increases when the plane is tilted more (α made larger) and when the path is directed *less* steeply up the plane (θ decreased). An increase of α can therefore be compensated by an increase of θ. Hunter (1931) interpreted the behaviour as a series of postural reflexes depending on these three forces, and he was able to show that rats on a horizontal surface respond in similar ways to forces applied by means of string.

On this basis the matter can be most vividly conceived by supposing oneself to be sprawled out on a steeply sloping roof, with the limbs stretched out as widely as possible. The body could then be subjected both to a rolling and to a pitching or somersaulting rotation compared with the primary orientation. This tilting would stimulate the statocysts and would also tend to throw the weight on to those limbs farthest down the plane and so stimulate the proprioceptors differentially. The tendency to roll could be reduced by orientating more nearly up and down the plane instead of across it, but this would increase the pitching. In such a position, animals having only proprioceptors would receive the information required for assuming a different orientation, and those having statocysts as well would receive the information from two distinct sources. The addition of weights to the body would affect the proprioceptors and might also tend to slew the body round mechanically (see pp. 239–41).

The question now arises as to what sort of compromise occurs between rolling and pitching. Most of the locomotory reflexes of animals are symmetrical, making allowance for phase differences in limb movements. Movement horizontally across the slope of an inclined plane involves asymmetrical complications in such reflexes. On the other hand, movement directly up the slope seems to present little difficulty to most animals, if there is good foothold. It is therefore not unexpected that a line involving no more than a certain degree of rolling is adopted. Pitching is avoided little if at all, as long as the tendency to roll is below a certain limit, and crawling appears to be otherwise unlimited in direction. If the animals are started off in a horizontal direction, they turn until they have passed the lower limiting value of θ, and they may or may not turn after that. If orientation angles are measured as soon as the animal crawls straight, then values clustering near the lower limit of θ may be expected. This is the kind of result obtained by Crozier and his pupils. If orientation is measured later on, values clustering round $\theta = 90°$ are to be expected, as found by Hovey (1928) and shown in Fig. 112, p. 240. When orientation is reached, the rolling component $g \sin \alpha \cos \theta$ is not constant for all values of α, either when only threshold values of θ or when all values of θ are counted, and it therefore seems that analysis of the situation is as yet incomplete.

We therefore reach the conclusion that the orientation of these animals on inclined planes is essentially due to postural reflexes. The transverse axis is not allowed to tilt by more than a certain amount, but the situation is complicated by activities other than this. This is the view adopted by v. Buddenbrock (1931 b, 1937). The animal cannot maintain its primary orientation on an inclined plane, but the greater part of the side to side symmetry is attained at the expense of fore-and-aft tilting. This posture is often complicated by forward movement. In the experiments animals which do not walk are not counted.

The principal alternative view is that the reaction is geotactic. On this view, as the plane is tilted the effectiveness of gravitational stimulation straight down the plane ($g \sin \alpha$) increases, and so the accuracy of orientation up the plane increases correspondingly. It is not easy to make a clear distinction between these two views, except by reference to cases of undoubted geo-taxis. It has been shown by Piéron (1928) for *Limax* under water and by Jäger (1932) for *Helix* under water, for *Arenicola marina* and for the turbellarian *Otoplana* that the steepest path is adopted even when the slope is not very steep. All these animals have statocysts, and proprioceptive effects must be small because of the support provided by the water. For the same reason there can be little tendency to roll over down the plane. It is hardly likely that the proprioceptors of animals in air are not sufficiently sensitive to enable a similar direct orientation up the steepest path to be made, for they are in constant use, making the most refined adjustments. In any case, rats and mice have statocysts as well so that their reactions at any rate are unlikely to be purely proprioceptive. If the reaction is really geo-tactic, therefore, some explanation is required for its inaccuracy.

XVII
MECHANICAL STIMULATION

O NE of the principal common characteristics of living organisms is that they are sensitive and responsive to mechanical stimulation. We include under the heading of mechanical stimuli those forces which deform or tend to deform organisms or their parts. Mechano-receptors are of several sorts, which are so distinct in their specific functions that we can subjectively distinguish a number of kinds of mechanical stimulation, each one having a name in ordinary language. There are thus light contact (touch), steady pressure, slowly alternating pressure (vibrations), and rapidly alternating pressure (sound); the mechanical force of gravity produces stimulation of contact receptors, pressure receptors, proprioceptors, and, most particularly, the special gravity receptors called statocysts. We are concerned with all these in this book only in so far as they affect the orientation of animals.

CONTACT

All animals moving about on solid surfaces normally maintain such a constant relation to the surface that it enables us to define a morphological side of the body; that side of the body which is kept nearest the solid surface is called the ventral surface. If almost any animal is turned over on to its back, it returns to its normal position by means of a characteristic reaction, commonly called a 'righting reflex'. This term is rather misleading, because a group or chain of reflexes is usually involved.

There are many animals which can walk about on a vertical surface or on the under side of a horizontal one, as flies do. Some animals will remain lying on their backs if some solid object is in contact with the feet, even if that object is movable. Clearly, therefore, it is not the absolute position of the body in space which initiates righting movements, and neither is it pressure due to the weight of the body on the dorsal surface. It has been shown for a number of animals that it is the absence of contact stimulation of the feet or of the ventral surface of the body which initiates the reaction (e.g. Weber, 1926, for snails; Fraenkel, 1928, for starfish; Hoffmann, 1933, for cockroaches).

The normal position of an animal on a surface is orientated with respect to the surface and we may regard righting movements as orientation reactions. Righting reactions initiated by contact are just as important to some animals as dorsal light and ventral gravity reactions are to others. When we try to classify the mechanism of the reaction, however, we find that all those classes which depend on the direction of the stimulus—like light and gravity—are ruled out. Similarly, it is only by distorting the facts that we could speak of a gradient of intensity of contact stimulation. When righting depends on contact, it proceeds actively or violently until the appropriate parts have recovered contact. There seems to be no evidence that contact is regained in the shortest possible way, or that it is guided at all.

When the animal has regained its primary orientation it brings the activity of righting to an end, but it is in a position to react to other stimuli by locomotor activity. There is a case, however, in which normal stimulation of the receptors of the legs by contact is sufficient to cause immobility. According to Hoffmann (1936), the flour-moth, *Ephestia kühniella*, often gets into this condition of reflex immobility. Such a reaction must be rare in animals, though the activity of *flying* in insects is certainly inhibited by contact stimulation of the feet (Fraenkel, 1932 *a*).

There are, on the other hand, plenty of cases in which contact on parts of the body other than the feet has an inhibitory effect on locomotion; in these cases the feet must be in contact with a solid as well. There are many animals which, during certain times of the day or certain seasons of the year, are only to be found in holes and crevices. In such places many parts of the surface of the body can be in contact with surrounding solid material. It seems to have been Loeb (1890) who first recognized the active measures taken by some animals to increase the amount of contact stimulation.

Crevices are generally places where the light intensity is low. Loeb (1890) showed that light is not necessarily the effective stimulus, for the noctuid moth, *Amphipyra*, crept into the small space between glass plates where the light intensity was not low at all. He mentioned other examples (Loeb, 1918) such as *Nereis* crawling into glass tubes (Maxwell, 1897). Cockroaches, bed-bugs, and scorpions react similarly. He called this type of reaction *stereotropism*. The prefix *stereo-* (στερεός, solid) appears to have been chosen to describe the fact that contact stimulation arises from a three-dimensional body instead of from one direction only. Loeb used the term *tropism* for a particular mechanism of orientation and also as a general name for orientation reactions, as if they all had the same mechanism. He never seems to have justified its use in describing the mechanism of stereotropism. The term *thigmotropismus*, which had already been used by Verworn (1889) for certain reactions of Protozoa, later came to be used synonymously. The prefix *thigmo-* (θίγμα, touch) is obviously preferable to *stereo-*, but neither *tropism* nor *taxis* can be justified, for the attainment of the final position is not directed at all, at any rate as far as contact stimuli are concerned. The animal moves about at random until it finds the crevice, and then it keeps still. This can quite properly be called *low thigmo-kinesis*, since a low intensity of stimulation by contact leads to high activity. It differs from chemo-, thermo-, and photo-kinesis in that the animal is not under the influence of the stimulus in question— except for the almost perpetual contact of the feet—until it finds the crevice in which it settles down.[1, 2]

In default of other suitable sources of contact stimulation, animals which show low thigmo-kinesis often aggregate together and gain contact with each other. This has been observed in many species of worms, particularly nemertines, which are often found entangled together in clumps of hundreds of specimens, even in their natural habitat in the sea (literature in Krumbiegel, 1932 *b*). Sometimes a single individual does the same kind of thing, coiling itself up so that it is in contact with itself at many points. This habit of the worm, *Gordius*, is responsible for the generic name (cf. Gordian knot). In dealing with these phenomena Krumbiegel (1932 *b*) has put forward a nomenclature in which *somato-thigmo-taxis*—reactions to the animal body—is distinguished from *topo-thigmo-taxis* or reactions to inanimate objects. Somato-thigmo-taxis is divided into three groups with prefixes *idio-*, *homoio-*, and *hetero-* to distinguish cases in which the animal reacts to its own body, to other members of the same species, and to members of other species respectively. The nomenclature seems superfluous unless it can

[1] See note 38, Appendix.
[2] See note 39, Appendix.

be shown that there are really four different reactions—otherwise one would have to give a new name whenever the animal was found to react to a new substance, like seaweed, stone, iron, and so on. In any case, it is by no means certain that the coiling of an animal on itself is the same kind of reaction at all.

It has already been pointed out that ortho-kinesis is an inefficient kind of reaction. Up to the time when the animal gains the crevice, contact stimulation does not guide it. Now crevices usually have dark entrances and so light can act as a token stimulus in guiding the animal, and in fact low thigmo-kinesis is almost always associated with negative photo-taxis, though *Amphipyra* is exceptional in this respect. Indeed, contact itself would seem to be a token stimulus for it does not seem to confer any direct benefit. Once an animal is in a crevice it is better off because it is sheltered from other forms of mechanical stimulation, such as currents of air or water and the violence of its enemies, and from harmful physical factors like temperature. It is quite likely that these are the selecting factors which have resulted in the evolution of thigmo-kinesis.

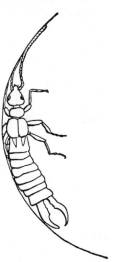

FIG. 113. The earwig, *Forficula*, coming to rest in a petri-dish, closely pressed into the corner where the bottom joins the walls. (From Wigglesworth, 1939, after Weyrauch, 1929.)

When the crevice has been reached, the animal commonly presses its body firmly against the available surfaces. Thus the earwig, *Forficula*, when in a petri-dish, presses its body against the wall so that it becomes curved to fit the wall (Fig. 113) (Weyrauch, 1929). In a similar situation scorpions even turn on to their sides so that the dorsal surface comes into contact with the wall (Fraenkel, unpublished). Moore (1929) has shown that the salamander, *Triturus torosus*, when stroked along the side of the body, rolls over so as to bring the dorsal surface into contact with the source of stimulation. When the tail is stroked, it bends round to the stimulated side. This has the effect of bringing the body into increased contact with surrounding objects (Fig. 114, p. 248). These reactions of the salamander are simple reflexes, for they appear regularly in the decapitated animal and even in the isolated tail.

A somewhat similar mechanism seems to underlie some contact reactions of certain millipedes, mealworms, and young mice and rats (Crozier & Moore, 1923; Crozier, 1924 b; Crozier & Pincus, 1926 a). These animals will creep along the base of a wall, rather than out in the open where they cannot get lateral contact. These workers used for the arthropods thick triangular glass plates, the edges of which acted as the walls;

FIG. 114. Effect of contact stimulation of the left side of the salamander, *Triturus torosus*. The body rotates on its longitudinal axis so as to bring the dorsal surface into contact with the stimulating object. The body is also bent to the left. (After Moore, 1929.)

boxes were used for the rodents. If a mealworm has been creeping along the edge of the plate and it reaches the end, or if the plate is suddenly removed, the animal turns towards the side which was previously in contact (Fig. 115). If it has been creeping in the narrow channel between two symmetrically placed plates, on emergence it crawls on straight ahead (Fig. 116, p. 250). If the plates are not symmetrically placed, the mealworm on emergence turns towards the side on which the contact area is more extensive. Rather similar reactions were performed by the other animals mentioned. This behaviour is interpreted by Crozier in terms of the tropism theory; unilateral contact stimulation leads to bending the body towards the stimulated side. This becomes apparent only when contact has at least partly ceased, for before that the presence of the solid wall prevents turning towards the stimulated side. 'The balanced action of equal zones of contact on either side results in the pursuit of a straight course.' We might reasonably apply the term tropo-taxis to this case and, for reasons given above (pp. 10, 245–6), we prefer to call it thigmo-taxis rather than stereotropism.

A clear distinction must be made between thigmo-taxis and low thigmo-kinesis; the former guides the animal during loco-motion, while the latter does not guide at all but determines where the animal shall stop. In thigmo-taxis the animal may actually leave a crevice, while in low thigmo-kinesis the essence of the reaction is that the animal remains in the crevice.

It was pointed out on p. 245 that this trapping effect of crevices is in action only under certain conditions. If it were

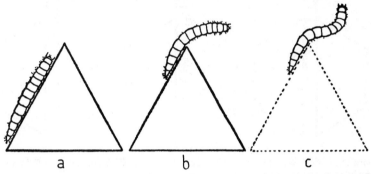

a   b   c

FIG. 115. 'Stereotropism' of *Tenebrio* larva. *a, b, c*, successive positions. After removal of the source of contact a 'homostrophic' reflex is released (i.e. the head end is placed parallel to the posterior end). (Crozier, 1924 *b*.)

always in action the animal would never be able to move about. Most reactions other than primary orientations are of this sort, dependent on other internal factors or physical factors in the environment. On the whole, however, animals which show low thigmo-kinesis during the appropriate periods also behave thigmo-tactically during locomotion, so that some reaction towards contact occurs in both periods. Rough handling leads to violent locomotion without thigmo-taxis (Crozier, 1924*b*), but it is just the sort of stimulus which is likely to lead, through other reactions, to concealment in crevices. Thus although there are points of similarity in the two reactions, they are easily dis-tinguishable.

RHEO-TAXIS

So far we have been dealing with contact between the animal and a solid surface; for small animals, such as insects, contact with a liquid surface may produce the same sort of results.

The fluid properties of water and of air make possible a kind of reaction which is impossible with solids—a reaction to flow. In swift streams many animals set the body in line with the flow of water and face upstream. This reaction to flow is called *rheo-taxis* (ῥέω, flow). Dewitz (1899) showed that such behaviour is very widely distributed among animals; it occurs in

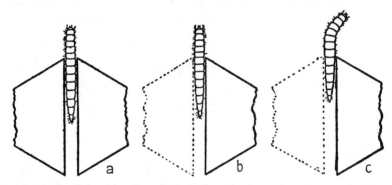

FIG. 116.   Balanced action of equal bilateral contact shown in pursuit of a straight course (*a*). Removal of contact on one side (*b*) is immediately followed by bending (*c*). (Crozier, 1924 *b*.)

planarians, gastropods, crustaceans, and fishes, and in the nymphs, larvae, and imagines of insects—in fact in practically all the active inhabitants of streams.

The way fishes lie with the head pointing upstream is familiar to anglers; it has been studied scientifically by a number of workers. It was naturally assumed at first that the fish orientate with the aid of mechanical stimuli produced by the flow of water. It is not immediately clear, however, how a fish out of contact with the ground could get any guidance at all through such stimuli. Indeed, as early as 1904, Lyon showed that *Fundulus* and other fishes, when not in contact with the ground, are guided solely by optical stimuli and not mechanically at all. He enclosed the fishes in a bottle which could be moved about freely on the end of a rope. If the bottle was kept still with respect to the banks, the fish swam about freely in all directions; when it was allowed to drift with the stream, they orientated up-stream; when it was towed upstream, they orientated down-stream. Under these conditions they could react only to optical stimuli. Blinded fish released in the stream were swept passively down until they touched bottom; they were then able to orientate and did so with the aid of contact stimuli from the solid ground.

The fish were also tested in an aquarium. A long strip of white paper with bold vertical black stripes painted on it could be moved horizontally along each side of the tank. When the strips were moved along together the fish swam along with them; it has already been pointed out that this reaction is very similar to the compensation reaction of an insect on a rotating turn-table and is in fact an optical fixation reaction (pp. 117, 257–8). Removal of both eyes abolished the reaction, but unilateral blinding had no effect (Lyon, 1909). Compass reactions and telotaxis had not been discovered at that time, but it seemed to Lyon that it was 'impossible to bring these observations into accord with the tropism scheme of one-sided response to one-sided stimulation'.

Lyon's results have been contested, particularly in the light of Hofer's (1908) claim that the lateral line is a receptor for currents. It has been repeatedly stated that fish out of contact with solids could orientate by means of the friction of the water as well as through optical stimuli (e.g. Steinmann, 1914). Analysis was made unnecessarily complicated by the use of currents in circular dishes, which can produce reactions mediated by the semicircular canals (Gray, 1937). It seems of little use to describe further this period of confusion. Dykgraaf (1933), in a careful investigation, confirmed Lyon's results in all essential respects, and extended them considerably.

Dykgraaf (1933) used the minnow, *Phoxinus laevis*, and made optical reactions impossible by blinding all the experimental animals. In addition to large currents which could carry the fish along, he used small currents produced with a pipette. He found that blind fish out of contact with solids could not orientate in water moving along bodily. If they touched the bottom, the frictional stimulation enabled them to orientate. When a sheet of muslin was dragged along the bottom of an aquarium, so as to simulate the relative motion of the bottom in a stream, if the blind fish came into contact with the muslin it swam jerkily with the muslin. It tended to keep a constant position with respect to a point on the muslin, just as a fish keeps its place relative to the bottom of a stream, so that it swam through the stationary water.

These reactions of minnows were unaffected by elimination of the lateral line system. But we see that orientation in a stream is already doubly assured by optical and tactile responses. May it not be further supported through the activity of the lateral line system? It has been shown that the semicircular canals are unaffected by linear movements or accelerations (Löwenstein, 1932), so only lateral line reactions are left. Dykgraaf (1933) made suitable tests on the minnow. He found that squirting water on to the side of the fish with a pipette led to turning towards the pipette, and this reaction no longer occurred if the lateral line was eliminated. It has since been shown by means of the cathode-ray oscillograph that the lateral line initiates action currents in its afferent nerves in response to changes of pressure, even if the changes are sufficiently rapidly repeated to be recognized by us as sounds (Sand, 1937). When a fish is drifting blindly with a current there can hardly be maintained differences of pressure on its two sides, though the chorus of pressure changes may alter as the animal drifts past obstructions in the stream bed. That side of the matter is considered below under the heading of indirect contact, but it is not relevant to experiments in smooth channels. On the other hand, if the fish comes into contact with the even stream bed as it drifts along, it is not immediately clear whether or not the lateral line could come into action. If the frictional contact acting on a fish drifting athwart the stream slows it down at all, then the pressure on the upstream side would be greater than that on the downstream side and the lateral line could come into action. If the direction of the friction itself is reacted to, forward swimming will only lead to a cessation of friction if the fish turns and swims directly into the stream. Any other direction would still leave a transverse component of the friction. That is to say, it is conceivable that suitable receptors could lead to orientation with the aid of friction alone, while the lateral line would only come into action in a smooth channel if the friction slowed the fish down appreciably. In fact Dykgraaf found that blind fish orientated equally well to contact stimuli whether the lateral line system had been eliminated or not. It seems that the direct contact reaction is so efficient that any lateral line reaction which might occur is not noticeable. The complementary experiment of putting out of action both the eyes and the contact receptors would be very difficult and has not been done, so that we can postulate a possible action of the lateral line in detecting gross pressure differences and so leading to orientation, but we can produce only indirect evidence of its possibility.

It seems, therefore, that the so-called rheo-taxis of a fish in a stream may have three components: as long as it can see, it can fix surrounding objects optically; in contact with the ground it can orientate truly rheo-tactically with the aid of mechanical stimuli; in a smooth channel the lateral line might come into action if the fish is already slowed down by friction, while in irregular channels containing obstructions it might use indirect contact through the same receptors. This, too, could properly be regarded as rheo-taxis.

As for the mechanism of these two possible varieties of rheo-taxis, orientation is so rapid and direct that klino-taxis is unlikely to be involved. It is easy to imagine a mechanism in which inequality of bilateral stimulation leads to a direct turn, both for contact receptors and for the lateral line. If the lateral line of one side is eliminated, stimulation with a stream of water from a pipette causes turning to the intact side but not to the operated one, so that tropo-taxis is almost certainly the mechanism for this system of receptors. On the other hand, complete unilateral removal of the contact receptors, which are usually free nerve-endings, must be practically impossible; telo-taxis mediated by these receptors seems unlikely, so we are driven to think that the contact reaction is also tropo-tactic in nature.

In the invertebrates, as far as position maintenance out of contact is concerned, the behaviour always depends on optic fixation, as it does in fishes. Hadley (1906) demonstrated this for the lobster, *Homarus americanus*, and Schulz (1931) for *Notonecta* by means of experiments very similar to those of Lyon. Fraenkel (unpublished) reached the same conclusion for certain mysids. If the water in a circular dish is swirled round, they head into the current. If they are tested in a dark-room with a solitary light, and if the light is moved round with the water, the mysids no longer show any reaction to the current.

In invertebrates which move about on the bottoms of streams, like *Asellus*, *Gammarus*, pulmonate molluscs, caddis worms, and so on, the tendency to head upstream is well known. The rheotaxis of such bottom-living animals has been best worked out for planarians. Pond species react poorly, and stream species vary according to the internal and external conditions as well as by species. *Planaria alpina*, which is generally considered to be a cold-water relic of glacial times in Europe, is positively rheotactic when the temperature is over 12° C. (Beauchamp, 1937). This results in a migration to the upper and usually cooler waters of the stream. Below 12° C. the condition of sexual maturity also leads to a rheo-tactic migration to the headwaters, where breeding takes place. Here the planarians are crowded and relatively starved after a time. Starvation results in the appearance of negative rheo-taxis, as long as the temperature is not above 12° C., and then the downstream migration begins (Beauchamp, 1933, 1937).

Planaria alpina, like the gastropod molluscs, lays down a carpet of mucus and moves over it by means of pedal waves. This slime provides a continuous anchorage during movement, and it is interposed like a cushion between the ground and the animal's contact receptors. It is, therefore, not surprising to find that it is not the receptors in contact with the ground but special current-receptors which are responsible for the rheotactic reaction. For that reason it is possible to investigate the reaction by means of small currents squirted from pipettes. This method was used by Doflein (1925) and Koehler (1932), whose results we give below. It is a useful extension of experiments with water rotating in a dish or flowing down a trough or a glass plate, because a greater variety of analytical experiments can be made with its aid.

If a current from a pipette is directed on a positively rheotactic specimen, the animal turns towards the pipette and follows its subsequent movements. If the current is a very fine one, it leads to orientation only if it plays on the anterior end of the animal (Fig. 117). It looks as if the receptors are localized anteriorly, but they are not; if the anterior end is cut off and the tests carried out before regeneration can occur, rheo-taxis still occurs as before. Moreover, stimulation of the *new* anterior end alone leads to a response. The receptors occur all over the surface, but they seem to be graded in sensitivity or in frequency from before backwards.

In these tactic responses the kinetic and orientation components can be separated. If the stimulus of a current is directed on to a resting specimen, it is first excited to activity and then it orientates into the current. *Rheo-kinesis*, unlike rheo-taxis, is largely a function of the anterior margin of the animal, including the tentacles, and of the brain. If either of these is removed,

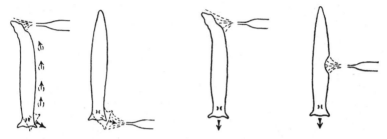

FIG. 117. Effect of stimulating a fresh-water planarian, *Planaria alpina*, with a thin jet of water applied locally on different regions of the body. When the head is stimulated, the planarian immediately becomes positively rheo-tactic; stimulation of the side or the tail end has no effect, but after some time, currents set up in the vessel stimulate the head. (After Koehler, 1932.)

or both of them, the animal is much less active and is difficult to excite with a current. It will sometimes orientate into a current without further locomotion.

As for the mechanism of orientation, it is difficult to imagine sense organs suitable for telo-taxis; the sense organs do not have any elaborate accessory apparatus and they are probably of a very simple type, like free nerve-endings in the skin. Turning into the current is very obviously direct, and turning ceases when the animal is orientated and so symmetrically stimulated, so we assume that the mechanism is tropo-tactic. Unilateral removal of sense organs is impossible because of their diffuse arrangement. It is possible, however, to carry out a test corresponding to the two-light experiment. Two identical pipette currents are directed on to the animal, one on either side (Fig. 118, p. 256). If the two currents are in line, but going in opposite directions of course, the animal crosses this line at right angles and so orientates between the two sources of stimulation. If the two currents make a right angle, *Planaria alpina* goes half-way between them (Fig. 119). This behaviour justifies us in naming the reaction *rheo-tropo-taxis*. In addition, if the intensity of stimulation is suddenly reduced, the animal tends to wave its anterior end about, and it is possible that this is a klino-tactic response.[1]

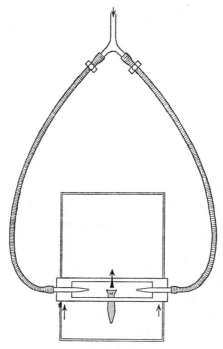

FIG. 118. Arrangement for testing the effect of two currents stimulating a planarian simultaneously. (After Koehler, 1932.)

ANEMO-TAXIS

Anemo-taxis (ἄνεμος, wind) is the reaction in air currents which corresponds to rheo-taxis in water, and was first described as such by Wheeler (1899). He observed that hovering flies, such as syrphids, bombyliids, and bibionids, always head into the wind. Midges and harlequin flies that form swarms do this too. If the velocity of flight is the same as the speed of the wind, then the insect does not move relative to the ground. It is inconceivable that this maintenance of position in moving air can

[1] See note 40, Appendix.

take place in any way except through the eyes, though there is little direct positive evidence, so that anemo-taxis is not a good

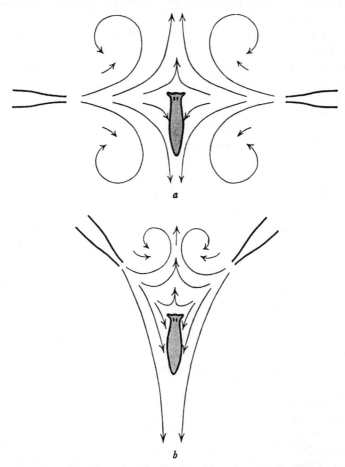

FIG. 119. Direction taken by *Planaria alpina* when stimulated by two currents. *a*. The currents act in opposite directions. *b*. The directions of the currents form a right angle. (After Koehler, 1932.)

term. Kennedy (1939*b*) found that mosquitoes tested in a wind, or with a moving background, would not tolerate movement over the retina of images of objects beneath them if this movement exceeded a rather low rate, and would not tolerate movement from back to front at all. Rapid backward movement of images might possibly occur if mosquitoes flew down wind near the ground, but they responded to such rapid movement of images by turning and flying into the wind, so that they became stationary or progressed slowly relative to the ground. Forward movement of images would occur if the mosquitoes faced up wind but could not fly fast enough to avoid drifting backwards. In that case, they landed. It is clear from this work that mosquitoes at any rate, once in the air, orientate entirely optically, both in maintaining position and in flying forward relative to the visible background. It is further interesting to notice that Kennedy found that chemicals which made the mosquitoes take to flight, whether attractant like host odours or repellent like citronella oil, did not alter this optical orientation; in both cases the mosquitoes flew up wind.

In forward flying, as distinct from hovering, direction is often determined by the wind. In a review of the whole subject of insect migration, Fraenkel (1932 *b*) showed, for example, that dragon-flies and hover-flies always migrate up wind, and that butterflies often do so. Williams (1930) has shown that butterflies sometimes but not always do so; the mechanism of orientation of many migratory butterflies remains mysterious. It is possible that they fix optically some object ahead and fly to that, then transfer to another object in the same line and so on. Again, they may orientate by means of the lines of movement of images on the ventral part of the retina. Mosquitoes keep these images constant or allow them to pass straight from front to back, parallel to the axis of the body.

We did not use the name *rheo-taxis* for the reaction of a fish to a stream, when that reaction was brought about solely through the eyes. It is true that the direction of flow of the stream determines body orientation, but it does not do so by stimulating the fish mechanically. To be consistent, we should abandon the term *anemo-taxis* as applied to the cases above, in which orientation is again entirely by means of the eyes. [1]

Practically nothing is known about the effects of wind on the orientation of animals on the ground. It has been observed, however, that insects resting in exposed places will often head up wind. Krijgsman (1930) and Krijgsman & Windred (1931) record this for the blood-sucking flies, *Stomoxys calcitrans* and *Lyperosia exigua*, when they are tested under experimental con-

[1] See note 41, Appendix.

ditions. According to Czeloth (1930), the newt, *Triton*, walks in the same direction as an artificial air-current. Cole (1917) found that *Drosophila melanogaster* sometimes walks against an artificial wind. Flügge (1934), while unable to confirm this

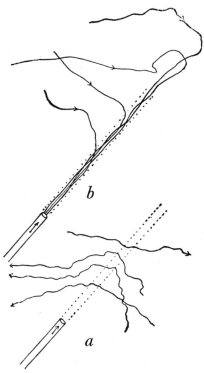

FIG. 120. *a. Drosophila* does not react to a current of pure air. *b.* The air current contains the smell of mashed pears, and *Drosophila* walks straight up wind. (From Wigglesworth, 1939, after Flügge, 1934.)

for pure air, found that *Drosophila* orientated very accurately into a wind containing the smell of mashed pears (Fig. 120). It seems probable that many olfactory reactions are only possible with the aid of such currents, both in water and in air, that the animal is stimulated to begin to orientate by the smell and that the only way to reach the source of the smell is to go against the current with the aid of either mechanical or optical stimuli.[1,2]

As for the mechanism of true anemo-taxis, no question of

[1] See note 42, Appendix.
[2] See also notes 45, 47 and 63.

dragging along the ground or of the stimulation of sensitive pressure receptors like the lateral line has arisen. An animal walking along at an angle to a wind tends to be bowled over by it; that is to say, extra weight is thrown on the legs to lee-ward. This extra force can be detected by proprioceptors or the like, and the situation is very like that of an animal walking across an inclined plane (see pp. 235–43). Orientation into the wind could take place by the same kind of mechanism as orientation up an inclined plane, by turning towards the side carrying less weight until the distribution of weight becomes approximately symmetrical.

INDIRECT CONTACT

A solid object may advertise its presence to an animal placed some distance away by setting up mechanical disturbances in the intervening solid or fluid material. For example, sounds can be detected by means of the sense of hearing. We shall deal with this function in a separate part of this chapter and, for the moment, confine ourselves to mechanical disturbances of the same essential nature as sound disturbances which are dealt with by an allied type of receptor.

Many animals are sensitive to mechanical disturbances in their surroundings and are able to localize the source of such disturbance very accurately. The sense involved has been called *Ferntastsinn*, that is distant-touch-sense (*tasten*—to feel one's way, to grope about) or indirect contact (Dykgraaf, 1933). It seems to occur mainly in aquatic vertebrates, but one or two other examples are known.

It has long been known that a spider can localize prey caught in its web. As early as 1880 Boys recognized that the main directing stimulus is the vibration in the web, caused by the wing-beat of the victim. A vibrating tuning-fork, brought into contact with the web, attracted the spider in just the same way. Barrows (1915) made similar observations on the large orb-weaving spider, *Epeira sclopetaria*, and he called the response *vibrotaxis*. He analysed the reaction into three parts—orienta-tion, approach, and attack. During the attack, the vibrating end of the tuning-fork was covered with web by the spider, just as if it were a fly. Meyer (1928) has extended these observations. The spiders *Aranea diademata* and *Argiope lobata* usually lurk in the centre of an approximately radially symmetrical web. When a fly gets caught in the web, the vibrations are transmitted along the radii to the spider at its lurking post. Other species, like *Zilla x-notata*, have a waiting post near the edge of the web, and this point is connected to the centre by a special signal-thread. In this case the spider goes to the centre before it turns to the fly. In either case orientation from the centre is rapid and precise. It is generally assumed that this orientation is made possible by special sense-hairs (trichobothria) on the legs. It is not aroused by any object lying passively in the web, but only by a continued vibration, like a buzzing fly or a vibrating tuning-fork.

There is one case known of an invertebrate which is able to localize disturbances in the water. According to Herter (1929), the duck leech, *Protoclepsis tesselata*, is attracted to any object moving through the water, and this is regarded as an adaptive response which leads the leech to its host, the duck.

The ability to locate mechanical disturbances is particularly well developed in certain of the fishes and amphibia. In investigating the reactions which occur it is necessary to prevent the occurrence of reactions to other kinds of stimulation. The animals used are therefore blinded. Some way must be found to make sure that chemical stimuli are not involved, and the disturbances are therefore sometimes produced by moving a metal disk. Suitable precautions were taken in all the work described below.

First of all, Wunder (1927) showed that blinded pike and eels were excited by mechanical disturbances of the water and were able to find the source of the disturbance quickly and accurately. Hungry pike would snap at a jerking fish from a distance of 5–10 cm., but not at a dead fish, so that the sense of smell was not responsible. A blinded eel-pout, *Lota vulgaris*, was able to follow a vibrating object around the aquarium. Minnows, *Phoxinus laevis*, were not so good at it and seemed to be much more dependent on their eyes.

Dykgraaf (1933) took the story further by using the conditioned reflex technique. An association is built up between feeding and some previously indifferent stimulus, and then the animal responds to the conditioned stimulus when food is not offered. In this way it is possible to establish the sensitivity of the animal to stimuli to which there is no spontaneous reaction, and it is also possible to test the power of discrimination between different intensities and qualities of the stimulus. Using the minnow, he showed that a moving disk can be located with astonishing precision. The minnow can also locate a fine jet of water from a pipette and, in swimming, it successfully avoids objects in its path. All these reactions were abolished by the elimination of the lateral line. According to Dykgraaf, the immediate stimulus in these cases is the movement of water on the lateral line.

In demonstrating the auditory function of the *pars inferior* of the labyrinth of minnows, von Frisch & Stetter (1932) found that individuals with the auditory nerve severed could still react to very low notes and that this reaction did not disappear when the lateral line was eliminated too. Later work by Hoagland (1933), Schriever (1935) and Sand (1937) shows that action currents are produced in the lateral line branch of the vagus nerve when the receptors are acted upon by a single pressure change or by repeated vibrations. The ultimate stimulus is the movement of fluid inside the lateral line canal (Sand, 1937).

In the light of all this work, it seems possible that in a suitable stream a fish could maintain its place by the use of the lateral line alone. A moving object can be followed through an aquarium; why should not a fish continually swim towards a stationary object in a stream? The flow of the water over a large stone must set up vibrations to which the fish could react, but it is possible that the chorus of such disturbances is too complicated to be of much use.

There is very little evidence to help us to decide which mechanism of orientation is involved in lateral line reactions of fishes. It has already been pointed out that orientation is rapid and direct (p. 253), so that klino-taxis is not in action. The lateral line can act as a one-way rudder, as shown by the experiment with a stream from a pipette, but no experiments with moving objects have been done after unilateral elimination, nor have tests been carried out with two sources of stimulation.

Aquatic amphibia make responses very similar to those described above. Nicholas (1922) reported that the axolotl, *Amblystoma tigrinum*, is easily attracted to any moving object even when blinded. Scharrer (1932) showed that this response depends on the integrity of the lateral line. Blinded larvae of

Amblystoma punctatum snap at a stream of water directed on to the head. If the stream is directed on to the flank of the animal, it turns at once and often bites the point of the pipette. This reaction appears to be valuable in the capture of food. Larvae which have had the rudiments of the eyes and of the olfactory organs removed during early development can still carry it out, but those which have had the rudiments of the lateral line system on the head removed cannot. As long as the lateral line is in action, they can catch a living worm (*Enchytraeus*) placed half a centimetre away, while they do not react to the chemical stimulation of a crushed worm. The newt, *Triton*, is also able to locate and catch moving prey in an aquarium, even when the olfactory organs are out of action (Matthes, 1924 *a*, *b*).

The most detailed analysis of the mechanism of such reactions has been carried out on the clawed toad, *Xenopus laevis*, by Kramer (1933). If a drop of water is let fall on to the surface, or if the finger is immersed, a blinded specimen turns and swims towards the site of the disturbance. If the side of the animal is touched lightly with a pencil, or if a mealworm is dropped on to the skin, the toad brings its mouth round to the place touched in a single quick movement. The efficiency of localization of distant disturbances is high. From a distance of 15 cm., *Xenopus* swims accurately towards a little ball of plasticene stuck on the end of a wire and immersed; the wire is held as still as possible in the hand, but the slight unavoidable movements make sufficient disturbance to enable the toad to locate it (Fig. 121, p. 264). Such a performance is possible only in a large aquarium, for otherwise reflection of the vibrations from the walls makes the sensory situation too complicated.

These reactions of *Xenopus* are entircly dependent on the integrity of the lateral line. If the organs of one side are put out of action by cautery and the animal is stimulated by two plasticene balls, one on each side, it always turns to the intact side, even if the ball on that side is five times as far away as the other. A unilaterally operated *Xenopus* is still able to locate a moving object straight ahead. This is due to the presence of parts of the lateral line system on the front of the head; if these are destroyed on both sides, stimulation from the front leads to a turn towards the side on which the posterior parts of the system are still

intact (Fig. 121 *d*). This is strongly suggestive of an organization of the individual receptors like that of the ommatidia in
an insect compound eye, so that some discrimination of direc-

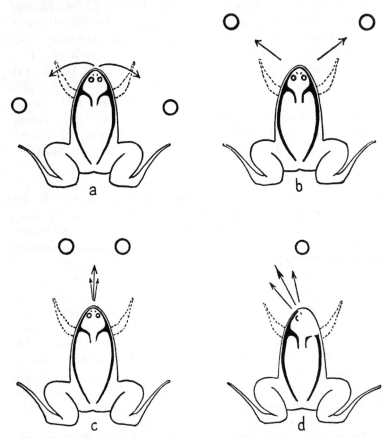

FIG. 121. *a*, *b* and *c*. Reactions of *Xenopus* when stimulated simultaneously by two
centres of disturbance in the water. The system of lateral lines is represented as
black lines. *d*. Scheme of the reaction of *Xenopus*, in which the lateral line of the
whole head region on the right, and of the mouth region alone on the left has been
destroyed, to a vibration stimulus set up exactly in front of the animal. It deviates
to the left. (Kramer, 1933.)

tion is possible without turning and with only one side in
action. It does not follow that the reaction is telo-tactic. The
proper test for telo-taxis is the two-source experiment. If two
stimuli are applied symmetrically, the response depends on

their distance apart. When the lines joining them to the tip of the mouth make an angle of more than 60°, *Xenopus* turns to one or other of them (Fig. 121 *a*, *b*), but if the angle is smaller, it goes between them (Fig. 121 *c*). Unfortunately this experiment is difficult to interpret. It may be that the animal inhibits one of the stimuli when the two are far enough apart to be distinguishable as two stimuli, and that when they are near together the sense organs are not sufficiently discriminating to make this possible. In that case, the reaction would be telotactic. On the other hand, when the sources are far apart, it may be that the animal is in a position similar to that of a positively tropo-tactic animal near two lights—the direction taken under the combined action of the two sources is so nearly directly to one source that it cannot be distinguished from the direct path. In that case the reaction would be tropo-tactic. Kramer (1933) came to the conclusion that the lateral line system is sufficiently differentiated and sufficiently well connected up in the central nervous system to allow direct localization of the stimulus to occur. That would make the case closely parallel to that of the light reaction of *Eristalis*, but in this case we cannot yet make the final decision about tropo-taxis and telo-taxis.

Sound

Just as there is no clear physical distinction between light and 'radiant heat', so there is none between the mechanical vibrations just dealt with and sound. An approximate subjective distinction can be made. We recognize light and heat as distinct, but of course light always has some heating effect. Similarly, we recognize sounds as such, but very low notes are also subjectively recognized as vibration. That has already been touched upon in connexion with the work of v. Frisch & Stetter (1932). In the vertebrates we can make an arbitrary distinction between those vibrations which are received by the *pars inferior* of the labyrinth of the ear, which we call sounds, and those which stimulate other receptors, which we could call mechanical vibrations. When we come to the invertebrates, for which we cannot well carry over our subjective experience, no such distinction can properly be made. The usual thing to do is to regard only vibrations above a certain frequency as sounds.

Responses to high-frequency mechanical vibrations seem to be fairly rare in the invertebrates. As far as we know, they are restricted to arthropods, and even then mainly to land insects. Apart from the buzzing noise of wings, few insects make much sound. Various families of Orthoptera stridulate by means of special organs, while the hemipteran cicadas have a membrane like a microphone diaphragm which is vibrated by muscular action. The crickets and both long-horned and short-horned grasshoppers have auditory organs provided with a tympanic membrane, while the auditory organs of other insects are not always so clearly recognizable as such. Probably the chordotonal organs in many insects have an auditory function, while Pumphrey & Rawdon-Smith (1936) have recently shown that certain hairs on the cerci of the cricket and the cockroach are auditory.

In only one case has the orientation response of an insect to sounds been thoroughly investigated. That example is provided by Regen (1912, 1913, 1923) for the field cricket, *Gryllus campestris*. The male stridulates and the female is able to find the male from a distance of 10 metres, guided entirely by sound. If the male stridulates into a telephone, the female orientates to the receiver placed in another room, just as if the receiver were the male itself. After removal of the two tympanal organs, the reaction disappears altogether. If only one organ is removed, the female is still able to find the male, but not so easily. During the reaction the cricket travels in a zigzag line; it walks a certain distance, stops, and then starts off again in a slightly different direction. The nearer it comes to the male, the straighter is its path. We do not know what the exact mechanism of localization of the source of the sounds is, but it looks as if the female cricket at first behaves klino-tactically and then tropo-tactically.[1]

The problem of the mechanism of sound localization has been studied extensively in mammals. It is a familiar fact that human beings can locate the source of a sound fairly accurately, especially if there are not many reflecting surfaces to complicate the situation. Many wild animals are extremely sensitive to sounds and they can turn their heads accurately towards a sound. The matter has been studied experimentally in dogs, cats, and domestic fowls (Keller & Brückner, 1932; Katz, 1937). Katz (1937) used well-trained Alsatian dogs and first built up an

[1] See note 43, Appendix.

FIG. 122. Arrangement for testing sound localization in the dog. The dog sits in the centre of a circle formed by thirteen screens. A buzzer is operated behind one screen at a time. (Original photograph, kindly supplied by Prof. D. Katz.)

association between the sound of a buzzer and a piece of meat as a reward. In one set of experiments sixty-four small black shields were arranged in a circle of diameter 5·75 metres, the buzzer was hidden under one shield and a piece of meat hidden behind the same one (cf. Fig. 122). The dog was then brought on to the scene, put into the centre of the circle, and given the signal to be on the alert. When the buzzer went, the animal turned and went to the right screen with unfailing accuracy, even if the sound lasted so short a time that the head hardly moved at all before the sound ceased. In another set of experiments there were only two screens, placed at the end of an alleyway. When they were 0·5 m. apart the dog could locate the one behind which the buzzer had sounded from a distance of 5 m., while when they were 0·75 m. and 1·5 m. apart it could locate the right one from 10 m. and 20 m. respectively. A cat could go to the right screen from 8 m. away when the two screens were 0·5 m. apart.

The mechanism of sound localization has been dealt with in great detail by v. Hornbostel (1926). There are three widely recognized facts which must be taken into account:

1. Localization is very much better with two ears than with only one.
2. Animals frequently make mistakes about 'above' and 'below' or about 'forwards' and 'backwards', but hardly ever about 'right' and 'left'.
3. Noises are more easily located than pure tones.

These facts lead to the first conclusion, that successful localization depends on a difference between the stimulation of the two ears. There are three main theories about the mechanism of localization. The first is based on the difference of intensity with which a sound reaches the two ears; this depends partly on the greater distance of one ear from the source, but mainly on the screening effect of the head. The second theory is based on the difference in timbre which a sound must acquire in reaching the more distant ear. The third theory depends on the difference in the time of arrival of a sound at the two ears. Hornbostel rejects the first two theories and supports the third for the following reasons. Success in localization is not much influenced by increasing the distance from the source; this changes the relative intensities with which the two ears are stimulated. A further observation against the intensity theory is that the relative intensities can be altered in other ways without much loss of efficiency; the sound can be supplied through two head-phones, one having more current and therefore a louder sound, or it can be supplied through two speaking-tubes, one wider than the other and so again giving a louder sound. Similar experiments tell against the timbre theory, for when the sound comes through tubes or from microphones the timbre cannot be affected by the head.

There are some experiments which support the time theory. For instance, if the distance between the ears is artificially increased by means of ear trumpets (principle of the sound ranger), the efficiency of localization is greatly increased. Again, the sound can be conducted to the ears in tubes, one of which can be extended like a trombone; as the length of path on one side is changed, the sound seems to travel round the head. A similar deceiving effect is produced if the two paths are identical in length, but one is heated up so as to accelerate the sound. The experiments mentioned still do not tell us whether it is the time interval between the arrival of gross changes in sound or the phase difference on the two sides which is effective, but it would take us too far to go into that (Rawdon-Smith, 1938).

If we accept the time theory, it is possible to estimate the time differences which can be utilized by various animals. The results are astonishing. A dog can locate a sound by means of a time difference as small as 0·000,0045 sec., while for the cat the figure is 0·000,0028 sec. These times are so short that one would have thought that they surpassed the best performance of nervous mechanisms, but, once more, we cannot go into that here.

In considering these reactions to sound from the point of view of the classification of taxes, it would clearly be wrong to treat them as examples of *Unterschiedsempfindlichkeit in der Zeit* (Koehler, 1932), for that phrase refers to the stimulation of one receptor at two different points in time, such as is involved in klino-taxis. For this purpose, stimulation of the two ears can be regarded as effectively simultaneous and, whatever the precise method, orientation involves simultaneous comparison of stimuli. That is to say, orientation is in fact tropo-tactic. It is rather striking to find tropo-tactic behaviour in the mammals.

This emphasizes the fact that orientation is limited by the capacity of the receptors, and that the mammals have generally been liberated from the more elementary types of reaction not only by their superior nervous organization but also by their superior sense organs.

XVIII

CHEMICAL STIMULATION

WE have seen that light as a stimulus can affect the orientation of organisms by varying in two different ways—in intensity and in direction. Radiant heat varies in the same two ways, while gravity hardly varies at all and its direction alone is commonly an effective directing stimulus for animals. On the other hand, chemical stimuli cannot act at a distance; they consist of material particles in contact with the surface of the animal, so that chemical stimuli can vary in intensity but they do not possess the property of direction at all. The *source* of chemical stimulation may be some distance away, but the animal cannot be stimulated chemically by that source unless there is an actual transfer of material—by diffusion or the like—from the source to the animal. In an ideal case the diffusion from the source would set up a gradient of concentration having concentric spheres of equal intensity, rather like the intensity gradient around a light source (p. 138); unlike the gradient of light intensity, however, the chemical gradient would become stable only after a very long time and would be upset instantly by currents in the air or water. Indeed, we have to deal more often with cases in which the chemical stimulation is delivered by a current than with the ideal diffusion case. The current itself may then play an important part in directing the reaction as well as in carrying the stimulating substance rapidly over a considerable distance. A well-known example of this is provided by the reactions of *Planaria alpina* in swift streams, which is dealt with elsewhere (p. 254 *et seq.*). There are also cases in which the initial excitation produced by molecules which arrive simply by diffusion is increased by means of a current which the animal itself produces. Something like this happens when a dog sniffs, and an even better example is provided by crabs (Luther, 1930, 1931) and hermit crabs (Brock, 1926, 1930); chemical stimulation of the first antennae immediately leads to a rhythmical beating of the palps of the maxillipedes, driving the water up to the antennules. These tricks, which help in localizing the source of stimulation, only serve to emphasize the non-directional nature of chemical stimulation. Although a single molecule diffusing in an otherwise complete vacuum would travel in a straight line and so could indicate the direction from which it started, in real cases the frequency of collision is so high that the most recent direction of the molecule gives no such indication at all.

The structure of chemo-receptors is very variable; there is no constant feature—like the pigment of photo-receptors or the statolith of statocysts—which makes them immediately recognizable. There is a constant feature of a negative sort, namely, that they are not direction receptors. It is this peculiarity of chemical stimulation and of chemo-receptors which makes responses like telo-taxis, compass reactions, and the dorsal light reaction impossible. We may therefore expect to find that the two kinds of kinesis and klino-taxis are the common types of response, though tropo-taxis is also theoretically possible. Thus when the gradient is sufficiently steep for two parts of the animal's body to be stimulated with different intensities, the information necessary for making a simultaneous comparison of intensities is available and a direct turn towards or away from the more strongly stimulated side is theoretically possible.

We are accustomed to make a distinction between taste and smell, although in ourselves taste in the mouth is commonly accompanied by a smell in the nose, giving a compound sensation. Nevertheless, the distinction is not altogether invalid, because not only the sense organs but also the brain centres concerned are in different places. On the whole, the sense of smell gives some warning of the chemical properties of a body placed some distance away, while taste only comes into action when the substance is in the mouth. A similar distinction can be made for some other animals, both vertebrates and invertebrates. Here we are concerned only with smell, since we are dealing only with locomotory reactions to more or less distant objects or places, and the reader is referred to other literature for a discussion of the relation between taste and smell (e.g. v. Buddenbrock, 1937; v. Frisch, 1926).

Animals in general use the sense of smell in finding food and in the search for a mate. More rarely it is involved in escape reactions. For some animals light is the most important stimulus, while the behaviour of others is largely guided in the natural state by chemical stimulation, particularly in food finding.

Fresh-water planarians fall into the latter category. If a dead frog, cut open, is placed in a swift stream, very soon large numbers of planarians leave their resting-places beneath the stones and crawl straight upstream to the bait. This reaction has been investigated by a number of workers, including Pearl (1903), Doflein (1925), Steinmann (1929), Voûte (1928, 1930), and Koehler (1932). We shall on the whole follow Koehler's very detailed descriptions and analyses. In a stream the behaviour is complicated by responses to the current of water, so it is more convenient to deal with the reactions of a pond form, *Planaria lugubris*.

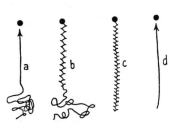

FIG. 123. Semi-schematic figure of the chemo-orientation of *Planaria lugubris* towards a bait. *a* and *b*. At first undirected crawling, then straight path to the bait. *b* and *c*. The final straight path is accompanied by continuous pendulations of the head. *a* and *d*. The last straight path is carried out without head movements. (After Koehler, 1932.)

The experiments were carried out in circular glass dishes 10 cm. in diameter. The bait consisted of freshly cut pieces of aquatic snails (*Limnaea, Planorbis*) or of *Asellus*, or of ox liver. A short time after bait was placed in the dish the planarian became 'excited'; instead of resting quietly on the bottom of the dish, it started crawling about this way and that. Gradually the path straightened out and the animal finally went straight to the bait. The last part of the track always led straight to the bait, though crawling might be interrupted from time to time while the animal raised its anterior end and swung it from side to side (Fig. 123).

Analysis shows that this complete reaction may be divided into separate phases. A resting planarian is considerably shortened, and the auricular organs—in which the chemo-receptors are located—are involved in the general contraction. The first sign of chemical excitation is a slow lengthening of the anterior end, which makes the auricular organs long and thin. Then the head becomes detached from the substratum and waves slowly, but with increasing amplitude, up and down, and symmetrically from side to side. After a certain time the head comes down again, the whole body lengthens, and crawling begins. The time taken for this series of movements to begin depends on the distance from the bait and so upon the time required for diffusion to raise the concentration of the stimulating substance to the threshold value; it is about 1 minute for 1 cm. and 10–50 minutes for 5 cm. The occurrence of an 'excited' condition is typical of reactions to chemical stimuli; it represents an ortho-kinetic response.

The next phase of the reaction is the crawling along a very convoluted path. Koehler describes this stage as undirectional, but it can be seen both from his figures (Fig. 123 *a*, *b*, p. 272) and from those of other authors that the animal does tend to approach the bait, though not directly. The general aspect of this stage is obviously similar to the behaviour of *Dendrocoelum lacteum* in a gradient of undirected light (Chap. V); turning occurs irregularly, but it is likely to occur a shorter time after the previous turn when the animal is going down the gradient than when it is going up. The animal is likely to turn soon if it is moving into a region of weaker smell and not so soon if it is increasingly stimulated by the smell. This results in a general drift towards the bait; it corresponds closely with the typical case of *klino-kinesis*, though it has not been analysed quantitatively since this category of reaction was first proposed.

During this klino-kinetic phase of the reaction the animal frequently stops and swings the anterior end from side to side; when it gets within a short distance of the bait—at the most 8 cm.—after one such halt it goes straight towards the bait. If the bait is only a short distance away at the beginning, crawling may be direct from the start and the klino-kinesis may be omitted. But even when the track is straight, at first it is only the posterior part of the body which keeps to the track; the anterior end makes regular swinging movements from side to side. In this phase the reaction is very similar to that of the blowfly maggot in its negative photo-taxis; it looks as if a regular comparison of intensities is being made, with the head alternately on one side and the other. This successive comparison of intensities leading to a direct movement towards or away from the source of stimulation is what we call klino-taxis. The appropriate movements of the head take place during the klino-kinetic phase, but presumably the difference of intensities in the alternate head positions is not then great enough to lead to an accurate turn in the direction of the bait. Klino-kinesis therefore continues until the information necessary for klino-taxis is available; the more efficient reaction can then take over.

Koehler also described cases in which the last few centimetres of the track were straight and in which there were no pendulating movements of the anterior end. The proper analysis of this last phase of the reaction became possible when the exact position of the sense organs involved was discovered. If the sides of the head, including the auricular organs, are cut off, the initial excitation is very much reduced and the bait is either not found at all or is found only after prolonged and apparently random movements. When the bait is reached, the examination of it and feeding on it take place normally. The deficiency in orientation is not due to a general effect of the operation, for removal of the central part of the anterior end has no effect on any of the phases of finding the bait; on the other hand, the latter operation does interfere with the final examination of the bait and with feeding. The interpretation of this is that the principal smell receptors are located at the sides of the head and the taste receptors in the centre of the front. There are, however, auxiliary receptors of both kinds scattered over the whole body surface.

The principal smell receptors—and especially the smell receptors which are involved in finding food rapidly—are thus localized in two concentrated and symmetrically placed groups at the anterior end. They can easily be removed without producing general harmful effects, and indeed they soon regenerate. There is therefore an excellent opportunity of applying one of the tests for tropo-taxis—namely, the elimination of the organ of one side to see if the animal makes circus movements when stimulated uniformly. In fact, a planarian with the left auricular organ removed, when tested in a dilute solution of *Planorbis* blood, made repeated turns to the right side; in a very dilute solution of sulphuric acid it circled in the opposite direction. This shows that *Planaria lugubris* has a suitable receptor apparatus and co-ordination system to enable it to perform chemo-tropotaxis. Not all the individuals tested gave this result; there was more turning to the expected side than to the other and the difference was statistically significant. The reasons for the irregularity of response are unknown. In addition to getting circus movements, it is possible to carry out an experiment which is closely parallel to the two-light experiment. First, if a capillary tube full of *Planorbis* blood is kept close in front of the animal, it follows the tube's movements like the donkey following the carrot. The distance between the open end of the tube and the anterior end of the worm must not be more than a few millimetres. Then, if the tube is bent and completely filled with the blood, it can be presented to the animal in such a way that the two open ends are equidistant from the animal and on opposite sides of it (Fig. 124). When this two-source stimulus is very slowly moved away from the animal, taking care that the open ends remain equidistant from it, the animal does not turn towards either end but heads between them. That is to say, turning does not occur if the receptors of the two sides are equally stimulated. A simultaneous comparison of intensities occurs, with a kind of cancelling out in the central nervous system, and the worm crawls straight on. If one auricular organ is cut out, this balance no longer occurs, the animal turns towards

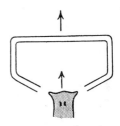

FIG. 124. Arrangement for simultaneous stimulation of a planarian with two chemical stimuli. The bent tube is filled with a solution of snail's blood. (After Koehler, 1932.)

the intact side and may thus reach one end of the tube. After 3-5 days, as regeneration of the auricular organ proceeds, the reaction of going between the two ends of the tube slowly reappears.

It is thus clear that if the gradient of intensity of the chemical stimulus is sufficiently steep, so that even when the head is kept still there can be an appreciable difference of intensities at the two sides of the body, then *Planaria lugubris* can carry out chemotropo-taxis. It can turn directly towards the source of stimulation and go straight towards it without deviations or trial movements of any kind. A gradient of sufficient steepness, however, occurs only in the immediate vicinity of the source— perhaps only within a few millimetres. When the gradient is less steep, the comparison must be made between two points farther apart than the two sides of the head; it is then that the head swings in a semicircle from side to side, and a comparison is made between the two points at the ends of the swing. In this case, the comparison is not between two stimuli which are delivered simultaneously on two separate organs, but between two stimuli which occur at two distinct points in time. The reaction then involves a repetition of that movement which previously led to the more intense stimulation, and a following up of that movement by crawling. These are the essential features of klino-taxis, bearing in mind that in *negative* reactions it is the lateral movement which leads to *less* intense stimulation which is followed up.

Another interpretation of these head pendulations is of the sort given by Loeb (1918) for similar cases. In reactions which we now classify as tropo-tactic, if the orientating effectiveness of the stimulus is low, then accidental deviations from the direct path may become considerable before they are corrected; Loeb uses the analogy of a down feather falling to the ground, not straight but swooping this way and that in its descent. This interpretation is very similar to the previous one, and they both involve the assumption that the animal is orientating by simultaneous comparison of stimuli on symmetrically placed receptors. An experiment of Koehler's, however, leads us to decide in favour of the other interpretation, namely, that the lateral deviations are an essential feature of orientation under certain conditions and that symmetry and balance are not essential. In that experiment one auricular organ was removed and the animal was tested with a single open tube of snail's blood, which was moved slowly away as the animal crawled forward. The planarian could follow the source of the smell, turning to either side as the tube was moved. There was a tendency to turn towards the intact side when the source had not been moved in that direction, and then the animal got lost, but this tendency could be overcome. When the tube was followed successfully, the head pendulations were carried out almost continually and the mechanism of orientation was clearly klino-tactic.

To sum up, we see that *Planaria lugubris* is able to perform chemo-tropo-taxis, provided the external conditions are suitably arranged. Suitable conditions—especially a steep gradient of stimulation—occur only over a short distance from the source. The whole reaction towards the food involves a series of phases—first a sort of awakening, the ortho-kinesis, then klino-kinesis, then, as the gradient becomes steeper, klino-taxis, and finally, in the steepest gradient near the source, the most efficient reaction of them all—tropo-taxis. *Planaria* thus makes an excellent example, for it performs reactions to chemical stimuli in practically all the possible ways.

The reactions of insects to smell have been more thoroughly investigated than those of any other group of animals. A number of insects find their food almost exclusively by means of smell, and the methods they use are so similar that a number of cases can be treated together. Recent work covers the method of finding dung used by the dung beetles *Scarabaeus* (Heymons & Lengerken, 1929) and *Geotrupes* (Warnke, 1931), the finding of the host in the parasitic hymenopteran, *Habrobracon* (Murr, 1930), and the orientation towards fermenting fruit in *Drosophila* (Barrows, 1907; Flügge, 1934), towards meat in the bluebottle, *Calliphora* (Hartung, 1935), and towards the host in the hog louse, *Haematopinus suis* (Weber, 1929). It is abundantly clear that the principal and probably practically the only site of smell receptors in insects is on the antennae (Marshall, 1935). Each antenna can usually be moved separately so as to investigate an approximately hemispherical space; sometimes they are too short to cover an extensive area, particularly in swift-flying forms like the dragon-flies and the brachycerous Diptera, while in other cases the surface area is greatly extended, as in pectinate and lamellate forms (Imms, 1934; Snodgrass, 1935). It is conceivable that long antennae are capable of indicating to the animal the existence of a gradient from one end of the antenna to the other, but usually it seems probable that the most they can do is to indicate when one antenna is more strongly stimulated than the other. This would provide the information necessary for reacting tropo-tactically.

The first sign of appropriate chemical stimulation is an 'alarm' reaction; when *Scarabaeus* is stimulated, it raises the head, extends the antennae diagonally sideways, and opens out the lamellae. *Geotrupes* behaves in this way too and then swings the head from side to side while the antennae move up and down rhythmically. After a certain time the beetle turns approximately in the direction of the source of stimulation and repeats the movements. The hog louse does not at first move the body, but swings the antennae until finally one of them is pointing at the source of stimulation and making swings of equal angle on either side of this line. *Habrobracon* first cleans the antennae and then moves them vigorously in the air so that their tips describe as large a part as possible of the surface of a sphere. *Drosophila*, if it is already walking, stops suddenly and cleans the head; then it turns quickly, facing first one way and then another. The antennae of *Drosophila* are very short, so that these movements of the whole animal correspond to antennal movements in the other insects. In all these cases, then, the animal is first activated or 'alarmed' and then it makes movements which—if there is a gradient—will subject the antennae to varying intensity of stimulation.

Frequently, however, the gradient is evidently not steep enough and the animal does not turn and walk straight off to the source. In such a case the tracks turn and twist and the animal wanders apparently at random; this type of meandering has been described for *Geotrupes* (Fig. 125), *Habrobracon*, *Drosophila*, and *Haematopinus* (Fig. 126). It is not yet clear whether these turnings are truly random, so that the animal gets into a higher concentration and a steeper gradient simply by chance, or whether they are essentially the same as the klino-kinetic wanderings of *Dendrocoelum* in a gradient of light intensity. Consider, for example, the familiar case of the arrival of blue-bottles when a piece of meat is exposed in the open air. Soon after the meat is put out, flies become visible where there were none before; they turn this way and that, getting nearer and nearer, until they finally settle. In the laboratory the space available is so small that the insect cannot get away and the chance of its finding the bait by purely random movements—without any systematic tendency to turn so as to move generally towards the bait—is much greater than it is in the open. In the open, if these movements were completely random, there is surely no reason why the majority of the approaching flies should not fly right away again. Most of the workers on this line have expressed the view that phobo-taxis is involved—the insect turning back when it begins to move into a lower concentration of the stimulating agent. Sometimes, however, the insect turns aside even when it is going directly towards the source (Fig. 126); this could only be regarded as a mistake on the part of the animal in the phobo-taxis scheme, but it is a normal feature of klino-kinesis. Without further investigation, then, we cannot say more than this: in low concentrations and when the gradient is not steep, it looks as if the bluebottle gets near the meat by a klino-kinetic mechanism. It would be interesting to discover if the mechanism is really the same as it is in *Dendrocoelum*, especially in respect of the important part played by sensory adaptation. It is more than likely, of course, that there are great differences in the *internal* mechanism, but the classification of reactions is not concerned essentially with that.

When we come to consider the reaction of the insect in a steep gradient near the source, the position is a little clearer but not much. The animal goes straight to the source of the appropriate smell from a distance of 10 metres for *Scarabaeus*, 50 cm. for *Geotrupes*, 23 cm. for *Drosophila*, 6·4 cm. for *Calliphora*, 5 cm. for *Haematopinus*, and 1·85 cm. for *Habrobracon*, each figure being an average or a representative figure of some kind. After removal of one antenna, most of the insects make circling movements towards the intact

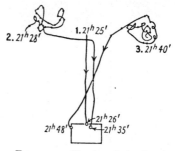

FIG. 125. Tracks of the beetle *Geotrupes* towards a smell (horse faeces). At the beginning, each track is convoluted; near the end, the tracks lead straight towards the bait. (After Warnke, 1931.)

side when stimulated by the smell, so that a number of authors have attributed the straightness of the last part of the track to a tropo-tactic reaction. They then call it *osmo-tropo-taxis*, to distinguish it from reactions to other kinds of chemical stimulation affecting organs of taste, for example. Thus *Geotrupes* when deprived of one antenna turns more often to the intact side than to the other, even during the klino-kinetic or wandering phase of the whole reaction. This gives us an important clue; clearly the wanderings are not tropo-tactic, for the animal is not then going straight to the source. It seems, therefore, that as long as the animal is equipped with the whole apparatus for making tropo-taxis possible, circus movements may be expected to occur after unilateral extirpation; but that is not to be interpreted as meaning that all the reactions to the same stimulus must be tropo-tactic. There is, in fact, no reason to suppose that any but the last few centimetres of the track are due to tropo-taxis. If *Geotrupes* with only one antenna gets near the source of smell, it is still able to localize the source by swinging the head from side to side—i.e. by klino-taxis.

Habrobracon, on the other hand, finds the *Ephestia* larva, on which it lays its eggs, just as well with one antenna as it does with two, suggesting that klino-taxis is more important here. This conclusion is completely unaffected by the fact that when one antenna is removed the insect tends to turn more towards

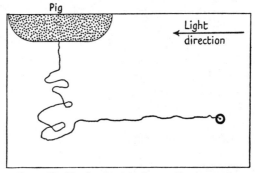

FIG. 126. Track of a hog louse, *Haematopinus suis*, towards a pig. In the first part, the track is directed away from the light; near the skin of the pig the louse first becomes alarmed and approaches the host along a convoluted path. Only the last part of the path is straight. (After Weber, 1929.)

the intact side than the other when placed in a chamber smelling of the larvae. When *Drosophila* has had one antenna cut off, it turns mainly towards the intact side in a smell to which it is positive (Fig. 127) and to the operated side in a smell to which it normally reacts negatively. Food substances having the appropriate smell are still successfully reached, but the last straight dash towards them is much shorter than with the normal fly. Similar results have been obtained from *Calliphora* (Fig. 128, p. 282)[1,2,3].

The striking feature of the orientation of many animals to chemical stimuli is the change over from one method of orientating to another as the conditions make it possible for the more efficient methods to come into action. Another unusual feature depends on the mobility of the antennae in the insects; in reacting klino-tactically, it is not necessary for the whole animal to make deviations alternately to each side and only the antennae need do this. The insect can then walk in a straight

[1] See note 44, Appendix.
[2] See note 45, Appendix.
[3] See note 46, Appendix.

line or in long curves, turning a little to one side if the antennae (or the single antenna, if one has been removed) are more strongly stimulated when they are swung over to that side. For both insects and other animals we conclude that circus movements after unilateral extirpation are an indication that the animal *can* perform tropo-taxis if suitable conditions are provided; they do not show that tropo-taxis is the sole mechanism in action all the time. If the animal is able to make directly for

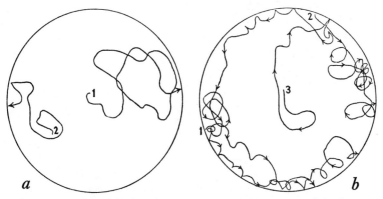

FIG. 127. Tracks of *Drosophila* with the left antenna amputated. *a.* In pure air. *b.* In an atmosphere of mashed pears. In the latter case circus movements occur frequently. (After Flügge, 1934.)

the source with the chemo-receptors of one side removed— always supposing that proper tests have excluded the possibility that other senses are responsible—then we must conclude that the receptor group on each side has a two-way action. In view of the small size of groups of chemo-receptors in general, and in particular in view of the thinness of antennae, it seems unlikely that they can have a tropo-tactic two-way action, like the eye of *Eristalis*. A very steep gradient indeed would be required to stimulate two receptors close together with different intensities. Since antennae and other parts bearing chemo-receptors are commonly waved about during a directed reaction, we must conclude that in these reactions klino-taxis plays a considerable part.

One of the best-known examples of orientation by smell is the finding of the female by the male of certain species of Lepidoptera. The distances covered appear to be far in excess of anything which has so far been discussed, and the method of orientation is unknown. It is possible that the moths keep flying into the wind—aided by an optical mechanism—as long as the smell is brought down to them and make random movements when they fly beyond the source, but that is pure conjecture. In two cases of orientation towards the female which have been described, the silkworm moth, *Bombyx* (Kellog, 1907),[1] and the

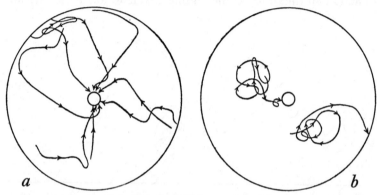

a   *b*

FIG. 128.   Tracks of the blowfly, *Calliphora erythrocephala*, reacting to meat. *a.* Intact animals. *b.* Left antenna amputated. Circus movements occur only in the amputated flies. (After Hartung, 1935.)

mealworm beetle, *Tenebrio* (Valentine, 1931), after unilateral removal of an antenna the male performs circus movements.

There are a few other cases of sufficient interest to be quoted. The fish leech, *Hemiclepsis marginata*, becomes active when fish slime is put into the water, but the wandering movements which follow are completely random (Herter, 1928). The cheese mite, *Tyrolichus casei*, reaches appropriate baits (meat juice, squashed caterpillars, dilute skatol) by means of a very devious path. Henschel (1929) concludes that the mites generally go straight on when travelling up the gradient of intensity and turn if they start to go down it; these are the obvious features of chemo-klino-kinesis. When first stimulated, the tick, *Ixodes ricinus*, starts by waving the front legs about; these legs bear Haller's organs, which are the chemo-receptors. The method of orientation seems to be the same in principle as that of *Tyrolichus* (Totze, 1933). Cephalopod molluscs detect and follow their prey mainly by means of their very well-developed eyes, but a blinded octopus

[1] See note 47, Appendix.

when stimulated by the smell of food extends the arms and searches with them. Each arm is capable of localizing food from a short distance; indeed, a severed arm has been observed to follow a stimulating source through the aquarium (Giersberg, 1926).

According to Copeland (1918) the first reaction of two proso-branch molluscs, *Alectrion obsoleta* and *Busycon canaliculatum*, to the smell of food (oyster juice) is to begin to crawl or to accelerate (ortho-kinesis). During this crawling the siphon swings from side to side. If oyster juice is pipetted into the water to one side of the advancing mollusc, no reaction occurs until the siphon turns to that side, and then the foot starts to turn in the appropriate direction. Water is drawn through the siphon into the mantle cavity, where the osphradial chemo-receptor lies, so that the siphon is continually obtaining samples of water to be tested by the osphradium. This continually shifting 'nostril' is an economical device, for it saves the additional ex-penditure of energy which would be involved if the whole body made the klino-tactic deviations instead of only the siphon, and it is not an important impediment to motion because the animal moves so slowly in any case. Another prosobranch, *Nassa reticulata*, is apparently incapable of klino-taxis, and finds the food by random movements which cease only when the end of the siphon comes practically on top of the bait. The con-tinual movement of the siphon simply increases the chance of finding the food (Henschel, 1933).[1]

There are a few cases known of elementary kinds of responses of vertebrates to chemical stimulation. There are many fishes which become 'excited', i.e. behave ortho-kinetically, when juices from their normal food are put into the water. Most authors believe that the actual finding of the food—at least in fishes which cannot see—is the result of purely random move-ments. In the case of the dogfish, *Mustelus canis*, however, Parker (1914) writes:

'When a fish in the course of its ordinary swimming approached to within a foot of the packet of crab meat, it usually made a sudden movement to one side with its head, swam at once to the bottom, and in quick circuitous turns, often in the form of a figure eight, swept the bed of the pen. In a short time it narrowed its search to the immediate vicinity of the packet. . . . Occasionally the packet

[1] See note 48, Appendix.

was not found and the fish then resumed its ordinary method of locomotion. . . .'

It appears from this description that something like klino-kinesis is involved. Parker concluded that there was an element of what we now call tropo-taxis, for after occlusion of one nostril turns towards the other side predominated.

The newt, *Triton*, is first of all activated by a suitable stimulus (e.g. the smell of fresh soil). It approaches the soil first along a convoluted route and then in a straight line. During the straight part it frequently stops and swings its head from side to side, so that it looks as if the initial klino-kinesis is succeeded by klino-taxis (Czeloth, 1930).

Some poisonous snakes are in the habit of releasing their prey after biting it, and then pursuing it. The pursuit is sometimes very wandering and there then seems to be no systematic orientation at all (Fig. 129 *a*); but *Vipera* is capable of following the track of a bitten mouse very closely. During the process, the head is swung continually from side to side (Baumann, 1929), giving a clear case of klino-taxis (Fig. 129 *b*). Indeed, a dog follows a trail by much the same method; the deviations are slight but obvious enough. There is no evidence of any tropo-tactic mechanism here—no one has so far observed the effect of eliminating one of the two nostrils.

So far we have dealt with cases in which the source of chemical stimulation is actually reached, if enough time is allowed (attractants), and have touched upon a few cases of chemo-negative behaviour (repellents). There are a few cases in which a chemical substance can be either an attractant or a repellent, according to the concentration. In such cases, if a suitably extensive range of concentration is available in the gradient, the animals may collect in an intermediate zone and thus show a preferred or eccritic concentration. Thus the cheese mite, *Tyrolichus casei*, reacts positively to putrefying protein and to one of its constituents, skatol; but on approaching a piece of filter-paper soaked in pure skatol, at a certain distance the concentration becomes too high and the reaction becomes negative. After moving away from the source for a short time the reaction again reverses, and so on, so that the mites collect in a ring around the filter-paper (Fig. 130) (Henschel, 1929). The same kind of aggregation in a so-called 'optimum' region (see

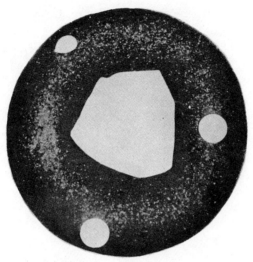

FIG. 130. Photograph of the aggregation of cheese mites, *Tyrolychus casei*, round a filter-paper soaked with a dilute solution of skatol. The mites are visible as small white spots. (Henschel, 1929.)

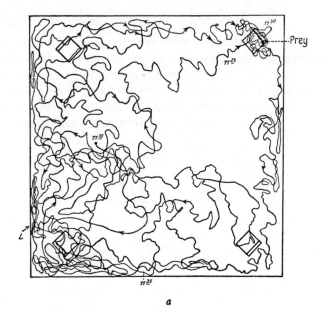

a

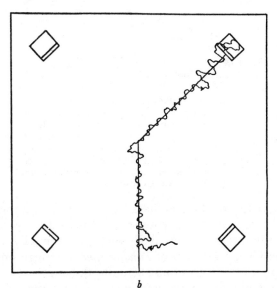

b

Fig. 129. Tracks of the snake, *Vipera aspis*, after it had attacked a mouse. The mouse was then taken away and hidden in the cage. *a*. The seeking movements were entirely directionless. *b*. The mouse was dragged over the ground and the snake was able to follow the track by means of continuous pendulations of the head. (After Baumann, 1929.)

Chap. XIV) is shown by ticks in a gradient of butyric acid vapour arising from a solution of 1 in 300,000 in water (Totze, 1933), (Figs. 131, 132). The explanations given by these authors follow closely that of Jennings (1904, 1906) for various similar reactions of certain Protista; the aggregation zone is an indifference zone, while at certain upper and lower limits

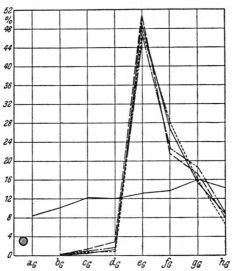

FIG. 131. Curves of distribution of the tick *Ixodes* in a gradient of smell (butyric acid). The various curves apply to larvae, nymphs, and adults. The thin line near the bottom represents a control experiment (without smell). Abscissa—distance from the source of smell; ordinate—number of ticks at each concentration as a percentage of all ticks present. (After Totze, 1933.)

avoiding reactions ('phobo-taxes') occur. Although this pheno-menon has not yet been reinvestigated with the new classification in mind, it seems very likely that it is essentially similar to the klino-kinetic reaction of *Dendrocoelum*, although once more the internal mechanism must be quite different.

One of Jennings's many experiments has become a classic and is worth a short description (Fig. 133, p. 288). A large cover-slip is supported at the corners by short plasticene legs and the space between it and the slide is flooded with a dense suspension of *Paramecium* in tap-water. A bubble of carbon dioxide, a drop of soda-water (i.e. CO_2 solution), or a drop of very dilute acetic acid solution ($N/10-N/100$) is then injected so as to lie under the centre of the cover-slip. In less than a minute the majority of the *Paramecium* form a dense ring at a little distance from the acid or the bubble. As the acid diffuses outwards, the ring moves away and eventually the animals are again uniformly distributed through the fluid. Observation of single individuals

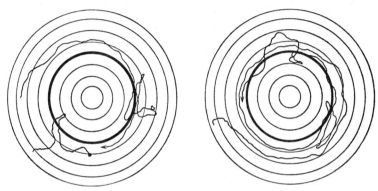

FIG. 132. Tracks of the tick *Ixodes* in a gradient of butyric acid, 1/100,000, diffusing from the centre of the experimental field. The ticks remain in an eccritic region. (After Totze, 1933.)

shows that they are active all the time, unless they fail to turn back and thus get into too concentrated acid; normally, they turn away from the acid at some short distance from it and then turn back at some greater distance. The reaction has been described so frequently that we need say no more about it.

An analogous case has been described by Fox (1921) for the flagellate, *Bodo sulcatus*, which reacts to oxygen concentration and not to carbon dioxide (Fig. 134, p. 289). The preferred concentration is lower than air saturation and the flagellates themselves reduce the concentration quite quickly if they are present in sufficient numbers. The result is that they aggregate first of all in the centre of the cover-slip. The resulting dense mass of flagellates reduces the oxygen concentration below the preferred value, so that they then form a ring which moves slowly outwards. At a certain distance from the centre this ring becomes stabilized, and at this distance the entrance of oxygen from the air around the edges of the cover-slip just balances the oxygen consumed by the flagellates.

It was the study of this kind of behaviour among the Protista which led Jennings (1904, 1906) to develop his 'Trial and Error Theory' for certain reactions. This has been very widely recognized, and Loeb (1918) admitted that the reactions which it described would neither fit into the tropism scheme nor under the name of *Unterschiedsempfindlichkeit*. Jennings's account is roughly this: the animal does not react until it reaches a certain intensity of stimulation, the marginal value. At the margin it stops, turns, and tries a new direction. If the new direction is an error, that is, if it does not lead immediately into a sub-marginal intensity, the trial reaction is repeated, and so on (Fig. 16, p. 56). This describes the reaction quite fairly and the only objection to it in many cases is that it has an anthropomorphic tinge (Viaud, 1938a). The limitations of this description have been dealt with in Chapter V, and we prefer to include this kind of reaction in our category of klino-kinesis.

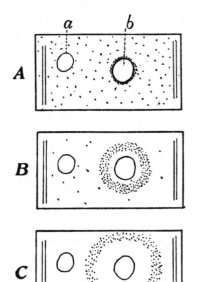

FIG. 133. Collection of *Paramecium* around a bubble, *b*, of CO_2. An air bubble *a* has no influence at all. As the CO_2 diffuses into the surrounding water, the *Paramecium* follow the preferred zone. B — 2 minutes later than A. C — 18 minutes later than B. (Jennings, 1906.)

The finding of food is essential to the survival of the individual and mating is essential to the survival of most species of animal. Another factor of increasingly recognized importance in survival is the humidity of the atmosphere. Many animals dry up and die if the air is too dry, while others are adversely affected by a very moist atmosphere (Buxton, 1932; Mellanby, 1935). It is therefore not surprising to find that some species react to humidity in such a way as to collect in places where these harmful effects do not occur. Little is known about the receptor mechanisms, and indeed it is only in the spiders (Blumenthal, 1935) and in the mealworm beetle, *Tenebrio molitor* (Pielou, 1940), that the position and form of hygro-receptors are known.[1] It seems rather improbable that the small amount of water exchange which can take place between the air and the receptor in the short time required for reaction can have a chemical effect; it seems much more likely that the effect is a physical one like the changes caused by humidity in paper, hair, and other fibres, and that the nerve-endings are stimulated mechanically. In classifying stimuli, however, we are not primarily con-

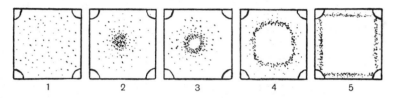

FIG. 134. Orientation of the flagellate *Bodo sulcatus* into a zone of reduced oxygen tension under a cover-slip. Explanation in text p. 287. (After Fox, 1921.)

cerned with the stages between the external stimulus and the activation of the nerve (i.e. the processes going on in the receptor) but with the external stimulus itself. Atmospheric humidity is presented as a certain concentration of molecules in a gas and is so similar to smell in this respect that we may regard. it as a kind of chemical stimulus.

Apart from experiments in which the humidity has been only imperfectly controlled and not measured at all, there are two main kinds of the apparatus which have been used for investigating humidity reactions, the transverse current apparatus (Shelford & Deere, 1913) and the diffusion gradient apparatus (Gunn & Kennedy, 1936). In the former a long narrow chamber is traversed by three air-currents, each of which may be varied in speed, humidity, and temperature. For example, the current across one end of the apparatus may be cold and moist, that across the other end warm and dry, and the one across the middle third of the apparatus, intermediate in both respects. The evaporating power of each current of air was measured directly. By means of this apparatus correlations have been found between the reactions of animals and the physical

[1] See note 49, Appendix.

conditions in their natural habitats (Shelford & Deere, 1913; Hamilton, 1917; Chenoweth, 1917; Heimburger, 1924). The methods of aggregation appear to depend mainly on ortho- and klino-kinesis; indeed, it is difficult to see how chemo-taxis could come into operation in such a transverse current.

The diffusion gradient apparatus has no currents of air, and it is made with a very low roof to prevent convection currents due to the humidity itself. The most convenient form of this apparatus is the 'alternative chamber', as described in Chapter II, after the style of Graber's apparatus, but made precisely to certain dimensions so as to facilitate comparison of work done on different insects and in different laboratories. In this apparatus an ortho-kinesis in woodlice (Gunn, 1937) and an avoiding reaction (klino-kinesis?) in mosquitoes (Thomson, 1938) have already been demonstrated. Kennedy (1937) obtained the curious result that the African migratory locust always aggregates at the drier side of the chamber, however dry that may be, although it has been shown that a fairly moist atmosphere is most favourable for the species (Hamilton, 1936).[1,2] There was a similar appearance of poor co-ordination between reaction and optimal conditions in Thomson's mosquitoes, and it seems likely in these cases either that humidity is not an important adverse condition available to the animals in their natural habitat or that they are preserved from harm by some other reaction, perhaps to a quite different type of stimulus. There is as yet no satisfactory evidence of hygro-taxis proper, though it seems likely that this type of reaction is possible in the spiders at least (Blumenthal, 1935; Savory, 1930).[3-14]

According to Czeloth (1930), the newt, *Triton*, is attracted to moist places. In still air, when stimulated by water vapour diffusing from a moist source, it first circles round, and eventually reaches the source by an indirect route. It can succeed from a distance of 70 cm. Czeloth suggested that the mechanism is tropo-tactic, but he did not carry out any crucial experiments.

We see, therefore, that chemical stimuli themselves do not lead to very efficient modes of orientation, mainly because the only reactions possible are reactions to intensity and not to direction. Even then, gradients of intensity are set up but slowly and are easily and quickly destroyed by currents in the air or water. It is not surprising that chemo-taxes are rare and

[1] See also Patlak's (1953 *b*) mathematical treatment of Kennedy's data.
[2] See note 50, Appendix.
[3-14] See notes 51 to 62, Appendix.

take rather a small part in chemo-reactions; the main work of locating the source is done by means of the two kinds of kineses. There are sometimes aids to orientation in the shape of mechanisms which sample the surrounding fluid; the sniffing of dogs, the siphon action of the prosobranchs quoted, and the currents thrown on to the antennules by the palps of the maxillipedes in crabs and hermit crabs are examples of this. Sometimes, instead of the animal making a sampling current, there is a current ready made, and then the animal can orientate towards the source simply by going directly against the current which carries the stimulating substance. In that case the reaction is initiated chemically and the direction is maintained through other receptors (rheo-taxis). This is true for *Planaria alpina* (Doflein, 1925). The marine gastropods, *Alectrion*, *Busycon*, and *Nassa*, which perform chemo-kinesis in still water, become positively rheo-tactic in running water carrying a suitable chemical, and thus find the bait by means of a directed reaction (Copeland, 1918). A simple air-stream has no influence on the direction of motion of *Drosophila*, but when the air carries an appropriate chemical substance the fly runs remarkably precisely into the current and so finds the bait directly (p. 259, Fig. 120) (Flügge, 1934).[1] Similarly the newt, *Triton*, in still air reaches the source of an appropriate smell (e.g. soil) only by a very devious route, but goes almost directly to the source if the smell is carried by a current of air. In a current of pure dry air *Triton* usually crawls with the current, but if the air is moist it equally often goes with and against it (Czeloth, 1930). In animals which swim or fly out of contact with solid objects, an upstream orientation can often be maintained optically, so that altogether there are a number of ways in which animals can overcome the special difficulties of reaching a source of chemical stimulation.

---

[1] See note 63, Appendix.

XIX

VARIATION IN BEHAVIOUR

IN a number of places in this book attention has been directed to the statistical outlook on the results of behaviour experiments. Thus in ortho-kinesis and klino-kinesis the results can be expressed precisely in statistical terms alone; there are no means of predicting exactly when *Dendrocoelum* will make its next turn in a gradient of light, but there are statistical methods available for judging what chance there is that the planarian will turn within a certain time (Chap. V). There is less chance that it will turn when going towards the dimly lit region than when going the other way, and this is the essence of the reaction. The behaviour of an individual animal at a particular instant is not predictable, but that of a sufficiently large number of animals over a suitable length of time is reasonably predictable on a statistical basis.

In the same way the movements of a particular electron cannot be reliably forecast but, under suitable conditions, the properties of a statistical assembly of electrons can be predicted with great accuracy on the basis of what can happen to a single electron. It is just as unnecessary to assume that the movements of animals are due to an unpredictable free will as it is to assume that free will controls the movements of atomic electrons. Some people take the view that because the motions of a single electron cannot be determined in advance, they are indeterminate in the sense that something analogous to caprice is affecting them; this view is not accepted by physicists to-day, but even if it were correct, it would not alter the determinacy of the behaviour of a large collection of electrons. Consequently, we conclude that even this free will can be described sufficiently well, by suitable statistical methods, to make prediction of mass behaviour reasonably sure.

If observations, calculations, and experiments did not yield reasonably constant and repeatable results and conclusions, then all scientific work would be a waste of time, as far as making further discoveries goes. Scientific work rests on the basic assumption that there is order in natural phenomena, and this assumption has been sufficiently justified by results. Even if free will exists in electrons and animals, it need not make research impossible or futile as long as this free will itself can be docketed, classified, and described statistically, as long as it is itself orderly in the mass. The disorder of individual electrons does in fact add up to a mass orderliness. In the same way the reaction of a single untested maggot to light cannot be stated in advance, but the chance that it will go away from light under specified conditions can be stated, and it is a big chance.

If free will is to be found anywhere, then it is operative in human beings and is a considerable factor in human reproduction. No one can predict a year in advance which couples are going to have babies; but as long as no important new factor intrudes—and this is a reservation which must be made in all prediction—the birth-rate in this country can be predicted with fairly high accuracy for a year or so ahead. It does not matter whether free will is operative or not—and that question is unanswerable if any question is—as long as in the mass it is not capricious; as long as it is statistically orderly, we can handle it like any other variable, even without knowing whether it exists or not.

Statistics, for this purpose, is the science of the description and analysis of variation. Consider, as an example, the variation in height in a group of human beings. If you add up all the heights and divide the total by the number of people measured, the answer is an average height for the group. If the group is sufficiently homogeneous, there are far more people of about the average height than of, say, a foot shorter or taller. Now height is determined by many factors under each of the headings of heredity, nutrition, disease, and so on, and these may all combine in favour of great height or against it. In most persons, however, some factors will be favourable and some unfavourable, so that the final height of an individual depends on a combination of a large number of small factors. Foreknowledge of how they would combine in a particular person would involve a complete and detailed knowledge of the whole universe and a fantastic game of chess with an infinite number of pieces. The neglect of the action of a pathological organism, a grain of poison, or something equally minute, would knock the whole calculation out of order. But when the final value of the variant depends on a large number of small factors, the group as a whole gives a curve of height distribution which is called the curve of normal variation; provided the incidence of disease and poison and so on remains about the same, this curve can be used for predicting the future of similar groups of people.

The same shape of curve can be obtained by tossing pennies or throwing dice, and this curve of chance or luck is of great importance in quantitative biology. If the variation is really normal, the curve can be completely described by means of two numbers—the average value and a quantity which measures the lateral spread (the standard deviation). Further, the standard error—which is obtained from the standard deviation and the number of observations—measures the reliability of the average. These figures are used in an invaluable method of comparing two groups of observations to see if they differ significantly, and so they can lead to the detection and assessment of factors affecting the size of the average. In short, some statistical analysis is often required in behaviour, and suitable methods are available for this analysis. Before the mechanism of a reaction can be described and before an estimate of its effects in nature can be made, it is frequently necessary partly to analyse and then to reduce the variation, so that fairly repeatable results can be obtained in a short time.

From what has been said it should be clear that occasionally unusual individuals are found which behave very differently from the majority and that these may be simply the extreme variants in a normal distribution. Thus it has been shown that animals behaving tropo-tactically under the influence of two lights do not all follow exactly the same path; the paths are normally distributed (Chap. VII). The extreme variants of this distribution go straight to one of the two lights, giving the appearance of telo-taxis, and some workers have in fact interpreted the behaviour as telo-tactic. Statistical analysis shows, however, that these extreme variants do not require a special explanation. That is to say, all the factors which can act in a particular direction are acting together in these individuals, while in most cases only some of such factors occur together. Until very detailed analysis enables us to identify and assess these factors, it is uneconomical to spend much time on exceptional behaviour. It is misleading to attach great importance to extreme variants and to appeal to higher modes of behaviour in order to explain them. This error appears to have been made by some of the members of the Marburg school. If, however, reasonably homogeneous *groups* of animals are found to behave differently from the majority, then these groups themselves offer opportunities for repeating experiments, for suitable statistical testing, and for finding out reasons why they differ from the majority of specimens..

In many cases the variation in a reaction is far from normally distributed. For example, when the angles of orientation to light of the nauplius larvae of the barnacle, *Balanus*, are measured, they are found to have a bi-modal distribution; some individuals are photo-negative and some photo-positive (Loeb, 1918). Such complete reversals of reaction are common (Rose, 1929) and do not require complex statistical analysis. Reversal and certain other kinds of variation are so striking and obvious that the causes of some of them are already well known. The account of some of these causes of variation which follows does not pretend to be complete, but it indicates the sorts of factors which may be responsible.[1]

One might classify the known causes of variation in behaviour into two main groups—external factors and internal ones. That is not very satisfactory, for the internal factors are themselves partly caused by external ones, perhaps acting immediately before and perhaps long before. It is then largely a matter of the length of the chain of events between the external stimulus and the resulting externally observable stimulus. A classification is put forward by Maier & Schneirla (1935).

First of all, the sense or sign of a reaction may be reversed by a change in the intensity of the stimulus; *Euglena* is photopositive in weak light and photo-negative in strong light (Mast, 1911, 1938). Consequently, in a gradient the organisms collect in a middle region, and Mast observed that in this region they are indifferent to light. The light has thus a double effect, presumably acting through the single receptor; the direction of the light controls the path of the animal and the intensity of the light controls the sense or sign of movement along that path. When the sign of reaction is uncontrolled, so is the path, so that in fact there is no reaction at all.

Again, some specimens of the cockroach, *Blatta orientalis*, are

[1] See note 64, Appendix.

hygro-negative. During a long sojourn in the dry air they lose water by evaporation and then they become hygro-positive. The continued action of the dry air—in the absence of food and of water to drink—has a physiological effect, so that the immediate cause of the hygro-positive reaction is internal (namely, the state of desiccation), but the ultimate cause is the external dryness. The sign of this reaction depends on the physiological condition, and that in its turn is determined by the external factor acting directly and not through receptors (Gunn & Cosway, 1938).

The light reaction of *Eristalis* is usually investigated experimentally when the animal has been kept in the dark for 20 minutes or so. The eyes are then fully dark-adapted and the reaction occurs with its greatest intensity. While the fly is being tested, it is of course exposed to light and the intensity of the reaction diminishes, though it never reverses. The continued action of the stimulus in this case causes a rapid decline in the reaction. We do not know if the migration of shielding pigment takes a part in this process of adaptation, but in any case some kind of sensory adaptation is involved (Chap. III).[1] Generally speaking, a stimulus may be expected to have the greatest effect on the nervous system when it first begins to act. Sensory adaptation may take on the appearance of learning; thus Minnich (1919) thought that the gradual elimination of circus movements in unilaterally blinded insects was due to learning, but Clark (1928) showed that it was due to sensory adaptation alone (p. 166).

In laboratory experiments it is usual to reduce the variation in reaction as much as possible by varying only one of the external factors and keeping the others as constant as possible. In a temperature gradient, however, it is extremely difficult or impossible to maintain a uniform humidity; normally the air gets progressively drier on passing from the cold end to the warm. Now those cockroaches which react to humidity alter their preferred temperature according to the air humidity. When the air is quite dry they give the pure preferred temperature, for individuals which do not react to humidity at all have the same preferred temperature. When the air contains some water vapour, humidity reactive specimens collect at a slightly higher temperature. That is to say, in moist air their whole

[1] See note 65, Appendix.

reaction shows a compromise between the pure reactions to temperature and to humidity (Gunn & Cosway, 1938). Such compromises are probably very common in nature, but there are also cases in which one kind of stimulus has far greater importance than all the others. Nevertheless, the observer must always be on the look-out for variable factors other than the one which is being investigated.[1]

A different kind of reaction to two stimuli at one time is shown by *Paramecium* (Fox, 1925). Under suitable conditions *Paramecium* is geo-positive in light and geo-negative in darkness. It does not matter whether the light comes from below or above or from the side, the animals go down. In nature the light would always come more from above than below, and then in going down the animals would be going away from it and into less intense light. It is only by means of laboratory experiments with test-tubes that the correct relations of the stimuli could be made out. The functional significance of the reaction in the normal life of *Paramecium*, if there is any, is not known.

Now had this effect of light been overlooked—as it might easily have been, for the situation is further complicated by a chemo-reaction to the acidity of the medium and by contact reactions of the animals to each other and to solid objects—it might have been considered that *Paramecium* is simply geo-positive. It is most probable that the common simplification of experimental conditions in the attempt to reduce variation has hidden other cases of the same kind. This is not an argument against performing laboratory experiments or against simplifying them, for had field observations alone been made, *Paramecium* might have been supposed to be simply photo-negative; it shows the danger of incautious application of laboratory results to natural life. Very many experiments have been done with the object of elucidating the mechanism of behaviour; it is to be expected that the behaviour will not be quite the same when the conditions have not the experimental simplicity. After the analysis the next stage is the synthesis—the investigation of the interrelations of various reactions and their importance in nature.

An analysis of the behaviour of *Littorina neritoides* in relation to natural conditions has been made by Fraenkel (1927 *b*). This animal is found several metres above high-water mark of

[1] See note 66, Appendix.

European seas. It is usually geo-negative and never geo-positive. When out of water it is always photo-negative. In the water it is too, except when it is upside down, and then it is photo-positive (Fig. 135). These reactions may be expected to guide the animal from the bottom of the water to rocks (dark) and then up the rock face (geo-negative); if the light is very bright, the animal stops and settles down at the water surface. In crawling up under water, if it gets into a deep horizontal cleft,

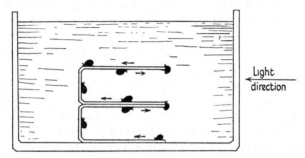

FIG. 135. The marine snail, *Littorina neritoides*, reacts photo-negatively while on the floor of a vessel in a horizontal position, geo-negatively while on the vertical wall, and photo-positively while hanging on the roof upside down. (Fraenkel, 1927 *b*.)

negative photo-taxis takes it inwards on the floor, negative geo-taxis upwards on the end wall, and positive photo-taxis outwards on the roof in the inverted position. Upward progress is therefore not barred by such a cleft. Above the water surface, the sign of photo-taxis does not reverse in this way, so the animal comes to rest in such a cleft. Under the influence of dryness and other unfavourable conditions the animal closes up; it may then fall back into the sea, but if conditions are not very unfavourable it may live for months out of water. This behaviour provides examples of taxes in opposition (gravity and light) and of one stimulus (the presence of surrounding water) affecting the response to another (light).[1,2]

For *Paramecium* light is simply a *background condition* for the gravity reaction. A striking instance of the importance of background conditions is provided by the light reaction of *Daphnia* (Loeb, 1906 *b*; Viaud, 1938 *b*). Individuals which are indifferent to light can often be caused to react strongly positively by adding carbon dioxide to the water. This relation between the back-

[1] See note 67, Appendix.
[2] See note 68, Appendix.

ground and the response to light may be of some value to
Daphnia in its ordinary life, for the light would normally guide
it to the surface of the water where the carbon dioxide tension
would usually be lowest. In a similar way, exposure to dry air
tends to alter the photo-tactic reaction of the woodlouse,
Porcellio, from negative to positive (Henke, 1930). It is possible
that here again light acts as a token stimulus in nature. The
velocity of the change of sign of the photo-taxis suggests that
Daphnia has receptors sensitive to carbon dioxide or that there
is a very rapid direct effect on the nervous system, while in
Porcellio the dry air has a slower physiological action of desiccation.

As a factor in behaviour age is rather difficult to classify. It
depends on the passage of time, in itself an unalterable factor;
but in poikilotherms, what may be called the *physiological age*
depends also on the rate of living and therefore on the past
series of temperatures (see p. 201). Consequently, age is best
regarded as a matter of physiological condition. The structure
and mode of life of a barnacle are so different from those of its
young nauplius larva that no question of similarity of behaviour
can be raised. Behaviour may depend on age, however, when the
two stages of the life-history are much more alike than those in
the example mentioned. Thus the newly hatched blow-fly
maggot is actually positive to weak light, and then soon becomes
negative (Herms, 1911). Presumably the first reaction has the
effect of scattering the newly hatched larvae a little, while the
later reaction keeps them sheltered from predators and from
extreme physical conditions.

Turning now to factors which are more clearly internal and
physiological, we find that the positive rheo-taxis of *Planaria
alpina* is shown most clearly when the animal has been well fed
and is approaching sexual maturity. It then makes its migration to the upper waters of the stream. The condition of sexual
development depends on external factors—the amount of food
available and the temperature (Beauchamp, 1933, 1937). In
the vertebrates many cases are known in which the complex
sexual behaviour—display, mating, nest building, migration,
&c.—is started off by internal factors in the shape of hormones.
These hormones, in their turn, are at any rate partly dependent
on external factors—amount of available food, temperature,

and duration of daylight—for their appearance at the appropriate time.

The external factors so far mentioned affect behaviour either because they have an immediate and transitory effect on the receptor-nervous-effector system or because they have an indirect effect on it through the physiological machinery of the body; there are other cases in which external factors and situations have an enduring effect on behaviour, but no other effect of a physiological nature. The resulting changes in behaviour may be generally classified under the various kinds of learning by experience.

Modification in behaviour due to experience takes place even in *Amoeba*. Thus Mast & Pusch (1924) showed that the delay in reacting to light decreased as the number of tests already made in the day increased. It is very striking to find that in this animal, in which there is no division of labour between differentiated cells, even the activity of learning by experience takes place. There are other cases in which the reaction diminishes instead of improving and in which neither fatigue nor sensory adaptation is the cause of the change. Thus a crawling snail normally withdraws its tentacles if a light is flashed on them; if the flash is repeated a number of times at suitable intervals, eventually the tentacles are not withdrawn in response, provided the flashes are not accompanied or closely followed by any noxious stimulation. The animal thus becomes *habituated* to the stimulus (Grindley, 1937).

Shock reactions to increase or decrease in intensity of light are very commonly found in animals (v. Buddenbrock, 1937); they are usually regarded as reflexes, but since habituation can take place they are not fixed and invariable. Photo-kinesis is perhaps the simplest kind of reaction involving locomotion and is remarkably constant in a number of animals; but even this reaction can be altered by suitable methods. Hovey (1929) used the turbellarian *Leptoplana*, which becomes active when the light is switched on in a previously dark room. If, however, it is touched on the snout each time it starts to move, after a large number of trials in a day it ceases to respond to the light and does not start to crawl, even if it is not touched. Even photo-kinesis can thus be inhibited, if suitable methods are used.

That raises the question of how far taxes and kineses in

general are learnt and not inherited or, if they are inherited, how far they can be discarded. Little information is available about this. According to von Frisch & Kupelwieser (1913) the reactions of different batches of *Daphnia* to light varied very much; responses were good and consistent in December and June and very variable in the Spring. Ewald (1910) reported that *Daphnia* from turbid ponds did not orientate to light at all under experimental conditions. Copeland (1930) trained *Nereis*, which is normally photo-negative, to come towards a light for food. These observations do not tell us whether or not taxes were learned or inherited in the first place, but they do tell us that taxes can sometimes be inhibited or unlearnt. On the other hand, Payne (1910, 1911) bred *Drosophila* in the dark (for 69 generations!) and found that they were photo-positive as usual at the first trial. It seems probable that certain reaction patterns are inherited by each species of animal, but that some or all of them may be modified as a result of experience gained during the individual's lifetime.

Instincts—that is to say, complex behaviour patterns as distinct from the basic urges or drives—are generally regarded as very fixed. Cocooning behaviour in Lepidoptera, web building in spiders, and egg-laying behaviour in Hymenoptera provide many examples in which all the members of the species carry out the same complex activities, though without contact with their parents or with each other; but even instinctive patterns may become more perfect on repetition. The young mammal or bird need not be taught to walk or fly; but these activities increase in efficiency with practice. Further, if the normal walking of a dog or a centipede is interfered with by putting one or more of the legs out of action, after a time a new co-ordination appears. The *plasticity* of co-ordination enables the activity to be carried out in a different way (v. Holst, 1935 *a*). Perhaps walking should be distinguished as an *acquired automatism* and not an instinct at all. Much work remains to be done before valuable generalizations can be made about the modifiability of instincts, taxes, and related reactions.

There are some activities which must always involve some kind of learning. Thus in many cases when locomotion is not random and not directed by light, temperature gradients, or the like, the direction taken depends essentially on previous experience. The simplest kind of training is carried out by punishing the animal whenever it does something you don't want it to do. An earthworm can be taught to turn to the left when crawling along a Y-tube by giving it an electric shock every time it turns to the right (Yerkes, 1912). After some hundreds of trials it turns to the left almost invariably, even if the brain is then removed. Domestic mammals can be taught to conform to a number of prohibitions by the same method. The number and kind of prohibitions which can be instilled into an animal depend not only on the sensory and nervous apparatus of the species but also on individual factors. Thus not only does the behaviour vary according to the past experience of the individual, but also according to the ability of the individual to profit by that experience. This phenomenon is even more familiar in human beings.

The Y-tube in which the earthworm was trained may be regarded as a very simple maze. A very large body of work has been done on the behaviour of animals in mazes. In the simplest case, there is one path through the maze to the goal, where the animal is fed; if the animal leaves this path, it enters a dead end and has to turn back eventually. Possibly the necessity for turning back acts like the electric shock in the earthworm experiment. Some animals, like cockroaches, learn the way through a maze rather slowly and forget again quickly (Turner, 1913), while others, such as rats, learn much more quickly (Maier & Schneirla, 1935).

No doubt something very like experimental maze running is a normal feature of the life of wild rats, and indeed of all animals which have any kind of home. In hive bees, home finding is carried out optically, with the aid of conspicuous features in the terrain, supplemented by a kinaesthetic sense (cf. p. 102). In ants, too, eyes are used in many species, both for recognition of landmarks and for performing the light compass reaction to the sun. The most reasonable explanation—though perhaps an incomplete one—of the successful homing of pigeons is that they recognize the lie of the land. On the other hand, the annual migrations of birds are not all susceptible to such easy explanation, for there are cases in which the young birds, which have never migrated before, leave after the older ones have gone and follow approximately the same routes.

Another kind of training or learning, which may be different in nature from that involved in maze running, is that known as conditioning. This kind of learning always starts with a reflex response to a given stimulus, the unconditioned stimulus; the training consists in substituting a different stimulus, the conditioned stimulus, for the unconditioned one in such a way as to lead to the same response. The classical example of this is provided by Pavlov's work on salivation in the domestic dog. The presence of food in the dog's mouth is an unconditioned stimulus for the secretion of saliva. In the experiment, a bell starts to ring and, while it is still ringing, the food is given to the dog. After a few trials, the bell is rung but no food is given; salivation occurs nevertheless. The sound of the bell has been substituted for the presence of food in the mouth as a stimulus for salivation. That does not mean, of course, that the presence of food in the mouth is any less effective in producing salivation than it was before, but simply that the ringing of the bell, which was previously ineffective, has become as effective as the food itself. The time relations of the experiment must be carefully observed, or it fails; the conditioned stimulus must start before the unconditioned one, and the two stimuli must overlap in time. If the bell starts to ring one second after the food is given, there is no conditioning effect.

Conditioning experiments have been used to demonstrate the existence of colour vision in fishes and in bees, and in a number of similar ways. The ability to substitute one stimulus for another is probably of great importance in natural behaviour. It enables animals to take short cuts, to eliminate much random behaviour, and to go straight towards food or away from danger. Although it is difficult to describe maze learning completely and satisfactorily in terms of conditioning, conditioning may very well be involved in the later stages of perfecting maze running. The analysis of such reactions is very difficult, but has attracted a good deal of attention because of its bearing on human behaviour.

Kineses and taxes are of very slight importance at most in the behaviour of mammals; instinctive patterns, too, take a much smaller part than they do in the arthropods, while the more variable kinds of reaction involving learning take a larger part. It is in the mammals, particularly the anthropoids, that completely new responses to new situations may occur at the first trial; the capacity for making such new responses is called *intelligence*, using the word in its restricted sense. In the wider sense, the intelligence of an animal is its capacity to learn in any way. The intelligence of chimpanzees, in the narrow sense, has been demonstrated by W. Köhler (1927).

Intelligent behaviour in the narrow sense is most obvious in man, though opinions vary as to its importance even in this species. There is no reliable evidence at all of its occurrence outside the Mammalia. Since the elementary reactions with which this book is concerned are of little importance in this class, presumably because they have been superseded by more complex and more adaptable modes of behaviour, intelligent action is probably not a cause of variation in taxes.

On the other hand, in the invertebrates there appears to be rather little modifiability of behaviour through individual experience, though successful maze running and simple learning of various kinds do occur in most of the groups. It may be that the ability to learn has not been looked for by suitable methods. What we do know is that kineses, taxes, and similar reactions are fairly consistently found amongst the individuals of those species in which they occur at all. That does not show that these reactions are inherent; but if they are not inherent, they are at least learnt by most of the members of a species. Practically speaking, there is only the work of Payne (1911) to show that in one case, at least, photo-taxis is not learnt. Before we can be dogmatic about the inherent nature of kineses, taxes, and the rest, work specifically designed to test the matter must be carried out. In the meantime, it remains possible that some of these reactions have to be learnt and that part of the observed variation is due to differences in learning. There are, however, so many other causes of variation in behaviour that most workers take the simplifying view that learning is not involved in these elementary reactions.

XX

GENERAL DISCUSSION AND CONCLUSION

THE great importance of the activities of the mind has been recognized since ancient times. There are several phrases in everyday speech in which an antithesis is made between 'mind' and 'body', setting an activity of the brain against the whole of the bodily structure. It has been clear for more than a generation, however, that whatever 'mind' may be, it is not observed independently of the organ of which it is an activity, and it is almost as logical to speak of *excretion and body* or of *digestion and body* as of *mind and body*. The phrase *mens sana in corpore sano* simply draws attention to the importance of the human brain, a structure so sensitive and so delicate that even in the absence of observable physical damage it may be sufficiently unhealthy to make the health of the rest of the body almost valueless. In general, the organs of the body react on one another to such an extent that the good health of one part is ultimately dependent on the health of the rest.

The brain, then, is a part of the body and its activity is only one of the interdependent bodily activities. Moreover, the brain is like the other organs in that it is not known to deviate from physical and chemical laws in any way. That is not to say that we know all about the activities of the brain, that we can construct a brain in the laboratory, or even that we can describe all its activities in precise physical and chemical terms —far from it. Considerable progress has been made in this direction, however, and that progress itself justifies us in neglecting the possibility that the mind is not amenable to scientific treatment.

It is generally assumed, then—and it is a pure assumption, though a valuable one—that organic activities conform to rules of a physical and chemical sort and may eventually be described in the fundamental terms of these branches of science. It is not necessary to await that distant day before investigating behaviour and describing it in terms of a different sort. Automobiles and their parts may be the legitimate subject of researches by an atomic physicist, a metallurgist, a mechanical engineer, a cost accountant, a traffic expert, and a sociologist.

Similarly, the nervous system and the results of its activities may be profitably studied on various planes—physical, chemical, morphological, physiological, psychological, and so on. It is possible to make extensive and valuable researches on one level, morphological for example, in complete ignorance of relevant knowledge on other levels; as knowledge increases, however, improvements in one field have an increasing effect on neighbouring fields, and the interdependence of the parts of natural science grows. Thus it is valuable to investigate the action currents set up by a receptor in a nerve even though the physical account of the nature of action currents is provisional and incomplete. Similarly, reflexes may be profitably examined without knowledge of anything more than the mere existence of some sort of transmission in nerve, though the information gained is more likely to lead to valuable generalizations when linked up with the other knowledge available.

In comparative psychology—which includes the study of the behaviour of whole animals and of parts of animals when that is helpful—it is usual to attempt to describe behaviour in the simplest terms. What is meant by 'simple' here is another story and a long one, but in practice physical and chemical terms are preferred; if these are insufficient in the existing state of knowledge, reflexes are brought in; if that is still not enough, as in maze learning, then a higher plane of behaviour has to be postulated, a plane of behaviour which is not at present capable of description in terms of lower planes except in very speculative fashion. Acting on this principle of parsimony, it often happens that descriptions are given in terms which are not demonstrably correct—for example, the descriptions of taxes in terms of reflexes—and it must be borne in mind that they are provisional. They are a convenience in summarizing existing knowledge and in making clear what the further problems are. Such hypothetical descriptions stand until they are demonstrated to be incorrect or until they are replaced by more satisfactory ones.

The atomic theory in chemistry and the Darwinian theory of evolution in biology gave to their subjects a new unity which was of the greatest value. In comparative psychology attempts have been made to provide such a universal key. The acceptance of evolutionary doctrine broke down the old distinction between man and the brute creation, and the resulting tendency was to attribute to other vertebrates and even to invertebrates the highest man-like qualities of mind. As an extreme reaction from this, beginning near the end of the last century, an optimistic and heroic attempt was made to interpret the whole of animal behaviour including that of man in terms of physics and chemistry.

Loeb (1859–1924) was the most conspicuous figure in this new movement. After about five years' work on brain function in vertebrates, in 1888 he published his first paper on invertebrate behaviour. He took over from the botanists wholesale, and without proper tests, the so-called tropism theory, setting up a theory of animal behaviour which even now has some supporters, and which we therefore discuss in the light of the information already set out. As can be seen from the quotations given in the first chapter of this book, two quite distinct ideas are involved in Loeb's theory and in the word *tropism*. The first is the general idea of forced movements and the absence of free will in behaviour; the second is a particular theory of the kind of mechanism involved in such movements.

Taking the idea of forced movements first, it is easy to see that it was useful in directing attention towards mechanisms of behaviour and diverting it from the vague and speculative methods of the older human psychologists. But neither Loeb nor any one else has ever demonstrated that any animal response is forced or in any way fixed and immutable. It may very well be that there is indeed no freedom of will in any animals. If that is so, then animals of the same hereditary composition and of the same individual history should react in identical fashion when subjected to identical conditions. Given time, money, and patience, it is not too difficult to get animals of practically identical heredity, nor is it very difficult to keep physical conditions reasonably constant; it would be much more troublesome to ensure that a number of individuals had all exactly the same experience. But supposing that the attempt were made and then the animals tested for identity of response. If the responses turned out to be identical, one might say either that behaviour is forced or, on the other hand, that such similar animals naturally like doing similar things; if the responses differed at all, one might say that the conditions were not really quite identical or that free will was causing the variation. The interpretation given is simply a matter of personal preference, and for that reason it is going too far to call any animal responses forced movements.

At the same time, it is worth noting that the more constant all the conditions are before and during an experiment, the more constant and repeatable are the results. If one could get conditions really constant, extrapolation of existing knowledge suggests that responses would be constant too. Once, however, Lloyd Morgan had enunciated the principle that higher functions should not be invoked in describing behaviour in a particular case, if lower functions are consistent with all the observations, then the work of the forced movement idea was done and the idea could have been dropped. The question of free will is a metaphysical one, and it cannot be answered by experimental methods. If, simply as an experimental method, one ignores the possibility of free will, then fruitful analysis of the causes of variation in behaviour can be carried out and real advances made, as has been shown in the previous chapter. That obviously does not justify us in treating an assumption as a fact and stating it dogmatically. As long as there is order in nature, we can fruitfully investigate it experimentally. Statistically speaking, even free will is orderly and is not beyond investigation; we can get on quite well without knowing whether it exists or not.

As for the particular mechanism of reaction postulated by Loeb, it is unfortunate that to-day the word *tonus* does not mean what he intended it to mean. As has been pointed out in the chapter on physiological machinery, tonus is the unvarying contraction of a muscle, while the locomotion and manœuvres of animals with muscles are usually controlled phasically and not tonically. It still remains to be demonstrated that tonus, in the modern sense, is an essential part of any one of the reactions which we call taxes, though there are a few cases in which it might be.

If, therefore, we turn to the alternative wording of Loeb's theory, we find great emphasis laid on symmetry of stimulation of receptors and symmetry of activity of effectors in the orientated condition. But we have seen that in telo-taxis the effectors work symmetrically when stimulation is asymmetrical, as in a two-light experiment; in light compass reactions the essential feature is the asymmetry of stimulation during orientated loco-motion; in tropo-taxis, orientation straight towards a single light may occur even when the effectors have been made asymmetrical by amputation of legs. In klino-taxis there often appears to be no structural basis on which the symmetry theory could be erected, and Loeb's treatment of such cases was plausible but shallow. Loeb himself recognized the inapplicability of the theory to what we now call kineses. In short, it is clear that the tropism theory has nothing like the universal application which was long claimed for it.

The posture of unorientated animals was a conspicuous feature of Loeb's theory. It was held that the first effect of asymmetrical stimulation is to induce an asymmetrical posture which is maintained tonically. When the animal begins to move, the symmetrical impulses for locomotion were thought to be superposed on the asymmetrical impulses for tonic posture and so to lead to turning in the appropriate direction. There are certainly cases in which such postures occur (Garrey, 1917, 1918; Löwenstein, 1936), but they are not known in a single case to take the entire responsibility for the appropriate turning. Mast (1923) has shown that the turn may be in a direction opposite to that expected from the posture. It seems at least as likely that the impulses for locomotion are asymmetrical and so lead to turning, as that tonus is involved in turning. It is too great a simplification to assume that if a kinesis is added to a posture, a taxis results. When locusts are tilted over in the basking posture, if they are stimulated to move by some other stimulus, the posture is completely abandoned and they do not tend to turn away from the sun. The posture may be retained during locomotion in some cases, but it does not necessarily determine the direction of motion.

There is one idea which is common to the tropism theory and to Kühn's category of tropo-taxis, namely, the idea of balance. That balance need not be symmetrical, any more than the yard-arm balance is. There is a striking contrast between Loeb's usual optimism about the fruits of experimental work and his pessimism about the possibility of describing behaviour in terms of reflexes; it is to reflexes, partial and total, that we must turn in place of tonus. Symmetrical reflexes may normally be expected to produce locomotion straight forward, and with these modifications we may use the idea of balance. It should be noted, however, that such reflexes are not fixedly quantitatively proportional to the stimulation leading to their activity; in particular, Mast (1923) showed that *Eristalis* with a leg out of action modifies the activities of its other legs so that it can still orientate.

The confusion of two ideas under the term *tropism* led to some curious results. For example, many workers who found quantitative relations in animal behaviour jumped to the conclusion that the mere fact that they were quantitatively repeatable was a demonstration of the truth of the tropism theory! Others, when they found out how unsatisfactory the theory was, went to the other extreme and tried to erect an alternative all-embracing theory in teleological or subjective terms. Perhaps the majority of zoologists took the moderate view that 'the term tropism is a convenient label for grouping reflexes concerned with bodily orientation in response to a particular type of stimulus' (Hogben, 1926, p. 158). Unfortunately, different workers attached very different meanings to the term.

Part of the violence of the reaction against Loeb's theory was due to the fact that his best examples were obtained from operations on the brains of vertebrates and from the effects of electric currents on animals. As we can see now, brain operations give us information about the localization of function in the brain, but they are too gross to tell us very much about refined co-ordination; they jump the receptor stage in the behaviour chain as well as more than one step in co-ordination. They interfere with both phasic and tonic reflexes and so do not discriminate between them. Similarly, the movements referred to as *galvano-tropism*, *electrotaxis*, *oscillotaxis*, are simply due to the direct action of electric currents on the nerve-trunks or the like. It is inconceivable that there are specific receptors for electric currents, and the experiments tell us nothing about normal behaviour. That is the reason for leaving galvano-taxis out of consideration in this book.

The greatest reaction against the Loebian attitude has occurred amongst those who are interested in animals in their natural haunts. It soon became clear, for example, that Loeb's generalizations about the migrations of planktonic marine organisms were far too sweeping.[1] Despairing of descriptions in

[1] See notes 3 and 68.

objective terms at all, some turned back to teleological ones. For example, Russell (1938) writes: 'It seems simpler and more illuminating to think of the worm's action as being an effort to get back . . .', and 'All these diverse actions are directed to one main end—escape from danger'. The relation between teleological explanations of behaviour and the evolution of behaviour has been discussed in the second chapter. It seems to be a matter of taste whether one regards such statements as either simple or illuminating. Descriptions of animal behaviour in terms of purpose may give a superficial sort of understanding of them, but objective study not only leads to a greater increase of information but may also enrich the study of man himself.

Any description of behaviour which attempts to include everything in one grand sweep is as yet premature. The kind of error of the mediaeval naturalist, who tried to squeeze ants into the vertebrate pattern by drawing them with four legs, is not too difficult to avoid. The principal guide is objectivity. The advantages of the objective attitude can be seen by comparing the text-book by Warden, Jenkins, and Warner (1934), in which that attitude is adopted, with the book by Washburn (1936), in which the attitude is frankly anthropomorphic. At this stage in the development of the study of animal behaviour we must describe, analyse, and on the basis of analysis, classify. The relations between the various kinds of behaviour will appear when we know more about the physiology of nervous systems. In the meantime, our information is not altogether isolated from the natural lives of animals and we are helping to increase the understanding of them.

The aim of science is not simply to amass information, but rather to co-ordinate it, to simplify knowledge by finding the relations between facts. One of the first steps in making generalizations is to classify the facts available, to put them into groups so that a short summary may be made of a large body of experience. It is too early to go very far in describing behaviour in terms of biochemical processes or nerve physiology, though knowledge in these fields is increasing rapidly. We can, however, classify responses to simple physical stimuli in terms of the nature of the stimulus, the capacity of the receptors, and the manœuvres made by the animals. Such a classification was first attempted by Kühn (1919) and it is certainly economical.

Neither this classification nor the modification of it which we are putting forward should be regarded as rigid or final. That would defeat one of the objects of making a classification at this stage.

Kühn's classification (Table VI, p. 317) included phobo-taxis, on the one hand, and topo-taxes, on the other. Topo-taxes were divided into tropo-taxis, telo-taxis, meno-taxis, and mnemo-taxis. *Phobo-taxis* is the term first used by Pfeffer (1904) for the 'trial and error' reactions of Jennings, while *topo-taxis* was used by the same author for behaviour in which the direction of movement was not random, as in phobo-taxis, but bore some constant relation to the direction of the source of stimulation. Now it is convenient to put together as kineses those reactions in which direction is random, so we call phobo-taxis by the new name of *klino-kinesis*. That makes it unnecessary to use any prefix to the word *taxis* for a directed reaction, so *topo-taxis* is simply replaced by *taxis*. In klino-kinesis the frequency of turning is affected by the intensity of stimulation while the ordinary kinesis, in which only linear velocity is so affected, is distinguished as *ortho-kinesis*. So far we have introduced two prefixes (ortho- and klino-) and got rid of two (phobo- and topo-).

In the subdivision of taxes the elimination of *mnemo-taxis*, or orientation with the aid of memory images, has been widely approved. That term is too dangerous in that it might seem to conceal a very complex phenomenon in a system of classification of simpler ones. *Meno-taxis* differs from the other taxes and is like the dorsal light reaction in that the animals orientate according to the direction of the source of stimulation but do not go straight towards or away from it. It makes the group of taxes more homogeneous if we therefore remove meno-taxis and call it by the perfectly good objective vernacular name of *compass reaction*. We are then left with tropo-taxis and telo-taxis.

Now both tropo-taxis and the old typical locomotory *tropism* involved directed orientation between two sources of stimulation and circus movements in uniform stimulation after unilateral elimination of receptors. These are the criteria which we have adopted. On these criteria some reactions which have been described as tropo-tactic must be removed from that category, for in these cases no such circus movements have been observed. When these extracted cases are examined, we find that there is a single receptor instead of a pair of them, or there is diffuse sensitivity, or we find that for some reason the receptors are not capable of providing the animal with the information required for the *simultaneous* comparison of intensities on the two sides of the body. We find, moreover, that in these cases the animals make deviating movements fairly regularly from side to side, so that a successive comparison of intensities can be made and a directed response result. We have therefore distinguished these cases as klino-taxes and separated them from the now restricted group of tropo-taxes.

When we come to telo-taxis we find ourselves in slight disagreement with Kühn (1919, 1929). Originally Kühn set up this category for reactions to shapes and movements, like a robber-fly following one midge while ignoring other midges. Now we are restricting taxes to reactions to uncomplicated stimuli—light as such, and not light from a moving object of a particular size—so if telo-taxis covered only such cases we should exclude it from our system. Since the category was first erected, however, a relatively small number of examples have turned up in which motion and form are not necessary for the reaction. The essential feature, then, of this restricted kind of telo-taxis is that when two sources of stimulation are available the animal ignores one and orientates to the other. Ignoring or inhibition is demonstrated satisfactorily if the animal from time to time switches over to the other source, thus following a zigzag path. Balance on the two sides is unnecessary to orientation. The two-source experiment gives a satisfactory criterion of telo-taxis, provided the animal is not tested too near the sources (pp. 148-53). Into the category of telo-taxis Kühn (1929) has put the behaviour of *Eristalis*. If this is done, no clear distinction can be made between tropo-taxis and telo-taxis. It was done because *Eristalis*, even when unilaterally blinded, can still go straight to one light, if there are no complicating reflections; but *Eristalis* goes between two lights and, as long as the lights are near enough together, it still does so when unilaterally blinded. On analysis, this behaviour fits in perfectly well with other cases of tropo-taxis and differs from telo-taxis. It is in this respect that we disagree with Kühn (1919, 1929).

Under taxes (topo-taxes) we have thus got rid of two prefixes (meno- and mnemo-) and brought in one new one (klino-).

We have thus ortho-kinesis and klino-kinesis, and klino-taxis, tropo-taxis, and telo-taxis. Each category is reasonably readily recognized and the only heterogeneous element is the invocation of inhibition in telo-taxis. As for the transverse orientations, namely dorsal light reaction, ventral gravity reaction, and light compass reaction, they are easily characterized and well named, and they are introduced because their mechanisms have features in common with those of taxes.

Klino-kinesis (phobo-taxis or 'trial and error') is a new name for an old category of reaction. The old names have the disadvantage that they do not fit into the rest of the scheme; no one has ever held that these reactions are directed (taxes), and when the 'trial and error' method is in use in a directed reaction, klino-taxis usually seems to be the appropriate term. The typical reactions under the old names were reactions at boundaries; the category of klino-kinesis covers such reactions and in addition brings into line reactions in smooth gradients when there is no boundary.

A large part of this book is concerned with terminology. That is not unusual in science, for it is necessary to give precise names to processes and things which are ignored in common language. It is also desirable to avoid giving a new and technical meaning to an ordinary word. When a layman describes an action as instinctive, he usually means that it took place without hesitation or taking thought. Many actions of this kind are technically called acquired automatisms, some are inborn reflexes, and only those which are both inborn and complex are technically called instincts. Even technically the word 'instinct' has the second quite distinct meaning of drive or urge. This sort of confusion is avoided if we invent a new word when we make a new class of action. At the same time, of course, it is desirable to keep the number of new words down to a minimum. We have borne these considerations in mind.

Loeb was very vigorous in pointing out that to call an action instinctive is merely to cover our ignorance. If ignorance is concealed by a name, it is better to discard the name. The names should be convenient tools and nothing more. In this respect Loeb's influence was probably very good at first, but in the end the new terms 'tropisms' and 'memory images' covered just as much mystery as the old ones had done.

In a similar way certain attitudes of mind are dangerous in concealing ignorance. Every one understands what I mean when I say that I do not like a certain thing, and my emotion might be used to explain my subsequent actions. But the less nearly related an animal is to man, the more unsafe it is to ascribe feelings to it and to use them as explanations of behaviour. 'Not infrequently we misinterpret the mental processes of our closest friends—why they do certain things—and have to be corrected by them. If we misinterpret the mental processes of salmon, we can have no hope that they will correct us' (Huntsman, 1938). Our perceptions are both too crude and too fine to allow us to make much progress in studying animals, if we attempt to feel the world with their senses and their emotions. We must usually confine ourselves to objective studies, in which emotions are ignored.

There may at first seem to be little difference between saying that '*Clepsine* is photo-negative and so goes to the bottom of the pond, where its food is', and saying '*Clepsine* goes to the bottom because its food is there'. In the latter statement, however, it is not clear whether the intention is to say that *Clepsine* has a purpose in mind or to shorten a long statement about the evolution of behaviour. There are many cases in which behaviour appears to some observers to be purposive because it leads to a biologically valuable result, as in many instinctive and reflex actions. Such actions are often observed when the individual animal cannot have received the information necessary for formulating a plan or purpose, and it cannot make bricks without straw. If purpose there be, it cannot then be in the mind of the animal, any more than it is supposed to be there in the layman's question 'What is the purpose of flies?' If, therefore, the statement can be ambiguous in this way, it is better to avoid it and use the first form.

On the other hand, purpose in the mind of an animal is a legitimate subject for study, though a difficult one. If a rat is put into a suitable maze, it can learn its way about. If it is then fed in the centre of the maze, on subsequent occasions it does not wander at random but goes to the centre. Is it any simpler or more parsimonious to say of this rat that it then reacts to memory images than it is to say that it goes to the centre on purpose to get food? This behaviour cannot be described otherwise than in terms of memory or purpose, whether they are overtly so or not. In any case Loeb was wrong in implying that purpose cannot be expressed quantitatively, for the incentive values of various situations have been successfully compared (Maier & Schneirla, 1935).

At the present day it has become clear that motivation, incentive, learning, and reasoning are useful and necessary conceptions in the study of mammalian behaviour. The general tendency is to extend their use in the study of invertebrates too. Care must be taken to see that these conceptions are not used when they are not necessary.

TABLE VI

KÜHN'S CLASSIFICATION OF THE ORIENTATION REACTIONS OF ANIMALS

Compiled from an article on responses to light (1929) and other articles by the same author (1919, 1932). Compare Table IV, pp. 133–5.

A. **TROPISMS.** Directed growth curvature movements of fixed animals, leading to equal intensities of stimulation of symmetrically placed parts of the body. *Eudendrium, Antennularia.*

> (Kineses are mentioned in a note only, referring to Engelmann (1883), as reactions in which the velocity of locomotion depends on the intensity of the stimulus.)

B. **TAXES.** Locomotory orientation reactions of motile animals.

   I. PHOBOTAXIS. (Phobic reactions, avoiding reactions, trial-and-error reactions, *Schreckreaktionen.*)

   Undirected reactions, initiated by temporal rather than spatial differences of intensity of stimulation. The response consists of a change of direction of movement and the new direction bears no special relation to the direction of stimulation; it occurs repeatedly in rapid succession until a direction is taken which leads to cessation of changes of intensity suitable for eliciting the reaction; it often leads to aggregation in an indifference zone or optimum. Ciliates, maggots.

   II. TOPOTAXIS. Directed reactions initiated by spatial differences of intensity of stimulation. The response consists of a turning movement into a position orientated in relation to the source or sources of stimulation. Reactions may be positive, negative, or transverse (e.g. dorsal light reaction).

   1. *Tropotaxis.* Symmetrical orientation. The animal turns so that symmetrically placed sense organs are equally stimulated. Asymmetry of stimulation leads to turning towards the symmetrical position. Sense organs of opposite sides of the body are linked with antagonistic turning effects; unilateral elimination of sense organs leads to lasting circus movements. With two sources of stimulation the animal orientates to both together and so moves along a line going between them. *Planaria gonocephala, Potamobius astacus* (transverse gravity orientation), *Armadillidium, Arenicola* larva, earthworm.

   2. *Telotaxis.* Goal orientation. Locomotion along the line joining the animal to the source of stimulation; maintenance of a certain part of the field of stimulation on a particular point of the sensory apparatus—the fixation point. In phototelotaxis the fixation point is usually the point of clearest vision. Orientation is still possible with only one of two symmetrically placed sense organs in action; circus movements may occur after unilateral elimination, if no source

suitable for fixation is present. With two sources of stimulation, in certain cases orientation is between them (*Eristalis*), and in other cases orientation is straight towards one or other of them and then the zigzag type of path may occur. Differs from tropotaxis in having as its basis the reflex map mechanism instead of simpler bilateral symmetry relations. Includes reactions to size, shape, colour, and movement, and also to conditioned stimuli. *Laphria* (robber-fly), *Eristalis, Vanessa* imago.

3. *Menotaxis.* Maintenance of a given direction of the body axis by preserving a certain distribution of stimulation over the sensory surface, using compensatory movements. This distribution and the resulting angle of orientation may be varied spontaneously, especially in the light compass reaction. Besides this reaction menotaxis includes the optic fixation reaction of fishes in streams and certain optically controlled compensation movements on the turn-table. *Vanessa* larva.

4. *Mnemotaxis.* Memory orientation. Placing the body in a previously experienced relation to a remembered source of stimulation and going through a series of such positions. Mnemotaxis was not mentioned in the article on reactions to light (1929) but was included in the other two articles (1919, 1932). Homing and returning to a feeding-place in bees and ants.

ADDITIONAL NOTES ADDED DECEMBER, 1960

Note 1 (p. 22)   An intertidal snail, *Leptochitona cinereus*, collects in shaded areas by an ortho-kinetic response. The animals move in light, and slow down and finally stop in darkness (Evans, 1951).

Note 2 (p. 22)   The suitability of 'high' and 'low' as qualifying 'kineses' has been discussed by Kennedy (1945) and Gunn (1945).

Note 3 (p. 23)   The vertical movements of *Daphnia*, a much-investigated example of plankton migration, have been recognized as being partly controlled by a photo-ortho-kinetic mechanism. Swimming of *Daphnia* consists of alternations of actively swimming upward and passively sinking downward, the orientation to gravity being maintained by a stable equilibrium. At certain low light intensities they swim most of the time and so move up, while with increasing light intensities the periods of active swimming decrease more and more in relation to those of passively sinking. At still higher light intensities they orient by photo-taxis. *Daphnia*, with the eyes removed, still shows a marked photo-kinetic response, but no longer reacts photo-tactically (Harris and Wolfe, 1955; Harris and Mason, 1956). (See also Note 68.)

Note 4 (p. 34)   The search for temperature receptors in the cockroach has led to the discovery of temperature-sensitive regions in the pad between the claws and on the first and fourth tarsal segment. They were localized by recording electrical responses to local stimulation in the nerve of the isolated limb. The activity increases as the temperature decreases, thus reacting like a cold receptor (Kerkut and Taylor, 1957). (See also note p. 27).

Note 5 (p. 53)   The question of whether adaptation is an essential feature of successful aggregation in an 'optimal' (cf. p. 201) zone of stimulation by klino-kinesis has been discussed by Ewer and Bursell (1950) and has been treated mathematically in great detail by Patlak (1953 *a,b*).

Note 6 (p. 55)   The 'phototropism' of planarians has been treated in great detail by Viaud (1950), without reference to the earlier work by Ullyott and the ideas expressed in this book. His lengthy discourse largely concentrates on the kinetic and 'photopathic' effects of light at various intensities and wave-lengths, with little reference to mechanisms of orientation.

Note 7 (p. 55)   Ewer and Bursell (1950), while conceding that shock-boundary reactions of planarians may be regarded as extreme cases of klino-kinesis with adaptation, consider it a mistake to regard klino-kinesis as necessarily underlying all 'shock' reactions. They point to a number of observations of an animal stopping at a boundary or even shrinking back, waving the antennae or forelegs or part of the body in different directions, and then turning round and walking off in a new direction, without klino-kinesis ever appearing to come into play. They propose an entirely new concept of a reaction at a boundary where klino-kinesis with adaptation does not apply, coining for it the term 'titubant reactions' (from Lat. *titubans*, dithering) with the following definition: 'A reaction made at a boundary by animals not showing klino-kinesis with adaptation and characterized by a marked slowing or cessation of movement, followed by orientation by some tactic mechanism.' That is to say, the new direction taken is not random, as in kineses, but is related in direction to the arrangement of the stimulus. (See also the mathematical treatment of the role of such boundary reactions by Patlak, 1953 *b*).

Note 8 (p. 57)   Preliminary work with *Paramaecium* indicated that the klino-kinesis scheme applies to its behaviour towards pH (Gunn and Walshe, 1941). The suitability of the word, instead of 'avoiding reactions', is discussed by Gunn (1942 *b*).

Note 9 (p. 57)   Klino-kinesis is the principal mechanism of orientation to the diffuse stimuli of temperature, humidity, smell, or contact in the body louse *Pediculus humanus*, according to Wigglesworth (1941). Entering a zone of adverse stimulation brings forth an increase in random turning movements. This may result in an immediate return to the favourable zone if the response is strong and immediate, or in a long convoluted course in the unfavourable zone if the response is weak or delayed. Sensory adaptation eventually straightens the course out, so the animal has a chance to get out of the unfavourable zone.

Note 10 (p. 64)   The photosensitive organs of fly larvae which in all probability are responsible for the negative klino-tactic orientation have since been discovered and described by Bolwig (1946). By means of minute operations, histological sections, and a specially constructed microflashlight, a cluster of rounded cells situated in a pocket of the cephalopharyngeal skeleton above the condyle spine was identified as the light-sensitive organ. In the second stage larva, these cells are not placed in such a pocket but are freely exposed to light coming from the side. This explains why second stage larvae, unlike third stage ones, cannot orient to light from two opposed sources. For achieving orientation, the shadow cast by the larva's own body, and even more so by the skeleton in the third stage larva, is of fundamental importance.

Note 11 (p. 69)   A very detailed analysis of the orientation to light in the termite *Calotermes flavicollis* was given by Richard (1951). In the early instars light has little orienting effect, beyond pronouncedly affecting the activity (ortho-kinesis). The sixth instar, however, orients very accurately in the direction of the light rays by negative klino-taxis. This response with regular pendular movements of the head closely resembles the familiar reaction of the photo-negative fly larva. The adult orients equally accurately *towards* the light. Negative and positive photo-taxis is essentially identical in parallel, converging or diverging light beams, showing that it is the direction and not the intensity of light which controls the response. Both in sixth instar larvae and the adult orientation in the presence of two lights follows strictly the direction of a resultant in a parallelogram of forces. In the seventh instar orientation is frequently lateral to a light beam. While claiming it to be '*intéressant de conserver les termes de la classification de Fraenkel et Gunn,*' this work is almost devoid of any critical experimentation by which the mechanism of these various orientation reactions could be demonstrated. Too little is said about orientation in the early instars to make klino-kinesis even a possibility. Neither is it stated whether positive photo-taxis in the adult is, like the negative reaction in the sixth instar larvae, by klino-taxis. The critical experiment of unilateral blinding was not performed.

Note 12 (p. 73)   Certain rotifers also fit surprisingly closely into this scheme (Viaud, 1940) • Branchionus pala, for instance, has one eye only and swims in a spiral path directly towards a light. In a two-light experiment it orients in between. Another species, Triartha mystacina, has two eyes but also swims towards a light in a spiral. Under the influence of two lights it usually goes in a direction between them. Only under certain circumstances, when one light is white and the other coloured, some individuals swim towards the green light as if disregarding the white, or towards a white light as if disregarding another which may be red, orange, or violet. Viaud interprets such cases as telo-taxis, which is surprising in an animal with eyes as primitive as those in question, and which swims in a spiral. In this particular case it appears probable that a white or coloured light has no effect because it is so much weaker than the other one.

Note 13 (p. 75)   This mechanism of photo-tactic movements as described here applies principally to Pelmatohydra. Chlorohydra orients mostly by a different mechanism whereby the animal periodically contracts and then extends in a new and apparently random direction. These contractions occur within 20 to 30 seconds and are sharp when inclined away from the light; they occur after 100 to 200 seconds if the orientation is athwart the light direction; and after 5 to 12 minutes and very gradually with the oral disk facing the light. In the latter case the extension is maximal and often twice that in the opposite direction. Locomotion then usually occurs in the position maintained the longest time, i.e., when facing the light. Haug interprets this behaviour as a case of 'trial and error.' It seems to us to be best explained by a combination of ortho- and klino-kinesis, where the speed and frequency of locomotory activity and the frequency of random turning depend on the intensity of stimulation. It shows that locomotion in an almost straight course towards the light can be achieved by a combination of kineses.

Note 14 (p. 75)   Klino-taxis is the usual reaction of the sheep-tick Ixodes ricinus to favourable or unfavourable stimuli of temperature, smell, or humidity, and involves the successive comparison of intensities by the sensillae borne on the forelegs. Orientation is still efficient after removing one leg. Good examples of negative orientation are the avoiding responses to high humidity, to warm air in the absence of a favourable smell (in the adult only), or to repellent smells like citronella. Positive responses occur to warm air (in nymphs and larvae) and to favourable smells in the presence of warm air (Lees, 1948).

Note 15 (p. 75)   The body louse (Pediculus humanus) which in a diffuse gradient reacts to various stimuli by klino-kinesis (note 9) orients by klino-taxis where there is a steep gradient between an adverse and favourable zone. It swings the body and antennae from side to side, and often orients along the line of the boundary. Examples are in chemical stimulation and in a sharp temperature gradient (Wigglesworth, 1941).

Note 16 (p. 89) Ewer and Bursell (1950) extend the meaning and definition of the term tropo-taxis to include cases where a simultaneous comparison of intensities is achieved not between symmetrically placed receptors, but between receptors located at the anterior and posterior end of an animal. The case in question concerned the reactions towards humidity by the oncopod *Peripatopsis moseleyi* (Bursell and Ewer, 1950). This animal, belonging to a group hypothetically deriving from a link between worms and arthropods, lives very much like a terrestrial isopod under moist boards and vegetable refuse, and in a choice chamber aggregates in the wet region by ortho-kinesis, being inactive at a high (minimal activity at 98 per cent relative humidity) and active at a low relative humidity. At a sharp boundary, as in crawling through a narrow hole from a wet towards a dry humidity, they frequently stop and after a short interval of time back up into the wet region. Such reactions occurred ten times more often between wet and dry than between dry and wet. The authors assume the animal to be capable of making a simultaneous comparison of the humidities at the two ends of the body and suggest such a type of orientation to be common in vermiform types of animals. To prove this hypothesis the authors smeared the anterior section of *Peripatopsis* over with petroleum jelly which would prevent transpiration and thus presumably create, to the humidity receptors, a situation similar to that in moist air. Under these circumstances a far larger number now backed from a wet atmosphere into the dry air than before. While this may be so, we do not feel that a strong case for this type of anterior-posterior comparison has been made, and that this behaviour cannot be equally well explained by klino-kinesis or klino-taxis, involving merely receptors on the head. Furthermore, to call such a reaction tropo-taxis, solely on the rather superficial criterion of simultaneous comparison, would appear unnatural, since the main emphasis has always been on the simultaneous stimulation of *symmetrically* placed receptors. Bursell and Ewer's work with *Peripatopsis* has been treated mathematically by Patlak (1953 *b*).

Note 17 (p. 91) The curious phototelotactic to-and-fro swimming movements of *Hemimysis lamornei* have been further analysed by Foxon (1940). They take place only under horizontal illumination. When the light is placed above or below, the action of the statocysts presumably prevents swimming in an up-and-down direction. Without statocysts the behaviour changes radically. At low light intensities, and when dark-adapted, they tend to swim upwards, and if suddenly illuminated, downwards, irrespective of the direction of the light. The light then stimulates a gravitational response. (See also note 20.)

Note 18 (p. 104) This particular experiment, illustrated in Figure 41 *b*, has not been confirmed. It has been shown that under similar circumstances bees compensate also for the movement of the sun during the period of imprisonment (von Frisch, 1952). This does not, however, affect the gist of the argument as presented here, namely that bees do use the sun as a compass in their orientation towards the hive.

Note 19 (p. 119) A curious influence of the elevation angle of a light source on the compass reaction has been described by Birukov and De Valois (1955). The dung beetle *Geotrupes silvaticus* frequently reacts to illumination from a horizontal direction by a typical compass orientation. If this light is then elevated by a certain angle the beetles deviate from their former course by the same angle. This deviation may be either to the right or to the left.

Note 20 (p. 125) A curious type of dorsal light reaction was described by Foxon (1940) in the pelagic mysid *Hemimysis lamornei*. This animal, as described on page 90, when illuminated from the side, shows remarkable to-and-fro swimming movements in the direction of the light. At the same time its normal horizontal orientation is maintained by the statocysts. After removing the statocysts (by removing the whole uropod) the behaviour to light changes radically. They now show a strong dorsal light reaction, turning their backs towards it, and at the same time exhibit negative photo-taxis, by swimming away from the light. Since they are already directed with their long axis at a right angle to the light, they swim away in this position, with the ventral side forwards, irrespective of the position of the light.

Note 21 (p. 126) A lucid analysis of the dorsal light reactions of two aquatic beetle larvae, *Acilius* and *Dytiscus* was given by Schöne (1951). They possess six ocelli on each side of the head. Blackening the anterior three on both sides causes swimming in dorsally directed loops, and that of the posterior three, in ventrally directed loops. Rolling around the longitudinal axis towards the blind side occurs when all six ocelli of one side are blackened. The normal dorsal light reaction is therefore achieved by a balanced action between the anterior and posterior ocelli, and the ocelli on the right and left side of the head.

Note 22 (p. 128) Without statocysts *Palaemonetes varians* reacts to light very much like *Acilius* (Schöne, 1952) (note 21). After blinding of one eye it rolls towards the seeing side. After blinding of the posterior or anterior zones alone of both eyes, the shrimps perform somersaults directed ventrally or dorsally, respectively.

Note 23 (p. 132) A dorsal light reaction in a flying insect was for the first time demonstrated by Mittelstaedt (1950). When dragonflies were suitably suspended in mid-air, in a manner which allowed free movements of the wings and also free rolling about the longitudinal axis, they turned their backs towards the light regardless of whether it came from above, below, or the side. This reaction still occurs when one of the eyes is blinded, which suggests a telo-tactic mechanism. Under diffuse light conditions, rolling then occurs about the long axis, as one would expect. A freely flying dragonfly cannot fly on its back, and usually crashes to the ground when suddenly illuminated from below in a dark room. But on side illumination it tends to incline the body and fly in upwards or downwards spirals.

Note 24 (p. 159)   The mechanism of tropo-taxis in *Eristalis*, as pictured in the reflex map of its compound eye (see Fig. 35, p. 88, and Fig. 74, p. 157) suggested to Mittelstaedt (1949) an ingenious experiment. He turned the head 180° by twisting it around the neck in the longitudinal axis and fixing it in this position with a drop of paraffin. The soft neck of this fly allows this operation to be performed without any harm to the insect. Such flies moved normally on a glass plate when illuminated from below and showed equilibrium disturbances when illuminated from above. This clearly demonstrated the working of a dorsal light reaction since the ommatidia which were in the normal fly directed upwards were, in the operated one, now directed downwards.

If, with the head inverted, the turning reflexes associated with local illumination still work in the same sense as in the normal fly, the fly should now turn away from the light instead of towards it. This is what indeed happened, in a general way. The fly never went straight towards the light and often moved away from it. After some time, however, frequently it moved *backwards* toward the light, i.e., with the head turning away from the light. The results obtained were best explained by assuming that the *sense* of turning elicited by individual ommatidia remained the same but that the *gradient* of sensitivity became inverted, with the least sensitive ommatidia now directed backwards. Mittelstaedt concludes that these reactions cannot be explained solely on the basis of fixed turning reflexes and sensitivity gradients, but involved some kind of integration by higher nervous centres.

Note 25 (p. 181)   One of the most striking cases of 'skoto-taxis' has been demonstrated in two mosquito species *Culex molestus* and *Anopheles maculipennis atroparvus* rendered wingless and tested on a horizontal plane (Rao, 1947). In an arena uniformly illuminated from below they moved towards vertical dark bands. The narrowest width of band to which they consistently responded was 0·5 cm. at a distance of 3·5 cm., corresponding to an angle of 8°. If the band was straight in front or about 45° to the side they moved straight towards it, while with a more posterior location the reaction became less and less consistent. When two bands were simultaneously offered they moved towards one of them, ignoring the other. In agreement with what has been said on p. 181, all these reactions conform to negative photo-tropo-taxis. In fact, tested in the presence of one light the mosquitoes walked straight away from it, and unilaterally blinded, moved in circles towards the blind side. However, when such a one-eyed mosquito in the course of circling came to face a dark band, it moved straight towards it. This would not seem entirely consistent with negative photo-tropo-taxis. Furthermore, if a new band came into view when the mosquito was already moving towards another, it frequently turned towards the new one. This may be interpreted as a primitive reaction towards a moving shape.

Note 26 (p. 182)   Skoto-tactic behaviour was described also by Lees (1948) for the sheep-tick *Ixodes ricinus*, and by Wigglesworth (1941) for the louse *Pediculus humanus*. Both organisms react normally photo-negatively;   skoto-taxis was always exhibited by such photo-negative individuals. One can easily understand how such behaviour fits into the life of *Ixodes*. This organism, when hungry, climbs to the top of grasses or herbs and responds to vibrations as are caused by a passing animal by 'questing' with the forelegs. A positive response to a passing shadow would reinforce such a reaction. The louse reacts negatively photo-tropo-tactically in a light beam and, when unilaterally blinded, moves in circles towards the blind side.

Note 27 (p. 194)   Slifer (1951 , 1953) has described sensory structures, situated on the head, thorax, and abdomen of many grasshoppers which, in all probability, function as the thermo-receptors which mediate orientation to radiant heat. They are segmentally and bilaterally arranged, and consist of areas where the cuticle is very thin, little or not at all sclerotized, with a single richly innervated layer of epidermal cells closely attached to it. Their distribution over many segments of the body, their exact location on the segments, together with the effect of extirpation and local thermal stimulation, strongly suggest that they function as thermo-receptors for radiant heat.

Note 28 (p. 196)   Herter (1942), describing similar orientation re-actions to temperature in the related Triatomid *Triatoma dimidiata*, attempted to identify the thermo-receptors by the systematic removal of the four segments of the antennae. The reaction seemed to be largely dependent on the presence of thin and short hairs which were missing on the first, and were most numerous on the third and fourth segments.

Note 29 (p. 203)   A strikingly sensitive location of an 'optimum' in a temperature gradient was demonstrated in the honey-bee (Heran, 1952). The receptors in question are located on the antennae. Nothing was stated about the mechanism of orientation.

Note 30 (p. 204)   Hungry sheep-ticks, *Ixodes ricinus*, are attracted to a warm tube of $37°$, and engorged ones are repelled. They react to the gradient of air temperature and not to radiant heat. Covering the tube with cloth to reduce radiant heat leaves the reaction unchanged. How-ever, a warm tube wrapped with freshly cut sheep's wool becomes more attractive, while the same wool at $20°$ is no longer attractive. Thus a favourable smell enhances the reaction to warmth. This applies chiefly to females. Nymphs and larvae react already maximally to an uncovered tube at $37°$. The mechanism of these reactions to temperature is largely by klino-taxis (note 14) (Lees, 1948).

Note 31 (p. 210)   The results of Nicholson (1934) are not peculiar to the blowfly, for essentially similar results have been obtained by Gunn and Hopf (1942) with a small beetle, *Ptinus tectus*.

Note 32 (p. 213)   The housefly larvae avoid $37°$ in moist air and $33°$ in dry air. These reactions very much resemble avoidance reactions to dry air, and have underlying mechanisms of ortho- and klino-kinesis, and of klino-taxis. At a sharp boundary between $8·5$ and $40°$ they move straight on the boundary line, exhibiting regular alternate turning movements to the hot and cold side (Hafez, 1950).

Note 33 (p. 217)   For further details see Fraenkel (1939) and Pringle (1948). Mittelstaedt (1950) has demonstrated that in a flying dragonfly the whole head, as it were, functions like a static organ, responding through its inertia to rolling of the body about the long axis, thus eliciting static compensatory movements of the wings. Any rotation of the head causes, under suitable experimental conditions, rolling of the flying insect.

Note 34 (p. 222) A more detailed analysis of the reactions to gravity by *Astacus* revealed that the statocyst is not quite as simply and invariably a one-way sensory receptor as had appeared from the well-known investigation by Kühn. Bending a certain group of sensory hairs in the statocyst gives opposite reactions with regard to eye and leg movements, according to whether they were bent inwards or outwards. When pushed outwards, the legs of the same side make swimming movements, and when pushed inwards those of the opposite side show these movements. The organs have therefore a potentially two-way action. Consequently, tilting of the animals evokes the same reaction originating from the two statocysts, since in a given position the statolith would bend a given group of hairs inwards in the one statocyst, and outwards in the other. The turning reactions, as controlled by the statocysts, therefore reinforce each other in the two statocysts, rather than work against each other (Schöne, 1954).

Note 35 (p. 227) A curious orientation reaction to gravity, elicited by pressure, was described by Hardy and Bainbridge (1951). Zooea and megalopoda larvae of *Carcinus* and *Portunus* swim upwards if subjected to an increase in pressure. The authors merely recorded the number of larvae present in the upper or lower half of a 20-inch long glass tube, and say nothing about the mechanism of the reaction. The opinion is, however, expressed that hydrostatic pressure may be involved in the vertical migrations of planktonic forms.

Note 36 (p. 227) A kind of compass reaction to gravity is implied in the now well-known discovery of von Frisch on how a bee communicates on return to the hive the localization of a food source to fellow workers in the hive. In the dark hive and on a vertical comb the returning worker directs her dance in a direction which deviates from the vertical by the same angle by which the direct line to the food outside deviates from the direction of the sun. Orientation is therefore to gravity, but in a manner in which any angle to the vertical can be maintained (von Frisch, 1951).

Astonishing as these orientation performances of bees are, they seem to have precursors in similar but simpler reactions. Birukov (1953) states that the dung beetle *Geotrupes silvaticus*, when moving on a horizontal surface, usually moves at a certain angle to a light source in a marked light compass reaction. If the board on which it is moving is suddenly tilted into the vertical, it then takes a course which deviates from the vertical by the same angle as that with which it had previously deviated from the light source, and also to the same side as that where the light formerly was. Negative photo-taxis then becomes negative geo-taxis, etc. The author interprets these phenomena as the preservation of a central-nervous equilibrium of excitation.

Note 37 (p. 227) The hitherto rather little understood mechanism of the gravity reactions of several aquatic bugs has been further elucidated by Rabe (1953). In *Notonecta*, *Corixa*, *Naucoris*, and *Plea*, gravity is perceived by the movements of an air cushion situated behind the antennae and on the underside of the head and acting through its pressure on the Johnson's organ in the pedicellus of the antennae. In *Notonecta*, which normally swims on its back, with the air cushion removed the position is reversed in the dark. In light it then gives a ventral light reflex. With the antenna of one side removed it rolls towards the missing antenna. With either both antennae or the air cushion removed it also loses its equilibrium but may then roll towards either side indiscriminately.

Note 38 (p. 246)   Thigmo-kinesis is the mechanism by which lice (*Pediculus humanus*) cluster on rough surfaces, when given a choice between rough and smooth. On crossing from rough to smooth the path becomes more convoluted, thus leading the louse usually quickly back to the rough surface where the path is straighter. There is also an ortho-kinetic element in this reaction. The lice are more active, and settle down less frequently, on a smooth surface (Wigglesworth, 1941).

Note 39 (p. 246)   Low thigmo-kinesis is also the mechanism by which unfed larvae of the sheep-tick *Ixodes ricinus* cluster together (Lees, 1948).

Note 40 (p. 256)   Barnacles in locations exposed to a regular current, e.g., when fixed to the hulls of boats, are commonly very accurately oriented with regard to the current. So adult populations of *Balanus balanoides*, *B. crenatus*, and *Elminius modestus* are oriented so that the carinae are pointing away from and the cirral net is facing the current. The same position was found in *Coronula diadema* (fixed on a whale). The current influences orientation during the growth of the metamorphosed barnacle (Crisp and Stubbings, 1957).

Note 41 (p. 258)   Weiss-Fogh (1948) finally discovered the mechanism of earlier reported observations on the stimulation to flight in insects by air currents. The locust *Schistocerca gregaria*, and presumably grasshoppers in general, have tufts of hairs on the front of the head which are sensitive to bending by air currents. Stimulating these hairs will cause the locust to fly if it is in a suspended position. If the air strikes the head horizontally from the side, the pitch of the wings is altered so as to turn the locust into the wind. These reactions are lost when these hairs are covered by a cellulose paint.

Note 42 (p. 259)   According to Kalmus (1952 *a*) the Drosophila species *D. virilis*, *americana*, *subobscura* and *funebris* orient and walk against an air current, while *D. melanogaster* and *buskii* do not react to air currents alone. (*D. melanogaster*, however, runs upwind if the air carries simultaneously an attractant chemical stimulus, p. 259). Kalmus's explanation for this difference in behaviour concerns the dark colour of the four first-named species which, by virtue of the higher degree of tanning in the cuticle, gives it a better protection against desiccation. The same author (1942 *b*) investigated also the anemo-taxis of several soft-skinned animals. Several slugs (*Agriolimax reticulatus*, *Arion subfuscus* and *hortensis*) in a gentle air current direct the head into the wind, raising it and testing the current with all four tentacles. In strong wind they contract the tentacles and eventually the head and turn downwind. Similar reactions were observed with *Helix hortensis* and *aspersa*, earthworms and fly maggots. Positive anemo-taxis may be important for olfactory orientation, and a negative reaction may reduce the rate of desiccation and lead the animal to shelter.

Note 43 (p. 266)   The literature contains many statements to the effect that male mosquitoes are attracted to the female through the sounds produced by the latter in flight and that Johnston's organ, which is very large in male mosquitoes, serves as the receptor for sounds. The truth of these statements has been fully proved through the investigations of Roth (1948). The most relevant section for our purpose of this very extensive work concerns the possible mechanisms of orientation to sound. To quote the author: 'The mosquitoes are so drawn to the [vibrating tuning] fork that the response reminds one of the inevitable attraction of iron filings to a magnet. The path taken by the flying male appears to be more or less a straight line.' Earlier authors had suggested a mechanism by which the sounds emanating from a female vibrated the fibrillae of the two antennae to a different extent, and that this asymmetry of stimulation led to orientation, an explanation corresponding to tropo-tactic mechanism. Roth, however, found that the males lacking one antenna would still fly to the vibrating prongs of a tuning fork, without showing continuous turning movements. It appears from these descriptions that the exact mechanism of orientation to sound has yet to be discovered.

Note 44 (p. 280)   The housefly larva moves towards horse or pig dung, ammonia, acetone, or amines and avoids acetic acid and other lower acids. This orientation is considered to occur mainly by a klino-tactic mechanism.   The larvae turn sharply at a boundary between a positive and negative smell. Unilateral extirpation of the so-called antennae, which are considered the seat of the sense of smell, does not lead to circus movements under olfactory stimulation (Hafez, 1950).

Note 45 (p. 280)   Otto (1951), working with *Drosophila melanogaster*, *Geotrupes silvaticus*, and *Vespa rufa* comes to the conclusion that tropo-taxis plays little or no part in chemo-orientation. *Drosophila*, under the influence of a stimulus, performs little more turning towards the one remaining antenna than towards the operated side. All the insects quoted find a source of smell about equally well with one as with both antennae. In both cases they orient by turning more frequently and sharply towards the stimulus than away from it. 'The animals react to successive differences in stimulation with turnings which approach them to the centres of stimulation. They avoid directions of turnings whereby the intensity of the stimulus decreases' (translation from German). This very closely corresponds to our definitions of klino-taxis. Otto also emphasizes the importance of air currents in chemo-tactic reactions of this kind.

Note 46 (p. 280)   The pine bark beetle, *Hylastes ater*, is attracted by lower concentrations of terpenes (α-pinene), a constituent of its natural food. When tested in an alternative chamber they spend most of the time on the scented side. Turning reactions occur on the boundary to scentless air as well as in the immediate vicinity of the substance where the concentration becomes too high. A similar sharp turning reaction, but in the opposite direction, on the boundary between scented and scentless air occurs in another species, *Hylurgos palliatus*, which is repelled by α-pinene at all concentrations. Perttunen (1957) interprets these turning reactions at the boundary as klino-taxis.

Note 47 (p. 282) Schwinck (1954) reinvestigated the mechanism by which the male of the silkworm *Bombyx mori* is attracted to the female. The sequence of reactions involved in successful orientation closely follows the scheme described for several insects on page 277 ff. The first manifestation of a reaction is a general stimulation which affects many phases of activity, like cleaning of the antennae, vibration of the wings, walking, flying, turning on the spot without any component of direction—ortho-kinesis in our terminology. This is followed, if the source of the smell is relatively near (about 50 cm.), by a convoluted path with continuous turnings by which in most cases the female is gradually approached. The phase of the gradual approach (called by the author 'Chemomacrostrophotaxis') seems to correspond closely to klino-kinetic mechanism. The males then run the last 10–20 cm. more or less straight towards the female, with continuous slight turnings of head and body, fulfilling the conditions of klino-taxis (though Schwinck calls it 'Chemomicrostrophotaxis'). Removing one antenna has no effect on this reaction, thus confirming the interpretation as klino-taxis. This was in contradiction to the findings of Kellog (1907), who had reported circus movements (p. 282) under such conditions.

Orientation became far more efficient when the chemical stimulus was carried by an air current. The males then oriented more or less in a straight run from distances of several yards. There was no reaction to an air current alone. In this and other respects the reaction resembles closely that of *Drosophila melanogaster* in an air current plus smell (Fig. 120, p. 259). The mechanism of this reaction is almost certainly 'anemo'-klino-taxis, as indicated by the wavy nature of the path, the occurrence of probing movements of antennae and head, and the essentially small effect on orientation after amputation of one antenna.

Note 48 (p. 283) The orientation of wireworms in response to chemical stimulation was investigated by Thorpe *et al.* (1947). Certain nutritious substances elicit biting reactions. When having a choice between merely wet sand or sand moistened with solutions of attractive substances, they moved faster in the former, thus aggregating in the latter. Crossing a boundary between water and an attractive substance elicited no visible reaction. Crossing in the reverse direction, they either backed along their tracks and then made a side turning or they proceeded forwards and made a turn back into the 'attractive' region. The authors had difficulties in reconciling this behaviour with either klino-kinetic or klino-tactic mechanisms.

Note 49 (p. 289) Humidity receptors have since been discovered and described in many insects and terrestrial arthropods. So in *Tribolium* (simple and branched peg organs of the type of basiconic sensillae on segment 7–11 of the antennae) and many other beetles (Roth and Willis, 1951 *a,b*), tuft organs on the antennae of *Pediculus* (Wigglesworth, 1941), Haller's organ on the forelegs of the sheep tick *Ixodes ricinus* L. (Lees, 1948).

Note 50 (p. 290) The humidity reaction of two grasshoppers *Melanoplus bivittatus* (Say) and *Camnula pellucida* (Scudd.) were studied in a similar apparatus as in the work with *Tribolium*. Normally fed larvae and adults preferred the drier, and starved ones and insects during a moulting period, the wetter of two humidities. The humidity receptors were localized on the first eight segments of the antennae. Removal of these segments caused a complete elimination of the responses. The grasshoppers reacted ortho- and klino-kinetically to humidity (Riegert, 1959).

Note 51 (p. 290) An elaboration and amplification of previous work on the orientation to humidity by various terrestrial isopods was given by Waloff (1941). The three following species were used: *Armadillium vulgare, Porcellio scaber* (formerly also used by Gunn, 1937), and *Oniscus asellus*. The resistance to desiccation in these three species decreases in the same order. Observations in a constant humidity revealed that the mechanism whereby the isopods collected in a humidity gradient in moist air was twofold: ortho-kinesis, with decrease in activity and speed of movement in moist air, and klino-kinesis, less frequent turnings, retaining them in regions of higher humidity. This is associated at high humidities with low thigmo-kinesis making the animals come to rest against surfaces, and negative photo-taxis, leading them into and retaining them in dark and damp localities. The klino-kinesis of *Porcellio*, for instance, showed an average number of turnings (1 turning $= 90°$) of $61·95$ per hour at 0–10 per cent R.H., and of $20·33$ at 98–100 per cent R.H. The per cent of time at rest was near zero between 0 and 60 per cent R.H. and near 100 per cent between 99 and 100 per cent R.H. Waloff's data were subsequently mathematically analysed by Patlak (1953 *b*).

Note 52 (p. 290) The adults of the mealworm *Tenebrio molitor* react to humidity, tending to collect in the drier region. This reaction is the stronger, the higher the highest humidity available between 70 and 100 per cent R.H., and is weak with the highest humidity below 70 per cent. The reaction has a strong ortho-kinetic component. In uniform humidities below 90 per cent R.H., 90 per cent and more of the beetles become inactive, while the activity increases between 90 and 100 per cent R.H. Animals approaching regions of high humidity show turning movements which have both an undirected component (klino-kinesis) and a directed component involving movement of the antennae (klino-taxis). Tropo-taxis does not occur. There are no circus movements after unilateral amputation of the antennae. (Gunn and Pielou, 1940; Pielou and Gunn, 1940; Pielou, 1940). These data have also been mathematically analysed by Patlak (1953 *b*).

Note 53 (p. 290) *Ptinus tectus*, another beetle infesting dried stored products, normally reacts in a humidity gradient by collecting in the drier regions. A kinetic mechanism of reaction is involved—the higher the humidity, the higher the locomotory activity. Desiccated animals are more active than normal ones. At low humidities they show a much weakened reaction towards drier air; at high humidities the beetles collect in the wetter region. Some of the humidity receptors appear to be located on the antennae, but attempts at identification were unsuccessful (Bentley, 1944).

Note 54 (p. 290) Orientation to humidity in wireworms of the genus *Agriotes* has been described by Lees (1943 *a, b*). In an alternative chamber these larvae avoid dry air and assemble in wet air. These reactions are better in accord with humidity differences when expressed as saturation deficiency than as relative humidity, suggesting that the reaction is mediated rather by 'evaporimeter' than by 'hygrometer' receptors. Two mechanisms of orientation could be discerned, one of ortho-kinesis, by which the activity was higher in moist than in dry air, and the other a more direct response interpreted as klino-taxis. 'On approaching the humidity boundary the larva hesitates, moves its head from side to side, and finally recoils backwards into the moist air.' Unilateral amputation of antennae and maxillipalps, the site of the humidity receptors, had no effect on orientation in the alternative chamber, and neither initiated circus movements. Distinct from reaction to air humidity, there were also migrations from dry into wet sand. 'This is due solely to differential effect of moisture on the burrowing activity [ortho-kinesis].'

Note 55 (p. 290) The sheep-tick *Ixodes ricinus*, when in a desiccated state, is active in dry air and comes to rest in moist air (ortho-kinesis). In the normal non-desiccated state, it avoids moist air by strong turning reactions. When crossing a boundary from dry to wet, it stops, waves the forelegs more or less violently, turns round, and moves away. Lees (1948) considers these reactions as klino-taxis, and believes that klino-kinesis rarely occurs in this tick.

Note 56 (p. 290) The housefly larva, according to Hafez (1950), selects a moist environment. Three mechanisms can be discerned in these reactions: ortho-kinesis—they move about twice as fast in dry as in moist air; klino-kinesis—they turn more frequently in dry air; klino-taxis—on crossing a sharp boundary from wet into dry they stop and turn back into the wet region. This latter reaction is reminiscent of klino-tactic behaviour in negative photo-taxis. These three mechanisms come simultaneously into play and cannot always very clearly be separated.

Note 57 (p. 290) The Talitridae, marine amphipods which live out of the water in the high-water zone, are very liable to desiccation in the air. When tested in a humidity gradient in an alternative chamber they spend most of the time in the moister region. This is accomplished by low hygro-ortho-kinesis—they move more quickly in dry than in moist air—and by klino-kinesis—they turn more often when moving from moist to dry than when moving from dry to moist air. The turns are not always *towards* moister or *away* from drier air (Williamson, 1951).

Note 58 (p. 290) Our knowledge of the hygro-receptors and the humidity reactions of various beetles, and especially of the genus *Tribolium*, has been greatly enlarged by the investigations of Willis and Roth (1950) and Roth and Willis (1951 *a, b*). An apparatus was constructed which essentially consisted of a horizontal chamber made of 40-mesh brass-wire screen, 2 cm. high, through which air conditioned to the desired humidity flowed down from two ports placed above the cage. Thus the insects were able to move freely between clearly defined regions of different humidities. Their reactions were very much dependent on their state of feeding and desiccation. Wet reactions increased with period of starvation and extent of desiccation. The probable humidity receptors were recognized in simple and branched peg organs of the type of basiconic sensillae, situated on segments 7–11 of the antennae. Removal of most of the peg organs did not abolish the reaction, but unilateral removal of one antenna caused circus movements towards the remaining antenna in desiccated insects in moist air.

The mechanism of orientation to humidity at a sharp boundary between dry and wet appears to be klino-taxis as shown in the following example, describing the march of starved and desiccated *Tribolium castaneum* towards a disk of moist filter paper. 'The animal with intact antennae generally approached the source of moisture over a somewhat tortuous path. The beetle hesitated or stopped walking, raised and swung its body from side to side, waved its antennae, and then continued to walk towards the moist paper' (Roth and Willis, 1951).

Note 59 (p. 290)   Perttunen (1951) tested the humidity preferences of eight species of Carabid beetles, using the ring gradient and the alternative chamber (Gunn and Kennedy, 1936). Some species showed at the beginning a strong dry response which gradually with desiccation changed to a wet response, while others always gave a wet response. The direction of the initial reaction and the rapidity of the aggregation in the moistest zone are closely correlated with the moisture condition in the natural habitat of these species. Amputation of the antennae reduced or abolished responses to humidity.

Note 60 (p. 290)   The common earwig *Forficula auricularia* changes its sign of humidity reaction with the seasons. Specimens collected in the summer showed a consistent preference for the dry side of the alternative chamber, but chose the wet side after desiccation. During the winter, although kept in a moist atmosphere, they preferred the wet side (Perttunen, 1952).

Note 61 (p. 290)   Perttunen's (1953) work on millipeds includes an extensive discussion and bibliography of work in this area after 1940. The alternative chamber (Gunn and Kennedy, 1936; Wigglesworth, 1941) was used as the principal method. Of three species used, *Orthomorpha gracilis* aggregated in the moist and *Schizophyllum sabulosum* in the dry area, while *Julus terrestris* proved indifferent. 'Both in uniform dry or moist atmosphere and in the alternative chamber *Orthomorpha gracilis* shows a clear ortho-kinetic response; its speed is always higher in the dry atmosphere than in the moist. In the alternative chamber both the distance covered and, to a still greater extent, the time spent are greater on the moist side. The frequency of the climbing reaction is much higher on the moist side and is a contributory factor slowing the speed in a moist atmosphere. The frequency of the random turning reaction is higher on the dry side; thus a klino-kinetic reaction also occurs. At the humidity boundary the animal shows a clear klino-tactic turning reaction [combined with a "titubant" reaction, see note 7] on coming from moist to dry: in the opposite direction this reaction almost never takes place.'

Note 62 (p. 290) *Drosophila melanogaster*, studied in an alternative chamber, preferred the lower humidity in a choice between 100 and 87 per cent, and the higher in a choice between 77 and 20 per cent R.H. In desiccated specimens the original dry reaction was reversed to wet (Perttunen and Salmi, 1956). The humidity reactions also changed with age (Perttunen and Ahonen, 1956). In a choice between 100 and 77 per cent R.H. young flies strongly preferred the dry side. The reaction decreases gradually to one of indifference in the course of two weeks, while subsequently a slight preference to wet may develop. Removal of the antennae destroyed all reactions to humidity (Perttunen and Syrjämäki, 1958).

Note 63 (p. 291) Steiner (1953, 1954) in work with the dung beetle *Geotrupes stercorarius* and *Drosophila hydei* also emphasizes the fact that chemical stimuli often have principally the function of releasing other mechanisms of orientation involving, for instance, an opto-motor reaction leading to flight against the wind, or anemo-taxis in orientation on the ground.

Note 64 (p. 295) The literature on the change in the sign of a taxis or kinesis and what factors cause such change is immense. To quote only a few recent examples: The bark beetle *Blastophagus piniperda* changes from photo-negative at low temperature (5–8°) to photo-positive at 20° (Perttunen, 1958). Adults and larvae of the mealworm *Tenebrio molitor* are commonly strongly photo-negative, but after prolonged desiccation the adults (but not the larvae) become photo-positive (Perttunen and Lahermaa, 1958). See also notes 11, 65 and 66. Dolley and Golden (1947) give a long list of investigations dealing with the effect of temperature on reversal of photo-taxis. Dolley and White (1951) remarked that 'for over seventy-five years physiologists have attempted without success to unravel the mechanism involved in the change of sign of reaction of organisms to light.'

Note 65 (p. 296) Even an organism as strongly photo-positive as *Eristalis* may react photo-negatively under certain conditions. Dolley and Golden (1947) and Dolley and White (1951), working with a light-dark choice chamber arrangement, found *Eristalis* highly photo-positive at temperatures between 10 and 30°, and becoming negative below and above these regions. The reactions also depended on age and sex of the fly and intensity of illumination. The arrangement of these experiments does not, however, allow us to decide whether the general mechanisms of the positive and negative orientation are the same.

Note 66 (p. 297) French authors, in various writings (Bohn, 1940; Chauvin, 1941; Grison, 1942, 1944; Viaud, 1938, 1940, 1948, 1950; Richard, 1951) have been dealing in great detail with the problem of 'phototropisme' in animals, with little regard to mechanisms of orientation, as expounded in this book. Instead they have concentrated more on the external and internal factors influencing such reaction, such as age and physiological state of the animals, temperature, light intensity, and effect of wave-length. Much use is made of the term 'capacité photopathique,' which signifies the tolerance of the animal to a certain exposure to light, and its faculty of adaptation to it, and also involves the phenomenon of the 'sign' (positive or negative) of orientation.

Note 67 (p. 298)   Another striking example of interaction between orientation to light and gravity, under the impact of stimuli of various kinds with great ecological significance in the life of the animals, is given by the so-called 'alarm' reaction of mosquito larvae. These insects normally exhibit alternate up-and-down movements in the water, as directed by the exigencies of feeding at the bottom (down) and breathing at the surface (up). However, when they hang on the surface and are either submitted to a mechanical disturbance or a shadow from above, they precipitately swim downwards. In this course they are guided by gravity and at the same time by strong negative photo-taxis. If the incidence of light is not from above, photo-taxis overrules geo-taxis. The stimuli vibration and shadow act independently. After having become accommodated to vibrations by repeated and continuous mechanical disturbance, they still react to the shadow, and vice versa. The reactions are made still more complicated by the fact that different mosquito species, or the same species at times, can be lighter or heavier than water so that a vertical movement in either direction may be performed by active swimming or passive floating (Folger, 1948; Thomas, 1950; Mellanby, 1958).

Note 68 (p. 298)   One of the most complicated examples in the literature of an orientation phenomenon in nature concerns the vertical plankton migrations of *Daphnia*, as analysed and described by Baylor and Smith (1957). 'Vertical migration is essentially a very complex combination of geo-taxis and photo-taxis which is influenced by a number of parameters of the environment. In various marine and freshwater zooplankters it can be induced by light intensity or wave length, pH, redox poising compounds, temperature or pressure. Sometimes all of these parameters are effective in a single species, such as *Daphnia magna*, and sometimes visible light has little effect, as for example certain marine zooplankters of the Inland Waterway of Florida. Since gravity is a constant force in the environment capable as serving as a behaviour cue along with radiant energy which is less constant, it is not wholly unexpected that geo-taxis and photo-tactic behaviour patterns have evolved in response to those parameters of the environment which have diffuse vertical gradients, as for example light, temperature, pressure, pH, and redox potentials. The gravitational field of force of the earth has been well exploited by the Cladocera and behaviour responses to nongradient situations are oriented not to the stimulus *per se* but to gravity. A nongradient situation has no spatial dimensions for cuing an oriented response but the stimulus serves to set off a gravitational response. When one considers thermal, chemical or radiant energy gradients of the environment in relation to the size of Cladocera, it is clear that the change in intensity of the gradient over the length of the animal is too small to be detected and resolved into directional information on which to base an oriented taxis. Hence, we have behaviour patterns like geo-taxes initiated by chemical or radiant energy stimulus. Radiant energy sources, on the other hand, may be localized if the animal has a receptor backed up by an opaque curtain. Gravitational receptors appear to be localized in the swimming antennae of *Daphnia magna* and monitor this force only when the animal is not swimming (Grosser, Baylor, and Smith, 1954).'

BIBLIOGRAPHY

(*Titles of papers are abbreviated in many cases.*)

ADAMS, J. A. 1937. *J. Sci. Iowa State Coll.* **11**, 259–65.
Temperature preference of the firebrat, *Thermobia domestica* (Thysanura).

ADRIAN, E. D. 1928. *Basis of Sensation.* London. 31 figs. pp. 122.

—— 1930. *Physiol. Rev.* **10**, 336–48.
The mechanism of the sense organs.

ALVERDES, F. 1922. *Studien an Infusorien über Flimmerbewegung, Lokomotion und Reizbeantwortung.* Berlin. 46 figs. pp. 130.

—— 1926. *Z. vergl. Physiol.* **4**, 699–765.
Stato-, Photo- und Tangoreaktionen bei zwei Garneelenarten.

—— 1928. *Z. wiss. Zool.* **132**, 135–70.
Lichtsinn, Gleichgewichtsinn, Tastsinn und ihre Interferenzen bei Garneelen.

—— 1930. *Z. wiss. Zool.* **137**, 403–75.
Die lokomotorischen Reaktionen von decapoden Krebsen auf Helligkeit und Dunkelheit.

—— 1932. *The Psychology of Animals in relation to Human Psychology.* London. pp. 156.

BARROWS, W. M. 1907. *J. exp. Zoöl.* **4**, 515–37.
The reactions of the pomace fly, *Drosophila*, to odorous substances.

—— 1915. *Biol. Bull.* **29**, 316–26.
Reactions of *Epeira sclopetaria* to rhythmic vibrations of its web.

BARTELS, M. 1929. *Z. vergl. Physiol.* **10**, 527–93.
Sinnesphysiologische und psychologische Untersuchungen an der Trichterspinne *Agelena labyrinthica*.

BARTELS, M., and BALTZER, F. 1928. *Rev. suisse Zool.* **35**, 247–58.
Orientierung und Gedächtnis der Netzspinne, *Agelena labyrinthica*.

BAUER, V. 1908. *Z. allg. Physiol.* **8**, 343–70.
Die reflektorische Regulierung der Schwimmbewegungen bei den Mysiden.

—— 1910. *Z. allg. Physiol.* **10**, 231–48.
Die anscheinend nervöse Regulierung der Flimmerbewegung bei den Rippenquallen.

BAUMANN, F. 1929. *Z. vergl. Physiol.* **10**, 36–119.
Geruchsinn und Beuteerwerb von *Vipera aspis*.

BAUNACKE, W. 1913. *Biol. Zbl.* **33**, 427–52.
Statische Reflexe bei Mollusken.

BEAUCHAMP, R. S. A. 1933. *J. exp. Biol.* **10**, 113–29.
Rheotaxis in *Planaria alpina*.

—— 1937. *J. exp. Biol.* **14**, 104–16.
Rate of movement and rheotaxis in *Planaria alpina*.

BĚLEHRÁDEK, J. 1935. *Temperature and Living Matter.* Berlin. 70 figs. pp. 277.

BERT, P. 1869. *Arch. Physiol.* **2**, 547–54.
La question de savoir si tous les animaux voient les mêmes rayons lumineux que nous.

Bethes Handbuch der normalen und pathologischen Physiologie. 1925–32. 18 vols. Berlin.

BETHE, A., and FISCHER, E. 1931. *Bethes Handb. norm. path. Physiol.* **15,** 1045–1130.
Die Anpassungsfähigkeit (Plastizität) des Nervensystems.

BIERENS DE HAAN, J. A. 1921. *Biol. Zbl.* **41,** 395–414.
Phototaktische Bewegungen von Tieren bei doppelter Reizquelle.

—— 1929. *Animal Psychology for Biologists.* London. pp. 80.

BLUMENTHAL, H. 1935. *Z. Morph. Ökol. Tiere,* **29,** 667–719.
Das Tarsalorgan der Spinnen.

BODENHEIMER, F. S. 1931. *Z. vergl. Physiol.* **13,** 740–7,
Die Beziehung der Vorzugstemperatur zur Luftfeuchtigkeit der Umgebung.

BODENHEIMER, F. S., and KLEIN, H. Z. 1930. *Z. vergl. Physiol.* **11,** 345–85.
Die Abhängigkeit der Aktivität bei der Ernteameise, *Messor semirufus,* von Temperatur und anderen Faktoren.

BODENHEIMER, F. S., and SCHENKIN, D. 1928. *Z. vergl. Physiol.* **8,** 1–15.
Die Temperaturabhängigkeiten einiger Insekten.

BOHN, G. 1905. *Mém. Inst. gén. psychol.* **1,** 1–111.
Attractions et oscillations des animaux marins sous l'influence de la lumière.

—— 1909. *Les Tropismes. Rapport VIème Congrès Internat. Psychol.* Genève. pp. 15.

BORING, E. G. 1912. *J. anim. Beh.* **2,** 229–48.
Note on the negative reaction under light-adaptation in a planarian.

BOYS, C. V. 1880. *Nature,* **23,** 149.
The influence of a tuning-fork on the garden spider.

BRAMSTEDT, F. 1935. *Zool. Anz.* **112,** 257–62.
Die Lokalisation des chemischen und thermischen Sinnes bei *Paramecium.*

BRANDT, H. 1934. *Z. vergl. Physiol.* **20,** 646–73.
Die Lichtorientierung der Mehlmotte, *Ephestia kuehniella.*

BROCK, F. 1926. *Z. Morph. Ökol. Tiere,* **6,** 415–552.
Das Verhalten von *Pagurus arrosor* während der Suche und Aufnahme der Nahrung.

—— 1930. *Z. vergl. Physiol.* **11,** 774–90.
Das Verhalten der ersten Antennen von Brachyuren und Anomuren in bezug auf das umgebende Medium.

BRUN, R. 1914. *Die Raumorientierung der Ameisen und das Orientierungsproblem im Allgemeinen.* Jena. pp. 242.

BUDDENBROCK, W. VON. 1912. *Biol. Zbl.* **32,** 564–85.
Die Funktion der Statocysten im Sande grabender Meerestiere (*Arenicola* und *Synapta*).

—— 1913. *Zool. Jb. Abt. allg. Zool. Physiol.* **33,** 441–82.
Die Funktion der Statocysten im Sande grabender Meerestiere II.

—— 1914. *Zool. Jb. Abt. allg. Zool. Physiol.* **34,** 479–514.
Die Orientierung der Krebse im Raum.

BUDDENBROCK, W. VON. 1915 a. *S. B. heidelberg. Akad. Wiss. Math.-Nat. Kl. Abt.* **6 B**, 1–10.
Über das Vorhandensein des Lichtrückenreflexes bei Insekten sowie bei dem Krebs *Branchipus grubei.*

—— 1915 b. *Biol. Zbl.* **35**, 481–506.
Die Tropismenlehre von Jacques Loeb, ein Versuch ihrer Widerlegung.

—— 1917. *S. B. heidelberg. Akad. Wiss. Math.-Nat. Kl.* **8 B**, 1–26.
Die Lichtkompaßbewegungen bei Insekten, insbesondere den Schmetterlingsraupen.

—— 1919. *Zool. Jb. Abt. allg. Zool. Physiol.* **37**, 315–60.
Analyse der Lichtreaktionen der Heliciden.

—— 1922. *Wiss. Meeresuntersuch. N.F. Abt. Helgoland,* **15**, 1–19.
Mechanismus der phototropen Bewegungen.

—— 1931 a. *Z. vergl. Physiol.* **15**, 597–612.
Lichtkompaßorientierung (Menotaxis) der Arthropoden.

—— 1931 b. *Gellhorns Lehrbuch der allgemeinen Physiologie,* 687–729.
Tropismen.

—— 1935. *Biol. Rev.* **10**, 283–316.
Die Physiologie des Facettenauges.

—— 1937. *Grundriß der vergleichenden Physiologie,* **1**.
Physiologie der Sinnesorgane und des Nervensystems. Berlin. 2nd Ed. 355 figs. pp. 567.

BUDDENBROCK, W. VON, and SCHULZ, E. 1933. *Zool. Jb. Abt. allg. Zool. Physiol.* **52**, 513–36.
Lichtkompaßbewegung und Adaptation des Insektenauges.

BUDER, J. 1917. *Jb. wiss. Bot.* **58**, 105–220.
Zur Kenntnis der phototaktischen Richtungsbewegungen.

BUXTON, P. A. 1932. *Biol. Rev.* **7**, 275–320.
Terrestrial insects and the humidity of the environment.

CAMPBELL, R. E. 1937. *Ecology,* **18**, 479–89.
Temperature and moisture preferences of wireworms.

CANDOLLE, A. P. DE. 1832. *Physiologie végétale.* Paris.

CHAPMAN, R. N. 1931. *Animal Ecology, with especial reference to insects*; with an appendix by V. Volterra, with 6 figs. New York and London. 137 figs. pp. 464.

CHENOWETH, H. E. 1917. *Biol. Bull.* **32**, 183–201.
The reactions of certain moist forest mammals to air conditions and its bearing on problems of mammalian distribution.

CLARK, L. B. 1928. *J. exp. Zoöl.* **51**, 37–50.
Adaptation versus experience as an explanation of modification in certain types of behavior (circus movements in *Notonecta*).

—— 1931. *J. exp. Zoöl.* **58**, 31–41.
Reactions of insects to changes in luminous intensity (*Dineutes assimilis*).

—— 1933. *J. exp. Zoöl.* **66**, 311–33.
Modification of circus movements in insects.

COGHILL, G. E. 1929. *Anatomy and the problem of behaviour.* Cambridge. 52 figs. pp. 113.

COLE, W. H. 1917. *J. anim. Beh.* **7,** 71–80.
The reactions of *Drosophila ampelophila* to gravity, centrifugation and air currents.

—— 1923. *J. gen. Physiol.* **5,** 417–26.
Circus movements of *Limulus* and the tropism theory.

COPELAND, M. 1918. *J. exp. Zoöl.* **25,** 177–228.
The olfactory reactions and organs of the marine snails, *Alectrion obsoleta* and *Busycon canaliculatum.*

—— 1930. *J. comp. Psychol.* **10,** 339–54.
An apparent conditioned reflex in *Nereis virens.*

CORNETZ, V. 1911. *Rev. suisse Zool.* **19,** 153–73.
La conservation de l'orientation chez la fourmi.

CROZIER, W. J. 1924 *a. J. gen. Physiol.* **7,** 123–36.
On the critical thermal increment for the locomotion of a diplopod.

—— 1924 *b. J. gen. Physiol.* **6,** 531–9.
On stereotropism in *Tenebrio* larvae.

—— 1929. *The Foundations of Experimental Psychology.* Chapter II. The study of living organisms, 45–127. Worcester.

—— 1935 *a. J. gen. Physiol.* **18,** 659–68.
On the geotropic orientation of *Helix.*

—— 1935 *b. J. gen. Physiol.* **18,** 729–38.
The geotropic response in *Asterina.*

CROZIER, W. J., and COLE, W. H. 1929. *J. gen. Physiol.* **12,** 669–74.
The phototropic excitation of *Limax.*

CROZIER, W. J., and KROPP, B. 1935. *J. gen. Physiol.* **18,** 743–53.
Orientation by opposed beams of light.

CROZIER, W. J., and MOORE, A. R. 1923. *J. gen. Physiol.* **5,** 597–604.
Homostrophic reflex and stereotropism in diplopods.

CROZIER, W. J., and PINCUS, G. 1926 *a. J. gen. Physiol.* **10,** 195–203.
Stereotropism in rats and mice.

—— —— 1926 *b. J. gen. Physiol.* **10,** 257–69.
The geotropic conduct of young rats.

—— —— 1928. *J. gen. Physiol.* **11,** 789–802.
Geotropic orientation of young rats.

—— 1929. *J. gen. Physiol.* **13,** 57–120.
Analysis of the geotropic orientation of young rats. Studies I and II.

—— —— 1933. *J. gen. Physiol.* **16,** 801–13.
Study VII.

—— —— 1935. *J. gen. Physiol.* **19,** 211–19.
Study IX.

—— 1936. *J. gen. Physiol.* **20,** 111–44.
Study X.

CROZIER, W. J., and STIER, T. J. B. 1929. *J. gen. Physiol.* **12,** 675–93.
Geotropic orientation in arthropods. II. *Tetraopes.*

CZELOTH, H. 1930. *Z. vergl. Physiol.* **13,** 74–163.
Raumorientierung von *Triton.*

DEAL, J. M. 1939. University of London Thesis for Ph.D.
Tropic reactions of insects, with especial reference to temperature preferences.

DELAGE, Y. 1887. *Arch. Zool. exp. gén.* (2), **5,** 1–26.
Sur une fonction nouvelle des otocystes comme organes d'orientation locomotrice.

DEMBOWSKY, J. 1929. *Arch. Protistenk.* **66,** 104–32.
Die Vertikalbewegungen von *Paramecium caudatum.*

DEWITZ, J. 1899. *Arch. Physiol.* (Suppl.) 231–44.
Über den Rheotropismus bei Tieren.

DIETRICH, W. 1931. *Z. wiss. Zool.* **138,** 187–232.
Die lokomotorischen Reaktionen der Landasseln auf Licht und Dunkelheit.

DOFLEIN, I. 1925. *Z. vergl. Physiol.* **3,** 62–112.
Chemotaxis und Rheotaxis bei Planarien.

DOLLEY, W. L. 1916. *J. exp. Zoöl.* **20,** 357–420.
Reactions to light in *Vanessa antiopa,* with special reference to circus movements.

DOLLEY, W. L., and WIERDA, J. L. 1929. *J. exp. Zoöl.* **53,** 129–39.
Relative sensitivity to light of different parts of the compound eye in *Eristalis tenax.*

DOUDOROFF, P. 1938. *Biol. Bull.* **75,** 494–509.
Reactions of marine fishes to temperature gradients.

DYKGRAAF, S. 1933. *Z. vergl. Physiol.* **20,** 162–214.
Funktion der Seitenorgane an Fischen.

ECKERT, F. 1935. *Lotos,* **83,** 1–30.
Die positiv phototaktische Einstellreaktion des Komplexauges von *Daphnia pulex* im Zweilichtversuch.

—— 1938. *Z. vergl. Physiol.* **25,** 655–702.
Die positiv phototaktische Orientierung von *Daphnia pulex.*

ELLSWORTH, J. K. 1933. *Ann. ent. Soc. Amer.* **26,** 203–14.
The photoreceptive organs of the flesh-fly larva, *Lucilia sericata.*

ENGELMANN, T. W. 1879. *Pflüg. Arch. ges. Physiol.* **19,** 1–7.
Über Reizung contraktilen Protoplasmas durch plötzliche Beleuchtung.

—— 1881. *Pflüg. Arch. ges. Physiol.* **25,** 285–92.
Neue Methóden zur Untersuchung der Sauerstoffausscheidung pflanzlicher und tierischer Organismen.

—— 1882. *Pflüg. Arch. ges. Physiol.* **29,** 387–400.
Über Licht- und Farbenperzeption niederster Organismen.

—— 1883. *Pflüg. Arch. ges. Physiol.* **30,** 95–124.
Bacterium photometricum. Vergleichende Physiologie des Licht- und Farbensinnes.

EVANS, C. L. 1933. *Starling's Principles of Human Physiology.* London. 6th Ed. 562 figs. pp. 1122.

EWALD, W. E. 1910. *Biol. Zbl.* **30,** 1–16, 49–63, 379–99.
Orientierung, Lokomotion und Lichtreaktionen einiger Cladoceren.

FLÜGGE, C. 1934. *Z. vergl. Physiol.* **20,** 463–500.
Geruchliche Raumorientierung von *Drosophila melanogaster.*

Fox, H. M. 1921. *J. gen. Physiol.* **3,** 483–512.
The causes of the spontaneous aggregation of flagellates.

—— 1925. *Proc. Camb. philos. Soc. biol. Sci.* **1,** 219–24.
The effect of light on the vertical movement of aquatic organisms.

Fraenkel, G. 1925. *Z. vergl. Physiol.* **2,** 658–90.
Der statische Sinn der Medusen.

—— 1927 *a. Naturwissenschaften,* **15,** 117–22.
Phototropotaxis bei Meerestieren.

—— 1927 *b. Z. vergl. Physiol.* **5,** 585–97.
Geotaxis und Phototaxis von *Littorina.*

—— 1927 *c. Z. vergl. Physiol.* **6,** 167–220.
Die Grabbewegungen der Soleniden.

—— 1927 *d. Z. vergl. Physiol.* **6,** 385–401.
Die Photomenotaxis von *Elysia viridis.*

—— 1928. *Z. vergl. Physiol.* **7,** 365–78.
Über den Auslösungsreiz des Umdrehreflexes bei Seesternen und Schlangensternen.

—— 1929 *a. Z. vergl. Physiol.* **10,** 237–47.
Geotaxis von *Convoluta roscoffensis.*

—— 1929 *b. Biol. Zbl.* **49,** 657–80.
Sinnesphysiologie der Larven der Wanderheuschrecke, *Schistocerca gregaria.*

—— 1930. *Z. vergl. Physiol.* **13,** 300–13.
Die Orientierung von *Schistocerca gregaria* zu strahlender Wärme.

—— 1931. *Biol. Rev.* **6,** 36–87.
Die Mechanik der Orientierung der Tiere im Raum.

—— 1932 *a. Z. vergl. Physiol.* **16,** 371–93.
Die Flugreflexe der Insekten und ihre Koordination.

—— 1932 *b. Ergebnisse der Biologie,* **6,** 1–238.
Die Wanderungen der Insekten.

Fraenkel, G., and Pringle, J. W. S. 1938. *Nature,* **141,** 919.
Halteres of flies as gyroscopic organs of equilibrium.

Franz, V. 1911. *Int. Rev. Hydrobiol.* (Biol. Suppl.) **3,** 1–23.
Phototaktische Lokomotionsperioden bei *Hemimysis.*

Friedrich, H. 1932. *Z. vergl. Physiol.* **16,** 345–61.
Gleichgewichtserhaltung und Bewegungsphysiologie bei *Pterotrachea.*

Frisch, K. von. 1926. *Bethes Handb. norm. path. Physiol.* **11,** 203–39.
Vergleichende Physiologie des Geruchs- und Geschmackssinnes.

—— 1931. *Aus dem Leben der Bienen.* Berlin. 2nd Ed. 96 figs. pp. 159.

—— 1936. *Biol. Rev.* **11,** 210–46.
Über den Gehörsinn der Fische.

Frisch, K. von, and Kupelwieser, H. 1913. *Biol. Zbl.* **33,** 517–52.
Einfluß der Lichtfarbe auf die phototaktischen Reaktionen niederer Krebse.

Frisch, K. von, and Stetter, H. 1932. *Z. vergl. Physiol.* **17,** 686–801.
Sitz des Gehörsinnes bei der Elritze.

FULTON, B. B. 1928. *J. econ. Ent.* **21**, 889–97.
Some temperature relations of *Melanotus* (Coleoptera, Elateridae).

GAMBLE, F. W., and KEEBLE, F. 1903. *Quart. J. micr. Sci.* **47**, 363–431.
The bionomics of *Convoluta roscoffensis*.

GARREY, W. E. 1917. *Proc. nat. Acad. Sci. Wash.* **3**, 602–9.
Proof of the muscle tension theory of heliotropism.

—— 1918. *J. gen. Physiol.* **1**, 101–25.
Light and the muscle tonus of insects.

GEISMER, A. 1935. *Zool. Jb. Abt. allg. Zool. Physiol.* **55**, 95–130.
Die lokomotorischen Reaktionen von *Helix pomatia* auf Helligkeit und Dunkelheit.

GIERSBERG, H. 1926. *Z. vergl. Physiol.* **3**, 827–38.
Über den chemischen Sinn von *Octopus vulgaris*.

GÖTHLIN, G. F. 1920. *J. exp. Zoöl.* **31**, 403–41.
Inhibition of the ciliary movement in *Beroë*.

GRABER, V. 1883. *S. B. Akad. Wiss. Wien*, **87**, 201–36.
Helligkeits- und Farbenempfindlichkeit augenloser und geblendeter Tiere.

—— 1884. *Grundlinien zur Erforschung des Helligkeits- und Farbensinnes der Tiere*. Leipzig. pp. 322.

—— 1887. *Pflüg. Arch. ges. Physiol.* **41**, 240–56.
Thermische Experimente an der Küchenschabe.

GRAY, J. 1937. *J. exp. Biol.* **14**, 95–103.
Pseudo-rheotropism in fishes.

GRINDLEY, G. C. 1937. *The Intelligence of Animals*. London. pp. 70.

GROSSMANN, E. F. 1929. *J. econ. Ent.* **22**, 662–5.
Thermotropism of the Mexican cotton boll weevil.

GUNN, D. L. 1934. *Z. vergl. Physiol.* **20**, 617–25.
Temperature and humidity relations of the cockroach.
II. Temperature preference.

—— 1935. *J. exp. Biol.* **12**, 185–90.
III. Temperature preference, &c., of *Periplaneta americana*, *Blatta orientalis* and *Blatella germanica*.

—— 1937. *J. exp. Biol.* **14**, 178–86.
The humidity reactions of the woodlouse, *Porcellio scaber*.

GUNN, D. L., and COSWAY, C. A. 1938. *J. exp. Biol.* **15**, 555–63.
V. Humidity preference of *Blatta orientalis*.

GUNN, D. L., and KENNEDY, J. S. 1936. *J. exp. Biol.* **13**, 450–9.
Apparatus for investigating the reactions of land arthropods to humidity.

GUNN, D. L., KENNEDY, J. S., and PIELOU, D. P. 1937. *Nature*, **140**, 1064.
Classification of taxes and kineses.

HADLEY, P. B. 1906. *Amer. J. Physiol.* **17**, 326–43.
The relation of optical stimuli to rheotaxis in the American lobster, *Homarus americanus*.

HAMILTON, A. G. 1936. *Trans. R. ent. Soc. Lond.* **85**, 1–60.
The relation of humidity and temperature to the development of three species of African locusts.

HAMILTON, C. C. 1917. *Biol. Bull.* **32,** 159–82.
Behavior of some soil insects in gradients of evaporating power of air, carbon dioxide and ammonia.

HARTUNG, E. 1935. *Z. vergl. Physiol.* **22,** 119–44.
Geruchsorientierung bei *Calliphora erythrocephala.*

HAUG, G. 1933. *Z. vergl. Physiol.* **19,** 246–303.
Die Lichtreaktionen der Hydren.

HEIMBURGER, H. V. 1924. *Ecology,* **5,** 276–82.
Reactions of earthworms to temperature and atmospheric humidity.

HENKE, K. 1930. *Z. vergl. Physiol.* **13,** 534–626.
Die Lichtorientierung und die Bedingungen der Lichtstimmung bei *Armadillidium.*

HENSCHEL, J. 1929. *Z. vergl. Physiol.* **9,** 802–37.
Reizphysiologische Untersuchungen an der Käsemilbe *Tyrolichus casei.*

—— 1933. *Wiss. Meeresuntersuch. Abt. Kiel,* **21,** 131–58.
Chemischer Sinn von *Nassa reticulata.*

HERMS, W. B. 1911. *J. exp. Zoöl.* **10,** 167–226.
The photic reactions of *Lucilia caesar* and *Calliphora vomitoria.*

HERTER, K. 1923 *a. Biol. Zbl.* **43,** 27–30.
Temperatursinn der Feuerwanze (*Pyrrhocoris apteris*).

—— 1923 *b. Biol. Zbl.* **43,** 282–5.
Temperatursinn der Hausgrille (*Acheta domestica*) und der roten Waldameise (*Formica rufa*).

—— 1924. *Z. vergl. Physiol.* **1,** 221–88.
Temperatursinn einiger Insekten.

—— 1925. *Z. vergl. Physiol.* **2,** 226–32.
Temperaturoptimum und relative Luftfeuchtigkeit bei *Formica rufa.*

—— 1926. *Bethes Handb. norm. path. Physiol.* **11,** 173–80.
Thermotaxis und Hydrotaxis bei Tieren.

—— 1927. *Z. vergl. Physiol.* **5,** 283–370.
Reizphysiologische Untersuchungen an der Karpfenlaus, *Argulus foliaceus.*

—— 1928. *Z. vergl. Physiol.* **8,** 391–444.
Reizphysiologie und Wirtsfindung des Fischegels, *Hemiclepsis marginata.*

—— 1929. *Z. vergl. Physiol.* **10,** 272–308.
Reizphysiologisches Verhalten und Parasitismus des Entenegels, *Protoclepsis tesselata.*

—— 1932. *Bethes Handb. norm. path. Physiol.* **18,** 280–2.
Nachträge zu Herter, 1926.

—— 1934. *Biol. Zbl.* **54,** 487–507.
Eine verbesserte Temperaturorgel und ihre Anwendung auf Insekten und Säugetiere.

—— 1935. *Verh. dtsch. zool. Ges.* **37,** 31–9.
Die Höhe des thermotaktischen Optimum als Art- und Rassenmerkmal bei Nagetieren.

—— 1936. *Z. vergl. Physiol.* **23,** 605–50.
Das thermotaktische Optimum bei Nagetieren, ein mendelndes Art- und Rassenmerkmal.

HERTER, K., and SGONINA, K. 1938. *Z. vergl. Physiol.* **26**, 366–415.
Vorzugstemperatur und Hautbeschaffenheit bei Mäusen.

HESS, W. N. 1925. *J. Morph.* **41**, 63–93.
Photoreceptors of *Lumbricus terrestris*.

HEYMONS, R., and LENGERKEN, H. VON. 1929. *Z. Morph. Ökol. Tiere*, **14**, 531–613.
Biologische Untersuchungen an coprophagen Lamellicorniern.

HOAGLAND, H. 1933. *J. gen. Physiol.* **16**, 695–714.
Electrical responses from the lateral line nerves of catfish.

HOFER, B. 1908. *Ber. bayer. biol. VersSta.* **1**, 115–64.
Die Funktion der Seitenorgane bei den Fischen.

HOFFMANN, R. W. 1933. *Z. vergl. Physiol.* **18**, 740–95.
Reflexgeschehen bei *Blatta orientalis*.

—— 1936. *Z. vergl. Physiol.* **23**, 504–42.
Einfluß von Druck- und Berührungsreizen auf Haltung und Verhalten der Insekten.

HOGBEN, L. T. 1926. *Comparative Physiology*. London. 44 figs. pp. 219.

HOLMES, S. J. 1905 *a*. *J. comp. Neurol.* **15**, 98–112.
The selection of random movements as a factor in phototaxis.

—— 1905 *b*. *J. comp. Neurol.* **15**, 305–49.
The reactions of *Ranatra* to light.

—— 1916. *Studies in Animal Behavior*. Boston. 11 figs. pp. 266.

HOLST, E. VON. 1935 *a*. *Biol. Rev.* **10**, 234–61.
Die Koordination der Bewegung bei den Arthropoden.

—— 1935 *b*. *Pubbl. Staz. zool. Napoli*, **25**, 143–58.
Über den Lichtrückenreflex bei Fischen.

HOMP, R. 1938. *Z. vergl. Physiol.* **26**, 1–34.
Wärmeorientierung von *Pediculus vestimenti*.

HONJO, I. 1937. *Zool. Jb. Abt. allg. Zool. Physiol.* **57**, 375–416.
Lichtkompaßbewegung der Insekten, insbesondere in Bezug auf zwei Lichtquellen.

HORNBOSTEL, E. M. VON. 1926. *Bethes Handb. norm. path. Physiol.* **11**, 602–18.
Das räumliche Hören.

HORTON, F. M. 1935. *J. exp. Biol.* **12**, 13–16.
The reactions of isolated parts of *Paramecium*.

HOVEY, H. B. 1928. *Physiol. Zoöl.* **1**, 550–60.
The nature of the apparent geotropism of young rats.

—— 1929. *Physiol. Zoöl.* **2**, 322–33.
Associative hysteresis in flatworms.

HUNDERTMARK, A. 1936. *Z. vergl. Physiol.* **24**, 42–57.
Helligkeits- und Farbenunterscheidungsvermögen der Eiraupen der Nonne (*Lymantria monacha*).

—— 1937. *Z. vergl. Physiol.* **24**, 563–82.
Das Formunterscheidungsvermögen der Eiraupen der Nonne (*Lymantria monacha*).

HUNTER, W. S. 1927. *Pedag. Sem. J. genet. Psychol.* **34**, 299–332.
The behavior of the white rat on inclined planes.

HUNTER, W. S. 1931. *J. gen. Psychol.* **5,** 295–310.
The mechanisms involved in the behavior of white rats on the inclined plane.

HUNTSMAN, A. G. 1938. *Nature*, **141,** 421.
Spawning urge, homing instinct, and waiting in salmon return.

IMMS, A. D. 1934. *Text-book of Entomology.* London. 3rd Ed. 624 figs. pp. 727.

—— 1937. *Recent Advances in Entomology.* London. 2nd Ed. 94 figs. pp. 431.

JÄGER, H. 1932. *Zool. Jb. Abt. allg. Zool. Physiol.* **51,** 289–320.
Die geotaktischen Reaktionen verschiedener Evertebraten auf schiefer Ebene.

JANISCH, E. 1931. *Z. Morph. Ökol. Tiere*, **22,** 287–348.
Wirkung der Umweltfaktoren auf Insekten. II.

JENNINGS, H. S. 1904. *Publ. Carn. Instn. Wash.* No. **16,** pp. 256. 81 figs.
Contributions to the study of the behavior of lower organisms.

—— 1906. *Behavior of the Lower Organisms.* New York. 144 figs. pp. 366.

JOLLY, W. A. 1910. *Quart. J. exp. Physiol.* **4,** 67–87.
The time relations of the knee jerk and simple reflexes.

JÖNSSON, B. 1883. *Ber. dtsch. bot. Ges.* **1,** 512–21.
Der richtende Einfluß strömenden Wassers auf wachsende Pflanzen und Pflanzenteile (Rheotropismus).

KALMUS, H. 1929. *Z. vergl. Physiol.* **9,** 703–33.
Die Bewegungen der Seesterne, *Asterina gibbosa*.

—— 1937. *Z. vergl. Physiol.* **24,** 644–55.
Photohorotaxis, eine neue Reaktionsart, gefunden an den Eilarven von *Dixippus*.

KATZ, D. 1937. *Animals and Men; Studies in Comparative Psychology.* London, New York, Toronto. 37 figs. pp. 263.

KELLER, H., and BRÜCKNER, G. H. 1932. *Z. Psychol.* **126,** 14–37.
Neue Versuche über das Richtungshören des Hundes.

KELLOG, V. L. 1907. *Biol. Bull.* **12,** 152–4.
Some silkworm moth reflexes.

KENNEDY, J. S. 1937. *J. exp. Biol.* **14,** 187–97.
The humidity reactions of the African migratory locust.

—— 1939 *a*. *Trans. R. ent. Soc. Lond.* **89,** 385–542.
The behaviour of the desert locust in an outbreak centre.

—— 1939 *b*. *Proc. zool. Soc. Lond.* **A 109,** 221–42.
The visual orientation of flying mosquitoes in still and in moving air.

KIRKPATRICK, T. W. 1935. *Amani Memoirs*, **1,** 1–66.
The climates and eco-climates of coffee plantations.

KLEIN, H. Z. 1933. *Z. wiss. Zool.* **144,** 102–22.
Zur Biologie der amerikanischen Schabe (*Periplaneta americana*).

KLEIN, K. 1934. *Z. wiss. Zool.* **145,** 1–38.
Helligkeitsreaktionen einiger Arthropoden.

KNIGHT, T. A. 1806. *Philos. Trans.* 99–108. [seeds.
On the direction of the radicle and germen during the vegetation of

KNOLL, F. 1921, 1922, 1926. *Insekten und Blumen.* Vienna. 3 vols. pp. 645.

KOEHLER, O. 1922. *Arch. Protistenk.* **45**, 1–94.
Über die Geotaxis von *Paramecium*.

—— 1932. *Z. vergl. Physiol.* **16**, 606–756.
Sinnesphysiologie der Süßwasserplanarien.

—— 1934. *Verh. dtsch. zool. Ges.* **36**, 74–84.
Beiträge zum Verhalten von *Paramecium*-Teilstücken.

KÖHLER, W. 1927. *The Mentality of Apes.* London and New York. Translated from 2nd Ed. 9 plates, 19 figs. pp. 336.

KRAMER, G. 1933. *Zool. Jb. Abt. allg. Zool. Physiol.* **52**, 629–76.
Die Sinnesleistungen und das Orientierungsverhalten von *Xenopus laevis*.

KREIDL, A. 1892. *S. B. Akad. Wiss. Math.-Nat. Kl. Wien,* **102**, 149–74.
Physiologie des Ohrlabyrinthes. II. Versuche an Krebsen.

KRIJGSMAN, B. J. 1930. *Z. vergl. Physiol.* **11**, 702–29.
Reizphysiologische Untersuchungen an *Stomoxys calcitrans*.

KRIJGSMAN, B. J., and WINDRED, G. L. 1931. *Z. vergl. Physiol.* **13**, 61–73.
Reizphysiologische Untersuchungen an blutsaugenden Arthropoden.
II — *Lyperosia exigua*.

KROGH, A. 1914. *Int. Z. phys.-chem. Biol.* **1**, 491–508.
Standard metabolism in insects.

KRÜGER, P. 1931. *Z. Morph. Ökol. Tiere,* **22**, 759–73.
Faktoren des Wärmehaushaltes der Poikilothermen.

KRUMBIEGEL, I. 1932 a. *Zool. Jb. Abt. Syst.* **63**, 183–280.
Untersuchungen über physiologische Rassenbildung.

—— 1932 b. *Zool. Anz.* **100**, 237–50.
Über die Bedeutung und Einteilung thigmotaktischer Erscheinungen im Tierreich.

KÜHN, A. 1914. *Verh. dtsch. zool. Ges.* **24**, 262–77.
Die reflektorische Erhaltung des Gleichgewichtes bei Krebsen.

—— 1919. *Die Orientierung der Tiere im Raum.* Jena. 40 figs. pp. 71.

—— 1929. *Bethes Handb. norm. path. Physiol.* **12/1**, 17–35.
Phototropismus und Phototaxis der Tiere.   [246–60.

—— 1932. *Claus/Grobben/Kühn—Lehrbuch der Zoologie.* Berlin and Vienna.
Das Verhalten der Tiere.

LAMMERT, A. 1925. *Z. vergl. Physiol.* **3**, 225–78.
Über Pigmentwanderung im Punktauge der Insekten, sowie über Licht- und Schwerkraftsreaktionen von Schmetterlingsraupen.

LANGENBUCH, R. 1928. *Zool. Jb. Abt. allg. Zool. Physiol.* **44**, 575–622.
Die Statocysten einiger Crustaceen.

LASHLEY, K. S. 1929. *Brain Mechanisms and Intelligence.* Chicago. 11 plates, 33 figs. pp. 186.

LLOYD, Ll. 1919. *Lice and their Menace to Man.* London. 13 figs. pp. 136.

LOEB, J. 1888. *S. B. phys.-med. Ges. Würzburg,* 1–10.
Die Orientirung der Thiere gegen das Licht und die Schwerkraft der Erde (thierischer Heliotropismus und thierischer Geotropismus).

—— 1890. *Der Heliotropismus der Thiere und seine Uebereinstimmung mit dem Heliotropismus der Pflanzen.* Würzburg. pp. 118.

—— 1891. *Pflüg. Arch. ges. Physiol.* **49**, 175–89.
Ueber Geotropismus bei Thieren.

LOEB, J. 1893. *Pflüg. Arch. ges. Physiol.* **54,** 81–107.
Ueber künstliche Umwandlung positiv heliotropischer Thiere in negativ heliotropische und umgekehrt.

—— 1894. *Pflüg. Arch. ges. Physiol.* **56,** 247–69.
Beiträge zur Gehirnphysiologie der Würmer.

—— 1905. *Studies in General Physiology.* Chicago. 2 vols. pp. 782.

—— 1906 a. *The Dynamics of Living Matter.* New York. pp. 233.

—— 1906 b. *Pflüg. Arch. ges. Physiol.* **115,** 564–81.
Die Erregung von positivem Heliotropismus durch Säure, u.s.w.

—— 1911. *Wintersteins Handb. vergl. Physiol.* **4,** 451–519.
Die Tropismen.

—— 1912. *The Mechanistic Conception of Life.* Chicago. pp. 232.

—— 1918. *Forced Movements, Tropisms and Animal Conduct.* Philadelphia and London. 42 figs. pp. 209.

—— 1928. *J. gen. Physiol.* **8,** LXIII–XCII.
Complete bibliography of Jacques Loeb from 1884 to 1924.

LÖWENSTEIN, O. 1932. *Z. vergl. Physiol.* **17,** 806–54.
Gleichgewichtssinn der Elritze (*Phoxinus laevis*).

—— 1936. *Biol. Rev.* **11,** 113–45.
The equilibrium function of the vertebrate labyrinth.

LÖWENSTEIN, O., and SAND, A. 1936. *J. exp. Biol.* **13,** 416–28.
The activity of the horizontal semi-circular canal of the dogfish, *Scyllium canicula*.

LUBBOCK, J. 1881, 1882. *J. Linn. Soc.* (*Zool.*) **16,** 121–7; **17,** 205–14.
The sense of colour among some of the lower animals.

—— 1889. *The Senses, Instincts and Intelligence of Animals, with special reference to Insects.* London. 118 figs. pp. 292.

LÜDTKE, H. 1935. *Z. vergl. Physiol.* **22,** 67–118.
Die Funktion waagerecht liegender Augenteile des Rückenschwimmers.

—— 1938. *Z. vergl. Physiol.* **26,** 162–99.
Die Bedeutung waagerecht liegender Augenteile für die photomenotaktische Orientierung des Rückenschwimmers.

LUDWIG, W. 1933. *Z. wiss. Zool.* **144,** 469–95.
Seitenstetigkeit niederer Tiere im Ein- und Zweilichterversuch. I — *Lymantria dispar*-Raupen.

—— 1934. *Z. wiss. Zool.* **146,** 193–235.
Seitenstetigkeit niederer Tiere. II — Menotaxis.

LUFTI, M. 1936. *Inaugural-Dissertation,* Berlin. pp. 1–38.
Das thermotaktische Verhalten einiger Reptilien.

LUTHER, W. 1930. *Z. vergl. Physiol.* **12,** 177–205.
Chemorezeption der Brachyuren.

—— 1931. *Zool. Anz.* **94,** 147–53.
Chemorezeption der Brachyuren und Anomuren.

LYON, E. P. 1904. *Amer. J. Physiol.* **12,** 149–61.
On rheotropism. I—Rheotropism in fishes.

—— 1909. *Amer. J. Physiol.* **24,** 244–51.
II—Rheotropism of fish blind in one eye.

MacArthur, J. W., and Baillie, W. H. T. 1929. *J. exp. Zoöl.* **53**, 221–68.
The Metabolic activity and duration of life in *Daphnia*.

Maier, N. R. F., and Schneirla, T. C. 1935. *Principles of Animal Psychology.*
New York and London. 107 figs. pp. 529.

Marshall, J. 1935. *Trans. R. ent. Soc. Lond.* **83**, 49–72.
The location of olfactory receptors in insects; a review of experimental evidence.

Martini, E. 1918. *Z. angew. Ent.* **4**, 34–70.
Verhalten der Läuse gegenüber Wärme.

Mast, S. O. 1911. *Light and the Behavior of Organisms.* New York and London. 34 figs. pp. 410.

—— 1912. *J. anim. Beh.* **2**, 256–72.
Behavior of fireflies, with special reference to the problem of orientation.

—— 1913. *Biol. Zbl.* **33**, 581–93.
Loeb's *Mechanistic Conception of Life.*

—— 1914. *Biol. Zbl.* **34**, 641–74.
Orientation in *Euglena*, with some remarks on tropisms.

—— 1915. *Arch. EntwMech. Org.* **41**, 251–63.
What are tropisms?

—— 1921. *J. exp. Zoöl.* **34**, 149–87.
Reactions to light in the larvae of *Amaroucium*.

—— 1923. *J. exp. Zoöl.* **38**, 109–205.
Photic orientation in insects, with special reference to the drone-fly, *Eristalis tenax*, and the robber-fly, *Erax rufibarbis*.

—— 1938. *Biol. Rev.* **13**, 186–224.
Factors involved in the process of orientation of lower organisms in light.

Mast, S. O., and Johnson, P. L. 1932. *Z. vergl. Physiol.* **16**, 252–74.
Orientation in light from two sources and its bearing on the function of the eyespot (*Euglena*).

Mast, S. O., and Pusch, L. C. 1924. *Biol. Bull.* **46**, 55–9.
Modification of response in *Amoeba*.

Matthes, E. 1924 *a*. *Z. vergl. Physiol.* **1**, 57–83.
Das Geruchsvermögen von *Triton* beim Aufenthalt unter Wasser.

—— 1924 *b*. *Biol. Zbl.* **44**, 72–87.
Die Rolle des Gesichts-, Geruchs- und Erschütterungssinnes für den Nahrungserwerb von *Triton*.

Maxwell, S. S. 1897. *Pflüg. Arch. ges. Physiol.* **67**, 263–97.
Gehirnphysiologie der Anneliden.

Mellanby, K. 1935. *Biol. Rev.* **10**, 317–33.
The evaporation of water from insects.

Mendelssohn, M. 1895. *Pflüg. Arch. ges. Physiol.* **60**, 1–27.
Über den Thermotropismus einzelliger Organismen.

—— 1902. *J. Physiol. Pathol. gén.* **4**, 393–410; 475–96.
La thermotaxie des organismes unicellulaires.

Merton, H. 1935. *Arch. Protistenk.* **85**, 33–60.
Versuche zur Geotaxis von *Paramecium*.

Meyer, A. E. 1932. *Z. wiss. Zool.* **142**, 254–312.
Helligkeitsreaktionen von *Lepisma saccharina*.

MEYER, E. 1928. *Z. Morph. Ökol. Tiere*, **12**, 1–10.
Neue sinnesbiologische Beobachtungen an Spinnen.

MILLER, D. F. 1929. *J. exp. Zoöl.* **52**, 293–314.
The effects of change in temperature upon the locomotor movements of fly larvae.

MINNICH, D. E. 1919. *J. exp. Zoöl.* **29**, 343–425.
The photic reactions of the honey-bee, *Apis mellifera*.

—— 1921. *J. exp. Zoöl.* **23**, 173–203.
An experimental study of the tarsal receptors of two nymphalid butterflies.

MITCHELL, W. H., and CROZIER, W. J. 1928. *J. gen. Physiol.* **11**, 563–83.
Photic orientation by two point-sources of light.

MOORE, A. R. 1929. *Z. vergl. Physiol.* **9**, 74–81.
The reflex character of stereotropism and galvanotropism in the salamander, *Triturus torosus*.

MÜLLER, A. 1925. *Z. vergl. Physiol.* **3**, 113–44.
Über Lichtreaktionen von Landasseln.

MÜLLER, H. L. H. 1924. *Zool. Jb. Abt. allg. Zool. Physiol.* **40**, 399–488.
Die Lichtreaktionen von *Julus fallax* und *Polydesmus complanatus*.

MURR, L. 1930. *Z. vergl. Physiol.* **11**, 210-70.
Über den Geruchssinn der Mehlmottenschlupfwespe, *Habrobracon juglandis*.

NICHOLAS, J. S. 1922. *J. exp. Zoöl.* **35**, 257–82.
The reactions of *Amblystoma tigrinum* to olfactory stimuli.

NICHOLSON, A. J. 1934. *Bull. ent. Res.* **25**, 85–99.
Influence of temperature on the activity of sheep blowflies.

NIESCHULZ, O. 1933. *Zool. Anz.* **103**, 21–9.
Die Bestimmung der Vorzugstemperatur von Insekten, besonders von Fliegen und Mücken.

—— 1934. *Z. angew. Ent.* **21**, 224–38.
Die Vorzugstemperatur von *Stomoxys calcitrans*.

—— 1935. *Zool. Anz.* **110**, 225–33.
Die Temperaturabhängigkeit der Aktivität und die Vorzugstemperatur von *Musca domestica* und *Fannia canicularis*.

NORTHROP, H. S., and LOEB, J. 1923. *J. gen. Physiol.* **5**, 581–95.
The photochemical basis of animal heliotropism.

OEHMIG, A. 1939. *Z. vergl. Physiol.* **27**, 492–524.
Orientierungsmechanismus bei der positiven Phototaxis von Schmetterlingsraupen.

PANTIN, C. F. A. 1935. *J. exp. Biol.* **12**, 119–64; 389–96.
The nerve net of the Actinozoa.

PARKER, G. H. 1914. *Bull. U.S. Bur. Fish.* **33**, 63–8.
The directive influence of the sense of smell in the dogfish.

—— 1919. *The Elementary Nervous System.* Philadelphia and London. 53 figs. pp. 229.

PATTEN, B. M. 1914. *J. exp. Zoöl.* **17**, 213–80.
A quantitative determination of the orienting reaction of the blowfly larva, *Calliphora erythrocephala*.

PATTEN, B. M. 1916. *J. exp. Zoöl.* **20,** 585–98.
The changes in the blowfly larva's photosensitivity with age.
—— 1917. *J. exp. Zoöl.* **23,** 251–75.
Reactions of the whip-tail scorpion to light.
PAYNE, H. 1910. *Biol. Bull.* **18,** 188–90.
Forty-nine generations in the dark.
—— 1911. *Biol. Bull.* **21,** 297–301.
Drosophila ampelophila bred in the dark for sixty-nine generations.
PEARL, R. 1903. *Quart. J. micr. Sci.* **46,** 509–714.
The movements and reactions of fresh-water planarians.
PFEFFER, W. 1883. *Ber. dtsch. bot. Ges.* **1,** 524–33.
Lokomotorische Richtungsbewegungen durch chemische Reize.
—— 1884. *Untersuch. bot. Inst. Tübingen,* **1,** 363–482.
Lokomotorische Richtungsbewegungen durch chemische Reize.
—— 1888. *Untersuch. bot. Inst. Tübingen,* **2,** 582–661.
Chemotaktische Bewegungen von Bakterien, Flagellaten und Volvocineen.
—— 1904. *Pflanzenphysiologie.* Leipzig. 2nd Ed.
PIELOU, D. P. 1940. *J. exp. Biol.* **17,** 295–306.
The humidity receptors of the mealworm beetle, *Tenebrio molitor.*
PIÉRON, H. 1928. *Ann. Physiol. Physicochim. biol.* **4,** 44–63.
Réactions géotropiques chez les Limaces.
PLATEAU, F. 1886. *J. Anat. Paris,* **22,** 431–57.
La perception de la lumière par les myriapodes aveuglés.
POUCHET, G. 1872. *Rev. Mag. Zool.* **23,** (sér. 2), 110–17; 129–38; 183–6; 225–31; 261–4; 312–16.
De l'influence de la lumière sur les larves de diptères privées d'organes extérieurs de la vision.
PRINGLE, J. W. S. 1938. *J. exp. Biol.* **15,** 101–31; 467–73.
Proprioception in insects. I, II, and III.
PUMPHREY, R. J., and RAWDON-SMITH, A. F. 1936. *Proc. roy. Soc.* **B. 121,** 18–27.
Hearing in insects.
RÁDL, E. 1901. *Biol. Zbl.* **21,** 75–86.
Über den Phototropismus einiger Arthropoden.
—— 1903. *Untersuchungen über den Phototropismus der Tiere.* Leipzig. pp. 188.
RAWDON-SMITH, A. F. 1938. *Theories of Sensation.* Cambridge. 18 figs. pp. 137.
REGEN, J. 1912. *Zool. Anz.* **60,** 305–16.
Das Gehör von *Liogryllus campestris.*
—— 1913. *Pflüg. Arch. ges. Physiol.* **155,** 1–10.
Über die Anlockung des Weibchens von *Gryllus campestris* durch telephonisch übertragene Stridulationslaute des Männchens.
—— 1923. *S. B. Akad. Wiss. Wien,* **132,** 81–8.
Über die Orientierung des Weibchens von *Liogryllus campestris* nach dem Stridulationsschall des Männchens.
RITCHIE, A. D. 1928. *The Comparative Physiology of Muscular Tissue.* Cambridge. 2 figs. 5 tables. pp. 111.

RIVNAY, E. 1932. *Parasitology*, **24,** 121–36.
The tropisms of the bed bug, *Cimex lectularius.*
ROMANES, G. J. R. 1883. *Mental Evolution in Animals.* London.
ROSE, M. 1929. *La Question des Tropismes.* Paris. 90 figs. pp. 469.
RUSSELL, E. S. 1938. *The Behaviour of Animals.* London. 2nd Ed. 26 figs. 6 plates. pp. 196.
SACHS, J. 1887. *Vorlesungen über Pflanzenphysiologie.* Leipzig. 2nd Ed. pp. 991.
SAND, A. 1937. *Proc. roy. Soc.* **B. 123,** 472–95.
The mechanism of the lateral line sense organs of fishes.
—— 1938. *Proc. roy. Soc.* **B. 125,** 524–53.
The function of the ampullae of Lorenzini, with some observations on the effect of temperature on sensory rhythms.
SANTSCHI, F. 1911. *Rev. suisse Zool.* **19,** 117–34.
Le mécanisme d'orientation chez les fourmis.
SARS, G. O. 1911. *Crustacea of Norway*, **5,** 102–16.
Copepoda. Family Thalestridae.
SAVORY, T. H. 1930. *J. Ecol.* **18,** 384–5.
Environmental differences in spiders of the genus *Zilla.*
SCHARRER, E. 1932. *J. exp. Zoöl.* **61,** 109–14.
The function of the lateral line organs in the larvae of *Amblystoma punctatum.*
SCHRIEVER, H. 1935. *Pflüg. Arch. ges. Physiol.* **235,** 771–84.
Aktionspotentiale des Nervus lateralis bei Reizung der Seitenorgane von Fischen.
SCHULZ, H. 1928. *Z. vergl. Physiol.* **7,** 488–552.
Bedeutung des Lichtes im Leben niederer Krebse.
SCHULZ, W. 1931. *Z. vergl. Physiol.* **14,** 392–404.
Die Orientierung des Rückenschwimmers zum Licht und zur Strömung.
SCHWARZ, F. 1888. *Ber. dtsch. bot. Ges.* **2,** 51–72.
Der Einfluß der Schwerkraft auf die Bewegungsrichtung von *Chlamydomonas* und *Euglena.*
SEIFERT, R. 1930. *Z. vergl. Physiol.* **11,** 386–436.
Sinnesphysiologische Untersuchungen am Kiemenfuß, *Triops cranciformis.*
—— 1932. *Z. vergl. Physiol.* **16,** 111–84.
Raumorientierung und Phototaxis der Anostraken Euphyllopoden (*Chirocephalus* und *Artemia*).
SHELFORD, V. E., and DEERE, E. O. 1913. *Biol. Bull.* **25,** 79–120.
Reactions of certain animals to gradients of evaporating power of air.
SHELFORD, V. E., and POWERS, E. B. 1915. *Biol. Bull.* **28,** 315–34.
An experimental study of the movements of herring and other marine fishes.
SIOLI, H. 1937. *Zool. Jb. Abt. allg. Zool. Physiol.* **58,** 284–96.
Thermotaxis und Perzeption von Wärmestrahlen bei der Bettwanze, *Cimex lectularius.*
SNODGRASS, R. E. 1935. *Principles of Insect Morphology.* New York and London. 319 figs. pp. 667.

SPOONER, G. M. 1933. *J. mar. biol. Ass. U.K.* **19**, 385–438.
The reactions of marine plankton to light.

STAHL, E. 1884. *Bot. Ztg.* **42**, 145–55; 160–75; 187–91.
Zur Biologie der Myxomyceten.

STEINMANN, P. 1914. *Verh. dtsch. zool. Ges.* **24**, 278–90.
Die Rheotaxis der Fische.

—— 1929. *Z. vergl. Physiol.* **11**, 160–72.
Vom Orientierungssinn der Tricladen.

STRASBURGER, E. 1878. *Jena. Z. Naturw.* **12**, 551–625.
Wirkung des Lichtes und der Wärme auf Schwärmsporen.

STUDNITZ, G. VON. 1932. *Zool. Jb. Abt. allg. Zool. Physiol.* **50**, 419–48.
Die statische Funktion der sogenannten „pelotaktischen Organe"
(„Schlammsinnesorgane") der Limnobiidenlarven.

SZYMANKSI, J. 1914. *Pflüg. Arch. ges. Physiol.* **158**, 343–85.
Eine Methode zur Untersuchung der Ruhe- und Aktivitätsperioden bei
Tieren.

TALIAFERRO, W. H. 1920. *J. exp. Zoöl.* **31**, 59–116.
Reactions to light in *Planaria maculata*, with special reference to the
function and structure of the eyes.

THOMSEN, E., and THOMSEN, M. 1937. *Z. vergl. Physiol.* **24**, 343–80.
Über das Thermopräferendum der Larven einiger Fliegenarten.

THOMSEN, M. 1938. *Stuefluen og Stikfluen.* Copenhagen. 107 figs. 13 plates.
pp. 352.

THOMSON, R. C. M. 1938. *Bull. ent. Res.* **29**, 125–40.
The reactions of mosquitoes to temperature and humidity.

TOTZE, R. 1933. *Z. vergl. Physiol.* **19**, 110–61.
Sinnesphysiologie der Zecken.

TREMBLEY, A. 1744. *Mémoires pour servir à l'histoire d'un genre de polypes d'eau
douce en forme de cônes.* Leiden.

TROTTER, A. P. 1911. *Illumination.* London. 209 figs. pp. 292.

TSCHACHOTIN, S. 1908. *Z. wiss. Zool.* **90**, 343–422.
Die Statocyste der Heteropoden.

TSCHAKHOTINE, S. 1936. *C. R. Soc. Biol. Paris,* **121**, 1162–5.
La fonction du stigma chez le flagellé *Euglena* étudiée au moyen de la
micropuncture ultraviolette.

TURNER, C. H. 1913. *Biol. Bull.* **25**, 348–65.
Behavior of the common roach in an open maze.

UEXKÜLL, J. VON. 1894. *Z. Biol.* **31**, 584–609.
Physiologische Untersuchungen an *Eledone moschata*.

ULLYOTT, P. 1936. *J. exp. Biol.* **13**, 253–78.
The behaviour of *Dendrocoelum lacteum*. I—Responses at light-and-dark
boundaries. II—Responses in non-directional gradients.

URBAN, F. 1932. *Z. wiss. Zool.* **140**, 299–355.
Der Lauf der entflügelten Honigbiene, *Apis mellifica*, zum Licht.

VALENTINE, J. M. 1931. *J. exp. Zoöl.* **58**, 165–228.
The olfactory sense of the adult meal-worm beetle, *Tenebrio molitor*.

VERWORN, M. 1889. *Psycho-physiologische Protistenstudien.* Jena. pp. 218.

VERWORN, M. 1891. *Pflüg. Arch. ges. Physiol.* **50,** 423–72.
Gleichgewicht und Otolithenorgan.
—— 1899. *General Physiology.* London and New York. 2nd Ed. 285 figs.
pp. 615.
VIAUD, G. 1938 *a. Le phototropisme animal.* Paris. 21 figs. pp. 127.
—— 1938 *b. Le phototropisme des Daphnies.* Paris. 32 figs. pp. 196.
VOLKONSKY, M. 1939. *Arch. Inst. Pasteur Algér.* **17,** 194–220.
Sur la photo-akinèse des acridiens.
VOÛTE, A. D. 1928. *Tijdschr. ned. dierk. Ver.* **1,** 69–71.
Einige biologische Beobachtungen an *Planaria alpina.*
—— 1930. *Doktor Diss. s'Gravenhage.*
De Nederlandsche Bach-Tricladen en de oorzaken van haar verspreiding.
WALTER, H. E. 1907. *J. exp. Zoöl.* **5,** 35–162.
The reactions of planarians to light.
WARDEN, C. J., JENKINS, T. N., and WARNER, L. H. 1934. *Introduction to Comparative Psychology.* New York. 90 figs. pp. 581.
WARNKE, G. 1931. *Z. vergl. Physiol.* **14,** 121–99.
Geruchssinn von *Geotrupes sylvaticus* und *G. vernalis.*
WASHBURN, M. F. 1936. *The Animal Mind; a Text-book of Comparative Psychology.* New York. 4th Ed. 17 figs. pp. 536.
WEBER, HEINZ. 1929. *Z. vergl. Physiol.* **9,** 564–612.
Biologische Untersuchungen an der Schweinelaus, *Haematopinus suis.*
WEBER, HERMANN. 1926. *Z. vergl. Physiol.* **3,** 389–474.
Über die Umdrehreflexe einiger Prosobranchier.
WEESE, A. O. 1917. *Biol. Bull.* **32,** 98–116.
The reactions of the horned lizard, *Phrynosoma modestum.*
WEISS, P. 1936. *Biol. Rev.* **11,** 494–531.
Selectivity controlling the central-peripheral relations in the nervous system.
WELSH, J. H. 1933. *Biol. Bull.* **65,** 168–74.
Light intensity and the extent of activity of locomotor muscles as opposed to cilia.
—— 1937. *Science,* N.S. **85,** 430–1.
The chemoreceptors of certain dipterous larvae.
WEYRAUCH, W. 1929. *Z. vergl. Physiol.* **10,** 665–87.
Sinnesphysiologische Studie an der Imago von *Forficula auricularia.*
—— 1936. *Zool. Anz.* **113,** 115–25.
Orientierung nach dunklen Flächen.
WHEELER, W. M. 1899. *Arch. EntwMech. Org.* **8,** 373–81.
Anemotropism and other tropisms in insects.
WIGGLESWORTH, V. B. 1939. *Principles of Insect Physiology.* London. 316 figs.
pp. 434.
WIGGLESWORTH, V. B., and GILLETT, J. D. 1934. *J. exp. Biol.* **11,** 120–39;
408.
The function of the antennae in *Rhodnius prolixus* (Hemiptera) and the mechanism of orientation to the host.
WILLE, J. 1920. *Biologie und Bekämpfung der deutschen Schabe.* Berlin. 62 figs.
12 tables. pp. 140.

354 BIBLIOGRAPHY

WILLIAMS, C. B. 1930. *Migration of Butterflies.* Edinburgh and London. 71 figs. pp. 473.

WINTON, F. R., and BAYLISS, L. E. 1935. *Human Physiology.* London. 2nd Ed. 221 figs. pp. 627.

WOJTUSIAK, R. J. 1929. *Acta Biol. exp.* **3,** 165–74.
Lichtreaktionen normaler und geblendeter *Acilius*-Larven.

WOLF, E. 1927. *Z. vergl. Physiol.* **6,** 221–54.
Heimkehrvermögen der Bienen. II.

WOLSKY, A. 1933. *Biol. Rev.* **8,** 370–417.
Stimulationsorgane.

WORTMANN, J. 1883. *Bot. Ztg.* **41,** 457–80.
Einfluß der strahlenden Wärme auf wachsende Pflanzenteile.

WUNDER, W. 1927. *Z. vergl. Physiol.* **6,** 67–98.
Nahrungsaufnahme bei verschiedenen Knochenfischarten.

YAGI, N. 1928. *J. gen. Physiol.* **11,** 297–300.
Phototropism of *Dixippus morosus*.

YERKES, R. M. 1912. *J. anim. Beh.* **2,** 332–52.
The intelligence of earthworms.

YOUNG, J. Z. 1935. *J. exp. Biol.* **12,** 229–70.
The photo-receptors of lampreys.

ZAGOROWSKY, P. 1914. *Z. Biol.* **65,** 1–12.
Die Thermotaxis der Paramäcien.

SUPPLEMENTARY BIBLIOGRAPHY, 1940-1960

BAYLOR, E. R., and SMITH, F. E. 1957. *Recent advances in invertebrate physiology.* Edited B. T. Scheer. University of Oregon Publications.
Diurnal migration of plankton crustaceans.

BENTLEY, E. W. 1944. *J. exp. Biol.* Vol. 20, pp. 152–58.
The biology and behaviour of *Ptinus tectus* Boie. (Coleoptera, Ptinidae), a pest of stored products. V. Humidity reactions.

BIRUKOW, G. 1953. *Rev. suisse Zool.* Vol. 60, pp. 535–40.
Photo-menotaxische Transpositionen bei *Geotrupes silvaticus.*

BIRUKOW, G. 1957. *Z. Tierpsychol.* Vol. 13, pp. 463–84.
Lichtkompassorientierung beim Wasserläufer, *Velia currens,* am Tage und zur Nachtzeit. 1. Herbst- und Winterversuche.

BIRUKOW, G., and BUSCHE, E. 1957. *Z. vergl. Physiol.* Vol. 14, pp. 184–203.
Lichtkompassorientierung beim Wasserläufer, *Velia currens* (Heteroptera), am Tage und zur Nachtzeit. II. Orientierungsrhytmik in verschiedenen Lichtbedingungen.

BIRUKOW, G., and DE VALOIS, R. L. 1955. *Naturwiss.* Vol. 42, pp. 349–50.
Über den Einfluss der Höhe einer Lichtquelle auf die Lichtkompassorientierung des Mistkäfers *Geotrupes silvaticus.*

BOHN, G. 1940. *Actions directrices de la lumière.* Paris. Gauthier-Villars, 74 pp.

BOLWIG, N. 1946. *Videns. Meddel. Dansk. Naturhist. For. Kopenhagen,* Vol. 109, pp. 80–212.
Senses and sense organs of the anterior end of the housefly larvae.

BURDON-JONES, C., and CHARLES, G. H. 1958. *Nature,* Vol. 181, pp. 129–31.
Light reactions of littoral gastropods.

BURSELL, E., and EWER, D. W. 1950. *J. exp. Biol.* Vol. 26, pp. 335–53.
On the reactions to humidity of *Peripatopsis moseleyi* (Wood-Mason).

CARTHY, J. D. 1957. *Animal Navigation: How Animals Find Their Way About.* New York, Scribner's. 154 pp.

—— 1958. *An Introduction to the Behaviour of Invertebrates.* London, George Allen & Unwin, Ltd. 380 pp.

CHAUVIN, R. 1941. *Bull. Soc. zool. France,* Vol. 66, pp. 27–32.
Variations du phototropisme du Criquet pélerin (*S. gregaria*) suivant différentes longueurs d'onde.

CLARK, L. R. 1949. *Bull. Commonw. sci. industr. Res. Org. Austr.* No. 245, 27 pp.
Behaviour of swarm hoppers of the Australian plague locust.

COLD SPRING HARBOR SYMPOSIA. 1960. *Biological Clocks.* Vol. 15, 530 pp.

CRISP, D. J., and STUBBING, H. G. 1957. *J. Anim. Ecol.* Vol. 26, pp. 179–96.
The orientation of barnacles to water currents.

DEAL, J. M. 1941. *J. Anim. Ecol.* Vol. 10, pp. 323–56.
The temperature preferendum of certain insects.

DOLLEY, W. L., and GOLDEN, L. H. 1947. *Biol. Bull.* Vol. 92, pp. 178–86.
The effect of temperature and age on the temperature at which reversal
in reaction to light in *Eristalis tenax* occurs.

DOLLEY, W. L., and WHITE, J. D. 1951. *Biol. Bull.* Vol. 100, pp. 84–9.
The effect of illumination on the reversal temperature in the drone fly
Eristalis tenax.

EVANS, F. G. C. 1951. *J. Anim. Ecol.* Vol. 20, pp. 1–10.
An analysis of the behaviour of *Lepidochitona cinereus* in response to
certain physical features of the environment.

EWER, D. W., and BURSELL, E. 1950. *Behaviour,* Vol. 3, pp. 40–7.
A note on the classification of elementary behaviour patterns.

FOLGER, H. T. 1948. *Physiol. Zool.* Vol. 19, pp. 190–202.
The reactions of *Culex* larvae and pupae to gravity, light and mechanical
shock.

FOXON, G. E. H. 1940. *J. Mar. Biol. Assoc.* Vol. 24, pp. 89–96.
The reaction of certain mysids to stimulation by light and gravity.

FRAENKEL, G. 1939. *Proc. Zool. Soc. London Ser. A.* Vol. 109, pp. 69–78.
The function of the halteres of flies (Diptera).

FRISCH, K. von. 1951. *Naturwiss.* Vol. 38, pp. 105–12.
Orientierungsvermögen und Sprache der Bienen.

—— 1952. *Verh. Deutsch. Zool. Ges. in Freiburg,* pp. 58–72.
Die Richtungsorientierung der Bienen.

GRISON, P. 1942. *Bull. Soc. Zool. France,* Vol. 67, pp. 181–4.
Effet kinetique de la lumière, et son intensité sur quelques Chryso-
melides à l'état d'insectes parfaits.

—— 1944. *Bull. Soc. Zool. France,* Vol. 68, pp. 100–5.
Rythme d'activité chez *Leptinotarsa decemlineata* et leur importance
pour l'étude du phototropisme.

GROSSER, B. I., BAYLOR, E. R., and SMITH, F. E. 1953. *Ecology,* Vol. 34,
pp. 804–5.
Analysis of geotactic responses in *Daphnia magna.*

GUNN, D. L. 1942 a. *Biol. Rev.* Vol. 17, pp. 293–314.
Body temperature in poikilotherms.

—— 1942 b. *Nature,* Vol. 149, p. 78.
Klino-kinesis in *Paramaecium.*

—— 1945. *Nature,* Vol. 155, p. 178.
Classification and nomenclature of animal behaviour.

GUNN, D. L., and HOPF, H. S. 1942. *J. exp. Biol.* Vol. 18, pp. 278–89.
The amount of locomotory activity of *Ptinus tectus* in relation to experimental and to previous temperatures.

GUNN, D. L., and PIELOU, D. P. 1940. *J. exp. Biol.* Vol. 17, pp. 307–16.
The humidity behaviour of the mealworm beetle, *Tenebrio molitor* L.
III. The mechanism of the reaction.

GUNN, D. L., and WALSHE, B. M. 1941. *Nature*, Vol. 148, p. 1564.
Klino-kinesis of Paramecium.

—— —— 1942. *J. exp. Biol.* Vol. 19, pp. 133–40.
The biology and behaviour of *Ptinus tectus* Boie. (Coleoptera, Ptinidae), a pest of stored products. IV. Temperature preference.

HAFEZ, M., 1950. *Parasitology*, Vol. 40, pp. 215–36.
On the behaviour and sensory physiology of the housefly larva, *Musca domestica*. I. Feeding stage.

HARDY, A. C., and BAINBRIDGE, R. 1951. *Nature*, Vol. 167, pp. 354–55.
Effect of pressure on the behaviour of decapod larvae.

HARRIS, J. E., and MASON, P. 1956. *Proc. Roy. Soc. B.* Vol. 145, pp. 280–90.
Vertical migration in eyeless *Daphnia*.

HARRIS, J. E., and WOLFE, U. K. 1955. *Proc. Roy. Soc. London* B. Vol. 144, pp. 329–54.
A laboratory study of vertical migration.

HERAN, H. 1952. *Z. vergl. Physiol.* Vol. 34, pp. 179–206.
Untersuchungen über den Temperatursinn der Honigbiene (*Apis mellifica*) unter besonderer Berücksichtigung der Wahrnehmung strahlender Wärme.

HERTER, K. 1942. *Z. Parasitenk.* Vol. 12, pp. 552–91.
Untersuchungen über den Temperatursinn von Warmblüterparasiten.

—— 1952. *Zool. Anz.* Vol. 148, pp. 139–55.
Weitere Untersuchungen über den Temperatursinn von Warmblüterparasiten.

—— 1953. *Der Temperatursinn der Insekten*. Berlin. Duncker & Humblot. 378 pp.

JANDER, R. 1957. *Z. vergl. Physiol.* Vol. 40, pp. 162–238.
Die optische Richtungsorientierung der roten Waldameise (*Formica rufa*).

KALMUS, H. 1942 a. *Nature*, Vol. 150, p. 405.
Anemotaxis in Drosophila.

—— 1942 b. *Nature*, Vol. 150, p. 524.
Anemotaxis in soft-skinned animals.

KENNEDY, J. S. 1945. *Nature*, Vol. 155, p. 178.
Classification and nomenclature of animal behaviour.

KERKUT, G. A., and TAYLOR,B. J. R. 1957. *J. exp. Biol.* Vol. 34 pp. 486–93.
A temperature receptor in the tarsus of the cockroach, *Periplaneta americana*.

KOEHLER, O. 1950. *Physiological Mechanisms in Animal Behaviour*. Symposia of the Society for Experimental Biology. No. 4. Academic Press, New York, pp. 268–302.
Die Analyse der Taxisanteile instinktartigen Verhaltens.

LEES, A. D. 1943. *J. exp. Biol.* Vol. 20, pp. 43–53, 54–60.
On the behaviour of wireworms of the genus *Agriotes* Esch. (Coleoptera, Elateridae). I. Reactions to humidity. II. Reactions to moisture.

—— 1948. *J. exp. Biol.* Vol. 25, pp. 145–207.
The sensory physiology of the sheep tick, *Ixodes ricinus*.

MELLANBY, K. 1958. *Ent. exp. & appl.* Vol. 1, pp. 153–60.
The alarm reaction of mosquito larvae.

MITTELSTAEDT, H. 1949. *Naturwiss.* Vol. 36, pp. 90–1.
Telotaxis und Optomotorik von *Eristalis* bei Augeninversion.

—— 1950. *Z. vergl. Physiol.* Vol. 32, pp. 422–63.
Physiologie des Gleichgewichtssinnes bei fliegenden Libellen.

OEMIG, A. 1940. *Z. vergl. Physiol.* Vol. 27, pp. 492–524.
Zur Frage des Orientierungsmechanismus bei der positiven Phototaxis von Schmetterlingsraupen.

OTTO, E. 1951. *Zool. Jahrb. Abt. Allg. Zoologie Physiology*, Vol. 62, pp. 65–92. Untersuchungen zur Frage der geruchlichen Orientierung bei Insekten.

PARDI, L., and GRASSI, M. 1955. *Experientia*, Vol. 11, p. 202.
Experimental modification of direction finding in *Talitrus saltator* and *Talorchestia deshavei*.

PATLAK, C. S. 1953 *a*. *Bull. Math. Biophys.* Vol. 15, pp. 311–38.
Random walk with persistence and external bias.

—— 1953 *b*. *Bull. Math. Biophys.* Vol. 15, pp. 431–76.
A mathematical contribution to the study of orientation of organisms.

PERTTUNEN, V. 1950. *Ann. Ent. Fenn.* Vol. 16, pp. 41–4.
Experiments on the humidity reactions of some tsetse fly species (Dipt., Muscidae).

—— 1951. *Ann. Ent. Fenn.* Vol. 17, pp. 72–84.
The humidity preferences of various carabid species (Col., Carabidae) of wet and dry habitat.

—— 1952. *Nature*, Vol. 170, p. 209.
Seasonal changes in the humidity reactions of the common earwig, *Forficula auricularia*.

—— 1953. *Ann. Zool. Soc. 'Vanamo'*, Vol. 16, pp. 1–69.
Reactions of diplopods to the relative humidity of the air.

—— 1957. *Ann. Ent. Fenn.* Vol. 23, pp. 101–10.
Reactions of two bark beetle species, *Hylurgops palliatus* Gyll. and *Hylaster ater* Payk. (Col., Scolytidae) to terpene α-pinene.

—— 1958. *Ann. Ent. Fenn.* Vol. 24, pp. 12–18.
The reversal of positive phototaxis by low temperatures in *Blastophagus piniperda* L. (Col., Scolytidae).

—— 1959. *Ann. Ent. Fenn.* Vol. 25, pp. 65–71.

Effect of temperature on the light reactions of *Blastophagus piniperda* L. (Col., Scolytidae).

PERTTUNEN, V. 1960. *Ann. Ent. Fenn.* Vol. 26, pp. 86–92.
Seasonal variation in the light reactions of *Blastophagus piniperda* L. (Col., Scolytidae) at different temperatures.

PERTTUNEN, V., and AHONEN, U. 1946. *Ann. Ent. Fenn.* Vol. 22, pp. 67–71.
The effect of age on the humidity reactions of *Drosophila melanogaster* (Dipt., Drosophilidae).

PERTTUNEN, V., and LAHERMAA, M. 1958. *Ann. Ent. Fenn.* Vol. 24, pp. 69–73.
Reversal of negative phototaxis by desiccation in *Tenebrio molitor* L. (Col., Tenebrionidae).

PERTTUNEN, V., and SALMI, H. 1956. *Ann. Ent. Fenn.* Vol. 22, pp. 36–45.
The response of *Drosophila melanogaster* (Dipt., Drosophilidae) to the relative humidity of the air.

PERTTUNEN, V., and SYRJÄMÄKI, J. 1958. *Ann. Ent. Finn.* Vol. 24, pp. 78–83.
The effect of antennectomy on the humidity reactions of *Drosophila melanogaster* (Dipt., Drosophilidae).

PIELOU, D. P., and GUNN, D. L. 1940. *J. exp. Biol.* Vol. 17, pp. 286–94.
The humidity behaviour of the mealworm beetle, *Tenebrio molitor* L. I. The reaction to differences in humidity.

PIERON, H. 1941. *Nouveau traité de Psychologie*, Vol. 8, 250 pp.
Psychologie zoologique.

PRECHT, H. 1942. *Z. wiss. Zool.* Vol. 156, pp. 1–128.
Das Taxisproblem in der Zoologie.

PRINGLE, J. W. S. 1948. *Phil. Trans. Roy. Soc. Lond.* B. Vol. 233, pp. 347–84.
The gyroscopic mechanism of the halteres of diptera.

RABAUD, E. 1949. *Le comportement. animal.* Collection Armand Colin, Paris. 2 vols.

RABE, W. 1953. *Z. vergl. Physiol.* Vol. 35, pp. 300–25.
Beiträge zum Orientierungsproblem der Wasserwanzen.

RAO, R. T. 1947. *J. exp. Biol.* Vol. 24, pp. 64–78.
Visual responses of mosquitoes artificially rendered flightless.

RICHARD, G. 1951. Thèse à la faculté des Sciences de l'Université de Paris.
Le phototropisme des termites en rapport avec leur anatomie sensorielle.

RIEGERT, P. W. 1959. *The Canadian Entomologist*, Vol. 91, pp. 35–40.
The humidity reactions of grasshoppers. Humidity reactions of *Melanoplus bivittatus* (Say) and *Camnula pellucida* (Scudd.): Reactions of normal grasshoppers.

ROTH, L. M. 1948. *Amer. Midland Naturalist*, Vol. 40, pp. 261–352.
A study of mosquito behaviour. An experimental laboratory study of the sexual behaviour of *Aedes aegypti* (L.).

ROTH, L. M., and WILLIS, E. R. 1951 a. *J. exp. Zool.* Vol. 117, pp. 451–87.
Hygroreceptors in coleoptera.

ROTH, L. M., and WILLIS, E. R. 1951 *b*. *J. exp. Zool.* Vol. 116, pp. 527-70.
Hygroreceptors in adults of *Tribolium* (Coleoptera, Tenebrionidae).

SAVORY, T. 1959. *Instinctive Living: A study of Invertebrate Behaviour.* Pergamon Press, London. 90 pp.

SCHNEIRLA, T. E. 1953. Chapters on Behavior, in K. D. Roeder (ed.), Insect Physiology. John Wiley & Sons, New York; Chapman & Hall, London.

SCHÖNE, H. 1951. *Z. vergl. Physiol.* Vol. 33, pp. 63-98.
Die Lichtorientierung der Larven von *Acilius sulcatus* und *Dytiscus marginalis*.

—— 1952. *Naturwiss.* Vol. 39, pp. 552-3.
Zur optischen Lageorientierung (Lichtrückenorientierung) von Dekapoden.

—— 1954. *Z. vergl. Physiol.* Vol. 36, pp. 241-60.
Statozystenfunktion und statische Lageorientierung bei Dekapoden Krebsen.

—— 1957. *Z. vergl. Physiol.* Vol. 39, pp. 235-40.
Kurssteuerung mittels der Statocysten (Messungen an Krebsen).

SCHWINCK, I. 1954. *Z. vergl. Physiol.* Vol. 37, pp. 19-56.
Experimentelle Untersuchungen über den Geruchssinn und Strömungswahrnehmung in der Orientierung bei Nachtschmetterlingen.

SLIFER, E. H. 1951. *Proc. Roy. Soc. B.* Vol. 138, pp. 414-37.
Some unusual structures in *Locusta migratoria migratorioides* and their probable functions as thermoreceptors.

—— 1953. *Trans. Amer. ent. Soc.* Vol. 79, pp. 37-68, 69-97.
The pattern of specialized heat-sensitive areas on the surface of the body of Acrididae. I. The males. II. The females.

SOULAIRAC, A. 1949. *Année biol.* Vol. 25, pp. 1-14.
Classification des réactions d'orientation des animaux (tropismes).

STEINER, G. 1953. *Naturwiss.* Vol. 40, p. 514.
Zur Duftorientierung fliegender Insekten.

STEINER, G., and WETTE, R. 1954. *Naturwiss.* Vol. 41, p. 172.
Über die Wirkung eines homogenen Duftfeldes auf optische Wahlen von *Drosophila hydei*.

THOMAS, I. M. 1950. *Austr. J. Sci. Res.* Vol. 3, pp. 113-23.
The reactions of mosquito larvae to regular repetitions of shadows as stimuli.

THORPE, W. H. 1956. *Learning and Instinct in Animals.* Methuen & Co. London. 493 pp.

THORPE, W. H., CROMBIE, A. C., HILL, R., and DARRAH, J. H. 1947. *J. exp. Biol.* Vol. 23, pp. 234-66.
The behaviour of wireworms in response to chemical stimulation.

TINBERGEN, N. 1951. *The Study of Instinct.* Oxford, Clarendon Press. 228 pp.

SUPPLEMENTARY BIBLIOGRAPHY 361

VIAUD, G. 1938. *Recherches expérimentales sur le phototropisme des Daphnies.* Strasbourg-Paris. 196 pp.

—— 1940. 1943. *Bull. Biol.* Vol. 74, pp. 249–308; Vol. 77, pp. 68–93; Vol. 77, pp. 224–42.
Recherches expérimentales sur le phototropisme des Rotifères.

—— 1948. *Le phototropisme animal.* Vrin, Paris, 98 pp.

—— 1950. *Behaviour,* Vol. 2, pp. 162–216.
Recherches expérimentales sur le phototropisme des Planaires.

VOLKONSKY, M. 1942. *Arch. Inst. Pasteur Alger.* Vol. 20, pp. 236–48.
Comportement du Criquet pélerin dans le Sahara.

WALOFF, N. 1941. *J. exp. Biol.* Vol. 18, pp. 115–35.
The mechanism of humidity reactions of terrestrial isopods.

WEISS-FOGH, T. 1949. *Nature,* Vol. 164, pp. 873–4.
An aerodynamic sense organ stimulating and regulating flight in locusts.

—— 1950. *Eighth Intern. Congr. Entomology* 1948, pp. 584–88.
An aerodynamic sense organ in locusts.

WELLINGTON, W. G. 1955. *Ann. ent. Soc. Amer.* Vol. 48, pp. 67–76.
Solar heat and plane polarized light versus the light compass reaction in the orientation of insects on the ground.

WELLINGTON, W. G., SULLIVAN, C. R., and GREEN, G. W. 1951. *Canad. J. Zool.* Vol. 29, pp. 339–51.
Polarized light and body temperature level as orientation factors in the light reactions of some hymenopterous and lepidopterous larvae.

WIGGLESWORTH, V. B. 1941. *Parasitology,* Vol. 33, pp. 67–109.
The sensory physiology of the human louse *Pediculus humanis corporis.*

WILLIAMSON, D. I. 1951. *J. Mar. Biol. Ass. U.K.* Vol. 30, pp. 73–90.
Studies on the biology of Talitridae (Crustacea, Amphipoda): Effects of atmospheric humidity.

WILLIS, E. R., and ROTH, L. M. 1950. *J. exp. Zool.* Vol. 115, pp. 561–88.
Humidity reactions of *Tribolium castaneum* (Herbst).

AUTHOR INDEX
Notes added in 1960 are not included in this index.

Adams, 200.
Adrian, 23, 31, 32.
Alverdes, 8, 99, 121, 127, 129, 174–5, 180, 200, 222.
Archimedes, 132.

Baillie, 201.
Baltzer, 111.
Barrows, 260, 277.
Bartels, 104, 111.
Bauer, 223, 229.
Baumann, 284–5.
Baunacke, 234.
Bayliss, 25, 27, 40.
Beauchamp, 254, 299.
Bělehrádek, 201, 207.
Bert, 4.
Bethe, 18, 99.
Bierens de Haan, 8, 175.
Blumenthal, 289, 290.
Bodenheimer, 202–3, 205, 212.
Bohn, 174–5.
Boring, 168.
Boys, 260.
Bramstedt, 200.
Brandt, 79–84.
Brock, 270.
Brückner, 266.
Brun, 102–3.
von Buddenbrock, 8, 10, 18, 92, 98–9, 104–6, 111, 114–16, 119–21, 127, 132, 153, 156, 162, 164, 175, 220–3, 232–4, 237, 243, 271, 300.
Buder, 145.
Buxton, 288.

Campbell, 200–1.
de Candolle, 5, 183.
Chapman, 11.
Chenoweth, 200, 290.
Clark, 93, 156, 163, 166–73, 226, 296.
Coghill, 36.
Cole, 21, 162–3, 259.
Copeland, 283, 291, 301.
Cornetz, 100–1.
Cosway, 202, 212, 296–7.
Crozier, 9–10, 69, 146, 162–3, 207, 209, 235–42, 248–50.
Czeloth, 259, 284, 290–1.

Darwin, 3.
Deal, 213.
Deere, 200, 289–90.
Delage, 223.
Dembowsky, 235.
De Meillon, 239.
Descartes, 3.

Dewitz, 250.
Dietrich, 174–7.
Doflein, 254, 272, 291.
Dolley, 96, 148, 155–7, 166, 170.
Doudoroff, 200.
Dykgraaf, 251–2, 260–2.

Eckert, 117–18, 144, 159.
Ellsworth, 59, 62, 64.
Engelmann, 5–6, 17, 317.
Evans, 25–6.
Ewald, 120, 301.

Fielde, 100.
Fischer, 99.
Flügge, 259, 277, 281, 291.
Forel, 100.
Fox, 235, 287, 289, 297.
Fraenkel, 9, 23, 90, 92, 107–13, 121, 143, 146, 148–53, 192–4, 217–18, 230–1, 234–5, 244–5, 247, 253, 258, 297–8.
Franz, 90.
Friedrich, 223.
von Frisch, 103, 118, 124, 223, 262, 265, 271, 301.
Fulton, 200.

Gamble, 231.
Garrey, 162, 166, 169, 309.
Geismer, 177.
Giersberg, 283.
Gillett, 196–8.
Göthlin, 229.
Graber, 4–5, 53, 201, 212, 290.
Gray, 251.
Grindley, 300.
Grossmann, 200.
Gunn, 11–12, 14–15, 18, 46, 64, 67, 200, 202, 206, 212–13, 289–90, 296–7.

de Haan, 8, 175.
Hadley, 253.
Hamilton, A. G., 290.
Hamilton, C. C., 200, 290.
Hartung, 277, 282.
Haug, 74.
Heimburger, 200, 290.
Henke, 83, 85, 87, 299.
Henschel, 205, 282–4.
Herms, 21, 59–60, 62, 67, 299.
Herter, 125, 200, 202–3, 205, 212, 214, 261, 282.
Hess, 73.
Heymons, 277.
Hoagland, 262.
Hofer, 251.

Hoffmann, 244–5.
Hogben, 310.
Holmes, 18, 44, 59, 62, 79, 166.
von Holst, 121, 130–2, 301.
Homp, 195, 198–200, 205.
Honjo, 115.
Hopf, Fig. 93.
von Hornbostel, 267.
Horton, 200.
Hovey, 20, 237–8, 240–2, 300.
Hundertmark, 181–2.
Hunter, 237, 239, 241.
Huntsman, 315.

Imms, 59, 155, 277.

Jäger, 237, 243.
Janisch, 201.
Jenkins, 311.
Jennings, 6, 8, 18, 43–4, 56–7, 63, 73–4, 286, 288, 312.
Johnson, 145, 148.
Jolly, 37.
Jönsson, 5.

Kalmus, 182, 235.
Katz, 266.
Keeble, 231.
Keller, 266.
Kellog, 282.
Kennedy, 14–15, 18, 46, 210, 257–8, 289–90.
Kirkpatrick, 11.
Klein, H. Z., 203, 212.
Klein, K., 178–9, 181.
Knight, 5.
Knoll, 182.
Koehler, O., 58, 200, 235, 254–7, 268, 272–6.
Köhler, W., 304.
Kramer, 263–5.
Kreidl, 219, 234–5.
Krijgsman, 200, 258.
Krogh, 207.
Kropp, 69.
Krüger, 192.
Krumbiegel, 213, 246.
Kühn, 9, 18, 44, 89, 97–8, 106, 127, 221, 309, 311–13, 317.
Kupelwieser, 118, 124, 301.

Lammert, 182.
Langenbuch, 234.
Lashley, 36.
Lengerken, 277.
Lloyd, 214.
Loeb, 6–10, 18–20, 23, 32, 42–3, 59, 62, 65–6, 69, 89, 148, 151, 161–3, 175, 183, 185, 190, 220, 234–5, 245–6, 276, 288, 295, 298, 307–10, 314, 316.

Löwenstein, 31, 116, 219, 223–5, 252, 309.
Lubbock, 4, 100.
Lüdtke, 148, 156, 166, 172–3.
Ludwig, 113, 115, 117, 143, 151–2, 182.
Lufti, 212.
Luther, 270.
Lyon, 250–1, 253.

MacArthur, 201.
Maier, 295, 302, 316.
Marshall, 34, 277.
Martini, 195, 200.
Mast, 9–10, 18, 21, 57, 59–64, 70–3, 79, 84, 86, 88–9, 145, 148, 153–4, 158, 183–4, 295, 300, 309–10.
Matthes, 263.
Maxwell, 245.
de Meillon, 239.
Mellanby, 288.
Mendelssohn, 200.
Merton, 235.
Meyer, A. E., 164.
Meyer, E., 260.
Miller, 21.
Minnich, 34, 91, 93–4, 166, 296.
Mitchell, 146.
Moore, 247–8.
Morgan, 308.
Müller, A., 86.
Müller, H. L. H., 164–5, 174.
Murr, 277.

Nicholas, 262.
Nicholson, 208–9.
Nieschulz, 200, 202–3, 212–14.
Northrop, 148.

Oehmig, 182.

Pantin, 35.
Parker, 35, 283–4.
Patten, 18, 21, 59–60, 64, 68–70, 146.
Paylov, 303.
Payne, 301, 304.
Pearl, 20, 272.
Pfeffer, 5, 10, 44, 312.
Pielou, 15, 18, 46, 289.
Piéron, 100, 237, 243.
Pincus, 236–7, 239, 248.
Plateau, 4.
Pouchet, 59, 62, 64.
Powers, 200.
Pringle, 217.
Pumphrey, 33, 266.
Pusch, 300.

Rádl, 117, 120–1, 124.
Rawdon-Smith, 32–3, 266, 268.
Regen, 266.

Ritchie, 26, 28.
Rivnay, 195.
Romanes, 4.
Rose, 57, 295.
Russell, 8, 311.

Sachs, 5–6, 183.
Sand, 31, 34, 225, 252, 262.
Santschi, 10, 101–2, 116.
Sars, 143.
Savory, 290.
Scharrer, 262.
Schenkin, 202–3, 205, 212.
Schneirla, 295, 302, 316.
Schriever, 262.
Schulz, E., 111, 115.
Schulz, H., 121, 124.
Schulz, W., 166, 253.
Schwarz, 5.
Seifert, 121, 125–7.
Sgonina, 212.
Shelford, 200, 205, 289–90.
Sherrington, 18.
Sioli, 195–6.
Smith, 32–3, 266, 268.
Snodgrass, 26, 59, 64, 155, 277.
Spooner, 184–6.
Stahl, 5.
Steinmann, 251, 272.
Stetter, 223, 262, 265.
Stier, 237, 240.
Strasburger, 5.
von Studnitz, 234.
Szymanski, 22, 206.

Taliaferro, 75, 89, 174.
Thomsen, E., 211, 213.
Thomsen, M., 211, 213.
Thomson, 201, 290.
Totze, 79, 200, 204–5, 282, 286–7.
Trembley, 74.
Trotter, 139.
Tschachotin, 223.

Tschakhotine, 70.
Turner, 302.

Uexküll 223, 236.
Ullyott, 20, 45, 47–8, 50, 55, 57, 184.
Urban, 91.

Valentine, 282.
Verworn, 6, 229, 246.
Viaud, 288, 298.
Volkonsky, 194–5.
Voûte, 272.

Walter, 20.
Warden, 311.
Warner, 311.
Warnke, 277, 279.
Washburn, 311.
Weber, Heinz, 205, 277, 280.
Weber, Hermann, 244.
Weese, 192.
Weiss, 36.
Welsh, 20, 64.
Weyrauch, 183, 247.
Wheeler, 256.
Wierda, 96, 148, 155–7.
Wigglesworth, 196–8, 247, 259.
Wille, 22.
Williams, 258.
Windred, 258.
Winton, 25, 27, 40.
Wojtusiak, 121.
Wolf, 103–4.
Wolsky, 19.
Wortmann, 6.
Wunder, 261.

Yagi, 156.
Yerkes, 302.
Young, 21.

Zagorowsky, 200.

SYSTEMATIC INDEX

Notes added in 1960 are not included in this index. The use of a generic name in this index is no indication of its validity; the names are those used by the authors quoted. The classification is intended to bring similar animals together, so that readers do not miss a reference to a particular animal because of the use of an unfamiliar generic or vulgar name; it is not intended to indicate our views on the classification of organisms, but is designed for convenience in use.

PLANTS, 5–6, 9–10, 183, 235, 328–9, 333–4, 337.
Bacteria, 6, 333.
   Bacterium photometricum, 5, 17, 323.
Myxomycetes, 5, 334.
Algae, 9.
   Diatoms, 5.
Swarm spores, 5, 9, 335.
Sperm of ferns and mosses, 5.

PROTISTA, Protozoa, unicellular organisms, 5–8, 29–30, 35, 43, 57, 70, 75, 246, 288, 323, 328, 331, 335.
Rhizopods.
   Myxomycetes, 5, 334.
   Amoeba, 5–6, 300, 331.
Flagellates, 5, 9, 324, 333.
   Chlamydomonas, 5, 334.
   Bodo, 287, 289.
   Euglena, 5, 70–4, 135, 145–6, 148, 151, 187, 295, 331, 334–5.
   Volvocines, 333.
Ciliates, 5, 317, 319.
   Paramecium, 5, 35, 43–4, 57, 135, 200, 235, 286–8, 297–8, 320, 323, 327, 329, 331, 337.
   Oxytricha, 56.
   Stentor, 230.

PORIFERA, Sponges, 30, 35.
   Stylotella, 35.

COELENTERATA, 29, 35.
Medusae, 217, 220, 324.
   Leuckartiara, 121.
   Scyphomedusae, 230–1.
   Cotylorhiza, 231.
   Charybdaea, 121.
Hydra, 74, 326, 335.
Chlorohydra, 74–5.
Eudendrium, 10, 317.
Antennularia, 317.
Siphonophores, 227.
Anemones, 332.
   Cerianthus, 234.
   Calliactis, 35.
Pennatula (sea-pen), 235.

CTENOPHORA, 217, 220, 228.
Beroë, 228–30, 325.
Pleurobrachea, 228.

NEMATOMORPHA.
   Gordius, 246.

NEMERTINEA, 246.

CHAETOGNATHA.
   Sagitta, 185.

BRACHIOPODA.
   Lingula, 234.

ECHINODERMATA, 35, 235.
Starfishes, 235–6, 244, 324.
   Asterina, 235–6, 322, 328.
Sea-urchins, 235.
Holothurians, 235.
   Synapta, 234, 320, 324.

PLATYHELMINTHES, 35.
Turbellarians, 327, 330.
   Convoluta, 218, 231–2, 234, 324–5.
   Otoplana, 243.
   Plagiostomum, 20.
   Leptoplana, 20, 300.
   Planarians, 19, 75, 89, 100, 154, 168, 184, 250, 254, 256, 272, 320, 323, 329, 333, 335–6.
   Planaria alpina, 254–5, 257, 270, 291, 299, 319, 336.
   P. maculata, 20, 89, 174, 335.
   P. lugubris, 272–6.
   P. torva, 19.
   P. gonocephala, 20, 317.
   P. dorotocephala, 20.
   Dendrocoelum lacteum, 20, 45–55, 65, 79, 135, 292, 335.

ANNELIDA, 246, 311, 331.
Polychaetes, 111.
   Polychaete larvae, 185.
   Arenicola larva, 73, 135, 317.
   Nereis, 245, 301, 322.
   Alciope, 121.
   Tomopteris, 121.
   Arenicola, 232–3, 243, 320.
   Branchiomma, 220, 232–3.
   Spirographis, 10, 220.
Earthworms, 73, 302, 317, 326, 337.
   Lumbricus, 327.
Leeches.
   Clepsine, 315.
   Hemiclepsis, 282, 326.
   Protoclepsis, 261, 326.

MOLLUSCA, 319.
  Lamellibranchs, 28.
  Venus, 26.
  Solen (razor-shell), 233, 324.
  Gastropods, 234, 250, 254.
  Prosobranchs, 336.
  Alectrion, 283, 291, 322.
  Busycon, 283, 291, 322.
  Nassa, 283, 291, 326.
  Littorina, 175, 234, 297–8, 324.
  Pterotrachea, 223, 324.
  Opisthobranchs.
  Elysia, 107–13, 135, 324.
  Pulmonates, 234, 254.
  Snails, 175, 220, 237–8, 244, 300,
    321.
  Helix, 111, 162, 164, 175–8, 234,
    243, 322, 325.
  Limax (slug), 163, 234, 237, 243,
    322, 333.
  Cephalopods, 154, 223, 282.
  Octopus, 282–3, 325.
  Eledone, 335.

ARTHROPODA, 29, 89, 101, 154,
    178, 187, 266, 303, 321, 325, 327.
  MYRIAPODA, 175, 333.
  Centipedes, 301.
  Lithobius, 179, 181.
  Millipedes (diplopods), 248, 322.
  Julus, 105, 164–5, 174, 178–9, 181,
    332.
  Parajulus, 207.
  Polydesmus, 332.
  ARACHNIDA.
  Limulus, 21, 148, 322.
  Scorpions, 246–7.
  Mastigoproctus (whip-tail scorpion),
    21, 332.
  Tyrolichus (cheese mite), 205, 282,
    284, 326.
  Ticks, 335.
  Ixodes, 79, 204–5, 282, 286–7.
  Rhipicephalus, 239–41.
  Spiders, 104, 111, 260, 288, 290, 301,
    320, 332.
  Agelena, 319.
  Aranea, 260.
  Argiope, 260.
  Epeira, 260, 319.
  Zilla, 261, 334.
  CRUSTACEA, 29, 38, 98, 250, 329.
  Branchiopoda, 125, 324, 334.
  Apus (*Triops*), 121, 125, 135, 334.
  Artemia, 121, 125–7, 135, 334.
  Artemia nauplius larva, 126.
  Chirocephalus (*Branchipus*), 120–1,
    125–6, 227, 321, 334.
  Lepidurus, 125–6.
  Cladocera, 323.

ARTHROPODA, CRUSTACEA (*cont.*)
  Daphnia, 4, 117–18, 120–1, 124,
    159, 201, 298–9, 301, 323, 331,
    336.
  Copepoda, 185.
  Nitocra, 186.
  Thalestridae, 334.
  Phyllothalestris, 143, 145–6, 148–
    51.
  Argulus (fish louse), 124–5, 135,
    326.
  Cirripedia.
  Balanus larvae, 148, 295, 299.
  Mysids, 223, 253, 319.
  Hemimysis, 90–2, 98, 324.
  Amphipods.
  Gammarus, 254.
  Corophium, 152–3.
  Isopods, 234.
  Asellus, 254.
  Aega, 92.
  Cyathura, 234.
  Woodlice, 11, 15–17, 43–5, 100,
    135, 159, 164, 175–7, 181, 290,
    323, 332.
  Oniscus, 105, 175–6.
  Porcellio, 11–13, 135, 175–7, 299,
    325.
  Armadillidium (pill-bug) 82–7, 121,
    123, 222, 317, 326.
  Decapods—larvae, 185.
  Prawns and Shrimps, 121, 127,
    219, 234–5, 319.
  Leander, 121, 127–9, 135, 222–3.
  Processa, 127–8.
  Lysmata, 127, 227.
  Homarus (lobster), 253, 325.
  Potamobius (crayfish), 135, 221,
    317, 329.
  Hermit-crabs, 92, 99, 270, 291,
    320, 330.
  Eupagurus (hermit-crab), 99, 121,
    135, 180–1.
  Pagurus (hermit-crab), 320.
  Crabs, 99, 119, 175, 270, 291,
    319–20, 329–30.
  Carcinus, 180–1.
  Uca (fiddler-crab), 237.
  INSECTA, 4, 7, 33–4, 98, 111–12, 117,
    132, 202, 217, 227, 234, 245,
    249–51, 258, 266, 277, 281, 296,
    320–1, 323–34, 336.
  Thysanura.
  Lepisma (silver-fish), 164, 331.
  Thermobia (firebrat), 319.
  Orthoptera, 266.
  Cockroaches, 206, 212, 244–5,
    266, 302, 325, 336.
  Blatta, 22, 295–7, 325, 327, 335.
  Periplaneta, 325, 328. Facing p. 30.

ARTHROPODA, INSECTA (*cont.*)
Stick insects.
Carausius (*Dixippus*), 156, 182, 328, 337.
Grasshoppers, 266, 336.
Locusts, 132, 194–5, 201, 290, 309, 325, 328.
Schistocerca, 192–5, 210, 324.
Crickets, 266.
Gryllus (*Acheta*, *Liogryllus*), 204, 212, 266, 326, 333.
Dermaptera (earwigs), 175.
Forficula, 179, 181, 247, 336.
Ephemeroptera (mayflies)—nymphs, 121.
Odonata (dragon-flies), 97–8, 258, 277.
Anopleura (lice), 190, 200.
Pediculus (human louse), 195, 198–9, 205, 214, 327, 329, 331.
Haematopinus (hog louse), 205, 277–80, 336.
Hemiptera.
Pyrrhocoris, 326.
Cimex (bed-bug), 190, 195, 246, 333–4.
Rhodnius, 190, 196–8, 336.
Ranatra, 79, 166, 327.
Notonecta (backswimmer), 87, 121, 135, 148, 156, 166–73, 184, 226, 253, 321, 330, 334.
Cicadas, 266.
Coleoptera.
Larvae.
Acilius larva, 121, 337.
Wireworms, 321.
Tenebrio larva (mealworm), 248–9, 322.
Imagines.
Carabus, 213.
Notiophilus, 183.
Dineutes (whirligig), 87, 156, 163, 170–2, 321.
Coccinellid (lady-bird), 105.
Photinus (firefly), 154, 331.
Melanotus, 325.
Tenebrio, 282, 289, 333, 335.
Tribolium (flour beetle), 205.
Chrysomelid, 105.
Tetraopes, 237, 240–1, 322.
Cotton-boll weevil, 325.
Lamellicorns, 327.
Scarabaeus (dung beetle), 277, 279.
Geotrupes (dung beetle) 114–15, 277–9, 336.
Trichoptera.
Caddis worms, 254.
Lepidoptera, 34, 281, 301.
Larvae (caterpillars), 116, 321, 329.

ARTHROPODA, INSECTA (*cont.*)
Ephestia larva, 79–84, 135, 153, 159, 164, 320.
Malacosoma larva, 237.
Vanessa larva, 104–6, 135, 318.
Lymantria larva, 113–14, 117, 181–2, 327, 330.
Porthetria (*Lymantria*) larva, 113–14, 117.
Porthesia (*Euproctis*) larva, 184, 190.
Butterflies, 258, 332, 336.
Vanessa, 166, 170, 318, 323.
Gonepteryx, 132.
Moths, 282.
Ephestia (flour moth), 245.
Bombyx mori (silkworm moth), 282, 328.
Macroglossa (humming-bird moth), 182–3.
Amphipyra, 245, 247.
Diptera (*see* flies, *below*).
Larvae, 335.
Limnophila larva, 234, 335.
Maggots, 59–73, 100, 135, 146, 187, 211, 230, 293, 299, 317, 332, 333, 336.
Stomoxys larva, 213.
Musca larva, 21, 59, 213.
Lucilia larva, 59, 323, 326.
Calliphora larva, 21, 59, 69, 280, 326, 332.
Sarcophaga larva, 21.
Imagines (flies), 3, 26, 217, 244, 277, 315, 324, 332.
Bibionids, Harlequin flies, Bombyliids, 256.
midges, 256.
mosquitoes, 257–8, 290, 328, 335.
robber fly, 166, 169, 313.
Laphria, 318.
Proctacanthus, 162.
Erax, 79, 331.
Syrphidae, 256.
Eristalis, 84–9, 93–100, 115, 121, 123, 135, 144, 148, 155–8, 160–1, 164–6, 169–70, 184, 187, 222–3, 226, 233, 265, 296, 310, 313, 318, 323, 331.
Drosophila, 259, 277–81, 291, 301, 319, 322–3, 333.
Musca (house-fly), 203, 214, 332.
Fannia (lesser house-fly), 214, 332.
Stomoxys (stable-fly), 202, 214, 258, 329, 332.
Lyperosia, 258, 329.
Blowflies, 3, 332.
Calliphora (bluebottle), 2, 277–80, 282, 326.
Lucilia, 208–10, 326.
Phormia, facing p. 202.

ARTHROPODA, Insecta (*cont.*)
Hymenoptera, 301.
Habrobracon, 277–80, 332.
Apis (honey bee), 26, 91–104, 118, 121, 123, 135–6, 161, 164–6, 201, 222, 302–3, 318, 324, 332, 335, 337.
Ants, 100–3, 135, 302, 311, 318, 320, 322, 334.
Lasius, 103.
Formica, 205, 326.
Messor, 320.

INVERTEBRATES, 3, 223, 253–4, 265–6, 304, 307, 316.

PROTOCHORDATES.
Tadpole larva of *Amaroucium* (ascidian), 73, 135, 331.

VERTEBRATES, 3, 29, 33, 38, 116, 154, 217, 219–20, 223–4, 260, 265, 283, 299, 307, 310, 330.
Cyclostomes.
Lampreys, 21–2, 337.
Fishes, 1–4, 33, 132, 200, 220, 224–6, 250–3, 258, 261–2, 283, 303, 318, 323–5, 327, 330, 334–5, 337.
Dogfish, 31, 226–7, 332.
Mustelus, 283–4.
Scyllium, 330.
Herring, 334.
Salmon, 315, 328.
Trout, 2.
Fundulus, 250.
Pike, 261.
Phoxinus (minnow), 251–2, 261–2, 324, 330.

VERTEBRATES, Fishes (*cont.*)
Catfish, 327.
Eel, 31, 261.
Lota (eel-pout), 261.
Crenilabrus, 121, 130–1.
Amphibia, 261–2.
Triton (newt), 259, 263, 284, 290–1, 322, 331.
Amblystoma (axolotl), 262–3, 332, 334.
Triturus (Salamander), 247–8, 332.
Frog, 24, 26, 29, 31.
Bufo (toad), 154.
Xenopus (clawed toad), 263–5, 329.
Reptiles, 212, 224, 330.
Vipera (adder), 284–5, 319.
Phrynosoma (horned 'toad'), 192, 194, 336.
Birds, 3–4, 132, 201, 216–17, 224, 301–2.
Domestic fowl, 44, 266.
Pigeon, 302.
Mammals, 3, 29, 55, 118, 195, 201, 216–17, 266, 268–9, 301–4, 316, 321.
Rodents, 212, 326.
Rats, 236–7, 239–41, 243, 248, 302, 315, 322, 327–8.
Mice, 237, 243, 248, 322, 327.
Dog, 1, 40, 44, 266–70, 284, 291, 301, 303, 328.
Cat, 37, 39, 124, 266–8.
Ape, 303, 329.
Chimpanzee, 304.
Man, 4, 8, 17, 37, 41, 43, 58, 111, 136, 188, 266–8, 293, 302–4, 306–7, 311, 315, 328.

GENERAL INDEX

Notes added in 1960 are not included in this index.

Acceleration, angular, 31, 116, 218–19, 224–6, 252.
acclimatization, 204–5. *See* adaptation.
acquired automatisms, 39, 301.
action currents, 29–32, 226, 252, 262, 306.
adaptation, accessory, 32.
  sensory, 31–3.
  altering intensity of reaction, 60, 85, 131, 296.
  asymmetry of, 152, 168–9.
  essential in klino-kinesis of *Dendro-coelum*, 46–57.
  in klino-taxis, 65.
  & loss of circus movements, 93, 96, 161–2, 166–73.
  & temperature, 204–5, 208–11.
  see evolution, plasticity.
after-discharge, 39.
age, physiological, 201, 299.
aggregation, 17–18, 21, 184, 202. *See* preferred temperature, &c.
  in *Dendrocoelum*, 46–55.
  in locusts, 192–5.
  in *Paramecium*, 57.
  in Protozoa, 43.
  in turbellarians, 20.
  in woodlice, 11–17.
akinesis, 195.
alarm reaction, 277.
all-or-nothing, 26.
alternative chamber, 13–14, 53–4, 201, 290.
anecdotes, 4.
anemo-taxis, 256–60.
  in *Drosophila*, 259.
  in mosquitoes, 257–8.
  & olfactory reactions, 258–9.
angular velocity, 45–6.
antennae
  in Crustacea, 270.
  in insects, 34, 195–8, 277–82.
antennules (Crustacea), 180, 221–2, 270, 291.
anthropomorphic view of behaviour, 4–8, 16, 44, 55, 190, 202, 288, 311.
asymmetrical animals, 8, 114, 152–3, 309–10. *See* circus movements.
asymmetry of stimulation, 8, 76, 308–9. *See* light compass reaction; telo-taxis.
auricular organs (planarians), 272, 274–5.
automatisms, acquired, 39, 301.
average linear velocity, 13–15.
averages, *see* statistical treatment.

avoiding reactions, 55, 63–4, 203–5, 211, 286, 290. *See* klino-kinesis.

Background condition, 298.
balance, asymmetrical in light compass reaction, 113–15, 118, 180, 309.
balance of reactions, 122, 124, 128, 130–1 241–3, 296–7.
balance of reflexes, 309–10.
  stable and unstable, 157–9.
  in tropo-taxis, 77–8, 81–2, 86, 89.
  in telo-taxis, 90–6.
  in skoto-taxis, 178–80.
  in compass reactions, 113–15.
  in dorsal light reaction, 123, 125–6, 128, 131.
  & tropisms, 89.
  in circus movements, 170–2.
  in fishes, 225.
balancing, *see* equilibrium.
behaviour effects of temperature, 207–11.
binocular vision, 95, 98.
boundary reactions, 54–7, 172, 182, 314. *See also* avoiding reactions; klino-kinesis.
brain, 41, 305.

Campaniform sensillae, 33.
catch muscle of lamellibranchs, 26, 28–9.
cathode ray oscillograph, 29, 226.
central nervous system, 35–41. *See* inhibition.
centrifugal force, 218, 234.
chemical stimulation, reactions to, 270–91.
  in *Bodo*, 287, 289.
  in crabs, 270.
  in dogfish, 283–4.
  in insects, 277–82, 288–90.
  in *Paramecium*, 286–8.
  in planarians, 272–6.
  in prosobranch molluscs, 283.
  in snakes, 284–5.
  in ticks, 286.
chemo-klino-kinesis, 282.
chemo-receptors, 33–4, 271.
chemo-taxis, 5.
chemo-tropo-taxis, 274–6.
choice chamber, 13–14, 53–4, 201, 290.
cilia, 24.
circus movements, 77–9, 83–6, 161–73, 312.
  modification of, 93–5, 165–73.

circus movements (*cont.*)
  & klino-taxis, 66–7.
  & tropo-taxis, 77–9, 161–2, 164–6, 173, 312.
  & telo-taxis, 93–5, 161–2, 164–6, 173.
  & dorsal light reaction, 125–6.
  in chemical stimulation, 274, 279, 281–2.
  in light:
    in *Armadillidium*, 83, 85.
    in bees, 93–5, 166.
    in *Dineutes*, 170–2.
    in *Ephestia* larvae, 81, 84.
    in *Eristalis*, 85–6, 164–6.
    in *Julus*, 164–5.
    in *Limax*, 163–4.
    in maggots, 65–7.
    in *Notonecta*, 166–9, 172–3.
    in planarians, 168.
  & temperature, 195, 197.
classification of reactions, 1–10, 18–19, 133–5, 311–14, 317–18. *See also* kinesis; taxis; transverse orientation.
clonus, 26–7.
colour vision, 303.
comparison, simultaneous, 77, 81, 154.
  simultaneous and successive, 64, 69, 196–7, 313.
  successive, 64–5, 73, 145.
compass reactions, *see* light compass reaction.
compensatory movements, 116–17, 250–1, 253, 256–8.
condensation of water vapour, 192.
conditioning, 303.
conduction of heat, 191–2.
contact, indirect, 252, 260–5.
contact stimulation, 244–9.
convection of heat, 191–2.
co-ordination, 38–42, 99.
crevices, 245–9.
criticism, *see* anthropomorphic; teleological.
criticism of Kühn's classification, 9, 44, 97–8, 312–13.
criticism of Loeb's theory, 7–10, 32, 42–3, 89, 162, 220, 246, 276, 288, 307–10, 314, 316.
curiosity, 4, 8.
currents, *see* senses.

Dark adaptation, 30–2, 60, 85, 161–2, 166–73. *See* adaptation, sensory.
dark-room, 46, 60, 96–7, 161.
Darwin's theory of evolution, 3.
decision point, 153.
diagonal path, 170–2.
diffusion gradient apparatus, 289. *See* alternative chamber.

directed reactions, 43, 58, 76. *See* taxis; transverse orientation.
direction receptors, 75, 116, 154.
direction of stimulus, reactions to, 75, 148, 154, 183–8, 290. *See* taxis; transverse orientation.
distant touch sense, 260.
divergence angle, 113–15.
dorsal light reaction, 120–32, 134, 216, 314.
  & tropo-taxis, 120–3.
  & telo-taxis, 120–1, 123.
  & light compass reaction, 120–1.
  in *Argulus*, 124–5.
  in Branchiopoda, 125–6.
  in *Crenilabrus*, 130–2.
  in *Daphnia*, 124.
  in flying animals, 132.
  in *Leander*, 127–9.

Eccritic concentration (chemical), 284, 287.
eccritic temperature, 202. *See* preferred temperature.
eco-climates, 11, 215.
electro-taxis, 310.
elimination of circus movements, 165–73.
emotion, 4–5.
Entscheidungspunkt, 153.
equilibrium, maintenance of, 42, 122, 132, 216–27. *See* primary orientation.
evaporation of water, 191–2. *See* humidity.
evolution, 3–4, 306.
  of behaviour, 16–17, 137, 190, 311, 315.
excitation and inhibition, 40–1.
experience, *see* learning.
experience, modifiability through, 93.
exteroceptors, 33.
eye, types of, 97–8, 154.
  compound, 125–6, 157–8, 178, 187, 194.
  cup, 107.
  flat cyclopean, 140–3, 154, 187.
  lateral flat, 144–7, 154.
  median, of *Apus*, 125.
  spherical, 138–9.
  see also receptors; photo-receptors; form; direction; intensity.
eyes, two-way, 86–8.
eyes, scheme of action of compound, 155–60, 178–80.

Facilitation, 35.
fear, 13.
Ferntastsinn, 260.
final common path, 40.

fixation reaction, 117–18, 124, 257–8, 291.
fixation region in eyes, 95–7, 118–19, 121, 124, 128, 164.
fixation region in statocysts, 222.
flagellum, 24.
of *Euglena*, 70.
forced action, 43, 307. *See* free will.
movements, 307–8. *See* free will.
form vision, 137, 181–3, 188.
free will, 8, 162, 238, 292–3, 307.
fright reactions, *see* avoiding reactions; klino-kinesis; phobo-taxis.

Galvano-taxis, 310.
galvanotropism, 6, 310.
geographical varieties, 212–13.
geo-kinesis, 219.
geo-taxis, 5, 216–17, 228–43.
in *Convoluta*, 218, 231–2, 234.
in ctenophores, 228–30.
in *Paramecium*, 235.
in polychaetes, 232–3.
in prawns, 234–5.
in Scyphomedusae, 230–1.
geotropic responses (Crozier), 235–43.
geotropism, 5.
geo-tropo-taxis, 231.
gradient of intensity, 134.
of chemical stimulation, 270, 278.
of humidity, 13, 212, 289–90, 296–7.
of light, 46–9, 52, 137–40, 147, 183–5.
of temperature, 189, 192–3, 195–206, 211–15, 296–7.
gradient of sensitivity in eyes, 155–60, 178–80.
gravity reactions, 216–43.
gravity receptors, 216–18.

Habituation, 300.
Haller's organ, 282.
halteres, 217.
hearing, *see* sound.
heat, 21, 191. *See* temperature.
heliotropism, 6, 76.
heredity, *see* inheritance, instincts.
homing of ants, 100–3, 302.
of bees, 102–4, 302.
of pigeons, 302.
of spiders, 104.
homoiothermal animals, 3, 189, 201.
hormones, 29, 299.
horo-taxis, 34, 182.
humidity, 211–12, 288–9.
humidity reactions, 11–17, 211–12, 288–90, 296–7.
humidity receptors, 34, 288–9.
hydrotropism, 5.
hygro-kinesis, 11–17, 290.
hygro-taxis, 290.

Immobility, 245. *See* ortho-kinesis.
impulses, nervous, 29–42. *See* action currents.
inclined plane, orientation on, 235–43, 260.
indifference zone, 202, 284, 286–7. *See* preferred temperature.
indirect contact, 260–5.
in *Amblystoma*, 262–3.
in fishes, 261–2.
in spiders, 260–1.
in *Xenopus*, 263–5.
inheritance of reactions, 3, 301. *See* instincts, evolution.
inhibition, central & peripheral, 29, 38.
inhibition, central:
in reflexes, 38, 40.
in telo-taxis, 87, 90–8, 121, 159, 164, 173, 313.
in light compass reactions, 110, 112–13, 115–16, 118.
in static reactions, 222.
inhibition of cilia, 229.
of locomotion, 152, 245, 300.
of photo-kinesis, 300.
by training, 300–2.
inhibitory contact stimulus, 22–3, 245.
insect migration, 258.
instinctive action, 6, 39.
instincts, 3, 301, 303, 314.
intelligence, 304.
intensity receptors, 58, 64, 73, 116, 134, 137, 154.
intensity of stimulus, 32, 295.
reactions to, 148, 183–8, 290.
interoceptors, 33.
isometric lever, 25.

Kinaesthetic sense, 100, 103, 302.
kinesis, 10, 18–19, 53, 100, 134, 184–5, 309, 312, 317. *See also* ortho-, klino-kinesis; akinesis; chemo-, geo-, hygro-, photo-, rheo-, thermo-, thigmo-kinesis.
kinesis, high & low, 22–3, 195, 246, 249.
klino-kinesis, 43–57, 134, 312, 314.
& ortho-kinesis, 44–5, 53.
in *Dendrocoelum*, 45–56.
in *Paramecium*, 43–4, 57.
& chemical stimulation, 271–88.
& humidity, 290.
& temperature, 199, 204–5, 211.
klino-taxis, 58–75, 134, 185, 187, 309, 313–14.
& tropo-taxis, 67, 76, 312–13.
in *Euglena*, 70–3.
in *Hydra*, 74–5.
in maggots, 59–70.
in other animals, 73.
& chemical stimulation, 75, 271–84.

klino-taxis (*cont.*)
  & light, 58–75.
  & rheo-taxis, 256.
  & sound, 266, 268.
  & temperature, 196–9, 206.
klino-tropo-taxis, 118.
knee-jerk, 33, 37–9.
Kühn's classification, 9, 311–14, 317–18.
  See criticisms.

Labyrinth, *see* maze.
labyrinth of fishes, 130–2, 223–6, 262.
  of mammals, 118.
  of vertebrates, 33, 224.
latent period, 39.
lateral line of amphibia, 262–5.
  of fishes, 33, 251–3, 261–2.
lateral line nerve, 22.
learning by experience, 3, 96, 166, 168, 226–7, 300–4.
Lichtkompassbewegung, 106. *See* light compass reaction.
Lichtrückenreflex, 120, 135. *See* dorsal light reaction.
light, convergent, 185–6.
  imperfect beam, 161, 166–8.
  parallel beam, 137, 184–5.
  perfect beam, 161, 164, 169, 173.
  radiating, 137–40.
  uniform, 93, 96, 161–2, 164, 169, 172–3.
  see also dark-room; eyes; photo-taxis; photo-kinesis.
light compass reaction, 8, 100–19, 134, 308, 314.
  & tropo-taxis, 113–16, 118.
  & telo-taxis, 109, 112, 116, 118–19.
  & meno-taxis, 106, 312.
  & tropo-meno-taxis, 115–16.
  in ants, 100–3.
  in bees, 102–4.
  in caterpillars, 104–6, 113–15.
  in *Elysia*, 107–10.
linear velocity, 13–15, 20–1, 46.
lines of equal electrical potential, 150.
  of equal intensity of light, 138–9.
  of equal temperature, 196–9.
locomotory activity, 207. *See* ortho-kinesis.
Loeb's theory, 6–10, 307–10. *See* tropisms; tropism theory; criticisms of Loeb's theory.
logarithmic graphs, 163, 236–7.
  spiral path, 113, 117.

Manege-Bewegung, 77. *See* circus movements.
maxillary lobes of maggots, 59, 64.
maze running, 302–4, 306, 315.
mechanical outlook, 16–17, 162.

mechanical stimulation, 244–69.
mechano-receptors, 33, 244.
memory, 8, 51, 65, 302, 316.
memory images, 315.
men-akinesis, 195.
meno-taxis, 106, 135, 312, 318. *See* light compass reaction.
metabolic effect of temperature, 207–11.
micro-climates, 11, 13.
migration, 299.
  of birds, 302.
  of insects, 258.
  of plankton, 310.
  see also homing.
mind, 51, 305.
mnemo-taxis, 312, 318.
modifiability, *see* adaptation; learning; variation.
motoneurone, 41–2.
muscle contraction, 24–9.
muscle of lamellibranchs, 26, 28–9.
muscle spindle, 28–9, 32–3, 37–8.
muscle tension, *see* tonus; tetano-tonus.

Negative reaction, 10, 22.
nerve, afferent, 30, 32.
  efferent, 29.
nerve endings, free, 30, 33.
nerve fibre, 29–30.
nerve-muscle preparation, 24–7, 39.
nerve net, 35, 228.
neurones, 41.

Ocelli of caterpillars, 80, 116, 182.
odours, *see* smell; chemical stimulation.
ommatidia of insect eyes, 93, 95–6, 101, 112, 116, 118, 155–9, 162, 164, 166, 169–73, 178–80, 187.
one-way action of eye, 84.
one-way statocyst, 222, 231.
optimum, 189, 201–2, 284, 290.
orientation angle, 107–9, 111–12, 115.
orientation, meaning of term, 1.
orientation, primary, 1–3, 216, 245, 249.
  secondary, 2–3.
orientation, stable & unstable, 152, 157–9, 178–80, 198, 216.
ortho-kinesis, 11–23, 134, 312, 314.
  & klino-kinesis, 44–5, 53.
  in maggots, 21.
  in planarians, 19–21.
  in *Porcellio*, 11–13, 15–17.
  in other animals, 21–2.
  & chemical stimulation, 271, 273, 276, 283.
  & contact, 247.
  & humidity, 290.
  & temperature, 206–11.

oscillo-taxis, 310.
osmo-tropo-taxis, 279.
osphradium, 283.
otocyst, 217.
oxygen, 6, 287, 289.

Parallelogram of forces, 149. *See* triangle of forces.
parsimony, principle of, 180, 306.
pedio-tropo-taxis, 144.
peripheral inhibition, 29.
phasic & tonic contractions, 41, 220, 225.
phengophil & phengophob, 5.
phobo-taxis, 44, 55–7, 135, 278, 286, 312, 317. *See* klino-kinesis.
phono-receptors, 33.
photochemical change, 187.
photochemical equilibrium, 51.
photo-horo-taxis, 182.
photo-kinesis, 5, 17–22.
photophil & photophob, 5.
photoreceptors of earthworm, 73.
    of *Euglena*, 70–1, 145.
    of maggots, 59, 62, 64.
photo-taxis, 5. *See* taxis; klino-taxis; tropo-taxis; telo-taxis.
photo-taxis, negative, 10, 60.
phototropism, 5.
physiological effects of temperature, 21, 201, 206–11.
pitching, 122–3.
plankton, 185–6, 217, 220, 223, 310. See *Systematic Index*.
plasticity, 99, 173, 301.
poikilothermal animals, 3, 189, 201.
positive reaction, 10, 22.
posture reactions, 79, 193–4, 220, 225, 309.
preference, 4.
preferred concentration (chemical), 284, 287.
preferred temperature, 199–206, 209, 211–14, 296.
primary orientation, 1–3, 216, 245, 249.
profil-tropo-taxis, 144.
proprioceptive impulses, 39.
proprioceptors, 33, 37, 41, 196, 234, 242–4, 260.
pseudopodia, 24.
psychical & psychological, 3–4.
purpose, 4, 8, 16, 311, 315–16.

Radiant heat, 19, 21, 136, 191–2, 194–200.
radiation, 136, 191.
random movements, 43, 50, 63, 76, 81, 103, 110, 148, 193, 219. *See* kinesis.
random turning, 45.
r.c.d., 45–55.

receptors, 30–4, 73. *See* antennae; antennules; auricular organs; eye; halteres; maxillary lobes; muscle spindle; ocelli; ommatidia; osphradium; otocyst; senses
receptors, intensity, direction & movement, 137.
recovery, 131, 164, 166, 225–6. *See* elimination of circus movements.
reflex immobility, 245.
reflex map in eyes, 155–60, 161–2, 173, 178–80.
    in tropo-taxis, 85–9, 155–60, 173.
    in telo-taxis, 97–9, 164.
    in skoto-taxis, 174, 178–80.
    in light compass reaction, 101, 118–19.
    in dorsal light reaction, 123–4, 128.
    & circus movements, 162, 164, 169.
    plastic, 99, 180.
    in bees, 97.
    in crabs, 99.
    in *Daphnia*, 159.
    in *Eristalis*, 85–9, 155–7, 160.
    in *Notonecta*, 156, 173.
    in other insects, 156.
reflex map in static reactions, 222–3, 233.
reflex republic, 236.
reflex sensitivity, 156. *See* reflex map.
reflex tonus, 28, 37.
reflex turning, 76–7, 93, 95, 155–7. *See* taxis.
reflexes, 7, 35–42, 44, 89, 306, 309.
    conditioned, 261, 303.
    dynamic or phasic, 41, 220, 225–6.
    locomotory, 242.
    Loeb on, 7.
    partial & total, 42, 309.
    phasic & tonic, 41, 220, 225, 310.
    postural, 242.
    static, 225.
    tonic, 41, 224.
refractory period, 31.
resultant force, 218.
resultant law, 141, 145–7. *See* triangle of forces.
reversal of reactions, 82, 295–8.
rheo-kinesis, 255.
rheo-taxis, 117, 249–56, 291, 299.
    in fishes, 250–3.
    in *Notonecta*, 253.
    in planarians, 254–6.
rheotropism, 5.
rheo-tropo-taxis, 256.
rhythms of activity, diurnal.
    in cockroach, 22, 206.
    in planarians, 20–1.
righting reaction, 124–8, 227, 244–5.
rolling, 122–6, 131.
rotation, 218, 232, 235.

Schreckreaktion, 203. *See* avoiding reaction; klino-kinesis; phobo-taxis.
scratch reflex of dog, 40.
secondary orientation, 2–3.
selection of random movements, 44, 63. *See* klino-kinesis.
semi-circular canals, 31, 33, 42, 116, 217, 220, 223–6, 251–2.
senses, *see* receptors.
  currents: anemo-; lateral line; mechanical stimulation; rheo-.
  hearing: lateral line; mechanical stimulation; phono-; sound.
  position: campaniform sensillae; dorsal light; equilibrium; geo-; gravity; kinaesthetic; labyrinth; mechanical stimulation; pitching; posture; primary orientation; proprioceptors; righting; rolling; semi-circular canals; stability; statocysts; thigmo-; transverse; ventral earth; ventral gravity; ventral light.
  sight: anemo-; dorsal light; eyes; fixation; form; light; photo-; reflex map; skoto-; two-light; ventral light.
  smell: chemical stimulation; chemo-; humidity; taste; two-source.
  taste, *see* smell, above.
  temperature: thermo-; two-source.
  touch: contact; mechanical stimulation; stereo-; thigmo-; vibro-taxis.
sensitivity gradient in eye, 155–60, 169.
sexual behaviour, 299.
shapes, reactions to, 181–3.
shock reactions, 18, 55, 64, 300. *See* klino-kinesis.
sight, *see* senses; light; photo-.
skoto-taxis, 174–83.
  & telo-taxis & tropo-taxis, 174–81.
  & shapes, 181–3.
  in crabs, 180.
  in *Helix*, 177–8.
  in *Julus*, 178.
  in *Littorina*, 175.
  in *Lymantria* larvae, 181–2.
  in woodlice, 175–7.
smell & taste, 33–4, 270–91.
somato-thigmo-taxis, 246.
somersaulting, 122, 124, 126.
sound, localization of, 265–9.
  in crickets, 266.
  in mammals, 266–9.
spinal nerve, 41.
stability of equilibrium, 122, 124, 127, 132. *See* equilibrium.
stable orientation, *see* orientation, stable.
  in negative reactions, 159, 178–80.

standard deviation & standard error, 203, 294.
statistical treatment, 80–1, 153, 203, 292–5.
statocysts, 33, 127–8, 134, 217–35, 242–4.
statolith starch, 235.
stepping reflex, 42, 44.
stereotropism, 246, 248.
stimulatory organs, 19.
stimuli, *see* receptors; senses.
stimulus, 29–34.
symmetry, bilateral, 6–7, 308.
synapses, 35–9, 44.

Tangent law, 144. *See* triangle of forces.
taste & smell, 33–4, 271. *See* chemical stimulation.
taxis, 9–10, 44, 53, 58, 60, 100, 134, 312–14, 317. *See also* klino-; telo-; tropo-taxis.
  horo-; klino-tropo-; meno-; mnemo-; oscillo-; pedio-tropo-; phobo-; profil-tropo-; topo-; tropo-meno-taxis.
  anemo-; chemo-; electro-; galvano-; geo-; hygro-; osmo-; photo-; rheo-; skoto-; somato-thigmo-; thermo-; thigmo-; topo-thigmo-; vibro-taxis.
taxis & tropism, 9–10.
tel-akinesis, 195.
teleological outlook, 4, 6, 16, 310–11, 315.
telo-taxis, 8, 90–9, 134, 308, 312–14, 317.
  negative, 174.
  & klino-taxis, 90–1.
  & tropo-taxis, 78, 86–7, 90–8, 161–2, 164–6, 173, 313.
  & circus movements, 93–7, 161–2, 164–6, 173.
  & chemical stimulation, 271.
  & gravity reactions, 219, 222, 230, 232.
  & indirect contact, 264–5.
  & light in bees, 91–8.
    in crabs, 99.
    in *Mysis*, 90.
  & rheo-taxis, 255.
  & temperature reactions, 197–8, 203.
temperature adaptation, 204–5.
temperature of body, regulation, 192, 194–5, 201–2. *See* homoiothermal animals.
temperature gradient, 189–215, 296–7.
temperature gradient apparatus, 200–1, 212.
temperature & humidity reactions, 211–12, 289, 296–7.

temperature optimum, 189, 201–2.
temperature, physiological effects of, 21, 201, 206–9.
temperature preferendum, 202. *See* preferred temperature.
temperature reactions, 189–215.
  & ortho-kinesis, 206–11.
  & klino-kinesis, 203, 205, 211.
  & klino-taxis, 196–9, 206.
  & tropo-taxis, 205.
  & telo-taxis, 203.
  & humidity, 211–12, 289, 296–7.
  in bed bugs, 195.
  in cockroaches, 206, 296–7.
  in crickets, 204, 212.
  in flies, 202–3, 208–11, 214.
  in lice, 195, 198–9, 205, 214.
  in locusts, 192–5, 210.
  in maggots, 211, 213.
  in parasites, 190, 200.
  in other insects, 205, 213.
  in *Paramecium*, 200.
  in *Phrynosoma*, 192, 194.
  in other reptiles, 212.
  in Rhodnius, 196–8.
  in rodents, 212.
temperature receptors, 34, 194–5.
temperature, two behaviour effects of, 207–11.
temperature zone, preferred, 202. *See* preferred temperature; temperature reactions.
Temperaturorgel, 200.
tension of muscle, *see* tonus; tetano-tonus.
terminology, 314.
tetano-tonus, 28.
tetanus, 26–8, 38.
thermal death, 201, 209.
thermo-couple, 195, 198, 210.
thermo-kinesis, 34, 203–11.
thermo-meno-taxis, 199.
thermo-receptors, 34.
thermo-tactic optimum, 202.
thermo-taxis, 195–9, 203–6, 211.
thermotropism, 6.
thigmo-kinesis, 23, 246–7, 249.
thigmo-taxis, 248.
thigmotropism, 6, 246.
threshold of stimulation, 24, 26, 32, 96, 170, 172–3.
token stimulus, 119, 137, 190–1, 200, 247, 299.
tonic contraction, 41, 163, 220.
tonus, 26, 28, 38, 42, 88–9, 308–9.
tonus theory, 6–10, 42, 88–9, 162–3, 220. *See* tropism theory.
topo-taxis, 10, 312, 317.
topo-thigmo-taxis, 246.
touch, *see* senses, contact.

touch receptors, 33.
training, 302–3.
transmission, neuroid & neural, 35.
transverse current apparatus, 289.
transverse gravity reaction, 220–6.
  in crayfish, 221–2.
  in fishes, 223–6.
  in *Leander*, 222–3.
transverse orientation, 10, 106, 134, 216, 314. *See* dorsal light; ventral light; light compass; transverse gravity; ventral earth; ventral gravity reactions.
trench fever, 214.
trial & error, 8, 44, 55, 63, 195, 288, 312. *See* klino-kinesis.
trial movements, 62, 77, 140, 147–8, 182, 194. *See* klino-kinesis; klino-taxis.
triangle of forces rule, 140–52, 155, 158, 218, 234.
trichobothria of spiders, 261.
tropism, 9–10, 317. *See also* taxis; kinesis; transverse orientation; galvano-; geo-; helio-; hydro-; photo-; rheo-; stereo-; thermo-; thigmo-tropism.
tropism & taxis, 9–10.
tropism theory, 6–10, 89, 162, 175, 183, 248, 307–11. *See also* criticism of Loeb's theory.
tropisms of plants, 6, 9–10.
tropo-meno-taxis, 115–16.
tropo-taxis, 76–89, 134, 185–7, 309, 312–14, 317.
  & ortho-kinesis, 79.
  & klino-kinesis, 79.
  & klino-taxis, 76, 78–9, 81, 312–13.
  & telo-taxis, 78, 86–7, 90–8, 161–2, 164–6, 173, 312–14.
  & chemical stimulation, 274–6, 277, 279, 281, 284.
  & contact stimulation, 248.
  & currents, 253, 255.
  & gravity, 222, 230–1.
  & humidity, 290.
  & indirect contact, 265.
  & light, 79–89.
  & sound, 266, 268.
  & temperature, 195, 197–8, 205.
  See also circus movements; reflex map; skoto-taxis.
tropo-taxis, asymmetrical, 114.
turning reflexes, 76, 118.
turn-table, 116–17, 234–5, 251.
two-light experiment, 67, 78, 135–60.
  & klino-taxis, 67–9.
  & tropo-taxis, 78–87, 151, 153, 159.
  & telo-taxis, 90–3, 98, 153–4, 159.

two-light experiment, (*cont.*)
  & dorsal light reaction, 123.
  & light compass reaction 110, 113, 115, 118.
  & *Armadillidium*, 83–4, 86.
  & bees, 91–3.
  & *Bufo*, 154.
  & *Corophium*, 152–3.
  & crabs, 99.
  & *Daphnia*, 118, 159.
  & *Ephestia* larva, 80–2.
  & *Eristalis*, 85–7, 155–7.
  & *Euglena*, 145–6.
  & maggots, 67–9.
  & *Mysis*, 90.
  & *Phyllothalestris*, 143, 146, 149, 151.
two-source experiment, 135, 312, 317–18. *See* two-light experiment.
  & chemical stimulation, 275.
  & sound, 268.
  & temperature, 197–9.
two-way action, 226.
two-way action of eyes, 78, 86, 95, 98, 147, 173.
two-way statocyst, 222, 232.

Undirected reactions, 43. *See* kinesis.

unilateral extirpation of receptors, 134, 161–73. *See* circus movements.
Unterschiedsempfindlichkeit, 18, 135, 288.
Unterschiedsempfindlichkeit in der Zeit, 268.

Variation in behaviour, 82, 292–304. *See* statistical treatment.
ventral earth reaction, 134, 216.
ventral gravity reaction, 314.
ventral light reaction, 120, 126–7, 134.
vibrations, 244.
vibro-taxis, 260.
view-point, 1–11, 13–19, 292–5, 305–16. *See* anthropomorphic; mechanical; teleological.
voluntary actions, 6.
Vorzugstemperatur, 202.

Wahltemperatur, 202.
walking, 40.
wave-lengths, 136.
web of spider, localization of prey in, 260–1.

Zigzag path, 92, 99, 135, 159, 178, 313, 318.

CATALOGUE OF DOVER BOOKS

Biological Sciences

AN INTRODUCTION TO GENETICS, A. H. Sturtevant and G. W. Beadle. A very thorough exposition of genetic analysis and the chromosome mechanics of higher organisms by two of the world's most renowned biologists, A. H. Sturtevant, one of the founders of modern genetics, and George Beadle, Nobel laureate in 1958. Does not concentrate on the biochemical approach, but rather more on observed data from experimental evidence and results . . . from Drosophila and other life forms. Some chapter titles: Sex chromosomes; Sex-Linkage; Autosomal Inheritance;; Chromosome Maps; Intra-Chromosomal Rearrangements; Inversions—and Incomplete Chromosomes; Translocations; Lethals; Mutations; Heterogeneous Populations; Genes and Phenotypes; The Determination and Differentiation of Sex; etc. Slightly corrected reprint of 1939 edition. New preface by Drs. Sturtevant and Beadle. 1 color plate. 126 figures. Bibliographies. Index. 391pp. 5⅜ x 8½. S306 Paperbound **$2.00**

THE GENETICAL THEORY OF NATURAL SELECTION, R. A. Fisher. 2nd revised edition of a vital reviewing of Darwin's Selection Theory in terms of particulate inheritance, by one of the great authorities on experimental and theoretical genetics. Theory is stated in mathematical form. Special features of particulate inheritance are examined: evolution of dominance, maintenance of specific variability, mimicry and sexual selection, etc. 5 chapters on man and his special circumstances as a social animal. 16 photographs. Bibliography. Index. x + 310pp. 5⅜ x 8. S466 Paperbound **$2.00**

THE ORIENTATION OF ANIMALS: KINESES, TAXES AND COMPASS REACTIONS, Gottfried S. Fraenkel and Donald L. Gunn. A basic work in the field of animal orientations. Complete, detailed survey of everything known in the subject up to 1940s, enlarged and revised to cover major developments to 1960. Analyses of simpler types of orientation are presented in Part I: kinesis, klinotaxis, tropotaxis, telotaxis, etc. Part II covers more complex reactions originating from temperature changes, gravity, chemical stimulation, etc. The two-light experiment and unilateral blinding are dealt with, as is the problem of determinism or volition in lower animals. The book has become the universally-accepted guide to all who deal with the subject—zoologists, biologists, psychologists, and the like. Second, enlarged edition, revised to 1960. Bibliography of over 500 items. 135 illustrations. Indices. xiii + 376pp. 5⅜ x 8½. T786 Paperbound **$2.25**

THE BEHAVIOUR AND SOCIAL LIFE OF HONEYBEES, C. R. Ribbands. Definitive survey of all aspects of honeybee life and behavior; completely scientific in approach, but written in interesting, everyday language that both professionals and laymen will appreciate. Basic coverage of physiology, anatomy, sensory equipment; thorough account of honeybee behavior in the field (foraging activities, nectar and pollen gathering, how individuals find their way home and back to food areas, mating habits, etc.); details of communication in various field and hive situations. An extensive treatment of activities within the hive community—food sharing, wax production, comb building, swarming, the queen, her life and relationship with the workers, etc. A must for the beekeeper, natural historian, biologist, entomologist, social scientist, et al. "An indispensable reference," J. Hambleton, BEES. "Recommended in the strongest of terms," AMERICAN SCIENTIST. 9 plates. 66 figures. Indices. 693-item bibliography. 252pp. 5⅜ x 8½. T1137 Paperbound **$2.00**

BIRD DISPLAY: AN INTRODUCTION TO THE STUDY OF BIRD PSYCHOLOGY, E. A. Armstrong. The standard work on bird display, based on extensive observation by the author and reports of other observers. This important contribution to comparative psychology covers the behavior and ceremonial rituals of hundreds of birds from gannet and heron to birds of paradise and king penguins. Chapters discuss such topics as the ceremonial of the gannet, ceremonial gaping, disablement reactions, the expression of emotions, the evolution and function of social ceremonies, social hierarchy in bird life, dances of birds and men, songs, etc. Free of technical terminology, this work will be equally interesting to psychologists and zoologists as well as bird lovers of all backgrounds. 32 photographic plates. New introduction by the author. List of scientific names of birds. Bibliography. 3-part index. 431pp. 5⅜ x 8½. T1128 Paperbound **$2.00**

THE SPECIFICITY OF SEROLOGICAL REACTIONS, Karl Landsteiner. With a Chapter on Molecular Structure and Intermolecular Forces by Linus Pauling. Dr. Landsteiner, winner of the Nobel Prize in 1930 for the discovery of the human blood groups, devoted his life to fundamental research and played a leading role in the development of immunology. This authoritative study is an account of the experiments he and his colleagues carried out on antigens and serological reactions with simple compounds. Comprehensive coverage of the basic concepts of immunology includes such topics as: The Serological Specificity of Proteins, Antigens, Antibodies, Artificially Conjugated Antigens, Non-Protein Cell Substances such as polysaccharides, etc., Antigen-Antibody Reactions (Toxin Neutralization, Precipitin Reactions, Agglutination, etc.). Discussions of toxins, bacterial proteins, viruses, hormones, enzymes, etc. in the context of immunological phenomena. New introduction by Dr. Merrill Chase of the Rockefeller Institute. Extensive bibliography and bibliography of author's writings. Index. xviii + 330pp. 5⅜ x 8½. S299 Paperbound **$2.00**

CULTURE METHODS FOR INVERTEBRATE ANIMALS, P. S. Galtsoff, F. E. Lutz, P. S. Welch, J. G. Needham, eds. A compendium of practical experience of hundreds of scientists and technicians, covering invertebrates from protozoa to chordata, in 313 articles on 17 phyla. Explains in great detail food, protection, environment, reproduction conditions, rearing methods, embryology, breeding seasons, schedule of development, much more. Includes at least one species of each considerable group. Half the articles are on class insecta. Introduction. 97 illustrations. Bibliography. Index. xxix + 590pp. 5⅜ x 8. S526 Paperbound **$3.00**

THE BIOLOGY OF THE LABORATORY MOUSE, edited by G. D. Snell. 1st prepared in 1941 by the staff of the Roscoe B. Jackson Memorial Laboratory, this is still the standard treatise on the mouse, assembling an enormous amount of material for which otherwise you spend hours of research. Embryology, reproduction, histology, spontaneous tumor formation, genetics of tumor transplantation, endocrine secretion & tumor formation, milk, influence & tumor formation, inbred, hybrid animals, parasites, infectious diseases, care & recording. Classified bibliography of 1122 items. 172 figures, including 128 photos. ix + 497pp. 6⅛ x 9¼. S248 Clothbound **$6.00**

MATHEMATICAL BIOPHYSICS: PHYSICO-MATHEMATICAL FOUNDATIONS OF BIOLOGY, N. Rashevsky. One of most important books in modern biology, now revised, expanded with new chapters, to include most significant recent contributions. Vol. 1: Diffusion phenomena, particularly diffusion drag forces, their effects. Old theory of cell division based on diffusion drag forces, other theoretical approaches, more exhaustively treated than ever. Theories of excitation, conduction in nerves, with formal theories plus physico-chemical theory. Vol. 2: Mathematical theories of various phenomena in central nervous system. New chapters on theory of color vision, of random nets. Principle of optimal design, extended from earlier edition. Principle of relational mapping of organisms, numerous applications. Introduces into mathematical biology such branches of math as topology, theory of sets. Index. 236 illustrations. Total of 988pp. 5⅜ x 8. S574 Vol. 1 (Books 1, 2) Paperbound **$2.50** S575 Vol. 2 (Books 3, 4) Paperbound **$2.50** 2 vol. set **$5.00**

ELEMENTS OF MATHEMATICAL BIOLOGY, A. J. Lotka. A pioneer classic, the first major attempt to apply modern mathematical techniques on a large scale to phenomena of biology, biochemistry, psychology, ecology, similar life sciences. Partial Contents: Statistical meaning of irreversibility; Evolution as redistribution; Equations of kinetics of evolving systems; Chemical, inter-species equilibrium; parameters of state; Energy transformers of nature, etc. Can be read with profit even by those having no advanced math; unsurpassed as study-reference. Formerly titled ELEMENTS OF PHYSICAL BIOLOGY. 72 figures. xxx + 460pp. 5⅜ x 8. S346 Paperbound **$2.45**

THE BIOLOGY OF THE AMPHIBIA, G. K. Noble, Late Curator of Herpetology at the Am. Mus. of Nat. Hist. Probably the most used text on amphibia, unmatched in comprehensiveness, clarity, detail. 19 chapters plus 85-page supplement cover development; heredity; life history; speciation; adaptation; sex, integument, respiratory, circulatory, digestive, muscular, nervous systems; instinct, intelligence, habits, environment, economic value, relationships, classification, etc. "Nothing comparable to it," C. H. Pope, Curator of Amphibia, Chicago Mus. of Nat. Hist. 1047 bibliographic references. 174 illustrations. 600pp. 5⅜ x 8. S206 Paperbound **$2.98**

STUDIES ON THE STRUCTURE AND DEVELOPMENT OF VERTEBRATES, E. S. Goodrich. A definitive study by the greatest modern comparative anatomist. Exceptional in its accounts of the ossicles of the ear, the separate divisions of the coelom and mammalian diaphragm, and the 5 chapters devoted to the head region. Also exhaustive morphological and phylogenetic expositions of skeleton, fins and limbs, skeletal visceral arches and labial cartilages, visceral clefts and gills, vacular, respiratory, excretory, and peripheral nervous systems, etc., from fish to the higher mammals. 754 illustrations. 69 page biographical study by C. C. Hardy. Bibliography of 1186 references. "What an undertaking . . . to write a textbook which will summarize adequately and succinctly all that has been done in the realm of Vertebrate Morphology these recent years," Journal of Anatomy. Index. Two volumes. Total 906pp. 5⅜ x 8. Two vol. set S449-50 Paperbound **$5.00**

A TREATISE ON PHYSIOLOGICAL OPTICS, H. von Helmholtz, Ed. by J. P. C. Southall. Unmatched for thoroughness, soundness, and comprehensiveness, this is still the most important work ever produced in the field of physiological optics. Revised and annotated, it contains everything known about the subject up to 1925. Beginning with a careful anatomical description of the eye, the main body of the text is divided into three general categories: The Dioptrics of the Eye (covering optical imagery, blur circles on the retina, the mechanism of accommodation, chromatic aberration, etc.); The Sensations of Vision (including stimulation of the organ of vision, simple and compound colors, the intensity and duration of light, variations of sensitivity, contrast, etc.); and The Perceptions of Vision (containing movements of the eyes, the monocular field of vision, direction, perception of depth, binocular double vision, etc.). Appendices cover later findings on optical imagery, refraction, ophthalmoscopy, and many other matters. Unabridged, corrected republication of the original English translation of the third German edition. 3 volumes bound as 2. Complete bibliography, 1911-1925. Indices. 312 illustrations. 6 full-page plates, 3 in color. Total of 1,749pp. 5⅜ x 8. Two-volume set S15, 16 Clothbound **$15.00**

Psychology

YOGA: A SCIENTIFIC EVALUATION, Kovoor T. Behanan. A complete reprinting of the book that for the first time gave Western readers a sane, scientific explanation and analysis of yoga. The author draws on controlled laboratory experiments and personal records of a year as a disciple of a yoga, to investigate yoga psychology, concepts of knowledge, physiology, "supernatural" phenomena, and the ability to tap the deepest human powers. In this study under the auspices of Yale University Institute of Human Relations, the strictest principles of physiological and psychological inquiry are followed throughout. Foreword by W. A. Miles, Yale University. 17 photographs. Glossary. Index. xx + 270pp. 5⅜ x 8. T505 Paperbound **$2.00**

CONDITIONED REFLEXES: AN INVESTIGATION OF THE PHYSIOLOGICAL ACTIVITIES OF THE CEREBRAL CORTEX, I. P. Pavlov. Full, authorized translation of Pavlov's own survey of his work in experimental psychology reviews entire course of experiments, summarizes conclusions, outlines psychological system based on famous "conditioned reflex" concept. Details of technical means used in experiments, observations on formation of conditioned reflexes, function of cerebral hemispheres, results of damage, nature of sleep, typology of nervous system, significance of experiments for human psychology. Trans. by Dr. G. V. Anrep, Cambridge Univ. 235-item bibliography. 18 figures. 445pp. 5⅜ x 8. S614 Paperbound **$2.35**

EXPLANATION OF HUMAN BEHAVIOUR, F. V. Smith. A major intermediate-level introduction to and criticism of 8 complete systems of the psychology of human behavior, with unusual emphasis on theory of investigation and methodology. Part I is an illuminating analysis of the problems involved in the explanation of observed phenomena, and the differing viewpoints on the nature of causality. Parts II and III are a closely detailed survey of the systems of McDougall, Gordon Allport, Lewin, the Gestalt group, Freud, Watson, Hull, and Tolman. Biographical notes. Bibliography of over 800 items. 2 Indexes. 38 figures. xii + 460pp. 5½ x 8¾.
T253 Clothbound **$6.00**

SEX IN PSYCHO-ANALYSIS (formerly CONTRIBUTIONS TO PSYCHO-ANALYSIS), S. Ferenczi. Written by an associate of Freud, this volume presents countless insights on such topics as impotence, transference, analysis and children, dreams, symbols, obscene words, masturbation and male homosexuality, paranoia and psycho-analysis, the sense of reality, hypnotism and therapy, and many others. Also includes full text of THE DEVELOPMENT OF PSYCHO-ANALYSIS by Ferenczi and Otto Rank. Two books bound as one. Total of 406pp. 5⅜ x 8.
T324 Paperbound **$1.85**

BEYOND PSYCHOLOGY, Otto Rank. One of Rank's most mature contributions, focussing on the irrational basis of human behavior as a basic fact of our lives. The psychoanalytic techniques of myth analysis trace to their source the ultimates of human existence: fear of death, personality, the social organization, the need for love and creativity, etc. Dr. Rank finds them stemming from a common irrational source, man's fear of final destruction. A seminal work in modern psychology, this work sheds light on areas ranging from the concept of immortal soul to the sources of state power. 291pp. 5⅜ x 8. T485 Paperbound **$2.00**

ILLUSIONS AND DELUSIONS OF THE SUPERNATURAL AND THE OCCULT, D. H. Rawcliffe. Holds up to rational examination hundreds of persistent delusions including crystal gazing, automatic writing, table turning, mediumistic trances, mental healing, stigmata, lycanthropy, live burial, the Indian Rope Trick, spiritualism, dowsing, telepathy, clairvoyance, ghosts, ESP, etc. The author explains and exposes the mental and physical deceptions involved, making this not only an exposé of supernatural phenomena, but a valuable exposition of characteristic types of abnormal psychology. Originally titled "The Psychology of the Occult." 14 illustrations. Index. 551pp. 5⅜ x 8. T503 Paperbound **$2.00**

THE PRINCIPLES OF PSYCHOLOGY, William James. The full long-course, unabridged, of one of the great classics of Western literature and science. Wonderfully lucid descriptions of human mental activity, the stream of thought, consciousness, time perception, memory, imagination, emotions, reason, abnormal phenomena, and similar topics. Original contributions are integrated with the work of such men as Berkeley, Binet, Mills, Darwin, Hume, Kant, Royce, Schopenhauer, Spinoza, Locke, Descartes, Galton, Wundt, Lotze, Herbart, Fechner, and scores of others. All contrasting interpretations of mental phenomena are examined in detail—introspective analysis, philosophical interpretation, and experimental research. "A classic," JOURNAL OF CONSULTING PSYCHOLOGY. "The main lines are as valid as ever," PSYCHO-ANALYTICAL QUARTERLY. "Standard reading . . . a classic of interpretation," PSYCHIATRIC QUARTERLY. 94 illustrations. 1408pp. 2 volumes. 5⅜ x 8. Vol. 1, T381 Paperbound **$2.50**
Vol. 2, T382 Paperbound **$2.50**

THE DYNAMICS OF THERAPY IN A CONTROLLED RELATIONSHIP, Jessie Taft. One of the most important works in literature of child psychology, out of print for 25 years. Outstanding disciple of Rank describes all aspects of relationship or Rankian therapy through concise, simple elucidation of theory underlying her actual contacts with two seven-year olds. Therapists, social caseworkers, psychologists, counselors, and laymen who work with children will all find this important work an invaluable summation of method, theory of child psychology. xix + 296pp. 5⅜ x 8. T325 Paperbound **$1.75**

CATALOGUE OF DOVER BOOKS

SELECTED PAPERS ON HUMAN FACTORS IN THE DESIGN AND USE OF CONTROL SYSTEMS, Edited by H. Wallace Sinaiko. Nine of the most important papers in this area of increasing interest and rapid growth. All design engineers who have encountered problems involving man as a system-component will find this volume indispensable, both for its detailed information about man's unique capacities and defects, and for its comprehensive bibliography of articles and journals in the human-factors field. Contributors include Chapanis, Birmingham, Adams, Fitts and Jones, etc. on such topics as Theory and Methods for Analyzing Errors in Man-Machine Systems, A Design Philosophy for Man-Machine Control Systems, Man's Senses as Informational Channels, The Measurement of Human Performance, Analysis of Factors Contributing to 460 "Pilot Error" Experiences, etc. Name, subject indexes. Bibliographies of over 400 items. 27 figures. 8 tables. ix + 405pp. 6⅛ x 9¼.   S140 Paperbound **$2.75**

THE ANALYSIS OF SENSATIONS, Ernst Mach. Great study of physiology, psychology of perception, shows Mach's ability to see material freshly, his "incorruptible skepticism and independence." (Einstein). Relation of problems of psychological perception to classical physics, supposed dualism of physical and mental, principle of continuity, evolution of senses, will as organic manifestation, scores of experiments, observations in optics, acoustics, music, graphics, etc. New introduction by T. S. Szasz, M. D. 58 illus. 300-item bibliography. Index. 404pp. 5⅜ x 8.   S525 Paperbound **$1.75**

PRINCIPLES OF ANIMAL PSYCHOLOGY, N. R. F. Maier and T. C. Schneirla. The definitive treatment of the development of animal behavior and the comparative psychology of all animals. This edition, corrected by the authors and with a supplement containing 5 of their most important subsequent articles, is a "must" for biologists, psychologists, zoologists, and others. First part of book includes analyses and comparisons of the behavior of characteristic types of animal life—from simple multicellular animals through the evolutionary scale to reptiles and birds, tracing the development of complexity in adaptation. Two-thirds of the book covers mammalian life, developing further the principles arrived at in Part I. New preface by the authors. 153 illustrations and tables. Extensive bibliographic material. Revised indices. xvi + 683pp. 5⅜ x 8½.   S1120 Paperbound **$3.00** (tentative)

ERROR AND ECCENTRICITY IN HUMAN BELIEF, Joseph Jastrow. From 180 A.D. to the 1930's, the surprising record of human credulity: witchcraft, miracle workings, animal magnetism, mind-reading, astral-chemistry, dowsing, numerology, etc. The stories and exposures of the theosophy of Madame Blavatsky and her followers, the spiritism of Helene Smith, the imposture of Kaspar Hauser, the history of the Ouija board, the puppets of Dr. Luy, and dozens of other hoaxers and cranks, past and present. "As a potpourri of strange beliefs and ideas, it makes excellent reading," New York Times. Formerly titled "Wish and Wisdom, Episodes in the Vagaries of Belief." Unabridged publication. 56 illustrations and photos. 22 full-page plates. Index. xv + 394pp. 5⅜ x 8½.   T986 Paperbound **$1.85**

THE PHYSICAL DIMENSIONS OF CONSCIOUSNESS, Edwin G. Boring. By one of the ranking psychologists of this century, a major work which reflected the logical outcome of a progressive trend in psychological theory—a movement away from dualism toward physicalism. Boring, in this book, salvaged the most important work of the structuralists and helped direct the mainstream of American psychology into the neo-behavioristic channels of today. Unabridged republication of original (1933) edition. New preface by the author. Indexes. 17 illustrations. xviii + 251pp. 5⅜ x 8.   S1040 Paperbound **$1.75**

BRAIN MECHANISMS AND INTELLIGENCE: A QUANTITATIVE STUDY OF INJURIES TO THE BRAIN, K. S. Lashley. A major contemporary psychologist examines the influence of brain injuries upon the capacity to learn, retentiveness, the formation of the maze habit, etc. Also: the relation of reduced learning ability to sensory and motor defects, the nature of the deterioration following cerebral lesions, comparison of the rat with other forms, and related matters. New introduction by Prof. D. O. Hebb. Bibliography. Index. xxii + 200pp. 5⅜ x 8½.   T1038 Paperbound **$1.75**

Prices subject to change without notice.

Dover publishes books on art, music, philosophy, literature, languages, history, social sciences, psychology, handcrafts, orientalia, puzzles and entertainments, chess, pets and gardens, books explaining science, intermediate and higher mathematics, mathematical physics, engineering, biological sciences, earth sciences, classics of science, etc. Write to:

Dept. catrr.
Dover Publications, Inc.
180 Varick Street, N.Y. 14, N.Y.